The Middle East in Transition

The Centrality of Citizenship

Edited by

Nils A. Butenschøn

Professor, Norwegian Centre for Human Rights, Faculty of Law, University of Oslo, Norway

Roel Meijer

Associate Professor, Radboud University, Faculty of Religion, Theology and Religious Studies, Nijmegen, the Netherlands

EE Edward Elgar PUBLISHING

Cheltenham, UK • Northampton, MA, USA

Published by
Edward Elgar Publishing Limited
The Lypiatts
15 Lansdown Road
Cheltenham
Glos GL50 2JA
UK

Edward Elgar Publishing, Inc.
William Pratt House
9 Dewey Court
Northampton
Massachusetts 01060
USA

A catalogue record for this book
is available from the British Library

Library of Congress Control Number: 2017960010

This book is available electronically in the **Elgar**online
Law subject collection
DOI 10.4337/9781788111133

Printed on 30% PCR Stock
ISBN 978 1 78811 112 6 (cased)
ISBN 978 1 78811 113 3 (eBook)
Printed and bound by Thomson-Shore, Inc.
Typeset by Servis Filmsetting Ltd, Stockport, Cheshire

Contents

Contributors

Salima Ahmadou is a Moroccan national and MA student in Development Studies at the International Institute of Social Studies, Erasmus University Rotterdam, the Netherlands. She has ample experience working with civil society organisations focusing on gender, youth, social movements and democratisation in the Middle East and North Africa (MENA) region.

Zeineb Alsabeehg is a young political scientist. She received her BA and MA in Political Science from the University of Oslo. Her fields of interest are the Middle East with an emphasis on the Gulf region, the Arab Uprisings, citizenship and statelessness. She engages with non-governmental organisations (NGOs) for the cause of human rights in Bahrain, and she writes in the Norwegian press about the situation in Bahrain and the Gulf. Her contribution to this book is based on her MA thesis, *From Citizen to Non-Existent: A Study of Bahrain's Politics of Citizenship* (2017).

Zahra Babar is Associate Director for Research at the Center for International and Regional Studies at Georgetown University in Qatar. Her current research interests include migration and citizenship in the Persian Gulf states. Babar has published several articles and chapters, including: 'The "Enemy Within": Citizenship-Stripping in the Post-Arab Spring GCC', *Middle East Journal*, Volume 71, No. 4, 2017, 525–43; 'The "Humane Economy": Migrant Labor and Islam in Qatar and the UAE', *Sociology of Islam*, Volume 5, Nos. 2–3, 2017, 200–23; (with Andrew Gardner) 'Circular Migration in the Gulf States', in *Impact of Circular Migration on Human, Political and Civil Rights: A Global Perspective* (Springer, 2016); 'Population, Power, and Distributional Politics in Qatar', *Journal of Arabian Studies*, Volume 5, No. 2, 2015, 138–55; and 'The Cost of Belonging: Citizenship Construction in the State of Qatar', *Middle East Journal*, Volume 68, No. 3, 2014, 403–20. She has served as editor for *Arab Migrant Communities in the GCC* (Oxford University Press/Hurst, 2017) and co-edited (with M. Kamrava) *Migrant Labour in the Persian Gulf* (Columbia University Press/Hurst, 2012).

Sylvia I. Bergh (a Swedish national) is Associate Professor in Development Management and Governance at the International Institute of Social

Studies (ISS), Erasmus University Rotterdam. She has published widely on local state–society relations in the MENA region, including: *The Politics of Development in Morocco: Local Governance and Participation in North Africa* (I.B. Tauris, 2017), and edited the book *The Redeployment of State Power in the Southern Mediterranean: Implications of Neoliberal Reforms for Local Governance* (Routledge, 2013). She also regularly teaches and consults on evaluations of development projects and programmes.

Nathalie Bernard-Maugiron is a Senior Researcher at the French National Research Institute for Sustainable Development (IRD/CEPED) and Associate Researcher at the Law Faculty of Paris Descartes University. She holds a PhD in Public Law from Paris University and wrote her thesis on the Egyptian Supreme Constitutional Court and the protection of human rights (published by Bruylant, 2003). She works on the transition processes after the 2011 Uprisings, the judiciary, and personal status law in Egypt and in the Arab World. She was co-director of the Institut d'études de l'Islam et des sociétés du monde musulman (IISMM) at the Ecole des Hautes études en sciences sociales (EHESS) in Paris from 2010 to 2014. She has edited several volumes: (with Baudouin Dupret) *Ordre public et droit musulman de la famille en Europe et en Afrique du Nord* (Bruylant/IRD, 2012) and *Egypt and its Laws* (Kluwer Law International, 2002); and *Judges and Political Reform in Egypt* (American University in Cairo Press, 2008).

Nils A. Butenschøn is Professor of Political Science and former Director at the Norwegian Centre for Human Rights, Faculty of Law, University of Oslo. Main research interests include nationality conflicts and state formation with the Middle East as focus. Publications include: Nils A. Butenschøn, Uri Davis, and Manuell Hassassian (eds.), *Citizenship and the State in the Middle East: Approaches and Applications* (Syracuse University Press, 2000); 'The Arab Spring and the "Iron Triangle": Regime Survival and the Conditions of Citizenship in the Arab Middle East', in Roel Meijer and Nils Butenschøn (eds.), *The Crisis of Citizenship in the Arab World* (Brill, 2017), 246–73; Nils A. Butenschøn, Øyvind Stiansen, and Kåre Vollan (eds.), *Power-Sharing in Conflict-Ridden Societies: Challenges for Building Peace and Democratic Stability* (Ashgate/Routledge, 2015); 'Arab Citizen and the Arab State: The "Arab Spring" as a Critical Juncture in Contemporary Arab Politics', *Democracy and Security* 11 (2015) 2: 111–28.

Lillian C. Frost is currently a PhD candidate in The George Washington University's Political Science Department, where her research focuses on citizenship, nationalism, refugees, and political identity. Her dissertation project explores variations in the sets of rights and forms of citizenship statuses host states offer to protracted refugees, including shifts in formal laws as well as the informal enforcement of these laws. She has received support for her research from the Fulbright US Student Program, Council of American Overseas Research Centers and American Center of Oriental Research, as well as The George Washington University's Institute for Middle East Studies and Department of Political Science.

Basak Ince is an Assistant Professor in the Department of Political Science and Public Administration at Bilkent University. She holds a PhD in Politics from the School of Oriental and African Studies (SOAS), University of London. She conducts research on citizenship, citizenship education, gender and citizenship, and sexuality and citizenship. She has articles published in journals such as: *Middle Eastern Studies* and *Oxford Review of Education*. Her book entitled *Citizenship and Identity in Turkey: From Atatürk's Republic to the Present Day* was published by I.B. Tauris in 2012. Currently she is working on a book project titled *Gender and Citizenship in Turkey from the late Ottoman Empire to the Present Day*.

Mariwan Kanie is a lecturer in Arabic studies at the Faculty of Humanities (University of Amsterdam). He teaches political and intellectual history of the Middle East and the modern Arab world. He is author of many books in Kurdish, and some of his publications are translated into Persian and Arabic. Among his publications are: 'Nationalism, Martyrdom and Body in the Modern Kurdish Politics and Culture', *Lijf en leden Gender en het historische lichaam Jaarboek voor Vrouwengeschiedenis* 28 (2008): 85–103; (with Michiel Leezenberg) 'Governing Iraq by Tribes and Constitutions: British Mandate Rule in Iraq', *IMISCOE Research* (2011): 89–110.

Roel Meijer is Associate Professor in Middle East history at the Department of Religious Studies at Radboud University, Nijmegen, the Netherlands. He has edited seven volumes, including: *Global Salafism: Islam's New Religious Movement* (Hurst/Columbia University Press, 2009, translated into Arabic and Chinese) and *The Muslim Brotherhood in Europe* (Hurst/Columbia University Press, 2012). He has published widely on social movements, the Islamist movement, and the political situation in Egypt, Saudi Arabia, Iraq and Bahrain. His latest interest is in concepts of citizenship in the Middle East. Recently he edited (with Nils Butenschøn), *The Crisis of Citizenship in the Arab World* (Brill, 2017). He is currently writing a monograph for Polity Press, *State and Citizenship in the Middle East*.

Valentine M. Moghadam is Professor of Sociology and International Affairs at Northeastern University, former director of the International Affairs Program (2012–2017) and directs the Middle East and

Mediterranean Studies Program. Her areas of research are globalisation, transnational feminist networks, civil society and citizenship, and gender and development in the Middle East and North Africa. Among her books are: *Modernizing Women: Gender and Social Change in the Middle East* (Boulder and London: Lynne Rienner Publishers, 1993, 2003, 2013) and *Globalization and Social Movements: Islamism, Feminism, and the Global Justice Movement* (Lanham, Maryland and London: Rowman & Littlefield, 2009, 2013). She co-authored the introductory chapter to the book *Women, Work, and Welfare in the Middle East and North Africa: The Role of Socio-demographics, Entrepreneurship, and Public Policies* (London: Imperial College Press, 2016). In 2017–2018 she has been involved in an ESRC-funded international research project on dynamics of inequality that examines low levels of female labour force participation in the Middle East, North Africa, southern Europe, and South Asia.

Zoltan Pall is a research fellow at the Middle East Institute at the National University of Singapore, and a former visiting Assistant Professor at the Gulf University of Science and Technology in Kuwait. Currently he is working on a research project that focuses on the activities of Kuwaiti and other Middle Eastern Islamic NGOs in Southeast Asia. He is the author of *Salafism in Lebanon: Local and Transnational Movements* (Cambridge University Press, in press) and *Lebanese Salafis between the Gulf and Europe: Development, Fractionalization and Transnational Networks of Salafism in Lebanon* (Amsterdam University Press, 2013).

Shirin Saeidi holds a PhD from Cambridge University, UK. She recently completed a post-doctoral fellowship at the Centre for Global Cooperation Research in Duisburg, Germany. She has published in the journal *Citizenship Studies* and *Gender & History*. She is currently an Adjunct Professor at George Mason University, Fairfax VA.

Ruth Hanau Santini is Assistant Professor at Università L'Orientale in Naples, where she teaches politics and international relations. Her research area covers international relations of the MENA region and in particular regional security and domestic and foreign policy of Tunisia and European foreign policy towards the MENA region. Her previous affiliations include associate fellowship at the Brookings Institution, Washington DC, and at Johns Hopkins, SAIS Europe and Bologna. Her most recent publications are: 'A New Regional Cold War in the Middle East and North Africa: Regional Security Complex Theory Revisited', *The International Spectator* (November 2017), and (with Francesco N. Moro) 'Civil–Military Relations and the State after the Arab Uprisings: Armed

Forces, Security Apparatus and Militias in Heterarchical Political Orders', in Ruth Hanau Santini and Reinoud Leenders (eds.), *Mediterranean Politics*, themed issue, November 2017.

Peter Seeberg is Associate Professor at the Centre for Contemporary Middle East Studies, University of Southern Denmark. He is also Director of the DJUCO-project, an academic cooperation project in Amman, Jordan. Peter Seeberg has published widely on relations between the EU and the Middle East, migration and security, etc. His most recent publications are Peter Seeberg and Musa Shteiwi (eds.), *European Foreign Affairs Review*, Special Issue: *New Challenges for the EU in the Arab Mediterranean and the Revision of the European Neighbourhood Policy* (Kluwer, 2017); Peter Seeberg, Martin Beck and Dietrich Jung (eds.), *The Levant in Turmoil: Syria, Palestine, and the Transformation of Middle Eastern Politics* (Palgrave Macmillan, 2016). His articles appeared in: *British Journal of Middle Eastern Studies, Democracy and Security, Democratization, European Foreign Affairs Review, Mediterranean Politics, Middle East Critique*, and *Middle East Policy*.

Musa M. Shteiwi is a Professor of Sociology and is currently the Director of the Center for Strategic Studies at the University of Jordan. His research focuses on political development and state building, political parties and civil society and gender issues. Most recently he has been working on radical and soft extremism and refugees. He is the editor of a joint policy study, *Migrants and Refugees: Impact and Future Policies: Case Studies of Jordan, Lebanon, Turkey and Greece*, published in 2016. He is also the co-author of the chapter titled: 'Economic and Social Integration of Migrants and Refugees in Jordan and Lebanon' in the above volume. He is currently finishing an empirical study on inter-communal relations between Jordanians and Syrian refugees.

Acknowledgements

This volume is one of two books produced as the result of the collaboration between Nils Butenschøn of The Norwegian Centre for Human Rights (NCHR), Faculty of Law, University of Oslo and Roel Meijer of Islam Studies, Faculty of Philosophy, Theology and Religious Studies, Radboud University, Nijmegen. The work started under the impression of the Arab Uprisings in 2011 and what appeared to us as a deep crisis of trust and confidence between rulers and the ruled in the region. This brought up the centrality of citizenship as the approach in our study. We wrote a state-of-the-art paper on citizenship as a field of study in the Middle East and invited colleagues from different parts of the world to join in developing the field further and to contribute to publications. The initiative was met with great interest among Middle Eastern scholars, and progressed into a large multidisciplinary project. The basic idea was to introduce and apply the citizenship approach both thematically and to case studies, including countries from across the region. The project developed into two main stages, the first with a particular view to challenges in the Arab region, the second with an extended perspective to include non-Arab countries, namely Turkey, Iran, and Israel. The editorial work commenced aiming at publishing two volumes: *The Crisis of Citizenship in the Arab World* (published by Brill in 2017), and the present volume with a broader perspective, *Middle East in Transition: The Centrality of Citizenship*. Maarten Danckaert joined us at an early stage as a research assistant, allocated by the NCHR, and did an invaluable job. The completion of the project was made possible by financial, institutional, and academic support from a number of sources. We received generous financial support from the Norwegian and Dutch Foreign Ministries, and academic and practical support from our home institutions in addition to the Institut Néerlandais au Maroc (NIMAR), the Centre Jacques Berque (CJB), Université Mohammed V, Rabat-Suissi, and the Norwegian Peacebuilding Resource Centre (NOREF). We are indebted to all the contributors who made this volume possible. Special thanks go to the editorial team at Edward Elgar for their professional and expeditious processing of our manuscript.

Nils A. Butenschøn and Roel Meijer

Introduction

The Middle East is currently undergoing the most dramatic transition since World War I. The crisis was unleashed by the Arab Uprisings (or 'Arab Spring') in 2010–2011, and is still (in 2017) unfolding in different violent and non-violent forms, from North Africa to the Gulf. What we witness in several parts of the Arab region is the implosion of states and state authority, leaving behind devastations, unprecedented suffering, and zones of power vacuum ready to be filled by non-state militias or external powers alike.

This book seeks to explore the condition of citizenship in the region as a core dimension of the crisis, a dimension that tends to be overlooked in the dramatic stream of events, also by academics. The Arab Uprisings brought to the surface a complex set of social, economic, and political grievances, but most of all a deep mistrust of citizens towards their own governments. The millions who occupied the streets in the early months of 2011 with demands of bread, dignity, and accountable government ignited an unprecedented crisis of legitimacy that threatened the local and regional political order. Locally, among most people, what happened is called a 'revolution'. Several rulers were indeed toppled, and modest reforms were achieved elsewhere, but the overall picture is currently that of counter-revolutionary forces hitting back mercilessly. Conflicts over the terms of citizenship understood as a social contract between rulers and the ruled are at the core of these developments and should be approached as such.

The variety of trajectories that the post-Uprising developments have taken clearly indicates a need for an open and multidisciplinary approach. Furthermore, the current crisis has wider regional ramifications that illustrate the contested nature of the state as the organising principle of political authority. The states and societies in the region, both Arab and non-Arab, are undergoing complex processes of transition, the outcomes of which are highly uncertain. The characteristics and historical patterns of Middle Eastern state formation are very different as compared with other regions, not least Europe. This invites a 'back to basics' approach in the analysis of the individual societies trapped in the crisis by keeping attention on how state–society relations have been formed; how ideas of 'citizen', 'nation', 'state', 'community', 'authority', and associated concepts – and the relations between them – contribute to our understanding of the complex developments now unfolding.

Citizenship is the mechanism that binds together state authority and citizens under its jurisdiction; a bond of trust or mistrust, of loyalty or opposition, of solidarity or oppression. In the age of the nation-state and the universal norms of citizenship rights (as standardised in the 1948 Universal Declaration of Human Rights and the human rights conventions that followed), holding a citizenship is the key to legal protection and basic human rights. It is 'the right to have rights'; the fundamental organising principle of the modern state together with the principle of state sovereignty.[1]

The two principles of citizenship and sovereignty are closely related and balanced in the overarching idea of the modern nation-state. With sovereignty comes state obligations of guaranteeing and protecting the basic rights of every individual under the jurisdiction of the state, citizens as well as non-citizens. We know, of course, that this ideal model of the nation-state is not implemented on the ground in many parts of the world, not least in the Middle East, in spite of the monitoring mechanisms of the UN organs and regional mechanisms on behalf of the international society. The balance between the two principles is in fact leaning heavily in favour of sovereignty and the associated principle of non-interference in internal affairs of the state, making it possible for the most notorious dictatorships to remain members of the UN with impunity and leaving their subjects in a very vulnerable and unprotected position. Persons without citizenship, stateless individuals, and those who have had their citizenship revoked for one reason or another, are in a particularly severe position, often as non-existent in any public records and without access to public services, to a passport, a bank account, etc.

The hypothesis of the project behind this book is not that there is one common pattern of state–citizen relations to be found throughout the Middle East; on the contrary, we seek to explore the variety of traditions and legacies, of state formations, regimes, and ideologies that form the overall picture of the region today.[2] However, one common denominator

---

[1] See Asbjørn Eide, 'Citizenship and International Human Rights Law,' in *Citizenship and the State in the Middle East: Approaches and Applications*, eds. Nils A. Butenschøn, Uri Davis, and Manuel Hassassian (Syracuse: Syracuse University Press, 2000) 88–123.

[2] The project was initiated by the editors of this book with a call for an international conference, 'Arab Citizenship in the New Political ERA', hosted by Université Mohammed V, Rabat-Souissi in May 2014. The first book from the

that makes it meaningful to study the Middle East as a crisis-ridden region is the unresolved and deeply entrenched divergences in the views of state authority and the social contract between rulers and the ruled. In short, it is the state itself as a sovereign organisation of territorial communities that is in crisis. Whereas the crisis is most exposed in the Arab part of the region, it is not limited to the Arab countries; also the Iranian theocracy, the Israeli ethnocracy, and the Turkish autocracy are states facing deep-seated challenges that should be studied through the lens of citizenship.

On another level, the centrality of citizenship related to the Middle East was underlined during the wave of refugees entering the EU in the summer of 2015 in search of refuge and possibly a new life as citizens of a European country. What they were hoping for in Europe was access to safety, protection, work and education, and to enjoy the rights of freedom of speech, belief and organisation. At the same time, we saw the reverse movement: Muslim youth from the United States and the EU travelling to join the Islamic State in Iraq and Syria (ISIS), where they acquired a new status as foreign fighters and demonstratively burnt their passports in a show of contempt of the secular states they believe are illegitimate and not ruled according to 'what God has sent down'. Or worse, reneging on their citizenship by executing attacks on citizens in the countries where they lived.[3] In addition, as hundreds of thousands of refugees entered Europe, established conceptions of citizenship in the European setting were also challenged and came to the forefront of political struggles there. Who is to be included, on what grounds and which conditions, to what extent and for how long?

Given this background it is surprising, for several reasons, that citizenship as a separate factor seldom figures in the debate on the crisis in the Middle East. In some of the recent important books published on the politics in the region citizenship is hardly mentioned. Factors relevant to citizenship such as authoritarianism, bad governance, poverty and other dimensions of underdevelopment are certainly discussed, but the political dynamics of citizenship as an important factor explaining the political crises in these countries are, in our opinion, not given sufficient, if any, attention.[4] Nor does citizenship play a significant role in Islamic studies. Authors mostly concentrate on identity, values, piety, norms, Islamic law,

---

project was *The Crisis of Citizenship in the Arab World*, eds. Roel Meijer and Nils Butenschøn (Leiden: Brill, 2017).

[3] Peter M. Berger, *The United States of Jihad: Who Are America's Homegrown Terrorists and How Do We Stop Them?* (New York: Broadway Books, 2016).

[4] Vincent Durac and Francesco Cavatorta, *Politics and Governance in the Middle East* (London: Palgrave, 2015); John Chalcraft, *Popular Politics in the Making of the Modern Middle East* (Cambridge: Cambridge University Press, 2016).

political Islam and social movements, but how these factors relate to such a crucial issue as citizenship and what that entails remains mostly unclear. This is all the more surprising as all Islamic thought in one way or another addresses substantive issues of citizenship, either by rejecting the state-centred conception of citizenship (as the alternative idea of 'citizens of God' in Salafism), or making citizenship in fact a central issue, but recognising it only in such terms as the 'common good' or 'promoting the good and preventing evil', or the 'rights of God'. In many ways, as elaborated elsewhere, elements of modern citizenship can be built on already existing Islamic thought and Islamic law.[5]

Furthermore, a broader awareness of the centrality of citizenship in the aftermath of the Arab Uprisings could have been expected when we consider how the study of citizenship rose to prominence in connection with the dramatic transitions in Europe after the dissolution of the Communist states in Eastern Europe in the early 1990s. In many ways this situation compares well with the current crisis in the Middle East as illustrated when Ronal Beiner explains the significance of the citizenship approach to the European crisis:

> These [European] political crises . . . are indeed central to an understanding of why the problem of citizenship is especially salient in our day. Ethnic and sectarian conflict in northeastern and southeastern Europe; a redefining of national states at the heart of Europe, in a post-Cold War epoch that might have been expected to diminish political turbulence but seems instead to have generated *more* of it; dislocating shifts of identity provoked by mass migration . . .: All these political dilemmas have raised anew deep questions about what binds citizens together into a shared political community. To these formidable challenges may be added what is probably the greatest challenge of all to contemporary citizenship, namely, persistent mass unemployment, which offers the surest prospect of excluding tens of millions of people . . . from a sense of full membership in civic community.[6]

THE CITIZENSHIP APPROACH

Analytically, the citizenship approach, whether applied to Europe or the Middle East, is located at the level in between the state/ruler (top down) and the individuals or group of individuals under the jurisdiction of the

---

[5] See Part II in this volume. See also Knut Vikør, 'Muslim Subjects and God's Law,' in *The Crisis of Citizenship in the Arab World*, eds. Roel Meijer and Nils Butenschøn (Leiden: Brill, 2017) 273–95.

[6] Ronal Beiner, 'Introduction: Why Citizenship Constitutes a Theoretical Problem in the Last Decade of the Twentieth Century' in *Theorizing Citizenship*, ed. Ronal Beiner (New York: State University of New York, 1995), 3.

state (bottom up). The aim is to identify and understand the dynamics of the interaction between the two levels as it can be studied both in terms of structural characteristics (laws and institutional frameworks, economic factors, cultural patterns) and agency (individual or collective strategic behaviour). Keith Faulks has suggested a useful categorisation of three main dimensions of citizenship: *Extent* (who are included in/excluded from membership in the political community; *content* (which rights and obligations are covered); *depth* (the level of commitment by the parties to citizenship as a social contract).[7] The citizenship approach should basically be seen as a method, not as a theory (even if there are theories *about* citizenship); it is an analytical approach that is context specific and applicable within different disciplines (social sciences, the humanities, law). It is well suited for comparative studies across empirical cases and, consequently, for theory development within individual disciplines. But it is not a discipline in itself. With this in mind this multidisciplinary book includes a number of case studies of countries and context specific issues that we consider to be of particular relevance, but certainly not exhaustive, in the study of the current crises – both in Arab and non-Arab parts of the Middle East and North Africa.

The case studies that follow are set in the general framework that includes a number of background issues, such as patterns of modern state building in the region; colonial legacies; identity formation and political loyalties; state sovereignty and transnational ideologies; and geopolitics.

CITIZENSHIP AND STATE FORMATION IN THE MIDDLE EAST

With the emergence of the modern state in the Middle East and North Africa from the beginning of the nineteenth century the significance of citizenship became progressively more apparent. This was an effect of the rise of the new relationship between state and society, the standardisation of bureaucratic procedures, the increased demands of the state on the population in the form of loyalty and the imposition of duties (taxes, conscription, education, identity, norms and values, political participation). The *Tanzimat* reforms (1839–1876), the rise of Ottomanism as a common identity and shared equal rights, as well as the struggle for independence of former Ottoman lands, cannot be understood without notions of citizenship and drawing literal and imaginary boundaries between those

---

[7] Keith Faulks, *Citizenship* (Abingdon: Routledge, 2000), 7.

who belong to the body politic and those who do not. This process was diffuse, highly irregular, constantly taking different shapes, particularly in certain countries and periods, fluctuating between collective and individual rights, and subsumed in different forms of unspoken pacts, or social contracts.[8]

The current crisis of the state in the Middle East has direct links to patterns of state formation under the influence of the Ottoman Empire and later colonial rule and geopolitical rivalries in the region. In the course of the breakdown of the Ottoman Empire and the struggle for territorial control among Western powers, the new states were established in several waves. The first wave was started in the early nineteenth century and ended in 1923 with the Treaty of Lausanne. At that point most of the region except for Turkey was under direct or indirect control of the colonial powers. The new states emerging from the post-World War I diplomacy had their borders, constitutions, and rulers to a large extent decided in uneven bargaining processes between colonial centres and local elites.

The new boundaries destroyed social, economic and cultural relations which had existed for centuries in empires whose boundaries were fluid. All at once a city like Aleppo found itself cut off from its hinterland and subordinated to Damascus. Aleppans had to find a new identity and identify with Arab nationalism and hate 'Turks', which was utterly strange to them. Turkish speaking members of the Greek Orthodox Church were subjected to forced emigration to Greece because they were regarded as Greeks. Kurds were dispersed over four countries: Syria, Turkey, Iraq and Iran, and in all these countries their identity was suppressed. Bedouin found themselves unable to reach their grazing grounds on the other side of a border. Arab Palestinians found themselves basically excluded in the British League of Nations mandate, when Palestine in 1922 for the first time was organised as a separate state territory. The provision in the Mandatory Regulations that a 'national home for the Jewish people' should be established in the country was unacceptable to the indigenous population, making it impossible for them to participate in the running of the country without undermining their claim to self-determination.[9]

---

[8] See, for example, Stanford J. Shaw and Ezel Kural Shaw, *History of the Ottoman Empire and Modern Turkey*. Volume II. *Reform, Revolution, and Republic: The Rise of Modern Turkey, 1808–1975* (Cambridge: Cambridge University Press, 1977).

[9] See Nils A. Butenschøn, 'The Paradox of Palestinian Self-determination' in *Where Now for Palestine? The Demise of the Two-State Solution*, ed. Jamil Hilal (London, New York: Zed Books 2007), 75–99.

Shiʿis in south of the Arabian Peninsula and the Hejaz found themselves in the new kingdom of Saudi Arabia.[10] With boundaries and the demand for loyalty, and new duties, 'majority' citizens were created with full rights and secondary citizens, or residents without rights created.

The second wave in the 1960s and 1970s saw the establishment of the Gulf states (from Kuwait in 1960 to the United Arab Emirates in 1970) after the British left, and a new definition of who were members and who were not took place. In between, several attempts were made, under the banner of Arab nationalism, to change borders imposed under colonial rule, such as the United Arab Republic (UAR) of Syria and Egypt 1958–1961 and other short-lived attempts to unify Syria and Iraq (1965) and Libya and Egypt (1971).[11]

On a parallel track, the State of Israel had been established in 1948, triggering the first Arab–Israeli war and making the previous British mandate into a continuous war zone. To top it off, theoretically Israel's potential citizens as defined by the Zionist state idea included world Jewry under the Law of Return issued in 1950, excluding Palestine's non-Jewish Arab population from full membership in the political community, and over the years preventing millions of refugees from returning to their homes. With its conquest of the rest of mandate Palestine under the Six Day War in 1967, what is known as the 'ingathering of the exiles' suddenly became a more realistic option, defining the Israel-Palestine conflict ever since.[12]

THE SOVEREIGN AND SOVEREIGNTY

The location of sovereignty is also not always clear. In monarchies it lies with the monarch or the royal family, who embody sovereignty, much as the French King embodied the state. The patrimonial '*l'état c'est moi*' still applies to most monarchies in the Middle East. Citizenship is a gift (*makrama*) that can be bestowed and rescinded at will, as Zeineb Alsabeehg

---

[10] Toby Matthiesen, *The Other Saudis: Shiism, Dissent and Sectarianism* (Oxford: Oxford University Press, 2015).

[11] For a well-known study of the early attempts, see Malcolm Kerr, *The Arab Cold War: Gamal Abd-al Nasir and His Rivals 1958–1970* (London: Cambridge University Press, 1971).

[12] The so-called Jerusalem Program, adopted as the platform of the World Zionist Organization in 1968, defined '[t]he ingathering of the Jewish people in the historic homeland, Eretz Israel, through aliyah [immigration] from all countries' as its central task. The New Jerusalem Program adopted in 2004 contains effectively the same provision. See http://www.wzo.org.il/The-Jerusalem-Program, accessed 3 May 2017.

shows in the example of Bahrain in this volume. Where the monarchy has evolved and moves in the direction of a constitutional monarchy, as is the case of Morocco, a hybrid form exists, as is expressed in the paradoxical term of Mohammed VI, who calls himself the 'citizen-king' (*le roi citoyen*), very much reminiscent of Louis Philippe in France (1830–1848). In this volume Mariwan Kanie demonstrates that even republican Iraq under Saddam Hussein fell back on this tradition, after the 1991 defeat, giving the country a modern authoritarian streak.

Sovereignty in other republics, however, is also not always clear. In many cases sovereignty is mediated. In Egypt, the Coptic Church is such an intermediary between the state and its religious followers. In Lebanon, the state is subjected to these mediators who determine the power/weakness of the state and divide its sovereignty among each other proportionally. In regions where tribal structures are still strong, as in Saudi Arabia or Jordan, tribes are maintained as intermediaries and held responsible for the conduct of their members. The religious establishment is another intermediary. In other cases, the creation of such mediators is a way to maintain the power of the state and co-opt civil society and exert patronage. One example is the cultural centre for the Amazigh minority in Morocco, officially controlled by the monarchy.[13]

CITIZENSHIP AND TRANSNATIONAL IDEOLOGIES

Sovereignty of the state has not been helped by the prevailing ideologies in the Middle East. Islamic political philosophy has never been very strongly developed and remained subordinated to religion. The Ottoman sultans developed administrative law, but that was to enhance the power of the state. There did exist a concept comparable to citizenship and notions of what can be called a *Rechtsstaat* in Islamic law. Otherwise the millet system supported a system of intermediaries who were largely autonomous but responsible for their community. The communitarian dimension was further enhanced by colonialism, which introduced systems of divide and rule in Lebanon, Syria, Iraq and Morocco. The subsequent nationalist ideologies in the era of anti-colonial liberation expanded the community from religious community to national, ethnic community, without developing individual rights, which are so crucial for citizenship. Especially influential has been the near universal retention of religious personal

---

[13] Francesco Cavatorta, 'Divided They Stand, Divided They Fail: Opposition Politics in Morocco' *Democratization* 16 (2009) 1: 137–56.

statute and family law, which has made civil marriage impossible in the region and has hampered equality and cross-sectarian marriages. Pan-Arabism was too wide to enhance individual rights. Syrian movements in favour of Arab unification, including the Baʿath party, did not produce a well-defined citizenship. Roel Meijer demonstrates in this volume a similar tendency within Islamist movements such as the Muslim Brotherhood and Salafism. Even where Sayyid Qutb's submission to God's sovereignty did allow for an opening up of the possibility of revolt against the state and agency, it did not lead to individual rights. A concept of the sovereignty of the people was finally developed, but this was ambivalent and retained strong sectarian overtones.

THE DEMOGRAPHIC FACTOR

A sign of weak sovereignty and legitimacy and the existence of many different unintegrated ethnic and religious minorities or even majorities has politicised demographic data. This is not abnormal and occurs in all countries. But nowhere are demographic data as sensitive and part of state security as in the Middle East. To a large degree the politics of citizenship concerns demographic management (with reference to Keith Faulks' 'extent of citizenship'-dimension mentioned above). The delicate balance between groups, the percentages of residents who as citizens could make claims are notorious. It has added significance to citizenship as a central dimension in Middle Eastern politics. Examples include the ethnocratic nature of the State of Israel, based on the premise of political hegemony of Jews as discussed by Nils Butenschøn in this volume. Demography, in particular the Jew/non-Jew ratio, represents a 'ticking bomb' under the current political system. Demography is also a core issue in the fragile power-sharing arrangement between Christians and Muslims that has regulated the Lebanese political system since independence. The National Pact of 1943 is a political contract between family-dominated religious sects based on the last census held in 1932. The 1990 Constitution that ended a 15-year civil war revised only moderately the system that had guaranteed Christian dominance in favour of the Muslims, indicating that the Lebanese are still not ready to dissolve the sectarian nature of the political system and establish a unified citizenship.[14] Moreover, the demographic factor will undoubtedly play a central role in the future

14 See for example, Nils A. Butenschøn, Øyvind Henden, and Kåre Vollan, 'Lebanon' in *Power-Sharing in Conflict-Ridden Societies: Challenges for Building*

political organisation of the war-ridden countries of Iraq and Syria (Who should be included in what arrangements, and where?). The position and role of the Kurds is a particularly salient question that will influence the integrity of these states and stability of the regional order.

Bahrain is another affected country. As Zeineb Alsabeehg makes clear in this volume perhaps as many as 200,000 Sunnis have been given Bahraini citizenship in order to turn the demographic balance between Sunnis and Shiʿis in that country.

CITIZENSHIP, AGENCY AND EMANCIPATION

Societies seldom develop in one direction only. Despite the forces working against equal citizenship, citizenship as a concept has gradually penetrated the public domain in the region. It is not difficult to identify parallel and conflicting tendencies, some pointing towards further disintegration of societies, public trust, and integrity of states, others pointing towards a higher awareness of social responsibility and active citizenship. In spite of immense setbacks this is made clear in the long-term perspective. Although the state's sovereignty might be marred by porous borders, intermediary institutions, communitarianism, collectivism, demographic disparity, ethnic and sectarian discrimination and exclusion, pervasive patronage, police repression, and deficient social contracts, notions of citizenship took hold already from the early nineteenth century. Later, with increasing demands made by states upon their subjects, identities also changed, and people formulated counter demands. With the emergence of the public sphere, people read newspapers, participated in political movements, became connected and started to live in 'imagined communities', which also meant they were citizens and could identify beyond their community, tribe, clan, religion, village and region.[15] They no longer mobilised only along tribal lines, but also based on professional identities and economic interests. Traditional Islamic notions changed character and became 'infected' by terms and concepts derived from the West, giving them a more abstract content adapted to the emergence of the citizen. Concepts such as reform and the common good indicated a change in the relations between state and subject, inferring a modern relation between

---

Peace and Democratic Stability (Farnham and Burlington: Ashgate, 2015), 105–135.

[15] Armando Salvatore and Dale F. Eickelman, *Public Islam and the Common Good* (Leiden: Brill, 2004).

citizen and state based on a negotiated social contract with the state working to the benefit of the citizen and the citizens having a responsibility to the larger good than his/her own community. It contained new notions of law, the position of women, the status of children, the role of education, and national economy, national and personal welfare.

Such patterns of modernisation were identified by Middle East scholars already in the 1950s and 1960s and led to general expectations that modernisation would continue to dominate the social, economic, political and cultural development, bringing Middle Eastern societies closer to the European patterns of development.[16] The tribal, patrimonial and sectarian traits typical of the traditional society would vanish together with personalised monarchical political systems. These expectations were not unreasonable at the time, particularly under the impression of the forceful mobilisation of Arab socialism that inspired millions across the region. But again, the counter-forces were strong, trapping the region in an 'iron triangle' whereby international, regional and local actors formed formal or informal alliances in order to secure that radical forces and threats to the regional order and interests of world powers would be neutralised (a pattern not very different from what we have observed in the current post-Arab Spring era).[17]

INCREASED AWARENESS OF CITIZENSHIP

What is clear is not only that citizenship is central but also that its forms fluctuate and its public prominence differs. Contesting unjust citizenship regimes can be done in many ways, based on different ideologies, concepts and notions, both in formal ways and informal ways. Informal political networks access the alternative avenues of participation and try to affect the distribution of goods and power relations.[18] Notions of citizenship can penetrate existing relations of power and subvert them and inspire change in relations of dependency.[19] Informal rights and concealed

---

[16] See for example, Daniel Lerner, *The Passing of Traditional Society* (Glencoe: Free Press, 1958); Manfred Halpern, *The Politics of Social Change in the Middle East and North Africa* (Princeton: Princeton University Press, 1963).

[17] See Nils Butenschøn, 'The Arab Spring and the "Iron Triangle": Regime Survival and the Conditions of Citizenship in the Arab Middle East' in *The Crisis of Citizenship in the Arab World*, eds. Roel Meijer and Nils Butenschøn (Leiden: Brill, 2017) 246–69.

[18] Diane Singerman, *Avenues of Participation: Family, Politics, and Networks in Urban Quarters of Cairo* (Princeton: Princeton University Press, 1989).

[19] Ward Berenschot, Henk Schulte Nordholt and Laurens Bakker (eds.), *Citizenship and Democratization in Southeast Asia* (Leiden: Brill, 2017).

notions of justice can express themselves in many ways ranging from 'quiet encroachment of the ordinary',[20] to what has been called 'everyday citizenship',[21] and 'acts of citizenship',[22] which are less organised and not always developed in relation to the state. Over time these can develop into social movements and even into political parties, transitioning from informal networks to formal organisations, with the danger that they lose their original purpose and become incorporated and depoliticised.[23]

We notice waves of increased awareness of citizenship in the beginning of the nationalist movement prior to Arab independence; Arab socialism 1950s to the 1970s; The Berber Spring 1981; the Palestinian Intifada 1987–1993; the Iraqi Intifada 1991; the Arab Uprisings 2010–2011.

What is crucial is that these developments highlight the importance of *agency* and the influence people have on the content, extent and depth of citizenship. They indicate a political awareness, conceptualisation of rights and notions of justice, and an increased self-reflexivity and attentiveness to the political environment. In this process, practices and concepts influence each other in ways that give hope for the future, even if the counter-forces such as those executed by the state and non-state actors on the national and local level in the form of patronage, repression, encapsulation and co-optation are always present as a threat.

What these examples further demonstrate is that the citizenship approach brings together not only the different conceptual dimensions of political authority, but also a wealth of experiences on the global, regional, and local levels that have, or should have, important policy implications. International standards of governance are centred on human rights, good governance, and the rule of law. These are universal norms and rules which are often at odds with the situation at hand. Their character as legalistic, formal, and procedural often makes them appear as external to the population and the values they uphold and practices they and local governments follow. They are a yardstick to measure 'progress' and 'regression' and compliance with external standards. But this tension between the external standards and the experienced world so often observed, this fundamental

---

[20] Asef Bayat, *Making Islam Democratic: Social Movements and the Post-Islamic Turn* (Stanford: Stanford University Press, 2007).

[21] Salwa Ismail, *Rethinking Islamist Politics: Culture, the State and Islamism* (London: I.B. Tauris, 2003).

[22] Engin F. Isin and Greg M. Nielsen, *Acts of Citizenship* (Chicago: Chicago University Press, 2008).

[23] As, for instance, happened with the Justice and Development Party (PJD) in Morocco. The failure of the Arab Uprisings is ascribed to the failure of this transition.

entfremdung, makes it difficult to identify mechanisms for effective realisation of the internationally accepted standards. The citizenship approach, in contrast, starts at, or at least delves into, the practices and notions of people themselves, their specific local forms, histories, cultural, political and economic environment and the national and international influences which have impinged on a specific citizenship regime. This does not mean that the citizenship approach neglects these international standards. It includes them because they all entertain and promote a certain concept of citizenship.

While some people support good governance, human rights, and the rule of law, *all* people and institutions entertain and affect notions and follow practices of citizenship. To discover what these are, which legal, social, economic, political, and ideological factors influence them, goes to the heart of politics. It analyses the 'actual situation' not the ideal situation and what is supposed to be.

CONTRIBUTIONS

We will use the distinctions Keith Faulks has suggested between three dimensions of citizenship rights – extent, content, and depth – to analyse the chapters of this volume and draw out their common themes.[24] *Extent* refers to the issue of who belongs to the community, and on what terms; *content* refers to rights of access to the services of the state; *depth* refers to what is demanded of members in the form of responsibility, participation and solidarity. These three dimensions cover crucial aspects of citizenship.

In **Chapter 1** Nils Butenschøn argues that the citizenship approach is sufficiently open in its theoretical orientation and precise enough as an analytical tool to capture the complexities of Israel as a state formation, and yet identify the distinct challenges this state poses in its relations with the various demographic collectivities that have claims to the territories under its current rule or control. The nature of these challenges and the controversies and conflicts they have sparked since the establishment of the state in 1948 can only be fully comprehended with a view to the extent, content and depth of citizenship as premised by Zionism as its ideological foundation and the historic conditions for creating a separate state for Jews in Palestine. Presenting some of the main academic discourses on Israel as an 'ethnic' state, 'democratic' state, and 'Jewish' state, Butenschøn maintains that whereas the legal and institutional fabric of the

[24] Faulks, *Citizenship*.

State of Israel unquestionably is ethnocratic in distribution of rights and resources, the state itself is still a state in the making, an unfinished state (by default, just like Palestine). This relates to the fact that neither its final borders nor the citizenship implication of its identity as a 'Jewish' state have been defined, leaving strings of controversies in relation to secular and religious Jewish societies and denominations, both locally and globally, as well as in relation to the Palestinians living in the State of Israel and in the Occupied Palestinian Territory, and the millions of refugees in exile. The larger picture is that of a state established against local and regional resistance, a state 'in the Middle East, but not of the Middle East' basing its survival on military hegemony; a 'programmatic' state seeking to integrate world Jewry but not the local non-Jewish population, gradually expanding its hold on Mandatory Palestine. This is the dynamic of a *frontier state* based on expanding ethnically exclusive settlements in conquered territory; in the contemporary world a unique challenge to the local, regional, and international order.

Chapter 2, by Basak Ince, is a good illustration of the changing character of citizenship and how it is influenced by internal and external dynamics in Turkey. She demonstrates how during the 1980s the secular and uniform concept of citizenship which Atatürk had imposed in the 1930s with its emphasis on duties and Turkish identity gradually became more pluralistic, recognising difference and becoming more receptive to the specific identities of Alevis, Kurds, and other minorities. In the words of Bryan Turner, 'formal', state definitions of citizenship were being replaced by 'radical' concepts of citizenship influenced by the people. With this move the emphasis changed from the legal aspect (extent of citizenship) to identity (content) and 'civic virtue' (depth). The last is represented by civic education and instilling in children notions and practices of equal citizenship. In this period Alevis, Christians, Jews, and Kurds demanded recognition of their religious institutions, freedom of religious education and equal access to the same funds of the state as the majority Sunni population. These changes were gradually put into practice after the Justice and Development Party (AKP) came to power in 2002. They were incorporated in its elections programme of 2007 and recognised as fundamental rights of citizens in constitutional amendments. In hindsight the draft Constitution of 2007 proved to be the high point of this trend. Since the Arab Uprisings and especially after the attempted coup in summer 2016 Turkey has drifted towards an authoritarian citizenship regime based on a populist, controlled, communitarian and deeply Turkish nationalist notion of citizenship.

If Turkey was largely successful in imposing concepts of citizenship from above, although Atatürk's legacy concerning extent, content, and depth of citizenship is still being contested, Iraq, as analysed in **Chapter 3** by Mariwan Kanie, represents a state where all attempts by the state to create a homogeneous population failed. The major difference was that Iraq did not emerge from a successful revolution and did not have a military leader who saved the country from occupation, as was the case in Turkey during the war of liberation (1920–1923). Iraq was also a more fragmented society between Shiʿis, Sunnis, Kurds and different Christian denominations, as well as smaller minorities such as Assyrians, Turkmen, Jews and Yezidis. Another difference was that Sunni leaders managed to retain power until the Americans invaded Iraq in 2003 and a dramatic shift took place in favour of the Shiʿis. As a result, the Sunni elite could pursue assimilationist policies as expressed in Satiʿal-Husri's pan-Arab educational project and forcefully repress the Kurdish and Shiʿi identity. The resistance against Sunni dominance continued throughout Iraq's modern history. The Communist Party of Iraq was one of the few political currents that embraced an active, participatory citizenship based on ethnic, religious, gender and social equality as well as cultural pluralism. After a brief period in the 1950s of widely supported social contract between the different ethnic groups in society, in the 1970s Saddam Hussein introduced a new phase of brutal repression of Pan-Arabism. Kanie gives an extensive analysis of the efforts of the Baʿath state to destroy any notion of rights and install a regime based on total fear and powerlessness of the citizen. In the end, the only thing that counted was loyalty to Saddam. No wonder that after the American invasion notions of shared citizenship hardly existed and fissures in society along ethnic and religious lines deepened. The establishment of ISIS in 2014 is a direct result of the failure of the Nouri al-Maliki government (2006–2014) to establish an inclusive, egalitarian but pluralistic citizenship regime.[25] In that context, it was not illogical that Sunni Iraqis tried to establish a homogeneous religious state based on Sunni religious exclusivity.

In **Chapter 4** Sylvia Bergh and Salima Ahmadou analyse the discourse of former members of the February 20 Movement in Morocco in relation to the concept of citizenship. Citizenship had been one of the central concepts of the February 20 Movement in 2011, which demanded equal civil, political and economic rights at the expense of the power of the *Makhzen* (power structures around the monarchy), condemning corruption, marginalisation and deprivation of dignity (*hogra*). As none of the grievances of the Arab Uprisings have been addressed, citizenship

[25] Toby Dodge, *Iraq: From War to a New Authoritarianism* (London: The International Institute for Strategic Studies, 2012).

continues to be the central demand after 2011, as is apparent from the Rif Uprisings and elsewhere in 2017. One of the reasons for the common theme of citizenship is that in Morocco, like in Tunisia, cross-ideological coalitions were formed between leftist, Islamist and non-political groups which had worked together in protest committees (*tansiqiyyat*). They express their grievances in 'acts of citizenship', in the form of 'taking to the street', 'freeing public space', and organising debates on public issues such as rising prices, corruption, profit of private investors and social justice. Learning from the failures of the February 20 Movement, activists pay more attention to defining more clearly the extent, content and depth of citizenship and formulating more concrete demands. The connection they make between socio-economic development and political citizenship reflects their increased political awareness. It is the arbitrariness of the authorities and their treatment as 'subjects' that provokes the greatest outrage.

In **Chapters 5** and **6** Zahra Babar and Zeineb Alsabeehg underline the centrality of citizenship for understanding core political dynamics in the Gulf states. Contrary to what is normally assumed by proponents of the so-called rentier state model, citizens in the Gulf are not passive but try actively to influence the extent, content and depth of citizenship in their own countries. Whereas it is well known that these oil-rich monarchies have 'bought' political loyalty by providing privileged citizens with basic social and economic needs through government stipends, subsidies, job guarantees, free education and health care, giving incentives for political inactivity and leaving legislative assemblies toothless (except in the case of Kuwait), this kind of social contract has been rejected by important segments of the population. They show that political contestation has always existed, and, in fact, has grown since the Arab Uprisings and that citizenship rather than democracy is central to that political struggle. The difference with liberal democracies is that illiberal states do not have formal channels for political contestation that are not under the control of the regime and that contestation assumes different forms. This is apparent from the way rulers define nationality, the criteria for access to citizenship, national identity, differentiating and privileging citizen rights, presenting rights as a 'gift' of the ruler, and increasingly, punishing opponents by revoking their citizenship. Here inclusion and exclusion are the tools of politics. The examples Zahra Babar and Zeineb Alsabeehg give of contestation relate to women's right to pass their citizenship on to their children, minority rights, and freedom of expression, and, most significantly, revocation of citizenship, leaving opponents of the regime stateless. These issues are tied up with national identity and belonging, split identities, dual nationalities on the one hand, and rulers' strategies for regime survival, on the other. It shows that while rulers have been forced to make concessions with regard to major issues such as passing citizenship to children, any attempt to deepen citizenship and create active citizenship to challenge content is punished by the ultimate sacrifice of revocation of citizenship.

In **Chapter 7** Nathalie Bernard-Maugiron shows that bringing about a new social contract after the Arab Uprisings was highly problematic and a key challenge to the political processes in the immediate post-Uprising situation. The old regimes had lost their popular legitimacy, but how should a new social contract be reflected and formulated in a constitutional language? While in Tunisia a near consensus on a new constitution was reached by the Constituent Assembly in January 2014 and free and fair elections organised in October that year, in Egypt – which is Maugiron's case study – the process failed to be inclusive and consensual. She compares the drafting process of the Constitution of 2012 under President Muhammad Morsi with the 2014 Constitution drawn up under Abd al-Fattah al-Sisi. Both were exclusive; the first dominated by Islamists, the second by opponents of the Muslim Brotherhood as represented in the 'Committee of 50' appointed by the military. The latter was less focused on religion and more on securing state powers and was called 'a short-term political deal rather than a long-lasting social contract'. This shows that in Egypt, unlike in Syria or Iraq, authoritarianism was able to legally secure its position by determining the extent, content and depth of citizenship. But it was not just the deep state that was able to reassert itself. Rather, what Nathan Brown calls the 'Balkanization of the Egyptian state', determines the rights of Egyptians. The Constitution of 2014 greatly limited the scope of the people's sovereignty by restricting the citizenry to followers of the 'divinely revealed religions', privileging the position of the military, and sanctioning the complete independence of the judiciary, making it even less accountable to the people. Specific elements of citizenship rights were also determined by the direct references to the status of citizens in different contexts. For example, while the Constitution of 2014 claims to secure equal rights of citizens, it regards women's natural position as the home; it recognises autonomy of non-Muslims and the special status of Copts (not as equal citizens), and the provision of Article 2 of Islam as state religion negates the provision of equality, and limits freedom of religion to followers of 'revealed religions' (Muslims, Christians and Jews).[26] On

---

[26] See Rachel Scott, 'Citizenship, Public Order, and State Sovereignty: Article 3 of the Egyptian Constitution and the "Divinely Revealed Religions"' in *The Crisis of Citizenship in the Arab World*, eds. Roel Meijer and Nils Butenschøn (Leiden: Brill, 2017) 375–405.

the whole, many provisions were vague, and much was left to legislation to determine the citizenship regime with regard to human rights and other matters. In the end, the repression of the Egyptian state installed a highly repressive citizenship regime, regardless of the constitutional provisions.

In the second part of the book the relationship between *Islam and citizenship* is analysed. It shows that Islamic movements have only recently contributed to modern notions of political citizenship. In **Chapter 8** Roel Meijer argues that fully articulated concepts of political citizenship depend on the recognition of the political as an independent field of human activity.[27] One of the characteristics of political Islam is that in its totalising ideological overreach politics is absorbed by religion and then diffused over ethics and religious practices. As a result of the eclipse of the political and denial of politics as independent activity separate from religion, extent, content and depth of political citizenship are not only defined in religious terms, they have become non-negotiable, non-debatable, and cannot be challenged in a rational manner in an open 'neutral' debate. Citizens in such movements as the Muslim Brotherhood have no rights, debates are restricted and dissent punished by banishment; leadership is unaccountable and political struggle is largely an issue of identity. Sayyid Qutb brings this trend to its logical conclusion by the absorption of all agency in God's sovereignty who determines extent, content, and depth of citizenship. In a nation-state, however, citizenship is a central issue, and subsequent thinkers were forced to address in a more realistic manner the fundamental relationship between citizen and state. The second General Guide of the Muslim Brotherhood, Hasan al-Hudaybi (1891–1973) was strongly opposed to the exclusionary doctrine of *takfir* and challenged the stark choice Qutb made between jihad and unbelief. Likewise, Yusuf al-Qaradawi (b. 1926) advocates the rationality of the *fiqh* of balances as an alternative to Qutb's jihadism. Younger generations go even further by liberating politics from Islam, either through the separation of the two, as Abdelwahhab El-Affendi advocates, or creating enough room for politics and citizenship to emerge through the method of the 'purposes of the sharia' (*maqasid al-shari'a*). Especially these last two routes show promising signs towards achieving an Islamic politics based on the sovereignty of the people, Islamic humanitarian ethics and inclusive, equal citizenship. In terms of extent, content, and depth, their discourse gives back agency

---

[27] For more on citizenship and the Wasatiyya trend, see Jakob Skovgaard-Petersen, 'Brothers and Citizens: The Second Wave of Islamic Institutional Thinking and the Concept of Citizenship' in *The Crisis of Citizenship in the Arab World*, eds. Roel Meijer and Nils Butenschøn (Leiden: Brill, 2017), 320–37.

to citizens, creates civility, recognises pluralism and a new intellectual openness.

In **Chapter 9** Zoltan Pall analyses Salafism,[28] a current in Islam that denies the relevance of citizenship as a relationship between state and citizen within the context of the nation-state. Instead, Salafis hold a universal, 'de-territorialised' concept of citizenship that includes the whole *umma*. Pall calls Salafism 'grounded utopianism', grounded in the sense that Salafis are connected to real situations, utopian because they strive for a return to the ideal society of the first three generations of Muslims. Their objection to the nation-state is its concept of sovereignty of the people and its demand of loyalty to a non-religious entity, fragmenting the *umma* into smaller units. In Salafi thought, extent and the question of who belongs to the community is a religious question and is limited to members of their own religious group; content is based on creed (*'aqida*) and is focused on the purification of doctrine and the emulation of the life of the first three generations of Muslims, who are the most pious and pure and are regarded as examples of a perfect life; depth, or what Salafis call *manhaj* (programme or methodology), demands a deep commitment through *da'wa*, preaching, and such practices as 'commanding good and forbidding evil'. However, as Pall shows, their groundedness and the reality of local political, social, religious and economic circumstances forces Salafis to make choices and compromises concerning the societal role of citizens. He compares two situations that have forced Salafis to adopt different strategies: in the first case, Lebanon, Sunnis are alienated from the sectarian state and feel threatened by the collapse of Syria and seek solidarity with Sunnis in Syria and Kuwait in a revival of the Sunni *umma* in their struggle against Hezbollah; in the second case, Salafis in Kuwait are more integrated and seek support from the state to help consolidate their institutions and the spread of Salafism internationally. Both cases demonstrate that Salafism is as much a product of the citizenship regimes in the region and rapid and deep political processes of change as it is a reflection of doctrine.

In **Chapter 10** Shirin Saeidi shows how citizenship works out in the case of Iran where citizenship acquires a deep ambivalence due to, on the one hand, its revolutionary legacy and sense of agency and rights that its founders Shariati and Khomeini have given to the people, and, on the other hand, the current repressive power of the state that demands obedience. Whereas Salafism mostly denies a discourse of rights, the

---

[28] See for more on citizenship and Salafism, Emin Poljarevic, 'The Ambiguity in Contemporary Salafism,' in *The Crisis of Citizenship in the Arab World*, eds. Roel Meijer and Nils Butenschøn (Leiden: Brill, 2017), 338–74.

strong revolutionary strain of (gnostic) 'critical thinking' in contemporary Shiʿism together with a much stronger rational philosophical dimension supports agency and acts of citizenship in Iran. It is the element of resistance in the service of the community and claim-making against the state that produces the notion of the citizen. The other element that works in favour of citizenship is the acceptance of a bounded entity of the Republic as a religious nation-state which clearly lays down specific relations between citizens and the state in a constitutional setting giving citizens equal rights. A third element that contributes to the strong ambivalence of citizenship rights in Iranian society is piety as a source of legitimacy and power. The idea that those who are more pious than others also have more rights – the same basis of Salafism (belonging to the 'saved sect') – lays the foundation for a hierarchy of rights and the rule of a religious elite over the majority of the people. This ambivalence between claims of citizens and their subjection to state power and state sanctioned pious hierarchy is reproduced in the Constitution. On the one hand it has a section on the 'The Rights of the People' who are called upon to defend the independence of the Republic, whereas on the other hand it stresses obedience to the state and respect for the religious political order. In the end, however, Saeidi argues it is not just rights per se that constitutes the potential for citizens to act and give them agency, it is the sovereignty of God that stands above the state that allows citizens to hold the state accountable to a supreme entity. This empowering principle has, of course, also operated in Europe during the Reformation, and in the Middle East has given Sayyid Qutb the power to develop jihad as a struggle for *hakimiyya* (sovereignty of God) against the secular state. In the second part of the chapter Saeidi gives several examples of how citizens have turned the more democratic principles of the Republic against it, both in its cultural institutions and in such highly ideologically loaded subjects as marriage, in this manner 'pushing the boundaries of autonomy and equality'.

The third part of the book focuses on the *international dimensions of citizenship*. In **Chapter 11** Ruth Hanau Santini analyses the effect of policies of the European Union (EU) towards the Middle East and North Africa on extent, content and depth of citizenship. In the first half of the chapter she argues that the EU, due to the diversity of the political background of its own member states, political inertia, and attempts to depoliticise democracy and make it non-controversial and exportable, never developed a coherent policy towards the Middle East and North Africa (MENA) region promoting democracy. The result has been that the EU pursues a policy that is unfavourable to citizens of MENA, supporting a neoliberal policy that undermines the agency of citizens. Hanau Santini differentiates between two models: Protective Liberal Democracy, which the EU promotes, and Developmental Liberal Democracy, which is more rooted in the region but is far too activist for the EU. Whereas the first supports individualist liberalism, procedural democracy, the market economy and a passive concept of citizenship, the second assigns a greater role to the state and advocates an active, participatory citizenship and is more substantive, or what has been called a 'thick' citizenship. It also acknowledges the importance of social and economic rights. In the second half of the chapter Hanau Santini analyses in greater detail the instruments the EU has developed, such as the European Neighbourhood Policy (ENP), the European Instrument for Democracy and Human Rights (EIDHR) and the European Endowment for Democracy (EED). Despite the new policy of promoting 'deep democracy', Hanau Santini argues that new measures of the EU based on human rights, good governance, civil liberties, fair and free elections, the rule of law, or what should be regarded as a 'thin' concept of citizenship, did little to support the Arab countries in their citizenship revolutions after the Arab Uprisings.

In **Chapter 12** Peter Seeberg analyses the position of the refugees from the civil war in Syria within the notion of citizenship and 'migration diplomacy'. Basically he analyses the agreement between the EU and Turkey of March 2016 in which Turkey grants Syrian refugees certain rights to have access to the Turkish labour market and provides certain services to refugees in the form of health care and education paid for by the EU (social and economic rights) in return for keeping Syrian refugees in Turkey and gradually integrating them into Turkish society. This agreement, which directly determines extent, content and depth of refugee status, provides a unique insight into citizenship policies of both the EU and Turkey and confirms the idea that citizenship is central to the current transformations in the Middle East. Seeberg argues that the refugee crisis has led to a greater interdependence between the EU and Turkey and greater complexity in their relations. In his words, it can lead to new a 'security partnership', but perhaps as important it confirms what Ruth Hanau Santini in the previous chapter points out: the EU's inability to develop a more substantive foreign citizenship policy is a reflection of its inability to formulate a common democratic internal one. In the case of the refugees, the EU's foreign citizenship policy can be regarded as a 'deferred' or 'transmitted' citizenship policy, allowing the Turkish government to determine the issues of extent, content and depth of the refugee problem rather than having the courage to organise that debate internally. The end result seems to be that the position of refugees has been far from settled and has become dependent on a power struggle between the EU, especially Germany, and Turkey. In this struggle, Erdoğan uses the refugee crisis as a lever to gain power over the EU and increase his popularity with his electorate. The Turkish electorat was promised to be able to travel freely without visas in Europe, while the refugees have acquired a second class status in Turkish society as a cheap labour force and are held hostage as a political instrument to exert pressure on the EU. Vague terms such as 'harmonisation', with which the governing party AKP describes the process of integration, remain too ambiguous to indicate clear rights.

In **Chapter 13** Lillian Frost and Musa Shteiwi highlight the refugee crisis and integration of refugees as citizens from a different angle. They analyse the position of Syrian refugees in Lebanon and Jordan with regard to content and social rights to education, health and work, as well as political participation. In contrast to Turkey, refugees in these two countries are less dependent on the power politics of a single politician in an economically strong country. Frost and Shteiwi analyse these refugees as 'non-citizens', whose rights are defended by international organisations in the context of two different local citizenship regimes. Lebanon and Jordan have developed their refugee policies against the background of the position of their own citizens and their local citizenship regimes. In the case of Lebanon, this is sectarianism and a weak state, whose capacity of interference and enforcement is limited. As a result, refugees have few formal rights, depend on the welfare of different religious groups and the development of informal relations for survival, finding a job and acquiring access to health and educational services. In Jordan, where the state is sovereign, relatively strong and centralised, the refugee regime is mostly determined by the Palestinian-Trans-Jordanian divide. The refugees benefit from a regime used to distributing welfare and providing for social rights. In both states the demographic factor weighs strongly and determines to a large degree the issue of extent (who belongs to the political community) and political rights. In Lebanon, refugees cannot be integrated and become citizens because it would upset the demographic weight in favour of the Sunnis who would become a majority. In Jordan, they cannot become citizens because they do not belong to the Trans-Jordanian tribal support group of the monarchy. Other factors of influence are the weak economic basis of these countries and insufficient resources to cope with such large numbers of refugees, and increasingly since the 2011 securitisation. Frost and Shteiwi show in the second part of their chapter the influence international treaties and international law have on the position of refugees as non-citizens and how it affects their civil, political and economic rights.

In **Chapter 14** Valerie Moghadam shows how globalisation has affected the economic rights of women in the Middle East and North Africa. While Frost and Shteiwi looked at the civil, social and economic rights of non-citizens, Moghadam analyses economic rights of women and investigates what chances women have in MENA to achieve economic citizenship. Her conclusion is that women have played a minor role in determining extent, content and depth of citizenship when it comes to their economic rights. In the first part of the chapter she analyses economic rights to employment and the right to freely find work of one's choice, which are hampered by patriarchy, family conventions and domestic duties; the second part deals with the effect the political economy has on women's rights. Rather than the so-called authoritarian bargain between authoritarian states and citizens, Moghadam argues that women were subjected to the 'patriarchal gender contract' which has kept women restricted to the household allowing men to become breadwinners. This arrangement was further supported by Islamic law, which strengthens patriarchal relations despite the many reforms of family law in the region. The weakening of the state and the introduction of the neoliberal economy in the 1980s further weakened existing economic rights of women. In the third part of the chapter Moghadam analyses the economic position of women on the eve of the Arab Uprisings. She shows that their position was much weaker than in other parts of the world in terms of labour participation. Women were also more highly concentrated in community, social and public services, leading to what she calls a 'feminisation of unemployment'. The final part of the chapter deals with women's organisations supporting women's economic rights. These were especially active in the Maghreb and it is there that women are able to exert some influence on the extent, content and depth of economic citizenship.

PART I

Local contested citizenship

1. Israeli ethnocracy and the Israel-Palestine citizenship complex

Nils A. Butenschøn

> We came to this land after having burned all our bridges behind us, and there is no return. The only way open for us – to advance, and when there is no possibility of advancing, we have no choice but to stand with our backs against the wall, and fight for our positions.
>
> David Ben Gurion[1]

INTRODUCTION

This chapter has three main parts. First, an attempt is made to identify basic principles of Israeli citizenship as it emerged in the extraordinary context of Zionist state-building in Palestine in the years prior to the establishment of the State of Israel in 1948. Second, I discuss how 'three generations' of Israeli political sociologists have conceptualised the relationship between the state and its citizens (and non-citizens). Finally, based on some of my earlier studies, I present a conceptualisation of Israel as an *ethnocracy* within the Israel-Palestine Citizenship Complex, demonstrating the interrelatedness of Israeli and Palestinian citizenship as elements not only in an intractable conflict but also in the future political organisation of state authority in Israel-Palestine.[2]

---

[1] David Ben Gurion, 'Planning Zionist Policy,' in *Jews and Arabs in Palestine: Studies in a National and Colonial Problem*, eds. Enzo Sereni and R.E. Ashery (New York: Hechalutz Press, 1936), 123.

[2] It seems that my coining of the concept of ethnocracy developed in parallel with works by the Israeli geographer Oren Yiftachel. In the late 1980s and early 1990s I published research papers defining the concept with particular reference to Israel, and a more elaborated version in Nils A. Butenschøn, 'State, Power, and Citizenship: A Theoretical Introduction' in *Citizenship and the State in the Middle East: Approaches and Applications*, eds. Nils A. Butenschøn, Uri Davis and Manuel Hassassian (Syracuse: Syracuse University Press, 2000), 16–28. I was not aware of Yiftachel's work until he published his important book *Ethnocracy: Land*

ISRAEL – IN THE REGION, BUT NOT OF THE REGION

In regional studies of the Middle East and North Africa the State of Israel is often not included because it deviates in so many ways from the states and societies in its surroundings. According to the late Leonard Fein: 'though *in* the region, Israel is not *of* the region'.[3] This fundamental regional alienation of Israel and the Israeli-Jewish society has its origins in Israel's nature as a mostly immigrant and settler-state, with its background in European models of state- and nation-building, and born in the bitter struggles over state-building in Palestine over the last century. Israel may not be of the region, but its presence is strongly felt, both as a dominant military power and as a source of regional instability. The struggle is still unfolding today as the last and undecided conflict between a European-style nationalist settler movement and a non-European local population over territorial control and entitlement to sovereign statehood.

This historical context has important implications for an analysis of the current conditions of citizenship in Israel in what I call the Israel-Palestine Citizenship Complex. As a settler-state in a regional environment that rejects its legitimacy Israel has had to mobilise sufficient internal strength, including military strength, and external support, from the moment it declared territorial sovereignty in 1948 in order to withstand potential attacks from any Arab war coalition.[4] This has been achieved partly by organising every Jewish citizen for the building and protection of the new state – defining citizenship in terms of a common destiny between state and

---

and Identity Politics in Israel/Palestine (Philadelphia: University of Pennsylvania Press, 2006).

[3] Leonard J. Fein, *Politics in Israel* (Boston: Little, Brown, 1967), 65 (emphasis added). James Piscatori and R.K. Ramazani give the following reason for excluding Israel in a study of the Middle East: '[. . .] official Judaism, European cultural affinities, the political strength of the Ashkenazi, and the intimate connection with the United States make Israel unique in, and thus different from, the region. As a result, we define The Middle East as excluding Israel, but including eighteen Arab states, Iran, and Turkey.' See J.P. Piscatori and R.K. Ramazani, 'The Middle East' in *Comparative Regional Systems: West and East Europe, North America, the Middle East, and Developing Countries*, eds. Gavin Boyd and Werner J. Feld (New York: Pergamon Press, 2016 (1980)), 275.

[4] The ambition of creating a Jewish state in Palestine was rejected almost unanimously not only by Palestinian Arabs, but throughout the region. When Israel declared independence on 14 May 1948, the Arab states immediately went to war as they had warned when a majority of the United National General Assembly voted for the partition of Palestine into a Jewish and an Arab state in November 1947.

its Jewish citizens – and partly by seeking security guarantees and military assistance from external powers, including from former colonial powers (thereby strengthening the regional perception of Israel as an alien entity and instrument of foreign domination). The lack of local and regional legitimacy, and confronted with a history of displacing large tracts of the non-Jewish Palestinians in times of war, a narrative justifying a separate state for Jews in Palestine has always been needed as a central theme in the building of Israeli citizenship as membership in a state with a historic mission for the Jewish people. The Israeli argument has been that Israel as a state for the Jews would not survive a military defeat since its legitimacy was rejected by the Arabs; it could lose a battle, but not a war. This is also why a strategic priority for the Israeli leadership has been to recruit as many immigrant citizens as possible from the pool of world Jewry, including the need to justify the Zionist state-building programme as a genuine 'Jewish' programme, either within secular or religious conceptions of the term.

Consequently, Israel needs to have not only a large contingent of its citizens, both men and women, mobilised and fully motivated as citizen-soldiers for military action on a short notice, but also to command an effective 'military edge' over the Arabs, at least as long as there is a credible external threat.[5] Furthermore, it needs to activate as much support as possible from external sources, both governments and public opinion. With references to the central geostrategic location of the country on the one hand, to ever-present 'existential threats' from neighbours, and to the tragic destiny of European Jewry on the other, this political-military doctrine, still operational today, resonates strongly with Jews in general, and also with influential segments of Western opinion. Among other motives, the doctrine reflects a world view that serves as a politico-moral shield against critics of Israeli human rights violations and violations of international law, and in support of requests for military, economic, and diplomatic support from European and Western powers in particular.

General Principles of Israeli Citizenship: A Context of Extraordinary State-Building

It follows from this introduction that Israeli citizenship can only be understood in the historical context of 'the Zionist Revolution' of

---

5 Michael I. Handel, *Israel's Political-military Doctrine* (Cambridge, Mass.: Harvard University Center for International Affairs, Occasional Papers in International Affairs, No. 30, 1973); Nils A. Butenschøn, 'Israel as a Regional Great Power' in *Regional Great Powers in International Politics*, ed. Iver. B. Neumann (London: Macmillan, 1990), 95–120.

(re-)creating a Jewish nation in historic Palestine. When the Zionist programme was first announced, almost the entire world Jewry was living outside Palestine, for the most part in Europe. The Zionist programme would imply, in a practical sense, moving Jews on a massive scale to a country totally different from Europe in terms of resources, climate, infrastructure, and culture and making them into an 'old-new' nation in an 'old-new' country.[6] And since the country was under Ottoman-Muslim rule (until after World War I) and already populated almost entirely by non-Jewish Palestinians, the country would somehow have to be made available and accessible for Jewish immigration and colonisation, whether through negotiations with Ottoman authorities or conquest. Negotiations failed; it was only after the British conquest of Palestine in 1918, and based on the promises of the British government to the Zionists the previous year of supporting the establishment of a 'national home for the Jewish people' in Palestine (the Balfour Declaration) that the Zionist programme became *realpolitik*.[7]

Mandatory Palestine is the state territory defined by the League of Nations as 'Palestine' in 1922 – including today's Israel within the 1949 ceasefire lines (the 'Green Line' or 'Israel proper'), the West Bank including East Jerusalem, and the Gaza Strip – as part of the post-Ottoman organisation of the Levant ino British or French Mandates. According to the Mandatory Regulations the Mandates were to be 'guided' towards independence by the Mandatory Power. In contrast to neighbouring countries (who got local governments) Palestine was to be ruled directly from London and the substance of the Balfour Declaration was included in the preamble of the Mandate for Palestine.[8]

From that point onwards defining state authority and citizenship in Palestine became an international issue and responsibility; a 'dual

---

6 See Theodor Herzl's utopian novel, *Altneuland* (Berlin: Verlag der Contumax, 2015 (1902)).

7 The Jewish population constituted only a small minority of about 65,000 persons (less than 10 per cent of the country, and many of whom were not necessarily sympathetic to the Zionists), and only a fraction of world Jewry. Zionism became *realpolitik* because the promise (albeit in conflict with other promises) was given by the coming Mandatory Power in Palestine, and because it was included in the League of Nations Mandatory Regulations for Palestine in 1922, reflecting that it was already accepted by other leading powers at the time (including US President Woodrow Wilson) and given a legal status.

8 The Balfour Declaration was issued in the form of a short letter to Lord Rothschild, a leading British Zionist, signed by foreign secretary Arthur Balfour on behalf of the government on 2 November 1917. The Declaration was controversial at the time and is so still today.

commitment',[9] as it were, by an international body that had promised self-determination and future statehood to the people of Palestine, on the one hand, and a 'national home' for the Jewish people in the same territory, on the other. The inherent inconsistency between the two commitments was never explicated and clarified or resolved at the time, leaving the Mandatory Power (Great Britain) with an escalating intractable conflict. Was the 'national home' meant to become a Jewish state, some restricted form of self-government, or merely the right to form autonomous religious and cultural institutions in the country? The World Zionist Organization headed by Chaim Weizmann, who had negotiated the declaration with the British government over several years, took the declaration to imply effectively British support for a Jewish state,[10] whereas the Palestinians protested against what they saw as an infringement of their rights of self-determination.

The Zionist programme was, in many ways, the most radical Jewish solution to 'the Jewish problem' in Europe, and did not gather much support among European Jews in the first stages of its history. Other solutions, not involving the uprooting of the Jewish societies in Europe were more popular.[11]

Convincing Jews to move to Mandatory Palestine, and rich sponsors to support the project would furthermore require propagating a narrative and an ideology that presented the Zionist programme both as a liberating continuity with references to millennia of Jewish history of 'exile', as well

---

9 Nils A. Butenschøn, 'The Paradox of Palestinian Self-Determination' in *Where Now for Palestine? The Demise of the Two-State Solution*, ed. Jamil Hilal (London and New York: University of Chicago Press, 2007), 75–99. For an excellent book on citizenship in pre-Israel Palestine, see Lauren Banko, *The Invention of Palestinian Citizenship, 1918–1947* (Edinburgh: Edinburgh University Press, 2016).

10 Weizmann described the Declaration as 'the Magna Charta of Jewish liberties', and in a letter to Balfour comparing it to the proclamation of Cyrus the Great called upon the Jews to return to Jerusalem and rebuild the Temple. Ronald Sanders, *The High Walls of Jerusalem: A History of the Balfour Declaration and the Birth of the British Mandate for Palestine* (New York: Holt, Rinehart and Winston, 1983), 616.

11 Responding at the time to European nationalism and anti-Semitism, including Russian, pogroms Jews chose different strategies. Between 1881 and 1914 a large wave of westward emigration of Jews from Central and Eastern Europe took place, about 2.6 million to the USA alone. Others chose to engage in political and other civil society organisations in their home country struggling for equality and freedom (for example, almost half of the delegates to the 2nd Congress of the Russian Social Democratic Party in 1903 had a Jewish background). Yet others, mostly Yiddish-speaking Jews in the so-called Pale of Settlement, mobilised for cultural autonomy for Jews in this region.

as being compatible with Jewish religious conceptions of 'redemption' on the one hand and secular universalism of modern nation-building, on the other. According to Theodore Herzl, the founder of modern political Zionism, the Zionist programme was not only a solution for the Jews, realising their potential as *one* people, but also for the European nation-states who would not or could not integrate or accommodate the Jews and Jewish societies in their midst.[12]

Rewriting Jewish history and constructing a functional modern Hebrew language were essential elements in the strategy of the 'practical Zionists' who took over from Herzl after his early death in 1904. The foundations were thus laid for a kind of Zionist and later Israeli patriotism of building the land and building the people, standards for Israeli citizenship in the historical struggle for survival. A clear expression of the task bestowed on the Israelis is the slogan *ein breira* – (we have) no choice: There was no choice but to build a state for the Jews, and the state had to be militarily strong enough to encounter whatever resistance came from the Palestinian Arabs or the Arab states. Consequently, the 1948–1949 Arab-Israeli war (War of Independence/Al-Nakba in Israeli and Palestinian parlance, respectively), the 1956 Suez War (when Israel for a short period occupied the Sinai Peninsula for the first time), the 1967 Six Day War/June War, and the 1973 Yom Kippur/October War were all understood by most Israelis as wars of an existential nature, wars of *ein breira*, whereas the 1982–1983 Lebanon war – presented by Prime Minister Menachem Begin as necessary under the motto of *ein breira* – was much more controversial among Israelis.[13]

Another dimension in the formative experience of Israeli citizenship is the spirit of the *settler*, the pioneer (*halutz*, pl. *halutzim*), the life and commitment associated with conquering the country bit by bit for the common good of the Jewish nation. In the pre-state period this was most famously organised in the form of the *kibbutz* (pl. *kibbutzim*): small collectivist agricultural communities, often set up overnight as vanguards of an expanding Jewish settler movement in Palestine, protected by Zionist militias.[14]

---

[12] There is a huge literature on the main trends in Zionist thought. One classical work is Arthur Hertzberg (ed.), *The Zionist Idea: A Historical Analysis and Reader* (Westport, Connecticut: Greenwood Press, 1959). See also Shlomo Avineri, *The Making of Modern Zionism: The Intellectual Origins of the Jewish State* (New York: Basic Books, 1981).

[13] Mark A. Heller, 'Israel's Dilemmas' *Survival* 42 (2000) 2: 21–34.

[14] See for example 'The Virtues of Ashkenazi Pioneering', Chapter 2 in Gershon Shafir and Yoav Peled, *Being Israeli: The Dynamics of Multiple Citizenship* (Cambridge: Cambridge University Press, 2002), 37–74.

Few have expressed the vision of 'the Zionist revolution' and the logic of its ethnic exclusionism in a more passionate way than David Ben Gurion, the leader of the pre-state Zionist institutions and later, as Israel's first Prime Minister, the foremost founder of the state.[15] In a well-known collection of articles, he underlines time and again the revolutionary nature of Zionism as a basis for building a completely new citizenship:

> Zionism in its essence is a revolutionary movement. One could hardly find a revolution that goes deeper than what Zionism wants to do to the life of the Hebrew people.
>
> . . .
>
> This transformation [in the life of the Hebrew people] does not limit itself to its geographical aspect, to the movement of Jewish masses from the countries of the Diaspora to the renascent homeland . . . it means taking masses of uprooted, impoverished, sterile Jewish masses, living parasitically off the body of an alien economic body and dependent on others – and introducing them to productive and creative life, implanting them on the land, integrating them into primary production in agriculture, in industry and handicraft – and making them economically independent and self-sufficient.[16]

Whereas the right-wing Zionists focused on the need to create a Jewish majority in Palestine and declare Jewish sovereignty as fast as possible, Ben Gurion and the socialist Zionists wanted a complete new *qualitative* start, basically rebuilding a new Jewish (or Hebrew) nation from scratch; the dominant idea both before and after the establishment of the state itself was that the new Jewish society would have to be built profoundly independent of the Arab Palestinian society. Realisation of Zionism in this view was a question of large-scale collective mobilisation of Jews, and the socialist model was considered best suited for the purpose.

The extraordinary fact is that a socialist movement, identified as the 'Labour Settlement Movement' by Shafir and Peled, came to play the dominant role in a settler-colonial project. They explain this terminology by tuning down the movement's socialist credentials:

---

[15] For a classical study of the founders of Zionism, see Arthur Hertzberg, *The Zionist Idea: A Historical Analysis and Reader* (New York: Doubleday, 1959; Philadelphia: The Jewish Publication Society, 1997 [Kindle edition 2014]). See also Shlomo Avineri, *The Making of Modern Zionism: Intellectual Origins of the Jewish State* (New York: Basic Books, 1981).

[16] Quoted from David Ben Gurion, *From Class to Nation* (1933) in Shlomo Avineri, *The Making of Modern Zionism: The Intellectual Origins of the Jewish State* (New York: Basic Books, 1981), 200. Avineri explains that 'Ben Gurion's usage of *Hebrew* rather that *Jewish* in referring to the new community in Palestine is indicative of this feeling of breaking with the exilic tradition'.

> The most distinguishing characteristic of the Jewish Labour Movement in Palestine was that it was not a labour movement at all. Rather, it was a colonial movement in which the workers' interests remained secondary to the exigencies of settlement. Keeping this observation in mind will allow us to properly describe the movements' dynamics and understand the variety of citizenship forms it fostered.[17]

Regardless of how the left-wing Zionists at the time are labelled, they came to play a dominant role in the pre-state Jewish society in Palestine (the *yishuv*) and for several decades after the establishment of the state. They introduced a concept of Israeli citizenship based on a collectivist republican model that laid the foundations for what they envisaged as a secular, democratic state for the Jewish people. That would only be possible, of course, if the Palestinian Arabs, who constituted the established majority of the country, were not to be included as equal citizens in this national revival of the Jewish people. There were only two logical solutions to this problem as seen from a Zionist point of view: The Palestinians would either have to leave the land projected as a Jewish state or accept a subordinate position recognising that Palestine is the homeland of the Jews and open for Jewish immigration.

Israel today has the character of a *frontier state*[18] to the extent that it applies its traditional Zionist strategy of 'ingathering the exiles' and 'creating facts (settlements) on the ground', developed in the pre-state period. This strategy was reintroduced by Israel after the victory in 1967 and the occupation of new territories. As occupying power Israel was in a position (however in contravention of international law) to expand its infrastructure and Israeli-Jewish civil population into the territories – as long as more powerful actors did not intervene to curb its expansionism – thereby confronting the indigenous Palestinians over the material foundation of society.

The State of Israel and Israeli Citizenship

When the State of Israel was declared in 1948 a civil war was already raging between Zionist and Palestinian militias and the military forces of the British Mandatory had just left the country. The entire Jewish

---

[17] Gershon Shafir and Yoav Peled, *Being Israeli: The Dynamics of Multiple Citizenship* (Cambridge: Cambridge University Press, 2002), 37.

[18] Daniel J. Elazar, *Israel: Building a New Society* (Bloomington: Indiana University Press, 1986), 2. See also, for more references, Nils A. Butenschøn, 'The Frontier State at Work. Models of Contemporary Israeli State-Building' *Journal of Theoretical Politics* 4 (1992) 4: 413–33.

population of the country in 1947 was about 650,000 (a ten-fold growth since 1917); the Palestinians comprised some 1.3 million (a two-fold growth since 1917), and would make up about 50 per cent of the population in the Jewish state projected in the United Nations Partition Plan of 1947. The demographic basis for a Jewish majority state in Palestine was fragile indeed, and with reference to the very purpose of Zionism of bringing the bulk of world Jewry to Palestine it was clear that the new state saw itself as the embodiment of that purpose. On 14 May 1948, on the date when Britain had decided to end its Mandate for Palestine, the State of Israel was declared at a meeting of the recently established Provisional National Council. David Ben Gurion, leader of the provisional National Administration, stated: 'By virtue of the national and historical right of the Jewish People and of the Resolution of the General Assembly of the United Nations we hereby proclaim the establishment of the Jewish state in Palestine to be called Israel.'[19] The laws and institutions of the new state were consequently designed to facilitate the recruitment, immigration and settlement of Jews. Due to a lack of consensus in the National Council and later in the Knesset, Israel did not get a constitution. A number of Basic Laws were enacted to implement a policy of Jewish nation-building and Jewish ascendancy within the new state.[20] Of these, the Law of Return (1950) is one that both by virtue of its ideological premises and policy implications most clearly expresses the *organic relationship* between the state and the non-territorial nation (world Jewry) that it takes upon itself to represent. The first article declares: 'Every Jew has the right to come to their country as an *oleh*.'[21] The word 'return' expresses the basic motive in the Zionist narrative; Jews living outside Palestine (Eretz Israel/the Land of Israel) are living outside their national homeland, which is an abnormal situation, so they should 'return' to the land of their ancestors. The same principle is expressed in the World Zionist Organization – Jewish Agency for Israel Status Law 1952 that portrays Israel as the succession of the pre-state Zionist institutions (rather than a successor state of the previous

---

19 Walter Laqueur, *A History of Zionism* (London: Weidenfeld and Nicolson, 1972), 586.

20 The controversial issue of adopting a constitution, and thereby conclusively defining the 'Jewish' nature of the state, is known as 'the religious status quo'; a modus vivendi whereby the religious camp accepts Israel as a secular state, and the secular camp recognises the Chief Rabbinate's prerogative to define who is a Jew for the purpose of issuing citizenship under the Law of Return. For a summary of arguments, see Yohoshua Freudenheim, *Government in Israel* (New York: Oceana Publication, 1967), 24–36.

21 *Oleh* – a person ascending towards Zion (pl. *olim*), a Jewish immigrant to Israel. See for example, Elazar, *Israel: Building a New Society*, 138–9.

Mandatory State of Palestine), and establishes that the World Zionist Organization and its agencies have the status as 'national institutions' in Israel. Article 1 stipulates that '[t]he State of Israel is considered to be the creation of the entire Jewish people; its gates are open, in accordance with the law, to every Jew who wishes to immigrate'.[22] The two said institutions 'will continue to operate in the State of Israel for the development and settlement of the country, the absorption of immigrants from the Diaspora and the coordination of the activities in Israel of Jewish institutions and organisations' (Article 4); and '[t]he mission of gathering in the exiles, which is the central task of the State of Israel and the Zionist Movement . . . requires constant efforts by the Jewish people in the Diaspora; the State of Israel, therefore, expects the cooperation of all Jews, as individuals and groups, in building up the state and assisting the immigration to it . . .' (Article 5). Finally, the Nationality Law was passed by the Knesset in 1952, giving detailed provisions for acquisition of citizenship with the prime purpose of securing that immigrants recognised as Jews have the automatic right to citizenship and settlement on arrival. Article 2 (a) declares: 'Every *oleh* under the Law of Return, 5710–1950, shall become an Israel national.'[23] The category 'Israel national' does not, however, imply a reference to an *Israeli nation*, a nation of all Israeli citizens, Jews and non-Jews. The 'national level' as understood in Israeli laws is the Jewish nation, an ethnic nation, not a territorial nation.

The other side of the coin, so to speak, in order to secure a Jewish majority in the country, and justify the claim of national self-determination on behalf of the majority, would be to prevent, as far as possible, Palestinian refugees from returning and acquiring citizenship in the State of Israel. The first Arab-Israeli war in 1948–1949 resulted in a massive flight of Palestinians, about 726,000 according to the United Nations Relief and Works Agency for Palestine (UNRWA), the UN institution that was given the humanitarian responsibility for the refugees. Eighty-three per cent of the Palestinians living in territories that came under Israeli control were made refugees.[24] Through a number of legal measures (among them the Law of Return and Nationality Law) the refugees as non-Jews were prevented from returning to their homes in what became Israel, in spite of UN Resolution 194 (III) of December 1948 stating that 'the refugees

---

[22] Claude Klein, 'A Jewish State or a State for the Jews?' *The Jerusalem Quarterly* 7 (1978) (Spring): 40–41.

[23] https://jewishvoiceforpeace.org/wp-content/uploads/2016/06/Citizenship-Law-1952.pdf (accessed 03.04.2017).

[24] Uri Davis, *Citizenship and the State. A Comparative Study of Citizenship in Israel, Jordan, Palestine, Syria, and Lebanon* (Reading: Ithaca Press, 1997), 40.

wishing to return to their homes to live at peace with their neighbours should be permitted to do so at the earliest practical date . . .'. In addition, hundreds of Palestinian villages were razed to the ground, and land and other properties of the refugees were confiscated, thus also erasing the traces of a major part of the Palestinian society.[25]

With most of the Palestinians and their old habitats out of sight, they were also easier to be kept out of mind as lawful citizens of the land, strengthening the Zionist narrative that Jewish immigration was politically feasible and morally justified. This *externalising* of the Palestinians was not least important in relation to the new immigrants who had never experienced the indigenous population and who for a large part were settled in areas previously inhabited by Arab Palestinians.

THE POLITICAL SOCIOLOGY OF ISRAELI CITIZENSHIP

Israel is an extraordinary, in many ways an exceptional case of state-building, as indicated in the previous section. But *as a state* it shares many basic characteristics with other states making comparative studies fruitful. Indeed, Israel is a laboratory for students of state formation, nation-building, and citizenship. It is a new state based on settlers and immigrants, an emerging state, born in conflict still unfolding, an expanding state with borders and a demographic composition still to be finally decided, and a contested definition as a 'Jewish' state – the programmatic *raison d'être* of the Zionist movement.

Israeli academics, largely originating and trained in the Western tradition, were from the beginning intimately involved as participants and interpreters of the state and society emerging around them. The debate among them as it has evolved is particularly interesting because it reflects both dominant Israeli self-perceptions at different points in time as well as some of the most critical assessments of Israeli state-building.

A main dividing line in this debate can be drawn between those who basically regard Israeli state-building as Jewish nation-building modelled on Western European democratic (liberal or socialist) patterns, on the one hand, and those who consider the settler-colonial aspect of Israeli state-building as the most significant aspect of the state-building project. Proponents of the latter position tend to be more or less critical of the whole Zionist endeavour.

---

[25] Benny Morris, *The Birth of the Palestinian Refugee Problem Revisited* (Cambridge: Cambridge University Press, 2004).

Analysing the State of Israel from a citizenship perspective should include both dimensions: In a historical perspective Israeli citizenship is clearly modelled on European experiences, both socialist and liberal, but uniquely set in the settler-colonial context in Palestine. This is a reflection of the two parallel processes of state-building that were necessary for the creation of a separate state for Jews in Palestine: The recruitment and organisation of massive immigration of Jews, and the acquisition, through whatever means available, of sufficient land, resources, and infrastructure for settling and incorporating the immigrants, while protecting them against resistance by the non-Jewish population and other neighbours in the region. So, while Israel is often portrayed and studied as a kind of Western political system,[26] alternatively in combination with post-colonial Third World systems,[27] the two processes mentioned create patterns of state-building completely different in important ways as compared to both, related basically to the frontier aspect of Israeli state-building.[28]

The Six Day War/June War of 1967 is a watershed event in this context. The striking Israeli victory and conquest of new large tracts of Palestinian territory meant a 'reopening of the Zionist frontier', i.e., the building of Israeli civil settlements in the occupied territories. The Israeli settlers continued to enjoy citizenship rights as Israeli Jews, the Palestinians were left without basic civil and political rights. They were not considered a serious challenge to Israel in this period, either politically or from a security point of view. In short, the Palestinians were *externalised* as a factor impacting the Israeli society; they were basically seen as irrelevant.[29]

Israel and Jewish Nation-Building: The Endogen Perspective

The first generation of Israeli political sociologists had as their dominant experience the post-1949 era characterised by the relative abolishment

---

[26] Arend Lijphart, *Patterns of Democracy* (New Haven and London: Yale University Press, 1999).

[27] Ian Lustick, 'Israeli State-building in the West Bank and the Gaza Strip: Theory and Practice' *International Organization* 41 (1987) 1: 151–71.

[28] For an elaboration of the argument, see Nils A. Butenschøn, 'The Frontier State at Work: Models of Contemporary Israeli State-Building' *Journal of Theoretical Politics* 4 (1992) 4: 413–33.

[29] During my first field work in Israel in the immediate aftermath of the 1973 war (as part of a larger Middle East project at the Norwegian Institute of International Affairs), I conducted a survey of Israeli politicians, among others. One of the standard questions was: 'How do you see a solution to the Palestinian problem?' One of the respondents (later to become president of Israel) answered: 'Palestinian problem? What Palestinians, what problem?'

of the threat by the Palestinians, the vast majority of whom had been incapacitated by the war as political and military actors. Israeli academics were mostly concerned with the enormous challenges of building the institutional, economic, social, and security infrastructure of the new state, and the absorption and integration of hundreds of thousands of new Jewish immigrants coming from the war-ridden Europe, soon also from Arab countries who had not experienced European anti-Semitism. These challenges of both organising sufficient absorption capacity and of identifying a common platform for citizenship in the new state defined the agenda of the first generation of Israeli political sociologists, foremost among them Shmuel N. Eisenstadt.[30]

In a brief introductory chapter to a book on studies of the Israeli society from 1980, Eisenstadt retrospectively presents his own approach, responding to critics from a younger generation of Israeli sociologists.[31] He presents himself solidly within the 'functionalist school' of the 1950s and 1960s. The focus was on nation-building as an essentially benign transitional process of modernisation from the 'traditional' society to 'modernity', 'a dichotomy between traditional and modern societies, a dichotomy which very often became closely identified with that between primordial and civil symbols as bases of legitimation of societies'.[32] The assumption was that the nation-state facilitated the diffusion of universalist values and modern (European) institutions, a dynamic civil society and equal citizenship, and that traditional elements in the society would be absorbed in the process. This was the appropriate model for Israel. Eisenstadt admits that the functionalist approach was inward-looking, basically concerned with processes *internal* to the dominant society, and that 'the construction of different types of criteria of membership and of boundaries of communities were mostly taken for granted as given, and were barely analysed'.[33] Israeli nation-building was Jewish nation-building with the Jewish people as the constituent *demos*. The Palestinians in Israel (or 'Arabs'; a separate Palestinian identity was not part of the vocabulary) were considered as a

[30] Two books by Eisenstadt are particularly well known: Shmuel N. Eisenstadt, *The Absorption of Immigrants* (Glencoe: The Free Press, 1953); Shmuel N. Eisenstadt, *Israeli Society* (New York: Basic Books, 1967).

[31] Shmuel N. Eisenstadt, 'Introduction: Some Reflections on the Study of Ethnicity' in *Studies of Israeli Society, Volume I. Migration, Ethnicity and Community*, ed. Ernest Krausz (New Brunswick: Transaction Books, 1980), 1–5. See also Uri Ram, *The Changing Agenda of Israeli Sociology: Theory, Ideology, and Identity* (Albany: SUNY Press, 1995).

[32] Schmuel N. Eisenstadt, 'Introduction: Some Reflections', 2.

[33] Ibid.

residual element of a traditional society leaving little or no imprint on the Israeli or wider Jewish society and therefore mostly left out of the analysis. Shafir and Peled observe that this analytical framework fitted very well with the agenda of the Israeli leadership, describing Israel 'as at once Jewish, Western, democratic and "revolutionary"'.[34] David Ben Gurion, Israel's first prime minister and leading strategist, saw the opportunity in using the new state and its institutions as foundations for a new collective identity for the modern Jewish people with the Israeli Jews as its vanguard. He was an exponent of a new ethos, *mamlachtiyut*, whereby the pioneering spirit (*chaltziyut*) of the pre-state settlers was to be converted into a republican, state-oriented citizenship, more or less expressing: 'Don't ask what the country can do for you, but what you can do for your country.'

> As understood in the context of *mamlachtiyut*, the uniform rule of law did not entail a neutral liberal state or a universal conception of citizenship. The state was to continue to be committed to the values of *chalutziyut* and to demand such commitments from its citizens.[35]

At this early stage there was a broad general agreement among scholars and leaders of the state that now, as the new state had been established, the imperative task of the state, if it were to survive, was to incorporate the many disparate groups of *Jews* with their different religious and cultural backgrounds and ideological cleavages.

Israel as a Plural Society – An 'Ethnic Democracy'?

Among the next generation of Israeli sociologists who entered the academic discourse relevant to citizenship in the 1970s and 1980s, Sammy Smooha stands out. His 1978 book *Israel: Pluralism and Conflict* challenges the dominant paradigm of the Eisenstadt school and analyses the Israeli society as a fragmented or 'plural' society.[36] He identifies three major cleavages: An ethnic cleavage (Ashkenazi (European) vs. Mizrachi ('Oriental'/non-European) Jews); a cultural-religious cleavage (Orthodox vs. non-observant Jews); and a national cleavage (Jews vs. Arabs).[37]

---

[34] Shafir and Peled, *Being Israeli*, 24.

[35] Ibid., 18.

[36] Lijphart, *Patterns of Democracy*. Lijphart was a leading proponent of the pluralist school in Western political sociology at the time.

[37] Sammy Smooha, *Israel: Pluralism and Conflict* (London and Henley: Routledge and Kegan Paul, 1978), 21–48. More recent works by Smooha include: *Arabs and Jews in Israel, Vol. I: Conflicting and Shared Attitudes in a Divided Society* (Boulder: Westview Press, 1989); *Arabs and Jews in Israel, Vol II: Change*

Contrary to the expectations of the functionalists, Smooha finds that the level of conflict between these different ethno-cultural groups increases and that a new integrated national identity under the dominance of a pioneering Ashkenazi Labour movement is not emerging. Furthermore, he concludes that Israel cannot be considered a democracy without qualifications due to systematic differences in citizenship rights, particularly along the Jewish/Israeli Arab cleavage:

> The Orientals and religious Jews are integrated into the broader society voluntarily, whereas Israeli Arabs are integrated involuntarily. Israeli political democracy is a reconciliatory 'consociational democracy' for the religious Jews, a restricted democracy for the Orientals, and a failing '*Herrenvolk* democracy' for the Israeli Arabs.[38]

Whereas the functionalists considered the State of Israel as a democratic nation-state on the route towards a fully integrated modernised nation, Smooha and a large group of younger scholars opened up a more critical perspective. Still, Smooha distanced himself clearly from the growing non- or anti-Zionist camp of Israeli and other scholars who 'portray Israel as a white settler, neo-colonial, theocratic *Herrenvolk*, an artificial entity which will not endure'.[39]

In later works he develops a conception of Israel as an '*ethnic democracy*', a term that has sparked a heated debate, not least among Israeli scholars. Smooha defines ethnic democracy as:

> a system in which two contradictory principles operate: 'the democratic principle,' making for equal rights and equal treatment of all citizens, and 'the ethnic principle,' making for fashioning a homogen[e]ous nation-state and privileging the ethnic majority.[40]

Importantly, he states that the state (Israel) is identified with a 'core ethnic nation' (i.e., the Jewish nation), *not with its citizens*. 'The state practices a policy of creating a homogen[e]ous nation-state, a state of and for a particular ethnic nation.'[41] In the Israeli context this implies that citizenship as an expression of *demos* extends over and beyond the borders of the state (irrespective of how these are defined) and includes the entire Jewish

---

and Continuity in Mutual Tolerance (Boulder: Westview Press, 1992); 'Ethnic Democracy: Israel as an Archetype' *Israel Studies* 2 (1997): 198–241.

38 Smooha, *Israel: Pluralism and Conflict*, 265.

39 Ibid., xvii.

40 Smooha, 'Israel as an Archetype', 200.

41 Ibid.

ethnos. Palestinians in Israel are accorded (second class) citizenship, but do not form part of the *demos* – of the collectivity for which the state primarily exists, and are not to be integrated in the demos because they are not Jews.[42] Israel is the nation-state of the Jewish nation, not the *Israeli* nation, since such a nation is not recognised by the State of Israel.[43]

Israel as an Ethnocracy

Is 'ethnic democracy' a meaningful categorisation of Israel as a political system? A number of Israeli scholars have taken part in that discussion; we can call them 'the third generation'. The debate tends to be politicised and heated because, in the final analysis, it addresses the question of whether Israel can be labelled a 'democracy' at all, and how an analysis of the Israeli political system should be structured. In their criticism of Smooha, Ghanem, Rouhana, and Yiftachel contend that he takes the boundaries of the State of Israel for granted as his unit of analysis, but operates, just like Eisenstadt, with world Jewry as *demos* and the subject of nation-building. 'Ethnic democracy' therefore entails 'a problematic mix' of *ethnos* and *demos* as principles of political organisation:

> 'Demos' denotes an inclusive body of empowered citizens within a given territory. It is a competing organising principle to that of the 'ethnos', where membership is determined by common origin. The term 'democracy' thus means the rule of the 'demos', and . . . points to an overlap between permanent state residency and political rights as a necessary democratic condition. Such overlap is the one and only way to enable the 'law of the land' to be equally imposed over all subjects. This entails the institutionalisation of clear and permanent borders. In other words, the state should belong to *all* its citizens and *only* to these citizens.[44]

The authors find that 'ethnocracy' is a term that better covers a description of Israel as a political system since it highlights the state's ethnic nature rather than its democratic nature.[45] A further basic point in the critique is that, in addition to systematic legal and institutional

---

[42] Klein states that 'the idea of the Jewish state is that the state can be defined over and beyond its mere geographic identity. In particular, it can be defined in relation to a particular ethno-political structure. See Klein, 'A Jewish State', 39.

[43] Yedidia Z. Stern and Jay Ruderman, 'Why "Israeli" is Not a Nationality' *Jewish Telegraph Agency*, 3 March 2014.

[44] As'ad Ghanem, Nadim N. Rouhana, Oren Yiftachel, 'Questioning "Ethnic Democracy": A response to Sammy Smooha' *Israel Studies* 3 (1998) 2: 261.

[45] Further on the coining of 'ethnocracy,' see note 2 above.

discrimination against non-Jews (which Smooha also accepts and has analysed), Israel advances and expands a process of 'Judaisation' both in parts of Israel 'proper' inhabited by Israeli Palestinians and in the occupied territories. The authors ask: 'Can a state which facilitates an ongoing process of ethnocratic colonisation and domination be considered an "archetype" ethnic *democracy*?'[46]

THE ISRAEL-PALESTINE CITIZENSHIP COMPLEX

Citizenship is the institution that regulates rights and obligations in the relationship between a sovereign state and its citizens, materialised in formal documents like a birth certificate and a passport. Everyone has the right to citizenship; no one should be left stateless.

This proposition, although enshrined in the founding documents of the United Nations,[47] is by no means self-evident or universally accepted and implemented by all UN member states. For example, in some states sovereignty is located in a royal family (as in the Gulf monarchies); in others in a religious leadership representing and interpreting a divine will (the Iranian theocracy and the Vatican mini-state). In yet other cases 'the people' is understood to mean 'the nation', and the nation might have different extensions, larger or smaller, than the actual inhabitants of a state. This means that the *state-idea*, the founding principles of a state, its constituent purpose (normally, but not always, reflected in the constitution of the state), is a major factor that determines the *extension* of citizenship. In this sense the state is a membership institution which administers territorial sovereignty, commands monopoly of coercive powers, and adopts laws and regulations that provide the legal basis for distributing rights and obligations among the inhabitants, on an equal basis or not; in short, the state as a membership institution defines who are included and who are excluded from access to public goods and political participation, in this way organising inhabitants in different legal classes on a more or less discriminatory basis.

The nature of Israel as a political system, whether it should be termed a 'democracy', 'ethnic democracy', 'ethnocracy', 'apartheid', or something else, is hotly debated both among academics and the general public. Liberating the debate from the grip of polarisation is probably

---

46 Ghanem et al., 'Questioning', 264.

47 Asbjørn Eide, 'Citizenship and International Human Rights Law: Status, Evolution, and Challenges' in *Citizenship and the State in the Middle East: Approaches and Applications*, eds. Nils A. Butenschøn, Uri Davis and Manuel Hassassian (Syracuse: Syracuse University Press, 2000).

not possible due to the 'existential' nature of conflicting narratives, but applying a citizenship approach gives an opportunity to identify major dimensions in what we can call the Israel Palestine Citizenship Complex. The basic consideration is that the political organisation of Mandatory Palestine is still today an unsettled question, raising questions of who should be included and who should be excluded as members of the polity that organises the territory. In short, who belongs to Palestine, who 'owns' it, who can claim the country as his or her homeland? To the extent, but only to the extent, that these questions are posed in *ethnically exclusionist* terms does the conflict become an unsolvable zero-sum conflict.

The Israel-Palestine Citizenship Complex Illustrated

We have so far discussed some major historical trajectories of Israel-Palestine as a state territory and theoretical debates related to alternative analytical frameworks of Israel as a state formation and how conceptions of citizenship have evolved. It should be clear by now that we are dealing with a very complex reality in terms of demographic and territorial entities, constitutional principles, and ethno-national political identities. I have tried to draw the threads together in Figure 1.1.

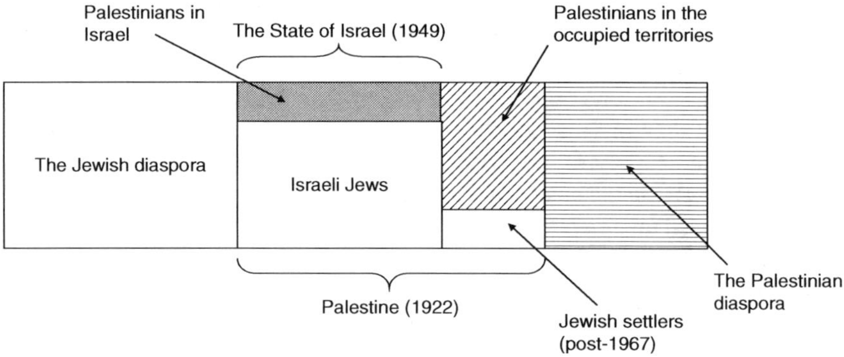

Notes: [a]The relative size of the individual boxes does not represent in any accurate way the actual sizes of groups. [b]An earlier and slightly different version of this figure appears in Nils A. Butenschøn, 'State, Power, and Citizenship in the Middle East: A Theoretical Introduction' in *Citizenship and the State in the Middle East. Approaches and Applications*, eds. Nils A. Butenschøn et al. (Syracuse: Syracuse University Press), 22.

Figure 1.1 Alternative demographic foundations for claims of self-determination and citizenship in Israel-Palestine. Parameters for final status negotiations between the State of Israel and the Palestine Liberation Organization

Of the six demographic entities in Figure 1.1, four are located within the territory of 1922 Mandatory Palestine – including today's Israel 'proper' within the 'Green Line' (1949–1967) and the Occupied Palestinian Territory (OPT; the West Bank, East Jerusalem, and the Gaza Strip). The other two represent the diasporas living outside the territory. Within Israel 'proper' Palestinian Arabs make up around 20 per cent of the population, within the OPT Israeli-Jewish settlers is a segment systematically being built up since 1967 and constitutes currently some 12 per cent of the population. Each of the groups represented have a particular status or relationship to the State of Israel and/or the Palestinian Authority. In addition, many individuals within these groups have citizenship, a non-citizenship refugee status, or some other status in other countries than Israel-Palestine. The peace process, in particular the final status issues, is all about a conclusive political organisation of Palestine 1922 and the distribution or sharing of rights and obligations between citizens included in the polity. In the political dispute between Zionists and Palestinian nationalists the different groups indicated in Figure 1.1 are included or excluded in the narratives, declarations, and negotiating positions of the parties in order to substantiate claims to all or parts of the 1922 Palestine state territory, or even beyond.[48]

Figure 1.1 represents just a first mapping of the 'ethno-political archaeology' of the Israel-Palestine Citizenship Complex. If we start digging beneath the surface we will discover yet new layers of subgroups, both within the Jewish and Palestinian sections, with or without particular legal statuses in a citizenship regime.[49] These groups have been formed as identity groups not least over the last century as participants and/or victims of conflict and war, but also because they have been ascribed rights, or denied rights, in a citizenship regime imposed by local or external powers in the struggle for Palestine. The relevance of the different groups and the cleavages that separate them with a view to the future political organisation of Israel-Palestine is difficult to predict. It will depend to a large extent on the conflict dynamics created by the further development of

---

48 In addition to the Syrian Golan Heights, occupied by Israel in 1967 and included in Israel's jurisdiction (if not formally annexed) in 1981, right-wing Zionists and left-wing Palestinians often refer to the national territory as including today's Kingdom of Jordan (the East Bank of Jordan, Transjordan), rejecting the League of Nations partition in 1922 of what was then (since the British conquest) Western and Eastern Palestine.

49 In the case of Israeli citizens, Jews and non-Jews, this has been studied in most detail by Sammy Smooha, see note 37 above.

Israel as an expanding frontier state, on the one hand, and the resistance by the Palestinians, on the other.

CONCLUSION

Israel and Palestine are currently two states-in-the-making; two state-building projects in the same territory, both unfulfilled according to the nationalist movements they represent, but otherwise very different in character and development. The conflict dynamic between them has many sources and drivers, with contested citizenship at the core. This is, on the face of it, not a unique situation; conflicts over territory and distribution of rights and resources in ethnically diverse societies are frequent in the world today.[50] In the case of Israel-Palestine, however, we are not dealing with clearly definable societies within an agreed-upon state territory. What is known as the 'final status issues' in this conflict relate to who are to be considered legitimate citizens with what kind of entitlements to which territories, including where the capitals of the two states are to be located.[51] In most debates within the framework of the so-called peace process introduced with the signing of the Oslo Agreement in 1993, the challenges are defined as primarily involving how a Palestinian state can by fitted into the existing political order, without endangering the security and integrity of existing states, including the State of Israel. But a conclusive solution to the final status issues will involve decisions on basic elements of Israel as a state formation that are still undecided. It will determine the borders of the country, the location of its capital, the composition of its future citizenry and the nature of Israeli citizenship, including the opportunities and limitations for the fulfilment of the diverse Zionist or non-Zionist blueprints for the country.

---

[50] Nils A. Butenschøn, Øyvind Stiansen and Kåre Vollan, *Power-Sharing in Conflict-Ridden Societies: Challenges for Building Peace and Democratic Stability* (Surrey and Burlington: Routledge, 2015). The book compares the cases of Burundi, Rwanda, Ethiopia, Lebanon, Bosnia and Herzegovina, Myanmar, The Philippines, and Fiji.

[51] 'Final status issues' concerns the issues referred for later negotiations in the Declaration of Principles (the Oslo Agreement) in 1993 between Israel and the Palestine Liberation Organization (PLO). The principles regulated relations and mechanisms for peaceful coexistence between the parties in the interim period of five years until the 'final status issues' had been solved. These included borders, security, the status of Jerusalem, Palestinian refugees, and water, all of which are determining factors for organising state authority, and all of which are still unresolved at the time of writing.

Israel has never declared an end to the 'Zionist revolution', of 'ingathering the exiles' and territorialising the Jewish people in Palestine/Eretz Israel – or, to put it in another conceptual language, the Zionist frontier has never been conclusively 'closed'.[52] There are strong voices among the Israelis (including among the 'third generation' discussed earlier) who demand an end to settlement expansion and ethnic exclusionism, arguing for a 'normalisation' of Israel as *a state for its citizens*, not for a privileged ethno-national group. But the right-wing nationalist forces, who have gradually strengthened their grip over Israeli politics since the 1967 occupation, are still pursuing a policy in line with the settler-colonial tradition seeking to alter the identity and demographic nature of Palestine, step by step. Israel is not a *status quo* state accepting to settle for the international consensus of a two-state solution, including recognising a sovereign, democratic and contiguous Palestinian state with the 1967 boundaries as defining lines between the two states. There are no prospects for a major change in this situation as long as the international society, with the United States at the centre, is not willing to exert substantial pressure on Israel. All diplomatic efforts at solving the Israel-Palestine conflict since the early 1990s have aimed at preparing the ground for the establishment of a Palestinian state in one form or the other. Huge resources have been invested with the hope of bringing the 'peace process' to a successful end. But all initiatives so far (mid-2017) have failed, bringing senior mediators to the verge of desperation.[53]

A basic element in a final solution to the Israel-Palestine conflict and the untangling of the Israel-Palestine Citizenship Complex will have to be

---

[52] This was clearly expressed in the Jerusalem Program, official platform of the World Zionist Organization, adopted at its World Congress in 1968, the first after the 1967 war. The two first articles read: '1. The unity of the Jewish people, its bond to its historic homeland *Eretz Israel*, and the centrality of the State of Israel and Jerusalem, its capital, in the life of the nation; 2. *Aliyah* (immigration) to Israel from all countries and the effective integration of all immigrants into Israeli society.' http://www.wzo.org.il/The-Jerusalem-Program (accessed 15 May 2017).

[53] US Secretary of State John Kerry's famous 70-minute speech on 26 December 2016, only days before the termination of the Obama administration, is considered one of the strongest criticisms a senior US official has ever expressed against the politics of an Israeli government, blaming Prime Minister Benjamin Netanyahu for the stalled peace process, and for undermining the two-state solution ('the only possible solution'). Kerry and his staff had used countless hours in efforts to forge a negotiated settlement, but had finally to conclude that the resources spent had been to no avail. See 'Kerry Rebukes Israel Calling Settlements a Threat to Peace', *New York Times* 28 December 2016, https://www.nytimes.com/2016/12/28/us/politics/john-kerry-israel-palestine-peace.html?_r=0 (accessed 23 March 2017).

built on agreements on the status of demographic and territorial entities and the rights and entitlements that follow: Who should be included in or excluded from rights to citizenship in which territory? These final status issues are as unresolved in 2017 as they were in 1917.

2. Remapping citizenship in Turkey: law, identity, and civic virtue 1980–2014

Basak Ince

INTRODUCTION

This chapter examines the evolution of the 'legal', 'identity', and 'civic' virtue aspects of citizenship in Turkey, focusing on the period since 1980. It addresses how the official definition of citizenship during the single-party period (1923–1946), based on a single religion (Sunni Islam) and single language (Turkish), was challenged in the 1980s by minority groups, particularly Alevis, non-Muslims and Kurds, who demanded that the state recognise their ethnic and religious identities. Given Turkey's ethnic and religious plurality, civic education potentially plays a very important role in promoting tolerance. After discussing 'legal' and 'identity' aspects of citizenship in Turkey I turn to Turkey's civic education textbooks to better evaluate the extent to which they promote human rights as shared values, and make positive references to ethnic, religious, and cultural diversity. Citizenship is everywhere a complex legal, political, and social category, particularly in societies as ethnically diverse as Turkey. The chapter examines the shifting meaning of citizenship in Turkey over recent decades and highlights a number of theoretical and historical issues at stake in the contemporary operations of citizenship in the Middle East.

The Ottomans ruled much of the Arab World for four centuries. Turkey and the Arab states had a common background in the Ottoman Empire but they have developed very differently since. The Turkish Republic was proclaimed on 29 October 1923. Mustafa Kemal (Atatürk) became the president, and devoted himself to reforms that would Westernise the country, of which secularism constituted the lynchpin. Education was completely secularised, the Latin alphabet and Western calendar were adopted, and the caliphate was dissolved. Although Atatürk was an important source of inspiration for the founders of most Arab states,[1] the radical transformation of the rump Ottoman territory into a modern nation-state by Atatürk was not easily reproducible in Arab countries because of its strong emphasis on cultural Westernisation and radical secularism. In the last three decades, however, a dramatic shift has occurred within the Turkish modernisation. Turkey's success in combining Islam and secularism, as well as in taking the military out of political and civilian life, has started to serve as a new model. Thus, the relevance of Turkey for developments in Arab countries, and especially its immediate neighbours, is increasing. Recent surveys such as the Turkish Economic and Social Studies Foundation (TESEV) poll clearly demonstrate that there is strong interest and demand from the Arab public for a Turkish model. The poll produced a striking result, as 66 per cent of respondents in the Arab world believe that Turkey can be a model for Middle Eastern countries.[2] However, as long as Turkey fails to meet identity demands coming from different sections of the society it can neither be a good example for the Arab world nor consolidate its democracy.

Up to the end of the 1980s the attitude of the state towards the identity claims of Alevis, Kurds and non-Muslim citizens continued to ignore differences among citizens, as the state was wary of abandoning its familiar construct of citizenship. As a result, non-Muslims, Alevis and Kurds felt they were second-class citizens while Sunni Muslim ethnic Turks were the real citizens of the Republic. Since the 1990s, official understandings of citizenship based on duties rather than rights and a particular vision of the 'Turkish citizen' deemed necessary for social cohesion, have increasingly come into conflict with demands for more liberal understandings based on the prioritisation of rights over duties and a new framework of citizenship emphasising the recognition of differences. This trend has been supported by the European Union, which has been a major force behind recent reforms to the understanding of citizenship in Turkey, though problems persist in the implementation of these reforms.

This study employs a variety of primary and secondary sources. Reviewing a number of recent theoretical approaches to citizenship, it draws on election manifestos and the party programmes of all the main political parties between 1980 and 2014 in order to explore the state's role

---

1 Nils A. Butenschøn, 'State, Power, and Citizenship in the Middle East: A Theoretical Introduction' in, *Citizenship and the State in the Middle East: Approaches and Applications*, eds. N.A. Butenschøn et al. (New York: Syracuse University Press, 2000), 15.

2 Mensur Akgün, Sabiha Şenyücel Gündoğar, Gökçe Perçinoğlu, and Jonathan Levack, *The Perception of Turkey in the Middle East, 2010* (İstanbul: TESEV Publications, 2011).

in the evolution of citizenship, as well as on civic education textbooks used between 1980 and 2013 in order to understand the kind of citizen the state imagined and hoped to create.

THE POLITICAL BACKGROUND

The evolution of citizenship as a legal, socio-cultural, and civic concept in the Republic of Turkey can be analytically divided into four periods: the single-party period (1923–1946), the period from 1946 to 1960, the interim between the 1960 and 1980 military interventions, and after the 1980 military intervention.

Mustafa Kemal (Atatürk) officially founded the Republican People's Party (*Cumhuriyet Halk Partisi*, CHP) on 9 September 1923 as a political expression of the war of national liberation, with the main aim of achieving national unity and integrity.[3] The CHP was the dominant political party in Turkey from 1923 to 1945, and ruled until the victory of the Democratic Party (*Demokrat Parti*, DP) in the general elections of 14 May 1950. 'One language, one culture, one ideal', the slogan of the Turkish Republic during the single-party period,[4] played a significant role in assimilating cultural differences among citizens and constructing the early idea of Turkish citizenship.

During its first years the DP amended and liberalised certain laws related to citizenship. In contrast to the CHP's long-standing elitist orientation, the DP's glorification of the 'national will' represented an attempt to bolster its image as the party of the common man. As such, one of its major contributions to Turkish democracy was the integration of citizens living in rural areas into the political process: Turkey's 'silent majority'. Due to economic problems and growing authoritarianism, the DP began to lose its support in the second half of the 1950s,[5] to which it responded by increasing its authoritarian measures against the opposition. The first

---

3 Quoted in Kemal H. Karpat, 'The Republican People's Party 1923–1945' in *Political Parties and Democracy in Turkey*, eds. M. Heper and J. Landau (London: I.B.Tauris, 1991), 42–64.

4 The 1931 programme of the Republican People's Party (*Cumhuriyet Halk Partisi*, CHP) defined nation as a 'political and social community formed by citizens bound by a unity of language, culture and ideal'. This definition of the nation, 'one language, one culture, one ideal', became the motto of the Republic; see *Cumhuriyet Halk Fırkası Programı'nın İzahı* (Ankara: Hakimiyet-i Milliye Matbaası, 1931).

5 William Hale, 'Modern Turkish Politics: An Historical Introduction' in *Aspects of Modern Turkey*, ed. W. Hale (London: Bowker, 1976), 3.

Turkish experiment with political democracy ended with the military intervention of 27 May 1960.

The period between 1960 and 1980 is of great significance in Turkish political history, as there were three military interventions in it: the 1960 coup, the 1971 memorandum, and the 1980 military intervention. These resulted in multiple constitutional changes. 1961 saw a new Constitution and a new citizenship law, inaugurating a more liberal understanding of citizenship, with individual rights given more emphasis than duties, a position guaranteed by law.[6] Although these rights were limited after the 1971 memorandum, there were clear improvements in citizenship rights and freedoms relative to the previous period. The second major development was the widening of the measure of representation. This enlargement had beneficial consequences, initiating, for instance, debates over the Kurdish issue by political parties, which had been taboo since the establishment of the Republic. Although the solutions proposed to the Kurdish problem were largely economic, it constituted a major step towards the realisation that there was a Kurdish issue. The third development involved a more moderate understanding of secularism, with the result that different sects, such as the Alevis, began to claim constitutional rights.

Since the 1980 military intervention and the consequent rewriting of the Constitution, Turkish politics has been defined by the clash between the foundational definition of citizenship, which is based on a single religion (Sunni Islam) and single language (Turkish) on the one hand, and new trends emphasising rights over duties and pluralism over a singular notion of identity on the other. Reforms to meet EU membership criteria have played an important role in these transformations, as has the presence of a majority government in Parliament. The winner of the 3 November 2002 national elections, the Justice and Development Party (*Adalet ve Kalkınma Partisi*, AKP) led by Tayyip Erdoğan,[7] received 34.3 per cent of votes, making it the first party since 1987 to secure an absolute majority in Parliament.[8] The aftermath of the 2002 elections saw a single-party

[6] The 1961 Constitution came into effect after a referendum held on 9 July 1961. It differed from its 1924 predecessor in several important respects: it attached more value to individuals; it emphasised citizenship rights more than citizenship duties; it limited the state's interference in the affairs of individuals; and it defined the state's duties towards individuals. See Bülent Tanör, *Osmanlı-Türk Anayasal Gelişmeleri* (İstanbul: Yapı Kredi Yayınları, 2001).

[7] Metin Heper and Şule Toktaş, 'Islam, Modernity and Democracy in Contemporary Turkey: The Case of Recep Tayyip Erdoğan' *Muslim World* 93 (2003): 157–85.

[8] Soli Özel, 'Turkey at the Polls: After the Tsunami' *Journal of Democracy* 14 (2003) 3: 80–94.

government formed by the AKP, the first non-coalition government since 1991.[9]

THEORISING CITIZENSHIP IN TURKEY

The origin and historical development of the concept of citizenship, often discussed in the context of Western European states, is the subject of an extensive and influential body of literature.[10] What distinguishes civil, legal, political and social rights in Turkey is their imposition from above, rather than acquisition of rights through claims and struggles from below.[11] Kahraman describes citizenship in Turkey as occurring 'at a dash', rather than as a process of gradual 'completion'.[12] In Marshall's terms, then, the civil element of citizenship emerged during the early Republican era, while its political dimension emerged after the transition to multi-party politics in Turkey.

Moreover, citizenship in Turkey represents an uneasy union between ethnic and civic conceptions of national identity and belonging. For this reason, the notion of citizenship in Turkey, seems, with Brubaker, akin to both the French conception of citizenship based on territory and the German conception of citizenship based on blood, as the Republican period saw periodic vacillations between *jus soli* and *jus sanguinis* principles. However, even if the definition of citizenship is legally based on *jus soli*, this does not imply tolerance or inclusiveness. The principle of homogeneity of membership, whether based on blood or territory, represses diversity and identity claims, assuming a commonality/homogeneity of culture that is inherently repressive and exclusionary.

Turner's distinction between radical and formal citizenship is helpful here. Radical citizenship emerges from the practical history of popular

---

9 K. Ifantis, 'Turkey in Transition – Opportunities amidst Peril?' *Journal of Southern Europe and the Balkans* 9 (2007) 3: 223–31.

10 See T.H. Marshall and T. Bottomore, *Citizenship and Social Class* (London: Pluto, 1992); W.R. Brubaker, 'Immigration, Citizenship, and the Nation-State' in *Citizenship and Nationhood in France and Germany* (London: Harvard University Press, 1992); Bryan. S. Turner, *Citizenship and Capitalism: The Debate over Reformism* (London: Allen and Unwin, 1986); Bryan. S. Turner, 'Outline of a Theory of Citizenship' in *Dimensions of Radical Democracy*, ed. Chantal Mouffe (London: Verso, 1992); C. Liauzu, 'Interculturalism: New Lands to Discover in France' *Intercultural Education* 4 (1993) 3: 23–31.

11 Ayşe Kadıoğlu, 'Citizenship and Individuation in Turkey: The Triumph of Will over Reason' *Cemoti* 26 (1998), 23–43.

12 Kadıoğlu, 'Citizenship and Individuation in Turkey', 41.

lived experience: class struggles, wars, migration, and the emergence of new egalitarian ideologies, which, in the European context, paved the way for revolutionary-democratic states. Formal citizenship, on the other hand, is envisioned and enacted by governments and seeks exclusion and control of the masses. This clarifies a key tension in Turkey's historical experience of citizenship. As Arat argues:

> Citizenship in Turkey appeared not as a revolutionary social struggle from the bottom up by the masses, who asked for their rights from those who did not grant it to them, but as a number of choices made by the ruling elite intelligentsia who tried to grant rights to the masses in order to increase social integration and to empower the state.[13]

This depiction, specific to Turkey, echoes Charles Taylor's work on the difference between liberal and civic Republican modes of citizenship. The former sees citizenship as a *status* mainly involving rights accorded to individuals, and the latter regards it as a *practice* involving responsibilities to wider society. 'To rule and be ruled', Taylor writes, 'in turn means that at least some of the time governors can be "us" and not always "them".'[14]

Yet citizenship is not limited to one's legal status or practices; it is a combination of these elements. Kymlicka and Norman identify three main elements in citizenship. The first is citizenship as legal status, defined by civil, political and social rights: the citizen as a legal person, free to act according to the law and enjoying its protection. It need not mean that the citizen takes part in the law's formulation, nor does it require that rights be uniform between citizens. The second dimension refers to citizenship as membership in a political community that furnishes a distinct source of identity. In many ways, the identity dimension is the least straightforward of the three elements of citizenship. The third dimension, civic virtue, considers citizens specifically as political agents, actively participating in a society's political institutions. These three ideas, conceptually and empirically linked, push us to see citizenship not only as a legal status but as inseparable from questions of identity and civic virtue, and underscore the inherent multidimensionality of citizenship.[15]

---

13 Yeşim Arat, 'Türkiye'de Toplumsal Cinsiyet ve Vatandaşlık', in *75 Yılda Tebaa'dan Yurttaş'a Doğru*, ed. Artun Ünsal (İstanbul: Tarih Vakfı Yayınları, 1998), 67.

14 Charles Taylor, 'The Liberal-Communitarian Debate' in *Liberalism and the Moral Life*, ed. N.L. Rosenblum (Cambridge, MA: Harvard University Press, 1989), 178.

15 Will Kymlicka and Wayne Norman, eds., *Citizenship in Diverse Societies* (New York: Oxford University Press, 2000), 30–31.

In the following section the 'legal aspect of citizenship' will be discussed. This section covers the definition of citizenship in legal documents (i.e. the official definition of citizenship) in Turkey. Then the 'identity aspect of citizenship' (challenges to the official definition of citizenship) will be discussed through an examination of the demands coming from Alevi, non-Muslim and Kurdish citizens. In order to explore the 'civic virtue' aspect of citizenship in Turkey, civic education textbooks of Turkey will be analysed. School textbooks – perhaps the most widely read books in Turkey – reflect not only the ideas of their authors but also the official viewpoint. In this context, civic education courses and textbooks are particularly important. In the conclusion comments on possible solutions to the demands for a more liberal understanding of citizenship in Turkey will be outlined.

Citizenship and the Law

The legal dimension of citizenship has undergone many changes since the 1980s. For the purpose of this chapter I will focus on the 1982 Constitution and amendments affecting citizenship rights of minorities.

The 1982 Constitution was the product of the 1980 military intervention and differed from its 1961 predecessor in many respects. It is a crucial document for understanding the shape of contemporary citizenship in Turkey.[16] Its primary aim was to restore the authority of the state and to maintain public order. Rather than protect the rights and liberties of its citizens against state encroachment, the new Constitution aimed to protect the state from the actions of its citizens.[17] It was more detailed, rigid and much longer, while the rights and liberties of citizens were significantly curtailed.[18]

The Preamble depicted the Turkish state as a 'sacred' and 'sublime' entity, suggesting a Hegelian absolutist state rather than a liberal limited state. In the original text of the Constitution, virtually every right was subject to limitations. The Constitution made citizens of Turkey more passive, created a less participatory democracy, and generally acted as a depoliticising agent.

For instance, Article 24 guaranteed the freedom of religion, provided this did not threaten the 'indivisible integrity of the state', and that no one

---

[16] Suna Kili and Şeref Gözübüyük, *Türk Anayasa Metinleri* (Istanbul: Türkiye İş Bankası Yayınları, 2000).

[17] Ergun Özbudun and Serap Yazıcı, *Democratization Reforms in Turkey (1993–2004)* (Istanbul: TESEV Publications, 2004).

[18] Ergun Özbudun, *Türk Anayasa Hukuku* (Ankara: Yetkin Yayınları, 2000).

be compelled to worship or to participate in religious ceremonies or rites. At the same time, the Constitution made religious courses compulsory in the curriculum of primary and secondary schools. State-controlled religion was upheld and religious education was limited to only one sect of Islam, Sunnism. Alevis, who do not belong to this sect, still suffer as a result of this decision.

Moreover, in Article 66 citizenship is defined as: 'Everyone connected to the Turkish state with ties of citizenship is a Turk. The child of a Turkish father or mother is Turkish.' Turkishness thus appears to be defined not in terms of ethnicity, but by geographical principles. In practice. however, ethnicity played a significant role in the definition of citizenship in Turkey.

The 1982 Constitution has been amended several times and a large number of ordinary laws have also been modified. The so-called Harmonisation Packages were passed in 2002 and 2003 in seven reform packages, and had the primary aim of fulfilling the Copenhagen political criteria necessary for EU membership. Constitutional amendments and reform packages related to the citizenship issue are very significant for understanding how the state responded to the demands for a more liberal understanding of citizenship and recognition of differences. For example, Article 13 was amended on 17 October 2001; the original text of Article 13 enumerated general grounds for restricting all fundamental rights and liberties of citizens, namely safeguarding the indivisible integrity of the state with its territory and nation. The 2001 amendment deleted the general grounds for these restrictions. The amended text reads as follows:

> Fundamental rights and freedoms may be restricted only by law and solely on the basis of the reasons set out in the relevant articles of the Constitution without infringing upon their essence. These restrictions shall not be in conflict with the letter and the spirit of the Constitution, the requirements of the democratic order and the secular Republic, and the principle of proportionality.

With this amendment, fundamental rights and liberties were protected and broadened by limiting possible restrictions. Furthermore, a constitutional amendment of 2004 stipulated that in cases of conflict between domestic laws and international agreements concerning fundamental rights and liberties, international agreements should take precedence. International agreements offer greater protection of citizens' rights in Turkey than the Turkish Constitution does, and citizens' rights and freedoms are increasingly better protected.

Although more than a third of the original text of the Constitution 1982 regarding the rights and freedoms given to citizens belonging to minority groups was subsequently amended, there are still many problems in the application of these laws. To a large extent, non-Muslim, Alevi and Kurdish citizens' demands for a more a liberal understanding of citizenship have not been met. This problem has been emphasised in the EU Progress Reports on Turkey since 1998. Consequently, the AKP promised to completely overhaul the 1982 Constitution and prepare a 'civil Constitution' in its 2007 election manifesto. Unlike the current Constitution, the draft Constitution of 2007 adopted a liberal and rights-based approach to the relationship between individual and state. The Preamble of the draft Constitution rejected every kind of discrimination by regarding 'differences as the source of cultural richness'. The draft Constitution also took crucial steps towards protecting citizenship rights and liberties. For instance, Article 4 stipulates that the principle aim and duty of the state is to remove all obstacles from the realisation of citizenship rights and liberties. The draft Constitution also redefined 'Turkishness'. Ergun Özbudun stated 'we did not characterise citizenship in the Constitution on the basis of blood ties'.[19] The phrase in Article 66 of the 1982 Constitution: 'Everyone bound to the Turkish state with the bond of citizenship is a Turk', was changed to 'Everyone bound to the Turkish Republic with the bond of citizenship is called a Turk regardless of religion or race'. If accepted, this draft Constitution could signify the turning point for the definition of citizenship in Turkey. However, because of disagreements among the AKP Members of Parliament, the AKP postponed the finalisation of the new Constitution after the 2011 general elections and again following the 2014 elections.

Another important legal document concerning the construction of citizenship in Turkey is the Citizenship Law (see below). Since the 1980s citizenship has been a significant issue for successive governments in Turkey. Initially, control over citizenship was used to punish people, especially leftists, who opposed the regime. From 1981 the government withdrew, on a large scale, the right of citizenship among both non-Muslims and leftists. Later, in the interest of greater democratisation as well as integration with Europe, Parliament discussed the issue of citizenship and enacted more democratic amendments to Turkey's Citizenship Law. For this reason, the existing Turkish Citizenship Law No. 403 of 1964 has been amended four times since its first enactment.

The conditions for permission to renounce Turkish nationality stated in Article 20 have been amended twice, firstly by Act No. 2383 of 2 February 1981 and secondly by the Act No. 4112 of 7 June 1995. The first amendment recognised that, in principle, Turkish citizens can voluntarily

---

[19] *Turkish Daily News*, 27 November 2007.

acquire a foreign citizenship without losing their Turkish one. However, in principle it is required that the respective person makes a request either for permission to renounce Turkish citizenship or permission for dual citizenship. Otherwise, Turkish citizens who voluntarily acquire foreign citizenship without obtaining the required permission may be faced with the sanction of the loss of their Turkish citizenship.

Significant changes were also made to Article 29 by new Act No. 4112 of 7 June 1995. This article, which stated:

> A person who has lost Turkish citizenship under this law is to be treated as foreigner as from the date of such loss. Such a person may only benefit from the rights of foreigners as recognised by Turkish law in matters such as residence, acquiring and transferring real estate, and inheritance and labour

was changed by adding this statement:

> However, those who held Turkish citizenship by birth, and acquired another country's citizenship after getting permission to withdraw from a decision of the Council of Ministers as well as their inheritors, may benefit from the rights of Turkish citizens in matters such as residence, acquiring and transferring real estate, and inheritance and labour, while the provisions for the national security and public order of the Turkish Republic are reserved.[20]

By looking at the legal reasoning of Act No. 4112 changing Article 29, one can easily discern the reasoning behind the amendment. In the minutes of the debates it is stated that:

> our citizens abroad wish to acquire the nationality of the state where they reside and work; but the respective states require the renunciation of Turkish nationality; whereas our citizens who had to obtain permission to renounce Turkish nationality in order to be able to acquire the nationality of the state of residence are made subject to the status of a foreigner in Turkey in accordance with Article 29 of the Turkish Nationality Act; this practice however has given rise to our citizens in question giving up their desire to acquire foreign nationality, and thus the Act No. 4112 has been precisely drafted for the purpose of removing this difficulty.[21]

During debates in Parliament over Article 29 some deputies warned that the changes would allow non-Muslims, such as Greeks, Jews and Armenians, who had lost Turkish citizenship in the 1920s, to re-claim

---

20 Rona Aybay, *Vatandaşlık Hukuku* (Istanbul: Bilgi Üniversitesi Yayınları, 2003), 387–8.

21 *TBMM Tutanak Dergisi*, LXXXVIII 842 (1) 1995.

their citizenship and demand that their property and former residences be returned.[22] These ex-citizens were regarded as a threat to the country's security.

Citizenship and Identity

Throughout the Republican period the state wanted to create modern, civilised, non-religious, egalitarian, passive, and duty-oriented citizens. Since the 1980s the official understanding of Turkish citizenship began to be challenged, especially by Alevis, non-Muslims and Kurds, who demanded that the state recognise their ethnic and religious identities.

The post-1980 period was marked by the rise of political Islam and an Islamic identity in Turkey. This had far-reaching consequences for non-Muslim citizens and citizens belonging to the Alevi sect of Islam, among them a large number of Kurds. Islam had been introduced by the military as an instrument for consolidating and institutionalising the post-1980 regime.

Alevis

Alevi religious practices and their interpretation of Islam are strikingly different from the practices and interpretations of the Sunnis. Although Alevism is the second largest sect in Turkey, many authors argue that the Alevi community has been oppressed and discriminated against ever since the founding of the Republic.

During the second half of the 1980s and 1990s there were significant political factors that renewed the interest of the Alevis in their identity. The first reason for the Alevi revival was the collapse of the Communist bloc in Eastern Europe. As a result, socialism, which was a strong ideological alternative for young Alevis, instead of religion, lost its importance. They rediscovered Alevism and began to define themselves as Alevis. The second reason was the rise of Islamic fundamentalism or political Islam in Turkey, and the third was the re-emergence of the Kurdish issue. No reliable figures exist for the size of either Turkey's Alevi or Kurdish population, but the proportion of Kurds among the Alevis as a whole can be estimated at around 10–20 per cent.[23] Alevi citizens claim they constitute 30 per cent of the population.[24]

---

[22] Aybay, *Vatandaşlık Hukuku*, 88–109.

[23] Reha Çamuroğlu, 'Alevi Revivalism in Turkey' in *Alevi Identity*, eds. T. Olsson et al. (Istanbul: Numune Matbaası, 1998), 79–85.

[24] Çamuroğlu, 'Alevi Revivalism in Turkey', 79.

The tension between the Sunni majority and the Alevi minority, which had traditionally supported secular politics, reached its peak during the 1990s. Alevi citizens felt increasingly threatened by militant Sunni Islamist movements. Following the 1980 military intervention, Sunni mosques were opened in Alevi regions in order to convert them to the dominant Sunni form of Islam.[25] The Alevis rejected these attempts at assimilation and, in their struggle against 'Sunni fundamentalism', their main political agenda became the preservation and development of Turkey's Republican principle of secularism.[26]

Their critique was also directed at Turkey's state Directorate of Religious Affairs (*Diyanet* for short), established in 1924. Alevis accused the *Diyanet* of only representing citizens belonging to the country's Sunni majority. Several Alevi citizens have called for equal representation in the bureaucratic structure of the *Diyanet*, whereas others have demanded the complete abolition of this institution.

The '*Diyanet* Debate' began in December 1991 following the publication of a report about an informal secret meeting called by the *Diyanet* with a number of Alevi intellectuals and religious leaders in order to learn the views of the Alevis. The report denied that there were significant differences between Sunnis and Alevis and declared that the existing disputes were the work of 'leftists'. In this way it tried to evade the demands Alevi citizens were making for the recognition of *cemevleri* (*cem* houses), Alevi houses of worship, the *ezan* (call to prayer) in Turkish, and their rejection of Sunni practices such as fasting. Alevi citizens criticised the *Diyanet* for trying to assimilate Alevism into Sunnism.

Because around one-third of the population is Alevi, Alevis demanded that 30 per cent of the *Diyanet's* budget should be reserved for Alevis and that 30 per cent of its personnel should be Alevis. They said that *cem* houses, where both men and women worship together, should be constructed by the state, and that compulsory courses on religion – always given by Sunni scholars – should either be abolished or Alevism taught on an equal basis. Responding to these demands, the *Diyanet* argued that it was impartial towards all forms of Islam and that it did not discriminate against Alevi citizens. Moreover, it rejected the need to establish equal representation of different sects within the *Diyanet* as there would be no end to such a practice.

---

25 Ruşen Çakır, 'Political Alevism versus Political Sunnism: Convergences and Divergences' in *Alevi Identity*, eds. T. Olsson et al. (Istanbul: Numune Matbaası, 1998), 64.

26 Çakır, 'Political Alevism versus Political Sunnism', 65.

The debate on the rights of Alevis grew more heated after the attack in Sivas in 1993. On 2 July 1993 an Alevi Pir Sultan Abdal festival was organised by members of Turkish and Kurdish Alevi organisations in Sivas. Events took a bloody turn when 37 people, most of them Alevis, were burnt to death when the Madimak Hotel was set on fire by Sunni radicals. This event had an adverse impact on Alevi and Sunni relations, leading to the escalation of violence. In 1994 Alevis attacked a commercial television station after derogatory remarks made by a host of a game show, and on 12 March 1995, three Alevi coffee houses in Istanbul's Gaziosmanpaşa neighbourhood were machine gunned.

The debate between Alevis and the *Diyanet* acquired an international dimension in 2000, when in meetings with members of the EU Commission representatives of the Alevi community voiced their complaints about the assimilationist policies of the state. This meeting was harshly criticised by the Ministry of Interior on the grounds that if the state gave rights to Alevis then citizens belonging to other sects might also demand rights.[27] In 2002, an important Alevi umbrella group composed of some 30 organisations was closed down for violation of Article 5 of the Law of Associations, which prohibits establishment of associations 'in the name of any religion, race, social class, or sect'. The ground for dissolution was that the Association's name contained the words 'Alevi' and 'Bektaşi', which unlawfully referred to Muslim religious minorities.

In another case of international interference, in 2007 the European Court of Human Rights (ECtHR) announced its detailed judgement on the case of Turkish Alevi citizen Hasan Zengin. He had appealed to the court in 2004 on the grounds that mandatory religious courses in the Turkish national education system, which predominantly teach the Sunni creed of Islam, are a violation of Article 9 of the European Convention on Human Right (ECHR).[28] The court decided that government policies contradicted the principle of the 'impartiality of the state', and thus were a violation of human rights.

Despite some recent attempts at reform by the government, Alevi citizens' demands have not been met. In the current textbooks on Religious Culture and Learning of Ethics Alevism is still defined as a 'Sufistic interpretation of Islam'. Promises to take positive steps are believed to be merely efforts to attract the votes of Alevi citizens during elections.

---

27 *Cumhuriyet*, 23 June 2000.
28 *Turkish Daily News*, 10 October 2007.

Non-Muslims

In contrast to the position of the Alevis, there have been some improvements in the state's approach to non-Muslim citizens of the Republic, especially in the second half of the 1990s. For instance, in 1999 President Demirel celebrated Christmas with Turkey's Christian citizens, a gesture that would have been unthinkable during the single-party period. Likewise, in November 2003 the office of the *Diyanet* in Antakya established a multi-religious committee aimed at developing a harmonious relationship between Muslims, Christians and Jews, and the dialogue between non-Muslim communities continued during the AKP government. However, as with the Alevis, reform has been sluggish and discrimination against non-Muslims continues.

The most persistent problem that non-Muslim citizens encounter is the legal position of their cultural and religious institutions, known collectively as *vakıflar* (religious foundations). As the funding of their religious, social, and cultural activities are dependent on these foundations, they are vital for the well-being of non-Muslim citizens. In 1912 the Ottoman Empire enacted a law that granted legal status to the foundations and enabled them to register the property they owned in their name. Article 40 of the Treaty of Lausanne (24 July 1923) explicitly confirmed these rights and granted non-Muslim minorities the right to manage and control their institutions. Following the establishment of the Turkish Republic, the Law of Foundations No. 2762 (hereinafter Law No. 2762), of 5 June 1935,[29] again called upon the foundations to declare and register with the state the property they owned. The religious and educational institutions of non-Muslim minorities were thereafter regulated by the Directorate General of Foundations (*Vakıflar Genel Müdürlüğü*, VGM), a government agency that supervises the operation of churches, monasteries, synagogues, schools, and charitable religious foundations, such as hospitals and orphanages. This direct state interference, however, violates the Treaty of Lausanne and the right of minorities to self-regulate their own foundations. The VGM demanded a *vakıfname* (foundation certification) concerning the property of non-Muslim citizens in 1972. Nevertheless, many did not have a *vakıfname* because they had been established by the sultan's *firman* during the Ottoman Empire. The VGM considered written statements from 1936 as a *vakıfname* in 1974. For this reason, properties acquired by non-Muslim foundations after 1936 were taken over, because they did not exist in the 1936 written statement.[30]

[29] The law was implemented in 1936.

[30] Baskın Oran, *Türkiye'de Azınlıklar* (İstanbul: TESEV Yayınları, 2004), 111.

A reform law package was put into force on 9 August 2002 that recognised the right of non-Muslim foundations to own immoveable properties and to dispose of them freely, a right which had been *de facto* taken away in 1936. This right was tied to the decision of the Council of Ministers and, with the fourth reform package of 2 January 2003, this right was tied to the VGM. Another reform package, that was put into force on 19 July 2003, recognised the right of non-Muslim communities to build places of worship, subject to the approval of the competent administrative authorities. Thus, non-Muslim foundations were given the right to own immoveable property and to meet their needs by these amendments. Despite this progress, however, these reforms were not able to solve the problems faced by non-Muslim foundations concerning their freedom from state interference in other fields. Religious foundations continue to be subject to interference of the *Diyanet*, which is able to dissolve the foundations, seize their properties, intervene in the management of their assets and accounting, and dismiss their board of trustees without a judicial decision.

Another major problem faced by non-Muslim citizens is the ban on the training of their clergy. Non-Muslim citizens encounter difficulties in sustaining their communities beyond the current generation. The Greek Orthodox Seminary on the island of Heybeliada (*Halki*) was closed in 1971, prohibiting the education of Orthodox priests in Turkey. Restriction on foreign nationality prevents non-Turkish clergy working for certain churches, such as the Syriac or Chaldean churches, while the public use of the ecclesiastical title of Ecumenical Patriarch is still banned and the election of the heads of some religious minority churches is still subject to strict conditions. Official religious textbooks have been redrafted in order to address the concerns of Christian minorities; however, clergymen and graduates from theological colleges continue to be barred from teaching in existing schools run by minorities. As in the single-party period, schools belonging to non-Muslim minorities are under strict control. In all minority schools, such as those belonging to expats, only 'ethnic Turks' can be appointed as principals. They are also granted more responsibility than the managers of these schools.[31]

Kurdish Nationalism

The rise of Kurdish nationalism was another development that challenged established definitions of Turkish citizenship. The intense fear of dissolution and separatism has been a cornerstone of Turkish nationalism. Although the military regime tolerated and even supported Islam, its

---

31 Oran, *Türkiye'de Azınlıklar*, 110.

attitude towards the Kurdish issue was one of intolerance.[32] Since the establishment of the Republic the existence of the Kurds had been denied and all expressions of Kurdish identity forbidden. A theory was formulated claiming that Kurds were 'mountain Turks'; their name came from the sound of the snow that crunched with a 'kurt kart' noise underneath their footsteps when they were walking.[33]

From the 1980s until the second half of the 1990s the Kurdish issue was equated with the threat of terrorism. The most radical Kurdish movement, the PKK/KADEK (Kurdistan Workers' Party/Kurdistan Freedom and Democracy Congress), was seen as the nation's main enemy. With the waning power of the PKK in the late 1990s and the government's emphasis on EU integration more moderate policies towards Kurdish citizens were adopted.

An increasing number of politicians have recognised the need for a peaceful solution to the Kurdish problem. The then President Turgut Özal, who broke many taboos in Turkey and brought unaddressed matters into the public consciousness, played a crucial role in offering a solution to the Kurdish question by arguing that this issue should be discussed freely. As a first step, he invited People's Democratic Party (*Halkin Demokrasi Partisi*, HADEP) deputies for a meeting and announced that 'we should discuss everything about the Kurdish issue, including federation'.[34] He also invited the Iraqi Kurdish leader Jalal Talabani to Ankara, which was an extraordinary event both for Talabani himself and for the Turkish public in general.[35] Özal was the first to suggest allowing radio and television broadcasts in Kurdish as well as the teaching of Kurdish as a secondary language in schools.[36]

In 1992 in Budapest, Özal's successor, Süleyman Demirel, went a step further and proposed 'constitutional citizenship' as a way to ensure internal peace in Turkey, a proposal that would later become a topic of heated debate among politicians and political scientists. In 1996, Demirel argued that the best way to produce harmony while recognising diversity was to establish an understanding of the nation

---

[32] Nilüfer Göle, 'Authoritarian Secularism and Islamist Politics: The Case of Turkey' in *Civil Society in the Middle East*, ed. A.R. Norton (Leiden: Brill, 1996), 20.

[33] Eyyup Demir, *Yasal Kürtler* (Istanbul: Tevn Yayınları, 2005), 43.

[34] Mehmet A. Birand and Soner Yalçın, *The Özal* (Istanbul: Doğan Kitapçılık, 2001), 455.

[35] Birand and Yalçın, *The Özal*, 465.

[36] Kemal Kirişçi and G.M. Winrow, *The Kurdish Question and Turkey* (London: Frank Cass, 1998), 137.

as a collective of citizens endowed with universal democratic rights. To underline his proposal he advocated the introduction of a notion of a form of citizenship that leaves no room for ethnic discrimination.[37] Yet, in 1999 during a visit to Israel, Demirel suggested that Turkey already had constitutional citizenship, so what he meant by the concept was not entirely clear.

These steps towards the recognition of diversity, however, did not go uncontested. The centre-right True Path Party (*Doğru Yol Partisi*, DYP), dominated by hard-liners, did not accept the Kurdish claims to cultural and political rights. The then DYP leader Tansu Çiller had a populist-opportunistic approach to the issue, like many politicians. When the Islamist Welfare Party (*Refah Partisi*, RP) gained popular success in Turkey's east and south-east, Çiller tried to take the wind out its sails by talking about the possibility of allowing private education and broadcasts to be held in Kurdish. After the elections she retracted these statements. However, to indicate that the sands were shifting and a renewed definition of citizenship had become inevitable in finding a solution to the Kurdish issue, on 31 December 1994 Çiller reformulated Atatürk's famous statement 'how happy is the one who says, I am a Turk', to 'how happy is the one who says, I am a citizen of Turkey'.[38]

Such changes over time are also reflected in the AKP's 2002 and 2007 election manifestos, which accepted cultural differences in the east and south-east as contributing to Turkey's 'cultural richness', and presented political solutions instead of economic ones. It supported broadcasts and publication in languages other than Turkish on condition that Turkish remained the official language and education continued to be in Turkish. It believed that all citizens of Turkey should be equal, without any distinctions. When Erdoğan first came to power he did not even identify the Kurdish issue as problem. For instance, when a worker in Moscow in December 2002 asked Erdoğan how he wanted to solve the Kurdish question, Erdoğan answered: 'We are saying that such a problem does not exist. According to you such a question exists. Thus you approach it with prejudice. I say that there is no such problem. We are all from Turkey.'[39] Certainly, Erdoğan's reply to another question about a possible Kurdish state in northern Iraq showed that he suffered from the same fear of separatism that all Turkish politicians suffer from: 'We are against a Kurdish

---

[37] Füsun Üstel, 'Anayasaya Vatandaşlık, Hangi Anayasaya Vatandaşlık?' *Radikal*, 17 December 1996.

[38] Ahmet İçduygu, 'Çokkültürlülük: Türkiye Vatandaşlığı Kavramı İçin Toplumsal Bir Zemin' *Türkiye Günlüğü* 33 (1997): 117.

[39] *Milliyet*, 24 December 2002.

state even if it is established in Argentina.'[40] In April 2005, in Norway, Erdoğan confirmed his Turkish nationalist credentials by stating: 'For us there is no Kurdish problem. It is an imaginary issue.'[41]

The above discussions of 'legal' and 'identity' aspects of citizenship in Turkey underline that only through the revision and redefinition of the early Republican concept of citizenship based on a single religion (Sunni Islam) and single language (Turkish) can the demands for rights coming from various sections of the society be met.

CIVIC VIRTUE (1980–2014)

Given Turkey's ethnic and religious plurality, civic education plays a very important role in promoting tolerance. After discussing 'legal' and 'identity' aspects of citizenship in Turkey I therefore turn to Turkey's civic education textbooks to better appreciate the extent to which they promote human rights as shared values, and make positive references to ethnic, religious, and cultural diversity.

Civic education is as contested as citizenship itself.[42] We are not born citizens, but become so through practice, in places of education and in everyday life.[43] Thus, one of the key elements in the creation of stable nation-states is the ability of states to socialise new generations into the role of citizen through a public process of mass-schooling.[44] Education has, in this framework, the function of conflict reduction, particularly in societies moving towards democracy, consolidating their democratic systems, or experiencing ethnic and religious strife. In Turkey, education has been vital for the modernising agenda and has played a crucial role in the production of citizens.[45]

Turkey has a highly centralised educational system. The Board of Education under the Ministry of National Education prepares the

---

40 *Radikal*, 1 June 2004.

41 *Milliyet*, 12 April 2005.

42 Audrey Osler and Hugh Starket, 'Learning for Cosmopolitan Citizenship: Theoretical Debates and Young People's Experiences' *Educational Review* 55 (2003): 289.

43 See Herman V. Gunsteren, *A Theory of Citizenship* (Boulder: Westview Press, 1998); Patricia White, 'Political Education in the Early Years: The Place of Civic Virtues' *Oxford Review of Education* 25 (1999) 1–2: 59.

44 See M.F. Astiz and G. Mendez, 'Education for Citizenship: The Argentine Case in Comparison' *Education, Citizenship and Social Justice* 1 (2006) 2: 175–200.

45 See Benjamin C. Fortna, *Imperial Classroom: Islam, the State, and Education in the Late Ottoman Empire* (New York: Oxford University Press, 2002).

curricula for all subjects and its approval of textbooks is required. As textbooks have to follow the guidelines of the board, they are all more or less identical and they fail to adequately reflect the general debate on citizenship-related issues in society.

Course books were reworked after the 12 September 1980 coup in order to reflect the military's perspective on social and political events. According to Kemal İnal, post-1980 education, both in general and in the textbooks, became a tool for ideological indoctrination.[46] The military made good use of the education system to portray itself as the natural guardian of the Turkish state, while its education policies were also influenced by the Turkish-Islamic synthesis. As a result, alienation of non-Muslim citizens and citizens belonging to different sects of Islam, e.g., Alevis, was supported.

The textbooks defined citizenship rights by uncritically presenting the constitutional limitations of the citizen rights in the 1982 Constitution. They argued that it was one of the duties of the state to limit the rights of its citizens under certain circumstances. Needless to say, the textbooks presented the existing situation as perfect[47] and did not mention domestic discussions of problems that citizens faced while trying to exercise their rights.

While citizenship rights were mentioned briefly, the emphasis was on duties, together with a host of larger responsibilities. The duties of citizenship were listed as: performing military service; paying tax; voting; obtaining a mindset that would prevent activities of a divisive or destructive nature; and securing national unity. The textbooks promoted a duty-based social order rather than a rights-based one and failed to address the importance of citizenship participation in the policy process, reducing democracy simply to the exercise of voting. Thus, civic education in Turkey became a means of sustaining an obedient society, rather than a way to introduce tolerance for diversity.

Not unexpectedly, these textbooks – like those published in previous periods – created a phobia of 'the enemy' in the minds of young people, which led to intolerance against the 'other', among both individuals and groups, as great emphasis was placed on 'enemies' and 'threats' in the textbooks. Unlike in previous periods, the textbooks warned not only of external enemies but also of internal ones who, said the books, seek to divide our nation along lines of race, class, and religious sect, and use

---

[46] Kemal İnal, *Eğitimde İdeolojik Boyut* (Ankara: Doruk Yayınları, 1996), 22.

[47] See F. Yılmaz and N. Yanıkoğlu, *İlköğretim Vatandaşlık ve İnsan hakları Eğitimi 7* (Istanbul: Okyay Yayıncılık, 2002).

various methods to do so, such as anarchy and terror. External threats were listed as smuggling, international terrorism – including Armenian terrorism – the historical and ideological designs of certain countries, such as Greece, Armenia, Syria, and Russia, and espionage.[48] The notion that Turkey was surrounded by enemies[49] was supported by the saying, 'Turks have no friends besides fellow Turks'.[50] Thus, civic education in Turkey was used as a tool to develop 'self-sacrificing' 'good citizens', who should always be on the alert for 'enemies' and vigilant in their protection of the unity of the nation. This burdened young citizens with great responsibilities and fostered xenophobia.

Some of the textbooks emphasised the importance of Islam. They mentioned only Sunni Islam, as well as Sunni religious rules governing the individual's relations with society. Such emphasis on the Sunni Islam, however, may have encouraged hatred against non-Muslim and Alevi citizens.

In 1998, *Citizenship and Human Rights Education* was incorporated as a required civics course. Though textbooks bear the name *Citizenship and Human Rights Education*, according to Fatma Gök these books contain items that are contrary to human rights.[51] For example, under Article 26 of the Universal Declaration of Human Rights, everybody has the right to receive an education, and under Article 42 of the 1982 Turkish Constitution, 'No one shall be deprived of the right of learning and education'. Nevertheless, according to Gök, the authors of these textbooks state that education should only be given in Turkish and completely ignore the feelings and perspectives of minority citizens.[52] The incorporation of citizenship education and human rights education in 2000 derived not so much from moral or ethical principles but because it is a mark of a civilised country.

Since the 2008–2009 academic year Turkey's Ministry of National Education has incorporated civic education into social studies textbooks for Grades Six and Seven. The current social studies texts also emphasise duties more than rights; connect ancient civilisations and the Turkish nation; and emphasise similarities between Muslim countries and Turkey.

---

[48] Nuri Bilgen, *8. Sınıf için Vatandaşlık ve İnsan Hakları Eğitimi* (Ankara: Mili Eğitim Bakanlığı Yayınları, 2001).

[49] Emin Ceylan, *İlköğretim Vatandaşlık Bilgileri* (Ankara: SEK Yayınları, 1996), 55.

[50] Ceylan, *İlköğretim Vatandaşlık Bilgileri*, 56–7.

[51] Fatma Gök, 'Vatandaşlık ve İnsan hakları Eğitimi Ders Kitapları' in *Ders Kitaplarında İnsan Hakları: Tarama Sonuçları*, eds. B. Çötüksöken et al. (Istanbul: Tarih Vakfı Yayınları, 2003).

[52] Fatma Gök, 'Vatandaşlık ve İnsan hakları Eğitimi', 159.

But there have also been some improvements, the most important of which concerns teaching techniques. The course supports class participation rather than rote learning. There is no talk of the 'enemies of Turkey', thus decreasing the likelihood of xenophobia. When discussing religious freedom, one text gives the example of Antakya, a city in Turkey, where three different religions peacefully co-exist. However, apart from this brief mention, the textbooks still do not discuss the ethnic and religious minorities living in Turkey and their identity claims. One text mentions *Nevruz*, the traditional celebration of the Iranian New Year, recounting it as if *Nevruz* is celebrated by ethnic Turks alone. However, Kurdish citizens traditionally celebrate *Nevruz*, despite being unable to do so openly until 2005. The holiday is now recognised in Turkey, but there is no mention in the texts of Kurds living in Turkey.

Although there have been certain improvements the current social studies textbooks do not place enough emphasis on civic information; continue to create dutiful citizens who uncritically obey all the state's dictates; and are not up to the task of cultivating the democratic and active citizens needed in the twenty-first century.

CONCLUSION

Citizenship is one of the most important but elusive concepts in modern political discourses and practice. It is important because citizenship, or the lack of it, determines people's political, legal, and social rights, and defines their membership in a political community. It is both a source and a result of inclusion and identification as it demarcates groups of individuals who have certain privileges and responsibilities in common. At the same time, it is also a source (and a result) of exclusion, as citizenship is not open to all but often can only be acquired by obeying elaborate rules and satisfying particular requirements.

The Kemalist revolution of the 1920s and 1930s had transformed the Ottoman Empire into a monistic nation-state. The empire had made room for many Turkish, Kurdish, Georgian, Abkhazian, Armenian, Greek, and Jewish sub-groups. Many were recognised by the state, but none of them coincided with the Ottoman supra-identity. The same sub-identities continued to exist in the Republic of Turkey, but the supra-identity was replaced by an ethnic Turkish one, creating an imbalance in favour of ethnic Turkish citizens.

Since the 1990s, however, in line with Bryan Turner's distinction, there has been a clash between formal and radical understandings of citizenship in Turkey. On the one hand, there is the official definition of citizenship, based on the Republican understanding of obligations to the state in return for rights. On the other hand, there are the demands for a more liberal understanding of citizenship, based on the priority of rights and recognition of differences in a new definition of citizenship. This clash has played itself out in the revival of the Kurdish, Alevi and non-Muslim identities, as citizens of these minorities began to question the fabricated and imposed monolithic citizenship identity of the single-party period. The common denominator of their demands is recognition of their social, cultural and political rights, which would end their cultural alienation. They demand a new form of citizenship based on constitutional rights rather than on nationality. It is within this context that the issue of 'constitutional citizenship', which represents something more than the formal legal status of membership, began to be discussed in the public sphere.

The demands formulated by different minorities in Turkey can be met through the concept of constitutional citizenship. In general, constitutional citizenship represents the idea that political loyalty should be based on the norms, values, and, more indirectly, procedures of a liberal-democratic Constitution. Thus, political allegiance is owed, primarily, neither to a national culture, as proponents of liberal nationalism have claimed, nor to 'the worldwide community of human beings'. Constitutional citizenship promises a form of solidarity distinct from both nationalism and cosmopolitanism. A form of citizenship that is purely formal, legal, and concerned with the relation of the citizen to the state, can secure the loyalty of distinct identity groups in a way that a concept of citizenship based on nationality cannot. Thus in countries like Turkey, where identity-based conflicts endanger the sense of unity, constitutional citizenship can secure the loyalty of distinct identity groups.

The concept of constitutional citizenship as founded on the articulation of identity claims with citizenship rights could provide an effective basis for the solution of the problems that Turkey faces. We should articulate identity claims within the context of constitutional citizenship that operates not only as a legal and political membership but also as an articulating principle for the recognition of group rights. The solution should not be sought in identity but in an attempt to articulate identity claims to citizenship rights within the context of a democratic and pluralist vision of Turkish modernity.[53] Only this kind of citizenship can create substantive equality, in addition to legal equality, in Turkey.

---

[53] Fuat Keyman, 'Articulating Citizenship and Identity: The "Kurdish question" in Turkey' in *Citizenship in a Global World*, eds. E.F. Keyman and A. İçduygu, (London: Routledge, 2005), 284.

The government should articulate the identity claims of Alevis, Kurds and non-Muslims to citizenship rights and seek democratic solutions to the problems in terms of a politics of recognition, attempting to reconstruct the Republican model of Turkish citizenship in such a way as to make it more flexible, differentiated and constitutional. Nevertheless, having 'constitutional citizenship' is not an easy task in diverse societies. As Ayşe Kadıoğlu rightly pointed out, citizenship has preceded and had prevalence over the notion of the individual in Turkey. Citizenship was embedded in national identity as well as defined in accordance with duties in a rather weak public space. Hence, it is rather difficult to envision citizenship as an empty space, as non-membership in Turkey.[54]

Turkey's success in combining Islam and secularism, as well as in taking the military out of political and civilian life, serves as a model for the new and evolving revolutionary regimes in the Middle East. However, until Turkey meets demands for a more liberal understanding of citizenship based on the priority of rights and recognition of differences it cannot be a good example for any evolving regime.

---

[54] Ayşe Kadıoğlu, 'Can We Envision Turkish Citizenship as Non-membership?' in *Citizenship in a Global World*, eds. E.F. Keyman and A. İçduygu (London: Routledge, 2005), 120.

3. Bringing about the non-citizen in Iraq: a genealogical approach

Mariwan Kanie

INTRODUCTION

The question of citizenship has been one of the major issues during the history of Iraqi state–society relations. Iraq was created in the aftermath of the First World War, and its arbitrary boundaries were drawn up by Great Britain and France. Since its creation this state has been confronted with religious, ethnic, social and political fragmentation. The main argument of this chapter is that both the state and society of Iraq have failed to create a common notion of Iraqi citizenship as a framework of moral and political identification. This structural failure is the result of specific technologies of rule and governmental techniques for controlling society that were based on social, cultural and political discrimination, the denial of the politics of rights, the perseverance of systems of patronage and clientelism, the excessive use of violence, the unbalanced distribution of resources, uneven representation of Iraqi's diverse population, and the near-absence of the language and discourse of citizenship, except in rare instances and among small groups of intellectuals.

These technologies of rule were linked to various grand political dreams, such as Pan-Arabism, Communism, one-party rule, semi-totalitarianism, and one-man rule, mixed with more traditional forms such as clientelism.

THE MONARCHY (1921–1958) AND THE COLONIAL STATE

Iraq is a modern colonial creation. During the Ottoman period the territories that make up present-day Iraq were the three autonomous provinces of Basra, Baghdad and Mosul, non of which were ever centrally controlled.[1] Britain did not intend to occupy these three provinces, let alone unite them into one state. Shortly after the outbreak of the First World War the British occupied the city of Basra in southern Iraq, with the aim of securing their interests in the Persian Gulf. However, 'what the British administration had started as a preventive action to secure British interests in the Persian Gulf ultimately led to the English occupation of the three provinces of Baghdad, Basra and Mosul at the end of 1918. During this process, the basis was set up for the establishment of an Iraqi state, and it was in this period that the history of the state commenced.'[2] Iraq received international recognition from the League of Nations as a new, legitimate member state under British mandate in 1921. In October 1932 the mandate was ended and Iraq recognised as an independent state, although Britain kept its political and military influence in Iraq through treaties and military bases.

When the Iraqi state was established in 1921 the country was inhabited by different ethnic groups including Arabs, Kurds, Turkmens, and Armenians, as well as various religious groups such as Shiʿis, Sunnis, different Christian denominations, Yazidis, and Jews.[3] King Faisal, the first ruler of Iraq, recognised the diversity of the country when, more than 10 years after its creation, he wrote that Iraqis are no more than 'unimaginable masses of human beings, devoid of any patriotic idea, imbued with religious traditions and absurdities . . . and prone to anarchy'.[4] Forcing all these different groups to gather under one political umbrella could only be achieved through significant levels of colonial and later post-colonial state violence. The seeds of the crisis of citizenship and the absence of a framework for national unity are to be found in this colonial project, which was also directly related to the significant role of violence in the political life of the newly created state.

Liberalism, Colonialism and Violence

However, liberal discourse was an important aspect of the colonial enterprise. Liberal notions of freedom, progress, autonomy and the right to self-determination – the basis of a new conception of citizenship – were

---

1 Charles Tripp, *A History of Iraq* (Cambridge: Cambridge University Press, 2002).

2 Tripp, *History of Iraq*, 56–7.

3 Sherko Kirmanj, *Identity and Nation in Iraq* (Boulder: Lynne Rienner, 2013), 5.

4 Efraim Karsh and Inari Rautsi, *Saddam Hussein: A Political Biography* (London: Futura Publications, 1991), 3; Fanar Haddad, *Sectarianism in Iraq: Antagonistic Visions of Unity* (New York: Oxford University Press, 2011).

important instruments in the hands of the colonial powers in their attempts to mobilise different ethnic groups against the Ottoman Empire during the First World War. This liberal message was disseminated through a large number of newspapers, published in different languages. For instance, when British forces occupied Basra on 22 November 1914 they seized the city's four newspaper printers and established the *Basra Times* in four different languages: Arabic, English, Persian and Turkish. In March 1917, four months after the occupation of Baghdad, the British published the Arabic-language newspaper *al-'Arab*, followed six months later by three other newspapers meant for the Iraqi public. The first was the English-language *Baghdad Times*, then the Persian daily *Iran*, and finally the Kurdish *Têgeîshtnî Rastî* (Understanding the Truth), published in the Sorani dialect.[5] The content of *al-'Arab* and *Têgeîshtnî Rastî* were very similar; these colonial newspapers highlight the period's zeitgeist; progress, independence, equality, freedom and justice. Nationalism, particularly, was portrayed as the modern driving force. Furthermore, these newspapers also discussed new risks and dangers seen at the time, risks that had either not existed in the past or had not done so in such a pronounced way, such as the domination of one nation by another, the danger of assimilation, or even the disappearance or 'eradication' (*mehu*) of a nation. The dominant notions that underpinned this worldview were the right to self-determination and the necessity of establishing an independent state for each ethnic group.[6] McDowall shows that the Anglo-French declaration of November 1918, in which both countries declared they would guarantee freedom for all peoples, resonated among Kurds and Arabs. According to this declaration, the allies aimed for 'the complete and final liberation of the peoples who have for so long been oppressed by the Turks, and that setting up of national governments and administrations that shall derive their authority from free exercise of the initiative and choice of the indigenous population'.[7]

The construction of this new political imagination and the promise of the creation of a new and just political order in the region planted the seeds of future problems for the newly created states, especially Iraq, where different ethnic groups had different political ideas and expectations. Emphasising freedom, progress, nationalism and the right to self-determination made the colonial project problematic from the

---

[5] Kemal Mezher, *Têgeîshtnî Rastî ū shwênî la rojnamegerî Kurdida*, ('Têgeîshtnî Rastî and its Place in Kurdish Journalism') (Baghdad 1978), 100–101.

[6] Mezher, *Têgeîshtnî Rastî*, 100–104.

[7] David McDowall, *A Modern History of the Kurds* (London/New York: I.B. Tauris, 1997), 163.

very beginning. Consequently, the use of violence and counter-violence became the main method of governing. The Kurds, from 1919 until 1932, and the majority of the Shiʿis in 1920 protested strongly against the imposition of a unified state under Sunni domination. To suppress these revolts, the colonial power was forced to use its military strength and inflict heavy casualties. Thus, from the beginning violence became an indispensable part of colonial rule, one which set a model for the rest of modern Iraqi history. As a result, it was not liberal citizenship and inclusion upon which the state was based; rather, the creation of the state was built upon violent subjugation, assimilation, counter-violence, military coups, alliances of one group against another, and/or exclusion. Equal rights were not the logic behind this newly created state.

The Colonial State as a Second-Hand State

Not only was violence one of the main instruments for administrating the colonial state, but this state lacked the power to act autonomously. Despite the formal aspects of government, such as the rule of law, rational administration, meritocracy and a liberal constitution, being present, foreign control of the colonial states 'undermined these liberal-rational notions' and its assumed forms of citizenship.[8] Parliaments in the mandates had little power, 'rather, decisions were made in London or Paris, subject to the vagaries of national politics in Britain and France'.[9]

Furthermore, the British in Iraq developed strong ties with the tribal leaders and used the segmented nature of society to their own political ends, supporting the existing patronage system, which blocked direct relations between the citizen and the state. 'In Iraq, the British rendered tribal leaders central to their strategy of political control. Tribal authority was strengthened by confirming tribal law and extending jurisdictional rights to tribal leaders, in addition to granting economic privileges.'[10] Finally, state power, for different social, political, and historical reasons, was monopolised by Sunni Arabs, a small minority who made up only 20 per cent of the total population of Iraq, and this Sunni elite tried to impose its concept of Arab identity on the whole of the population. I will elaborate

---

[8] Nicola Pratt, *Democracy and Authoritarianism in the Arab World* (Boulder: Lynne Rienner, 2007), 27

[9] Pratt, *Democracy*, 27.

[10] Pratt, *Democracy*, 28.

this point later when I discuss Sati'al-Husri and his Sunni educational project as an instrument of fostering Pan-Arabism in the country.

This combination of factors made the country ungovernable and unstable. For example, from 1932, when Iraq became formally independent, to 1939, 12 cabinets were formed; two cabinets per year. Across the whole period of the monarchy, between 1921–1958, 59 cabinets governed the country, 1.6 cabinets per year. In addition, politics in Iraq was deeply sectarian. Of the 59 cabinets during the monarchy, 53 were led by Sunni Arabs, while there was only one Shi'i Prime Minister, who was in power for little more than one year and 10 months, while a Kurdish Prime Minister led a cabinet for two months.[11] In contrast to many other countries, the Sunni domination of the army undermined its task of integrating the different ethnic and religious segments of Iraqi society into a unified Iraqi citizenship. But this failure also applies to the state in general. Zubaida notes that what is remarkable about Iraq in this period 'is the feeble part played by the state in the ideological and cultural construction of the nation, a weakness only reversed under the Saddamist Baath in the 1970s'.[12]

In short, on account of the perpetual internal power struggle within the fragmented elite, the politicisation of the army, and the weakness of the state in its efforts to create an Iraqi nation, nation-building never got off the ground. A real political commitment of the state to the principle of citizenship and the establishment of a close relationship between citizen and state based on trust and loyalty was never achieved. As a result, Iraq lacked a viable social contract both between its citizens and between the state and its citizens. This does not mean that the state did not attempt to develop another form of Iraqi patriotism, but this was undermined by the Sunni pan-Arabism that was upheld by the ruling elite, major state institutions such as the Ministry of Education, and the army.[13] Iraqi state policy was characterised by the Arabisation and the Sunnification of the state rather than the development of common notions and practices of citizenship based on equal civil, political and cultural rights; this could have been achieved under a different citizenship regime, such as a federal state or a state with a more open framework for political participation.

---

[11] Kirmanj, *Identity and Nation*, 28 and 87.

[12] Sami Zubaida, 'Iraq: History, Memory, Culture' *International Journal of Middle East Studies* 44 (2012): 334.

[13] For a nuanced reading of the monarchist period in Iraq and the realities between pan-Arabism, Iraqi nationalism, and Kurdish nationalism, see Kirmanj, *Identity and Nation.*

Sati'al-Husri and the Sectarian Education System in Iraq

That the Iraqi state was unsuccessful in creating a common Iraqi citizenship identity does not mean that it did not attempt to solve the problem of ethnic, religious, and provincial fragmentation and impose a unified concept of citizenship and belonging. The introduction of the secular ideology of pan-Arabism, particularly under the guidance of the intellectual Sati'al-Husri, must be considered an attempt to bridge the sectarian divide between the Iraqi Sunni and Shi'i Arabs. From 1921 to 1941 al-Husri was responsible for developing a national educational programme and, like King Faisal, al-Husri wanted to instil in future Iraqi generations a Sunni, pan-Arab identity.[14] He was, however, ill-informed about the complexity of the different ethnic and religious groups in Iraq and their historical relationships and, in consequence, his assimilation programme failed. The Kurds, whose political leader Sheikh Mahmud had, a decade earlier, expressed his desire that Kurdistan not be 'a part of Iraq nor the Kurds as Iraqis', instead favouring direct rule by the British, were particularly alienated.[15]

The Iraqi Shi'is, too, were not taken in by al-Husri's educational reform. Sati'al-Husri was not only an extreme secularist, but he was also highly suspicious of Shi'i religious connections with Iran. As a result, the Shi'is regarded him as an anti-Shi'i state official who discriminated against them.[16] This opinion was confirmed, in their eyes, when al-Husri fired many Shi'i schoolteachers due to their 'Iranian background'. For instance, he blocked a plan to establish a teacher's college in Babylon simply because the majority of the inhabitants of the city were Shi'is, and he was afraid that they would use the college to develop a pro-Shi'i curriculum. For the same reason he brought the Provincial Education Administration for the Middle Euphrates (a Shi'i area) under the control of the (Sunni) Baghdad Provincial administration.[17] However, what was particularly irksome for the Shi'i was al-Husri's curriculum of Arab and Islamic history, which was denigrating to them. Under al-Husri's influence the Iraqi government also began to suppress Shi'i religious holidays and rituals, which led to a mass uprising in the mid-1930s. If the Shi'is already had a strong feeling of political exclusion, al-Husri's educational

---

14 Bassam Tibi, *Arab Nationalism: Between Islam and the Nation-state* (New York: St. Martin's Press 1990), 122.

15 Kirmanj, *Identity and Nation*, 23.

16 Ferhad Ibrahim, *al-Ta'ifiyya wa al-Siyasa fi-l-'Alam al-'Arabi* ('Sectarianism and Politics in the Arab World') (Cairo: Maktaba al-Madbuli, 1996), 130.

17 Ibrahim, *al-Ta'ifiyya wa-l-Siyasa*, 231.

reforms also strengthened a sense of cultural and religious exclusion among them.[18]

Citizenship and the Iraqi Communist Party

One of the few political movements that did develop a comprehensive concept of citizenship in this period was the Communist Party of Iraq (CPI).[19] The first Marxist cells in Iraq were formed in Baghdad in 1924, the CPI was officially founded in 1935, and by the 1940s this had become a mass movement. In his standard work on the social and political history of modern Iraq, Hanna Batatu observes: 'In the forties communism became a factor in the life of Iraq. It did not implant itself in the visible citadels of power but in the hearts and minds of youth. In terms of continuity, organisation, and number of supporters and sympathizers, it rose to first rank among political movements.'[20] The CPI developed the idea of Iraqi-ness as a shared identity and Iraq as shared political framework for its heterogeneous population. It established different branches for different communities, such as Kurdish and Armenian branches, while creating horizontal 'central committees' for workers, students and the military, based on class and profession rather than ethnic difference.[21] The party constituted a cultural melting pot where Shiʿis, Kurds, Christians, Jews, Sunni Arabs, and other ethnic and religious groups could meet, debate shared interests, and struggle for a common future, and it was one of the few political organisations that represented the ethnic and religious heterogeneity of Iraq. In absolute numerical terms, the dominant place in the party belonged to underprivileged Shiʿi Arabs, while Kurds also constituted a relatively high proportion of its members.[22] However, in March 1938 the Iraqi government issued a law making membership of the CPI a crime; despite such harsh repression, communism continued to be consolidated, and its membership increased over time.

---

18 Mariwan Kanie, 'Martelaarschap tussen Natie en Religie: Politieke Liefde, Poëzie en Zelfopoffering in Koerdisch Nationalisme' ('Martyrdom between Nation and Religion: Political Love, Poetry and Self-Sacrificing in Kurdish Nationalism') (PhD diss., University of Amsterdam, 2010).

19 Many leftist political groups, segments of civil society, and intellectuals appealed to Iraqi patriotism. As well as the CPI, the National Democracy Party was also in favour of such patriotism; this party was licensed in 1946 and subsequently banned in 1954; see Kirmanj, *Identity and Nation*, 73–4.

20 Hanna Batatu, *The Old Social Classes and the Revolutionary Movements of Iraq* (London: Saqi, 2004), 465.

21 Batatu, *Old Social Classes*, 630.

22 Batatu, *Old Social Classes*, 650.

The CPI was not only 'colour blind' as a consequence of its programme of land reform, nationalisations, universal education and equal rights; it also projected a more inclusive idea of citizenship. For large sections of the Iraqi population the CPI became a source of inspiration for social and political change, the gaining of new social and political rights, and for sharing a vision of Iraq's future and identity. It also offered new conceptual instruments for understanding and influencing the development of their world, such as colonialism, nation-states, class struggle, new social formations, and new identities. The CPI's ideology was further popularised by the formation of numerous anti-colonial, national liberation movements in the aftermath of the Second World War, and, subsequently, the establishment of the Third World as a progressive block in world politics. In the eyes of many Iraqis the CPI's fight against oppression and colonialism, its programme to reform Iraqi society, end feudalism, support trade unions, implement social justice, liberate women, and recognise the rights of minorities all constituted a departure from the previous elitist politics based on sectarianism, patronage and the support of colonial powers. By calling Iraq the 'homeland' (*watan*) of all its inhabitants, regardless of their ethnic and religious background, the CPI provided an opportunity in which a common imagined community, with some sense of Iraqi identity and a common notion of citizenship, could be created. Moreover, after the Second World War the CPI helped create an active civil society, a civic culture of debate, and an active and dynamic public life.[23] In the end, the CPI project failed because it encountered the dominant interests of the state elite and the real holders of power in the country. As a result, the alternative version of a common citizenship, which in many ways resembled T.H. Marshall's notions of citizenship (including his concept of social rights), was suppressed.[24]

THE REPUBLICAN PHASE: 1958–1968

Through a successful military coup on 14 July 1958, under the direction of general Abd al-Karim Qasim, Iraq became a republic. The fact that he himself was part Kurd (his mother was a Faili/Shiʿi Kurd and his father a Sunni Arab) was particularly important. This multi-religious background was also reflected in the membership of the first cabinet, which was

---

23 Zubaida, 'Iraq: History, Memory', 333–45.

24 T.H. Marshall, *Citizenship and Social Class* (Cambridge: Cambridge University Press, 1950).

composed of six Sunnis, five Shi'is, and four Kurds.[25] According to Sami Zubaida, the intellectuals and leaders of the public debate, as well as the CPI, 'came to the fore under Qasim after 1958 and assumed prominent positions in some ministries, the school system, the professions, the media, and the general political fields . . .The relative openness of this cultural regime not only promoted an effervescence but also heightened ideological contests, breaking into violence on occasion.'[26] Gradually, however, the old, politically divisive problems reappeared, and political instability became the hallmark of the first 10 years of the republic. From 1958 to 1968 three military coups occurred, and the ideological battle between Iraqi patriotism ('Iraq first') and pan-Arabism and Kurdish nationalism came to a head, with all its attendant negative consequences for the question of loyalty and citizenship in Iraq. The military struggle of the Kurds for greater autonomy began in 1961 and would continue for decades, with short periods of negotiation. The tragic history of this struggle and the heavy, violent reaction of the rulers of Iraq alienated the Kurds still further from the Iraqi state and society.

The successful military coup of 1958 and the establishment of the republic also increased the role of the army in politics, while the Ba'athist coup of 1963 put an end to the more inclusive and reform-minded period of Abd al-Karim Qasim. In 1968 the Ba'ath Party led a new and successful military coup, managing to stay in power until the American invasion of Iraq in 2003; their reign had disastrous consequences for any attempts to build an inclusive Iraqi citizenship based on civil, political and social rights, as well as a common Iraqi identity.

BA'ATHIFICIATION 1968–1991

When the Ba'ath Party came to power in 1968 no one expected it to rule the country for the next 35 years. Their military coup was perceived as being just one more in a long line of military takeovers in Iraqi history. 'The Ba'ath leadership', wrote Karsh and Rautsi, 'was largely anonymous to the Iraqi people . . . Grassroots support for the party was meagre. According to Ba'athi estimates, in 1968 the Party numbered approximately 5,000 full members, and even this modest figure seems lavish.'[27] Their means of achieving domination was not the creation of

---

25 Kirmanj, *Identity and Nation*, 96.
26 Zubaida, 'Iraq: History, Memory', 335.
27 Karsh and Rautsi, *Saddam Hussein*, 37.

Iraqi citizens with legal and political rights, as these rights were not part of the language and rhetoric of the Baʿath party;[28] rather, it was through a massive, imposed Baʿathification of every aspect of the Iraqi state and society. Once in power, the Baʿath Party penetrated and took over every aspect of both. This Baʿathification differs from creating a sense of national identity or belonging to a country and community, as it was a technique of governing through which the Baʿath party tried to impose its own vision of history, politics and community on Iraqi society, and to demand complete loyalty to itself. It was, in fact, its leaders who were the focal point of loyalty, not Iraq. Baʿathification's crucial technique of governing was fear. 'Immediately after coming to power', writes Sassoon, 'the Baʿath began to imbue the population with the fear of spies everywhere and warned that the people should be vigilant and inform about anyone they suspected of spying'.[29] Kan'an Makia's book *The Republic of Fear* provides important insights into the technique for destroying society through conspiracy, cruelty and fear.[30] This was done by introducing the Iraqi masses to public executions of spies. 'As the terror struck deeper into the population', writes Makia, 'withdrawal, cynicism, suspicion, and eventually pervasive fear replaced participation as the predominant psychological profile of the masses'.[31] This new ruling technique created great distrust within Iraqi society, even between members of the same family. It is difficult to speak of even a minimum sense of citizenship without having a minimum degree of trust between people. In the end, a highly sophisticated system of reward and punishment were developed to create the new Baʿathist individual in Iraq.[32]

All these instruments of rule had one goal: the elimination of all opponents of the Baʿath Party and its leader. The Baʿath Party did not tolerate any form of dissent. Mass surveillance of the society was introduced, and the Baʿath implanted a loyalist in every part of society's social fabric.

---

28 Ofra Bengio, *Saddam's Word: Political Discourse in Iraq* (Oxford/New York: Oxford University Press, 1998). In this important book the author studies the political language of the Baʿath Party, notions such as *inqilab* (coup), *intifada* (popular uprising), *thawra* (revolution), *ridda* (deviation) etc. were widely used, but there is no mention of the notion of citizen and citizenship in Saddam Hussein's political lexicon.

29 Joseph Sassoon, *Saddam Hussein's Ba'th Party: Inside an Authoritarian Regime* (New York: Cambridge University Press, 2012), 117.

30 Samir Al-Khalil, *Republic of Fear: The Politics of Modern Iraq* (Berkeley/Los Angeles: University of California Press, 1990), 46–72. Samir Al-Khalil is the pseudonym of Kan'an Makiya.

31 Al-Khalil, *Republic of Fear*, 58.

32 Sassoon, *Saddam Hussein's Ba'th.*

This process of Baʿathification went hand in hand with the creation of a political and military elite whose loyalty to Saddam Hussein personally was unquestionable. From the very beginning, the narrow popular support-base of the party, and one faction of the party's fear of another, required significant coercive methods to subject the Iraqi people to the will of the party, and the will of party to that of the tiny group who stood at its apex.[33]

Elimination of Opponents

The total subjection of Iraqi society took place in steps. The first task was to bring the military under the control of the party and to protect the ruling elite from the permanent threat of ambitious military factions. The Baʿathification of the army was the first and most important step in bringing it under control. Following the Soviet model, a system of 'political commissars' was developed, which was directly connected to the Security Apparatus and whose loyalty was exclusively to Saddam Hussein. Implanted in the army, these young political commissars were 'effectively bypassing the formal chain of command and tightly controlled by Saddam Hussein'.[34] The Baʿathification of the army undermined its role as an institution for creating a common citizenship and instilling a sense of belonging and loyalty; instead it became an agent through which the Baʿath Party could dominate Iraqi society.

The next step was to attack the dissident political factions within the Baʿath Party itself; when Saddam deposed Ahmad Hasan al-Bakr and became the president of Iraq in 1979 one of the first measures he took was to arrest and assassinate dozens of the most prominent members of the Baʿath Party.[35] The third step was to eliminate the Kurdish resistance. In 1970 the Baʿath Party reached an agreement with the Kurds that gave the latter relative autonomy. However, in 1975 the Baʿath reneged on this agreement and a new round of fighting was initiated. After a year of heavy conflict, the Baʿath Party destroyed the Kurdish resistance and started to expel tens of thousands of the Shiʿi (Faili) Kurds to Iran, thus denying them their status as Iraqi citizens. At the same time, the deportation of Sunni Kurds to the south and west of Iraq began. A policy of systematic Arabisation and Baʿathification of different Kurdish areas

33 Karsh and Rautsi, *Saddam Hussein*, 37.

34 Ibid., 40–41.

35 According to Charles Tripp, Saddam Hussein has purged and executed 500 senior party officials. Tripp, *History of Iraq*, 222.

was implemented by the mass transfer of Shi'is from southern Iraq to Kurdish areas such as Mosul and Kirkuk.[36] Finally, after the elimination of the Kurds the Ba'ath regime took on the Iraqi Communist Party, its last opponent. This process reached its conclusion when Saddam became president of Iraq in 1979, as he decided to eliminate the CPI and Ba'athify its constituency. Thousands of Iraqi communists were arrested, tortured and killed; many were forced to leave the country, while some joined the Kurdish resistance.

Iraqi Civil Society

Iraqi civil society was the last independent bastion that the Ba'ath Party had to defeat. Within the span of one decade (1968–1979), the state/party reigned in the civil society, including the country's economic, cultural, and political life. All professional organisations and trade unions, whether they organised by students, workers, peasants, youth, or women, were brought under the control of the Ba'ath Party. The press, chambers of commerce, and industrial organisations underwent the same fate. Even sport organisations and clubs were Ba'thified. Transforming the youth into loyal Ba'athists had always been a dream of the party. Saddam Hussein was very clear about this: 'Some fathers slipped away from us for many reasons and factors, but the small boy is still in our hands.'[37] Sassoon analyses how Saddam Hussein introduced a new national curriculum in which the youth, even those in kindergarten, should be instructed 'about the party's leadership and achievements'.[38] The Ba'ath Party surrounded Iraqi youth with its three grand strategies, based on fear, reward and idealism. Sassoon argues correctly that 'the Ba'ath's ideology was not as dominant as the communist ideology, and none of its three slogans of unity, freedom, and socialism was ever enacted'.[39] On the other hand, this ideological deficit was compensated by developing a seductive system of rewards,[40] and producing a strong system of surveillance, buttressed by a policy of zero tolerance for dissidents.

Finally, in its totalitarian aspirations the Ba'ath Party tried to replace tribal, religious and ethnic affiliations with loyalty to the party – traditional mechanisms for patronage and loyalties outside the state. Sami Zubaida

---

36 McDowall, *A Modern History.*
37 Sassoon, *Saddam Hussein's Ba'th*, 268.
38 Ibid., 268.
39 Ibid., 227.
40 Sassoon, *Saddam Hussein's Ba'th*, 278.

argues that 'it was under the Baath regime after 1968 that the state took charge of culture, by fiercely repressing alternative sources and instituting its own cultural centers, media, and institutions, all supported by generous allocation of resources, made possible after 1973 by the gushing of oil revenues'.[41] Akin to the authoritarian bargain analysed elsewhere in this volume, according to him, 'the 1970s were the high point of Baʿathist rule: a government well supplied by oil revenues engaging in an accelerated developmental drive and instituting a welfare state and an elaborate cultural apparatus. This was accompanied by a highly authoritarian and violent security regime.'[42] The main difference after Saddam Hussein took power in 1979 was that the political system took on a strong personalist character and was dominated by 'a single familial, clan, ethnic, or regional group'.[43]

In short, within a decade the Baʿath Party had succeeded in eliminating all political parties, brought the army to heel and the party under the control of a tiny ruling elite, and eliminated any chance for the development of a strong sense of citizenship in the population, except as an opposition to the regime.

The Absence of the Language of Rights

What was conspicuously absent in all aspects of the Baʿathification process was the language of civil, social, cultural, and especially political rights. The Baʿath party developed a form of power that radically dismissed the notion of rights; delivering rights or having a discourse of citizens' rights were not part of Baʿathist ruling techniques. In the absence of any rights, and following the whittling away of modern horizontal and traditional vertical forms of protection against the state, nothing remained between the state and the individual, who stood alone against it, the party, and, ultimately, the will of the dictator. Even the relative economic well-being of some parts of population after the oil boom in 1973 was not rationalised in terms of economic and social rights and entitlements, but was seen as a *makrama*, a concept that should be translated as 'gift' or 'noble deed'.[44] *Makrama* was an alternative for rights and was regarded as a form of personal beneficence Saddam Hussein provided

---

41 Zubaida, 'Iraq: History, Memory', 335.

42 Zubaida, 'Iraq: History, Memory', 335.

43 Sassoon, *Saddam Hussein's Ba'th*, 276.

44 Nagih Al-Obaidi, 'No More Charity: How to Make Iraq's Oil-rich Economy Work' *Niqash: Briefings from Inside and Across Iraq*, 2011. Accessed 25 September 2015, http://www.niqash.org/en/articles/economy/2901/.

to the people. *Makrama* had but a single purpose: to create the idea that what citizens received from the state was not their right as citizens but was instead the personal gift from the head of state, who was represented as a shepherd who takes care of his flock. The Iraqi press played a significant role in promoting the concept of *makrama* and the disappearance of the language of rights.

That is not to say, however, that while the Baʿath party was heavily engaged in destroying all of its rivals and implementing the policy of *makrama* it did not introduce a considerable set of welfare measures to win the loyalty of Iraqi society. The 1970s were the era of oil and the developmentalist agenda of the state and the huge increase in oil revenues gave the regime an opportunity to create a reasonable level of prosperity. These developments were presented as the 'achievements of the revolution' (*injazat al-thawra*). *Munjazat* was the expression of the revolutionary will of the party and its leader in the fields of the economy and development. Subsequently, *makrama* was a consequence of the subordination of the economy to the needs of the ruling Baʿath party and the personalisation of power. For Saddam Hussein, the economy was an effective vehicle for rallying popular support behind the regime and bolstering his own political position.[45] Policies of full employment and public programmes were developed, as well as free education, free public health services, and reasonably priced housing. But all of these went hand in hand with increasing social inequality as the result of pervasive political clientelism, corruption and special privileges for specific tribes and people personally bound to Saddam Hussein. *Injazat* and *makrama* were the leading concepts in this rationalisation, and they were also strongly linked to the power of the Baʿath party, and especially its leader.

The Baʿathification policies were part of a wider strategy of domination that destroyed political life in Iraq, and consequently destroyed any real sense of citizenship. In this phase of Iraqi history, the state developed a mafia-like system, with the family of Saddam Hussein and his clan from Tikrit at the top. They considered the state's institutions and income as their own personal property and Iraqi society as a grateful flock (*riʿaya*), which received the generous *makrama* of the rulers. *Makrama* was also used in another way as an effective ruling technique; by combining *injazat*, revolutionary achievements, with *makrama* Iraqi citizens were reduced to the premodern position of subjects who obeyed the ruler, with the difference that even in medieval Iraq the believer was protected by the *Shariʿa*.

45 Karsh and Rautsi, *Saddam Hussein*, 90.

THE RETRIBALISATION AND SECTARIANISATION OF POLITICS

The first Gulf war (1989–1990), the uprising of 1991, and the international sanctions (1990–2003) changed the social structure of Iraq, sectarian relations, and the economic and political strategies of the ruling elite. The country was already weakened by the long eight-year war with Iran (1980–1988), but the uprising of 1991 and its aftermath brought an end to the semi-totalitarian character of the Ba'ath regime. The uprising had a clear Shi'i and Kurdish character; all the Shi'i provinces in the south and all the Kurdish provinces in the north of Iraq liberated themselves, and the infrastructure of the Ba'ath state was seriously damaged, if not totally destroyed. The official buildings of the security and intelligence forces, Ba'ath Party headquarters, and army barracks were attacked and gutted. Thousands of active members of the Ba'ath Party and security forces were killed, and many more forced to flee. Just as importantly, the immense quantity of information that had been gathered over the years by the Ba'ath Party and its security agencies regarding the political loyalty of large segments of the Iraqi population was destroyed. For a modern, authoritarian, one-party system, information was an important aspect in its efforts to instil fear. Monitoring and collecting information about different aspects of Iraqi society, including the economy, religion, education, Iraqi immigrants living abroad, and even children, was essential for the domination of Iraqi society by the Ba'athist state.[46]

The drastic decline of resources following the uprising and subsequent sanctions forced the Ba'ath regime to develop new techniques of governing. In practice, this meant the restructuring of the Ba'ath Party itself and the retribalisation of both society and relations between society and the state. The new strategy was to make membership of the Ba'ath Party more attractive; it became a basis of privilege. As the result of the huge loss of life and materials, the Ba'ath Party made full membership 'simpler and quicker'. The time it took to obtain full membership shrank from five years to less than 12 months.[47] In addition, party membership was, more than ever before, linked to different types of material benefits. For example, 'section members' (*'uduw al-shu'ba*) received a monthly stipend of roughly $250 in 2002, a significant sum.[48] But party members did not

---

[46] Sassoon, *Saddam Hussein's Ba'th*, 114–15.

[47] Miranda Sissons and Abdulrazzaq Al-Saiedi, *A Bitter Legacy: Lessons of De-Baathification in Iraq* (International Center for Transitional Justice, 2013), 5.

[48] Sissons and Al-Saiedi, *A Bitter Legacy*, 5.

only enjoy economic benefits; their authority also increased. They began to 'possess extrajudicial power over other Iraqi citizens, such as detaining criminal suspects, the right to possess weapons', as well as 'controlled preferential access to a host of important social resources, including government jobs, seed banks, professional associations, and technical training'.[49] Subsequently, party membership became more important than being a citizen, while within the party, in what has been termed graded citizenship, the hierarchy determined the degree of access to resources and power.

The retribalisation of Iraqi society and power relations was another strategy that was introduced to meet the huge challenges to the regime after its defeat in 1991. Incorporating tribes into the political process was not new in Iraq. From the beginning of the 1980s 'the centrality of loyalty for Saddam Hussein and the Baʿath Party led inevitably to significant reliance on tribal, familial, and kin associations. The intelligence services, for instance, recruited relatively many among large numbers of clans that owed loyalty to Saddam Hussein.'[50] The difference was that in the 1990s the Baʿath regime sought alliances with the tribes because state power had declined.[51] Desperate, the regime went so far that, in May 1996, it drafted a plan that proposed the installation of 'a high council of tribal chiefs with direct access to the president, and the granting of small arms, land, diplomatic passports, and military exemptions to shaykhs [and their tribes] in exchange for their absolute loyalty'.[52] In this way, the Baʿathist state started to delegate different state responsibilities to tribes allied with the regime. Armed units in civilian clothes and tribal headdress were deployed at strategic points in Baghdad and other cities to assist special security forces carry out contingency plans. Such activities, as Faleh Jabar explains, 'were previously the duty of the Popular Army (the party militia)'.[53]

But the significant process of retribalisation created serious new challenges to Iraqi society. The increasing power of local actors and the increase of tribal power structures resulted in chaos and insecurity, and enhanced the tendency of Iraqis to seek refuge in primordial relations, sectarianism, and ethnic and communal identities. In the 1990s premodern loyalties not only won new ground but became the dominant form of loyalty, as Iraq entered a new phase of radical fragmentation. People became highly dependent on their tribes, clans, and religious communities

---

49 Ibid.

50 Sassoon, *Saddam Hussein's Baʿth*, 11.

51 Faleh A. Jabar, 'Shaykhs and Ideologues: Detribalization and Retribalization in Iraq, 1968–1998'. *Middle East Report* 215 (2000): 28–31 and 48.

52 Jabar, 'Shaykhs and Ideologues', 31.

53 Jabar, 'Shaykhs and Ideologues', 31.

when interacting with the state and each other. This marked a retreat to a premodern mechanism of governing in which there is no space for notions such as citizen and citizenship. The politics of retribalisation, according to A. Jabar, 'has produced contradictory results: a clash between the state and the tribes, a clash between the tribalized and detribalized section of society, a clash among tribes themselves and clashes within the state'.[54]

POST-SADDAM SECTARIANISM

The period after 2003 has been one of extreme sectarian violence and serious internal social, political and religious divisions. At the time of writing Iraq is on the road to total disintegration and the country has become the arena in which competing internal, regional and international powers contend with each other. The Iraqi army has disintegrated and various powerful militia groups control different parts of the country. War crimes and human rights violations are occurring on a huge scale.[55]

The 'passive' or 'latent' sectarianism that has always been part of the Iraqi state and politics has been greatly exacerbated since the 1990s, and particularly since 2003, with disastrous consequences for inter-religious and ethnic relations in the country.[56] The minimal level of moral and political uniformity is lacking, and particularistic sectarian and non-sectarian identities are flourishing. The year 2006–2007 saw the climax of Sunni–Shi'i violence; the average of civilian death toll was 2,300 per month.[57] Kirmanj enumerates the huge problems confronting Iraq:

> political reconciliation between different ethnic and religious groups; laws needed to regulate the distribution of revenue gained from the country's natural recourses; management of Iraq's oil reserves; resolution of the long-standing territorial dispute between the Kurdistan region and the rest of Iraq, including the fate of the oil-rich areas around Kirkuk; the issue of federalism; and the request for amending the Iraqi constitution, especially the articles concerning Iraq's identity and structure.[58]

Developing a shared national vision of the future, a shared governance, and a sense of national unity or identity based on a new social contract

---

54 Jabar, 'Shaykhs and Ideologues', 31.

55 Human Rights Watch, 'World Report 2015: Iraq. Events of 2014'. Accessed 25 September 2015, http://www.hrw.org/world-report/2015/country-chapters/iraq.

56 Haddad, *Sectarianism in Iraq*, 25–30.

57 Kirmanj, *Identity and Nation*, 8.

58 Kirmanj, *Identity and Nation*, 8.

between citizens and the state and among citizens is, in these fragile conditions, a huge challenge. The invasion of the so-called Islamic State (IS) into Iraq and its occupation of huge swathes of Iraqi territory in 2014 has made the scene darker still, and the possibility of the total disintegration of Iraq as a country is much more likely.

CONCLUSION

The view of Iraq as a static and monotonous society in which three unchanging dominating sectarian identities rule is a simplistic fallacy. Such a static model does not acknowledge the changing character of the Iraqi state and society following its establishment after the First World War. In this chapter modern Iraqi history has been divided into five major phases. In each phase different ruling techniques were implemented, with different social and political consequences. Citizenship was never an essential part of the intruments of government of the country. In each phase the Iraqi state, for varying social and political reasons, did not seriously attempt to create Iraqi citizens who would be the bearers of different social and political rights and obligations. Loyalty to a party, a political leader, or religious or ethnic groups remained, and reproduced power relations that were in opposition to notions of citizenship. It was only during the later period of the monarchy that the notion of a common citizenship became the project of Iraqi opposition groups and civil society, but this was repressed by the state and its ruling elite. During the first republican phase an improvement in citizenship rights did occur, but with the emergence of the Baʿath Party as rulers after 1968 Iraq changed dramatically. The Baʿathist state was completely opposed to any notions of dignity that citizenship entailed, as the Baʿathification of the state and society was its main – and only – political aim. A Baʿathist vision was imposed on Iraq through the monopolisation not only of public offices and the main institutions of the state, but also through the crushing of Iraqi civil society, controlling the economy, and destroying political life. These processes were brought about by the development of a regime of fear, cruelty and violence, as well as developing a system of patronage, an effective system of reward and punishment, and a significant retribalisation of Iraqi society in the 1990s.

Currently, Iraq is witnessing deep ethnic and sectarian divisions. The social and political damage of the 1990s has been so significant that it is to be wondered whether the country will ever be reunited, and whether the creation of a common citizenship is possible. Could citizenship really be a remedy for all of the social, political, religious and ethnic ills that are plaguing Iraq?

BIBLIOGRAPHY

Al-Khalil, Samir. *Republic of Fear: The Politics of Modern Iraq*. Berkeley/Los Angeles: University of California Press, 1990.

Al-Obaidi, Nagih. 'No More Charity: How to Make Iraq's Oil-Rich Economy Work' *Niqash: Briefings from Inside and Across Iraq*, 2011. Accessed 25 September 2015. http://www.niqash.org/en/articles/economy/2901/.

Batatu, Hanna. *The Old Social Classes and the Revolutionary Movements of Iraq*. London: Saqi, 2004.

Bengio, Ofra. *Saddam's Word: Political Discourse in Iraq*. Oxford/New York: Oxford University Press, 1998.

Haddad, Fanar. *Sectarianism in Iraq: Antagonistic Visions of Unity*. Oxford/New York: Oxford University Press, 2011.

Halliday, Fred. 'Crises in het Midden-Oosten: 1914, 1967, 2003' ('Crises in the Middle East 1914, 1967, 2003'). *Eutopia: Internationale Venster op Politiek, Cultuur en Kunst* 17 (2007): 7–14.

Human Rights Watch. 'World Report 2015: Iraq. Events of 2014'. Accessed 25 September 2015. http://www.hrw.org/world-report/2015/country-chapters/iraq.

Ibrahim, Ferhad. *al-Ta'ifiyya wa-l-Siyasa fi-l-'Alam al-'Arabi* ('Sectarianism and Politics in the Arab World'). Cairo: Maktaba al-Madbuli, 1996.

Jabar, Faleh A. 'Shaykhs and Ideologues: Detribalization and Retribalization in Iraq, 1968–1998'. *Middle East Report* 215 (2000): 28–31 and 48.

Kanie, Mariwan. 'Martelaarschap tussen Natie en Religie: Politieke Liefde, Poëzie en Zelfopoffering in Koerdisch Nationalisme' ('Martyrdom between Nation and Religion: Political Love, Poetry and Self-Sacrifice in Kurdish Nationalism') PhD diss., University of Amsterdam, 2010.

Karsh, Efraim, and Inari Rautsi. *Saddam Hussein: A Political Biography*. London: Futura Publications, 1991.

Kirmanj, Sherko. *Identity and Nation in Iraq*. Boulder: Lynne Rienner, 2013.

Marshall, T.H. *Citizenship and Social Class*. Cambridge: Cambridge University Press, 1950.

McDowall, David. *A Modern History of the Kurds*. London/New York: I.B. Tauris, 1997.

Mezher, Kemal. *Têgeîshtnî Rastî ū shwênî la rojnamegerî Kurdida* ('Têgeîshtnî Rastî and its place in Kurdish Journalism'). Baghdad, 1978.

Pratt, Nicola. *Democracy and Authoritarianism in the Arab World*. Boulder: Lynne Rienner, 2007.

Sassoon, Joseph. *Saddam Hussein's Ba'th Party: Inside an Authoritarian Regime*. Cambridge: Cambridge University Press, 2011.

Sissons, Miranda, and Abdulrazzaq Al-Saiedi. *A Bitter Legacy: Lessons of De-Baathification in Iraq*. International Center for Transitional Justice, 2013.

Tibi, Bassam. *Arab Nationalism: Between Islam and the Nation-State*. New York: St. Martin's Press, 1990.

Tripp, Charles. *A History of Iraq*. Cambridge: Cambridge University Press, 2002.

Zubaida, Sami. 'Iraq: History, Memory, Culture'. *International Journal of Middle East Studies* 44 (2012) 2: 333–45.

4. Claiming spaces for acts of citizenship: recent experiences of activists in Morocco

Sylvia I. Bergh and Salima Ahmadou

INTRODUCTION

A new generation of young activists entered the political scene in Morocco in the spring of 2011 to demand democratic change.[1] On 20 February 2011, protests with a reported 300,000 participants were held in 53 towns simultaneously – something that had not been witnessed since the kingdom's independence. Two weeks later, King Mohamed VI announced the reform of the Constitution responding to the pressure generated by what came to be known as the February 20 Movement (F20M). A referendum on the new Constitution was held on 1 July 2011, in which 98.4 per cent of the voters voted in favour. While protests had continued throughout the period February to July 2011, they were attracting fewer people, especially after the King called for new parliamentary elections on 30 July 2011. During the elections, held on 25 November, the Islamist Justice and Development Party (PJD) emerged as the clear winner and Abdelilah Benkirane was appointed prime minister shortly afterwards.[2]

A key actor in the 'Arab Spring' in Morocco was the Moroccan Association of Human Rights (*Association marocaine des droits humains*, AMDH, created in 1979) which had a long track record of denouncing specific cases of human rights violations and boasted more than 90 regional branches. Since 2006, the AMDH and other non-governmental

---

[1] According to Haim Malka, the February 20 movement (F20M) protesters called for a constitutional monarchy in which the monarch's political and economic power would be substantially diminished to a more symbolic role. They also called for socio-economic justice, equality and an end to corruption. See Haim Malka 'Power and Authority in Morocco', *Adelphi Series* 55 (2015) 452: 69.

[2] Ahmed Benchemsi, 'Morocco's Makhzen and the Haphazard Activists', in *Taking to the Streets: the Transformation of Arab Activism*, eds. Lina Khatib and Ellen Lust (Baltimore: The John Hopkins University Press, 2014), 199.

organisations (NGOs) had also been campaigning for economic justice, represented by the now defunct National Coordinating Committee against the High Cost of Living (*Comité contre la cherté de la vie*). Supported by leftist parties, labour unions and anti-globalisation groups, the AMDH organised a series of sit-ins to protest the increases in the price of staple goods and basic services such as transportation, water, and electricity. Based on the popular success of these protests, more than 70 local coordinating committees (*tansiqiyyat mahalliyya*) were set up, which soon functioned independently from the national structure. A group called ATTAC Maroc also gained popularity with its struggle against French companies (such as Lydec and Amendis) holding urban water and electricity concessions in Casablanca, Tétouan, and Tangier.[3] More or less the same coalition of 40 political and civil society groups which had created the *tansiqiyyat* five years earlier, also formed the National Council for Support of the February 20 Movement (*Conseil national de soutien au mouvement du 20 février*).[4]

While most observers quickly realised that the new Constitution would leave the *Makhzen's*[5] powers mostly intact, the concessions in terms of giving official status to the Amazigh language and the pardoning of political prisoners by the King in April 2011 meant that the King had taken some of the wind out of the sails of the F20M supporters.

The reasons for the decline of the F20M can therefore be summarised as follows: the monarchy's rather favourable and swift response in terms of announcing a new constitution, the decrease in the number of protest marches, the internal tensions within the movement (and especially the withdrawal of the Islamist movement *al-'Adl wa-l-Ihsan* (AWI – *Justice et Bienfaisance*, or Justice and Charity Organisation) from F20M in December 2011), the refusal to elect F20M representatives, which led to a 'strategic paralysis', the smear campaigns against the activists by 'young royalists' (who created a group called March 9 Movement), as well as the *Makhzen's* surveillance and infiltration activities, and finally, the election of the PJD into government, which left many F20M activists with the feeling that their movement and cause had been taken away from them. In

---

3 Benchemsi, 'Morocco's Makhzen' 203–4. For the case of water privatisation and social mobilisation in Casablanca, see Mohamed Said Saadi, 'Water Privatization Dynamics in Morocco: A Critical Assessment of the Casablancan Case', *Mediterranean Politics* 17 (2012) 3: 376–93.

4 Benchemsi, 'Morocco's Makhzen', 216.

5 *Makhzen* refers to the power structures and patronage networks surrounding the monarchy. For the interviewees, this is the power structure or system that governs the country in practice, rather than the (elected) government.

addition, the regional context including the armed conflicts in Syria and Libya contributed to fears of national disintegration on the part of many Moroccans if the protests would continue. In short, after less than a year's time, the F20M no longer existed.[6]

However, while many activists were left disappointed and demotivated, others continued their struggles by joining other groups (including the PSU party (*Parti socialiste unifié*), which offered one-fifth of its congress seats to F20M activists in December 2011),[7] or creating new ones. The new groups included the Student Union for the Change of the Education System, known as UEX (*Union des étudiants pour le changement du système éducatif*) and the Theatre of the Oppressed (*Théâtre de l'opprimé; Massreh el-mahgour*), both established in 2012, as well as the Prometheus Institute for Democracy and Human Rights (*Institut Prometheus pour la démocratie et les droits humains*) set up in 2013, and others.[8]

---

[6] Sarah Larik, 'Maroc: cinq ans après le Mouvement du 20 février, la jeunesse a-t-elle arraché ses droits?' *Middle East Eye* (édition française), 19 February 2016, accessed 6 June 2017, http://www.middleeasteye.net/fr/reportages/maroc-cinq-ans-apr-s-le-mouvement-du-20-f-vrier-la-jeunesse-t-elle-arrach-ses-droits; Benchemsi, 'Morocco's Makhzen', 219–27. Benchemsi on page 226 describes how the lack of organisational structure and legitimate leadership in the local groups led them to be hijacked by their most radical members. This gradual radicalisation of the movement in turn led to a decrease in public support. See the *Privacy International* country page for Morocco for numerous examples of the government's use of Internet monitoring and surveillance activities targeting political activists and journalists (accessed 7 June 2017, https://www.privacyinternational.org/node/971). See also Samia Errazouki, 'Under Watchful Eyes: Internet Surveillance and Citizen Media in Morocco, the Case of Mamfakinch', *The Journal of North African Studies* 22 (2017) 3: 361–85.

[7] Benchemsi, 'Morocco's Makhzen', 231; but Ghassan Waïl El Karmouni, 'Mouvement du 20 février: Quels enseignments à tirer pour la gauche marocaine?' document dated 12 March 2012, accessed 7 June 2017, https://www.rosalux.de/fileadmin/rls_uploads/pdfs/Themen/Arabellion/20120315_ghassan_wail_maroc.pdf, in footnotes 28 and 29, points out that only ten former F20M activists joined the PSU national council and no one joined the political bureau. Furthermore, the established party members reportedly continued their 'paternalistic' discourses towards them and some tried to contain them, hamper their initiatives, or even discredit them.

[8] Larik, 'Maroc.' See also Assia Boutaleb, 'The Narrow Path: Acts of Citizenship by the Arab Youth: Lessons from Egypt and Morocco', in *The Crisis of Citizenship in the Arab World*, eds. Roel Meijer and Nils Butenschøn (Leiden: Brill, 2017), 481. The UEX was created to discuss and propose reforms to the Moroccan educational system. One of its main initiatives is the Popular University which is open to all, and mostly organised in public spaces such as parks. Similarly, the Theatre of the Oppressed holds plays in public spaces on issues such as corruption, racism, and violence against women. The Prometheus Institute works to promote

Indeed, scholars and observers agree that while the institutional gains brought about by the F20M are limited, and state–society relations entered a new phase of repression, the events of 2011 did bring about a fundamental change in the relations between the citizen and the state in Morocco. Citizens are no longer afraid of the *Makhzen*, both at the discursive and physical level – i.e. both in terms of what they dare to say in public, as well as in terms of occupying public space for sit-ins and protests.[9]

In addition, the underlying grievances that fuelled the 2011 protests are still in place: high levels of corruption (in Transparency International's Corruption Perception Index 2016, Morocco is ranked 90th, down from 52nd in 2002[10]), unemployment, and popular dissatisfaction with public services. All of these can be subsumed under the term *hogra*, a colloquial Derija Arabic term for deprivation of dignity because of official abuses, nepotism, corruption, and marginalisation.[11]

---

values of citizenship and human rights, as well as the monitoring and evaluation of public policies, especially those concerning youth. Similarly, the group 'One Hour of Reading' organises public reading sessions followed by a discussion on current issues. The 'Collectif Aswat' works on defending LGBT rights in Morocco, and is mostly active on social media.

9 Larik, 'Maroc'; Benchemsi, 'Morocco's Makhzen', 221; Francesco Cavatorta, 'Morocco: the Promise of Democracy and the Reality of Authoritarianism', *The International Spectator* 51 (2016) 1: 91; Anja Hoffmann and Christoph König, 'Scratching the Democratic Façade: Framing Strategies of the 20 February Movement', *Mediterranean Politics* 18 (2013) 1: 1–22. For a good overview of so-called 'revenge arrests' against activists, see Maati Monjib, 'Morocco's Illiberal Regime and Fragmented Political Society', *Arab Citizenship Review* 10, *EUSPRING* (October 2015), no page numbers.

10 Benchemsi, 'Morocco's Makhzen', 230 and https://www.transparency.org/news/feature/corruption_perceptions_index_2016 (accessed 7 June 2017).

11 Reuters, 'Thousands of Moroccans rally against corruption', *Middle East Eye*, 18 May 2017, accessed 7 June 2017, http://www.middleeasteye.net/news/thousands-north-morocco-rally-against-corruption-622375250; James Sater, 'Patronage and Democratic Citizenship in Morocco', in *The Crisis of Citizenship in the Arab World*, eds. Roel Meijer and Nils Butenschøn (Leiden: Brill, 2017), 168–9. For a discussion of the term *hogra*, see Abdelmajid Hannoum, 'Tangier in the Time of Arab Revolutions: An Ethnopolitical Diary', *The Journal of North African Studies* 18 (2013) 2: 274–5. For data on corruption and (dis)satisfaction in/with the health and education sectors in Morocco, see Hana Brixi et al., *Trust, Voice and Incentives: Learning from Local Success Stories in Service Delivery in the Middle East and North Africa* (Washington DC: The World Bank, 2015): figure 0.4 on p. 7 and figure 1.7 on p. 26 (corruption), figure 1.5 on p. 25 (satisfaction levels), figure 2.8 on p. 43 (rural-urban inequities in access to health services). See also Nabil Mouline (ed.), *Le Maroc vote: Les élections législatives en chiffres (1963–2011)* (TAFRA), 45 for some relevant results of the Afrobarometer survey 2013 in Morocco; e.g., 75 per cent of those surveyed reported finding it difficult to get hospital treatment.

This point is vividly illustrated by the protests that broke out both in social media and on the streets following the King's pardoning of a Spanish paedophile in the summer of 2013. While the street protests were violently dispersed by police forces, the King was forced to reverse his decision.[12]

Similarly, current protests in the historically neglected and marginalised northern Rif region are the largest since the F20M protests in 2011. They were triggered by the death of a fishmonger in Al Hoceima in October 2016, who was crushed inside a garbage truck while trying to salvage his fish that had been confiscated by police. Since then, demonstrators have been demanding more and better public services and railing against corruption, repression and unemployment. A grassroots movement, the Popular Movement (*al-Hirak al-Sha'bi*) has emerged, led by Nasser Zefzafi, who was arrested at the end of May 2017 on charges of 'attacking internal security'. Zefzafi was also put on trial for having interrupted the sermon of an imam in the main mosque of the city, accusing him of inciting the congregation against the protest movement. Scores of other protesters have been arrested as well.[13] As Mohammed Masbah points out in an online column, 'the protests have coincided with, and were sparked by, the six-month political deadlock that began after elections in October. The absence of a government since then has hindered the possibility of a genuine engagement with protesters and their demands. It has also left a void that was filled by the Ministry of Interior using repressive measures . . .'[14]

As a report by *Middle East Eye* points out, 'fishmonger Mouhcine Fikri's death has become a symbol for frustrations about official abuses and revived the spirit of the F20M that led pro-democracy rallies in 2011 and prompted King Mohammed VI to cede some of his powers'.[15] While demonstrations were initially confined to the Rif, the country is now witnessing a spate of violence in Al Hoceima and the Rif region, as well as in the country's largest cities of Casablanca, Rabat, Marrakech, Meknes

---

12 Larik, 'Maroc'.

13 MEE and agencies, 'Thousands Rally in Morocco for Release of Zefzafi and Ending Corruption', *Middle East Eye*, 3 June 2017, accessed 7 June 2017, http://www.middleeasteye.net/news/thousands-rally-north-morocco-release-zefzafi-and-end-corruption-914957953; Amnesty International, 'Morocco: Rif Protesters Punished with Wave of Mass Arrests', 2 June 2017, accessed 7 June 2017, https://www.amnesty.org/en/latest/news/2017/06/morocco-rif-protesters-punished-with-wave-of-mass-arrests/.

14 Mohammed Masbah, 'What Morocco's Monarchy Should Do Instead of Repressing Protesters', *Middle East Eye*, 19 May 2017, accessed 7 June 2017, http://www.middleeasteye.net/columns/moroccos-rif-protests-are-about-corruption-and-abuse-power-1658399521.

15 MEE and agencies, 'Thousands Rally in Morocco'.

and others. Live footage shows several thousand people marching in each of these demonstrations.[16] Current events thus add to the topicality of this chapter, as it aims to further our understanding of how and why 'ordinary citizens' mobilise to demand their rights from the state.

There is now quite a substantial body of scholarly work on the F20M, including on its use of social media, the constitutional reform it brought about, and the reasons for its decline.[17] However, not much is known about the activities of former F20M activists and other young Moroccans since 2011, and in particular about their search for alternative understandings and practices of citizenship. How did they keep the 'spirit' of the F20M alive and how are their 'acts of citizenship' claiming

---

[16] Fatima-Zohra El Malki, 'Morocco's Hirak Movement: The People Versus the Makhzen', *Jadaliyya*, 2 June 2017, accessed 7 June 2017, http://reviews.jadaliyya.com/pages/index/26645/moroccos-hirak-movement_the-people-versus-the-makh.

[17] This body of work includes among others: Mounah Abdel-Samad, 'Why Reform not Revolution: A Political Opportunity Analysis of Morocco 2011 Protests Movement', *The Journal of North African Studies* 19 (2014) 5: 792–809; Fadma Ait Mous, Olivier Deau, and Maâti Monjib, 'The Debates On Citizenship in Morocco: Social Movements and Constitutional Reform', *Euspring Working Paper* 4, undated; Benchemsi, 'Morocco's Makhzen', 199–235; Ahmed Benchemsi, 'Morocco: Outfoxing the Opposition', *Journal of Democracy* 23 (2012) 1: 57–69; Mounia Bennani-Chraïbi and Mohamed Jeghllaly, 'La dynamique protestataire du Mouvement du 20 février à Casablanca', *Revue française de science politique* 62 (2012) 5: 867–94; Sylvia I. Bergh and Daniele Rossi-Doria, 'Plus ça Change? Observing the Dynamics of Morocco's "Arab Spring" in the High Atlas', *Mediterranean Politics* 20 (2015) 2: 198–216; Lenie Brouwer and Edien Bartels, 'Arab Spring in Morocco: Social Media and the 20 February Movement', *Afrika Focus* 27 (2014) 2: 9–22; Matt Buehler, 'Continuity through Co-optation: Rural Politics and Regime Resilience in Morocco and Mauritania', *Mediterranean Politics* 20 (2015) 3: 364–85; Emanuela Dalmasso, 'Apolitical Civil Society and the Constitutional Debate in Morocco', in *Informal Power in the Greater Middle East: Hidden Geographies*, eds. Luca Anceschi et al. (London: Routledge 2014), 145–58; Thierry Desrues, 'Moroccan Youth and the Forming of a New Generation: Social Change, Collective Action and Political Activism', *Mediterranean Politics* 17 (2012) 1: 23–40; Thierry Desrues, 'Mobilizations in a Hybrid Regime: The 20th February Movement and the Moroccan Regime', *Current Sociology* 61 (2013) 4: 409–23; El Karmouni, 'Mouvement'; Driss Magharoui, 'Constitutional Reforms in Morocco: Between Consensus and Subaltern Politics', *Journal of North African Studies* 16 (2011) 4: 679–99; Malka, 'Power and Authority', 59–78; Adil Moustaoui Srhir, 'Le mouvement 20 février au Maroc: entre l'autolégitimation et la délégitimation de l'état. Une analyse critique du discours', *Nómadas* 49 (2016), no page numbers, accessed 7 June 2017. http://dx.doi.org/10.5209/rev_NOMA.2013.v39.n3.48322; for an account of women's role in the F20M, see Abdellatif Zaki, 'Reflections on the 20–February Movement: Hope Renewed, Hope Frustrated for Women', in *Women's Movements in Post-'Arab Spring' North Africa*, ed. Fatima Sadiqi (New York: Palgrave Macmillan US, 2016), 299–312.

public spaces? How do they understand the concept of citizenship as compared to the state's discourse? What are the state's reactions to their activities, and how do the groups in turn respond to them? Finally, what, if anything, does the 2011 Constitution mean to these activists? These are the questions we aim to address in this chapter. By doing so, we aim to update and deepen the analysis started by some scholars into how young independent activists are 'engaged in processes of new meaning making, connecting the local with the global, and at the same time, developing their citizenship skills'.[18] We also want to probe the wider argument that opportunities to engage in political activism and practice political citizenship are limited in Morocco due to deep-seated systems of patronage and the relatively stable consensus around the King.[19]

Following the body of critical studies on citizenship, we adopt the lens developed by Engin Isin to focus on the acts through which subjects constitute themselves as citizens, as those to whom the right to have rights is due. This constitutes a shift from the institution of citizenship (as a legal status of membership in the state) and the citizen as individual agent to acts of citizenship, i.e. collective or individual deeds that rupture social-historical patterns.[20] Isin defines 'acts of citizenship as those acts that transform forms (orientations, strategies, technologies) and modes (citizens, strangers, outsiders, aliens) of being political by bringing into being new actors as activist citizens (claimants of rights and responsibilities) through creating [or transforming] new sites and [stretching] scales of

---

[18] Brouwer and Bartels, 'Arab Spring in Morocco', 20, citing W. Lamer, 'Twitter and Tyrants: New Media and its Effects on Sovereignty in the Middle East', *Arab Media and Society* 16 (2012): 10. See also Assia Boutaleb, 'The Narrow Path', 471–87; and the contribution by Dörthe Engelcke on the Sada Middle East Analysis site of the Carnegie Endowment for International Peace ('Morocco's Changing Civil Society', 7 January 2016, accessed 28 April 2017, http://carnegieendowment.org/sada/?fa=62417). See also Taieb Belghazi and Abdelhay Moudden, 'Ihbat: disillusionment and the Arab Spring in Morocco', *The Journal of North African Studies* 21 (2016) 1: 48. They call for more research on the dynamics generated by political failures and their impact on both demobilisation and re-mobilisation of social movements. See also Joseph Hivert, 'Se désengager du mouvement du "20 février": Le cas des étudiants du supérieur de la coordination de Rabat', *European Journal of Turkish Studies* 17 (2013): 13ff, accessed 28 April 2017, http://ejts.revues.org/4811, for a detailed ethnographic account of F20M activists' disengagement.

[19] Sater, 'Patronage', 156.

[20] Egin F. Isin and Greg M. Nielsen, 'Introduction: Acts of Citizenship', in *Acts of Citizenship*, eds. Engin F. Isin and Greg M. Nielsen (London: Zed Books, 2008), 2; and Engin F. Isin, 'Theorizing Acts of Citizenship', in *Acts of Citizenship*, 16.

struggle'.[21] We argue in this chapter that the acts of former F20M activists constitute such 'acts of citizenship' and that this concept can help explain how the activists enact themselves in solidaristic, agonistic or alienating modes of being with each other.[22] More broadly, by adopting this theoretical lens, we aim to understand how former F20M members 'act and perform when contesting the prevalent citizen regimes and when developing new experimental citizenship forms'.[23]

INTERVIEWS

Methodology

Our research methodology relies on three weeks of fieldwork in Morocco in February 2017 by the second author, during which interviews were held with a total of 24 activists in Rabat, Casablanca and Tangier. Most of the interviewees were engaged in the F20M and/or with the protests against Amendis, the French company in charge of providing water and electricity in Tangier, and its practice of raising prices, and subsequently joined or set up new groups. Table 4.1 below gives an overview of the interviewees' main affiliations.[24] For the sake of ensuring their anonymity, in the text we refer to the number of the interviewees in our list rather than giving his/her name.

The interview guide for the semi-structured interviews included questions on the definition and experiences of citizenship and acts of citizenship; the nature of the spaces and activities used to perform 'acts of citizenship'; the discursive as well as physical reactions of state authorities towards the groups' actions; and finally, the interviewees' views on the 2011 Constitution in terms of the extent to which it is granting more rights and possibilities to claim rights (e.g. with regard to the right to submit petitions etc.).

It is clear that by relying heavily on interviews with a group of respondents in the main cities of Morocco that was sampled using a snowball

---

21 Isin, 'Theorizing Acts of Citizenship', 39; and Engin F. Isin, 'Citizenship in Flux: The Figure of the Activist Citizen', *Subjectivity* 29 (2009) 1: 383.

22 Isin, 'Theorizing Acts of Citizenship', 37–8.

23 Roel Meijer, 'Citizenship, Social Pacts, Authoritarian Bargains, and the Arab Uprisings', in *The Crisis of Citizenship in the Arab World*, eds. Roel Meijer and Nils Butenschøn (Leiden: Brill, 2017), 95.

24 The second author contacted a representative of Amendis as well as a member of AWI, but both refused to talk to her.

Table 4.1 List of interviews and research respondents – numbers and affiliations

Interview No.	Affiliations
1	Lawyer defending activists who were arrested during the protests and activist in F20M
2	Young activist arrested in Tangier during the Amendis protests
3	Journalist for Anwal website and activist in F20M
4	Member of PSU and activist in F20M
5	Involved in the anti-Amendis mobilisations in Tangier and activist in F20M
6	A citizen from Birr Chifa neighbourhood in Tangier involved in the anti-Amendis mobilisations
7	Activist in F20M and participated in anti-Amendis protests in Tangier
8	Activist in F20M and member of ATTAC Maroc in Tangier
9	Member of Prometheus Institute for Democracy and Human Rights and F20M
10	Member of Prometheus Institute for Democracy and Human Rights and F20M
11	Activist in Amazigh Movement (Tawada) and F20M
12	Journalist and activist in F20M
13	Activist in UEX and F20M
14	Activist in F20M
15	Member of Theatre of the Oppressed and F20M
16	Activist in F20M and member of ATTAC Maroc
17	Member of One Hour of Reading, Association Dibaja, and F20M
18	Activist in F20M and AMDH
19	Activist in F20M and other organisations
20	Working for an international NGO in Morocco
21	Activist in Amazigh Movement, UEX, and F20M
22	Activist in UEX, Collectif Aswat, and F20M
23	Member of Theatre of the Oppressed and F20M
24	Activist in F20M and member of youth section of FMAS (*Le Forum des Alternatives Maroc*)

Note: Interviews 1 and 6 were not cited in this chapter.

sampling technique, this contribution gives a view that is biased in favour of well-educated, secular, youth.[25] Indeed, many of the young secular activists in the F20M first formed in 2009 as a group of Internet users

25 Conducting a thorough analysis of social media postings was beyond

defending individual freedoms, especially after the MALI incident.[26] The most active members of this 'underground community' were middle class students or recent graduates from politically engaged families in Casablanca and Rabat. They engaged in online advocacy campaigns to defend victims of police abuses and corrupt (and nepotistic) government practices. Some of them had links with the AMDH and radical leftist parties. While the latter helped with logistics during the F20M protests (e.g. by letting them use their offices), the F20M kept its independence from established organisations.[27] Our interviewees are thus mostly part of what Driss Maghraoui calls 'subaltern politics' which is 'outside the control and orbit of the authoritarian state and quiescent political parties with a generally corrupt and cooptable leadership'.[28] However, as we can see from Table 4.1, a few of our respondents are members of (leftist) political parties such as the PSU.

The choice of Tangiers in addition to Rabat and Casablanca as a fieldwork location was motivated by the observation that the F20M in Tangiers was arguably the best organised group in the country. This is mainly because of its history of close coordination between leftist parties, Islamist organisations, and labour unions in organising protests against the US invasion of Iraq in 2003, and the Israeli attacks on Lebanon in 2006 and Gaza in 2009. According to Benchemsi, 'Tangiers was also the only big city in Morocco where Islamists were invited to participate in the *tanseeqiat* [*tansiqiyyat*] against rising prices'. The cross-partisan

---

the scope of this chapter, but it would have undoubtedly enriched the findings presented here.

26 The Alternative Movement for Individual Freedoms (known under its French acronym MALI) was launched on Facebook on 2009, and it organised a public daytime picnic during the month of Ramadan (which is a legal offence in Morocco) so as to open a debate on the freedom of conscience. The six activists were prevented from holding the picnic by a heavy police force and brutally interrogated. The event generated a massive conservative uproar and dominated the news for several days. Two thousand people joined the MALI Facebook page within two days, and for many leaders of the later F20M, this was a catalyst event that propelled them into political activism. See Benchemsi, 'Morocco's Makhzen', 206–7 and also Srhir 'Le Mouvement', for an account of pre-2011 mobilisations.

27 Benchemsi, 'Morocco's Makhzen', 205–6. As Adria K. Lawrence observes, 'many first movers [people who plan, publicise and initiate anti-regime protest] came from families that had previously suffered at the hands of the regime for their political activities'. See, Adria K. Lawrence, 'Repression and Activism among the Arab Spring's First Movers: Evidence from Morocco's February 20th Movement', *British Journal of Political Science* 47 (2017) 3: 3 and 8. See also Hivert, 'Se désengager', 1–30.

28 Magharoui, 'Constitutional Reforms', 687.

collaboration also supported ATTAC Maroc in mobilising big crowds for daily demonstrations against Amendis.[29] The eight interviews conducted with respondents in Tangiers thus focused mostly on their experiences in the anti-Amendis protests, which have flared up now and then for the last few years. The research more generally took place in a period in which there were regular clashes between protesters and state authorities in Al Hoceima and neighbouring areas, and this fact may have influenced the responses.

Capturing the Public Space: 'Taking (to) the Street'

This section presents the findings related to the claiming of public space as an 'act of citizenship' itself. Our interviews confirm that since the F20M, the occupation of public space has become 'normal'.[30] As Interviewee 19 said, 'since 2011 things changed. The first thing is that people are not afraid anymore to take to the street and the second thing is that people are actually interested to participate. They are aware of their rights and understand the political issues'. This is echoed by Interviewee 4, who observed that in Tangier, 'people were not afraid anymore and people became aware of claiming their rights . . . People understood that in this country you cannot get anything done without going to the street (*prendre la rue*/*tayakhdu al-shari'*)'. Interviewees 4, 7, and 8 also referred to despotism, corruption and loss of trust in the government and the local authorities to explain this trend.

This appropriation of the public space (the real and virtual one) also gave rise to expressions of 'acts of citizenship'. In the words of Interviewee 13, who is active in the UEX, 'freeing the public space [i.e. liberating it from state control] and occupying it is how we express our citizenship (*citoyenneté*, *muwatana*). We are transforming this public space into an agora of debate with people coming from different social classes and backgrounds.' Similarly, Interviewee 21 observed that 'all spaces are invaded with debate and discussion . . . when we are in the street people now come and listen and speak which they were not used to do before 2011.' This former F20M activist presents this public discussion of solutions as major lessons he and his contemporaries learnt from their 2011 experience:

---

29 Benchemsi, 'Morocco's Makhzen', 214–15, quote on p. 214. See also Hannoum, 'Tangier', 273.

30 For a historic overview of social protests in Morocco and their use of public space, see also Abderrahmane Rachik, *Les Mouvements de protestation au Maroc: de l'émeute à la manifestation* (Rabat: Forum des Alternatives Maroc, 2014).

> What we discovered after 2011 is that the youth speak about politics but hate the political parties. At the same time, people were protesting about lots of things but F20M was not bringing any propositions or alternatives. As they used to say, 'F20M knows [only] what they do not want.' I think in our activities, we try to establish new spaces to bring alternatives through debates and sharing.

Interviewee 16 frames these new forms of organising as 'new expressions of citizenship not in the formal "normal" processes (parties and trade unions) but in new ones that are expressed through the public space'. He went on to explain that these new types of activities, like Philosophy in the Street and Theatre in the Street represent a new approach to citizen participation developed by a younger generation which stand in contrast to (and sometimes in conflict with) the 'traditional models of participation' by the older generation of activists.

Socio-economic Rights versus Political Rights

Our findings also show a clear tendency by the activists to distinguish between 'acts of citizenship' to claim socio-economic rights, and those that are claiming political rights and changes in the political system. In their minds, the latter type of claim seems to have been dominant in 2011 but is now much more difficult to make (at least at the time of fieldwork – the current protests, i.e. in June 2017, may mean that this is now changing).

As Interviewee 5 puts it in the context of Tangier (similar to Interviewees 7 and 16):

> there are no more political protests in Morocco [to change the Constitution or the government] but all the social issues and problems are in the street now. A lot of people who got their first experience in F20M led the demonstration against Amendis, and gave their support and experience to better organise these spontaneous protests. They did so because they were concerned as citizens about the expensive bills. And it was also an opportunity to go back to [i.e. revive] the street after the calm in the wake of the 2011 protests. The difference between the F20M and Amendis protests is that the second one is about a social issue that affects the people in their pockets [money], so it is easy to mobilise them for it. People were willing to take the street in order to resolve this problem.

Interviewee 16 points out that in general, mobilisations are fragmented around professional or other social groupings: 'we see categories of society that have common interests emerging in the public space: teachers, students, and so on. We see a kind of coordination in all these categories. People can gain some rights but this lack of solidarity and clear political frame is a weakness in itself as well.'

Indeed, this trend signifies the continuation of the dominant earlier modes of popular mobilisation. As Benchemsi points out, even though many of their activists were members of anti-*Makhzen* political organisations, 'the success of ATTAC and the *tanseeqiat* (*tansiqqiyyat*) was largely based on their reputation as apolitical movements . . . Up until 2011, Moroccan citizens were eager to protest against their economic conditions as long as it didn't mean directly challenging the monarchy.'[31] Moreover, protests over socio-economic issues have become the norm in Morocco since 2011. One estimate in 2014 suggested that Morocco witnesses approximately 50 unrelated demonstrations every day throughout the country.[32]

Nevertheless, as the former F20M activists are involved in many of these 'issue-based' protests, they are trying to insert a more political dimension into them. As Interviewee 15 explained, while the protesters with limited and specific demands just want to resolve their own problems and disappear from the street:

> we have to be aware that those groups are supported and in lots of cases coordinated by groups of young people that were part of the F20M and learnt a lot there, so they are trying not to repeat the same mistakes [i.e. a lack of leadership, making vague and undefined political demands]. These groups try to link the demands of those protests with the slogans of the F20M such as dignity, freedom, and social justice. In Tangier for example, one of the slogans was: 'how are we considered as citizens if we don't have health or education?' (*bech ehna mouwatinin, la sehha la ta'alim*). The people who were involved with the F20M were able to make the link between the specific demands of those protesters with the large and political slogans of the F20M, however they could not give it a larger perspective as once the demands are realised the people stop going back to the street.

The King

A further interesting dimension is the distinction made between protesting against the government institutions as opposed to against the King. 'People are not going out to the streets to be against the state. Citizens go sometimes to the street to communicate directly with the King as they perceive him as the only one who can resolve their problems and not necessarily as someone who guarantees their rights as citizens' (Interviewee 12). Apart

---

31 Benchemsi, 'Morocco's Makhzen', 204.

32 B.S., 11 June 2014, 'Protest Culture in Morocco', *The Economist*, accessed 25 June 2017. http://www.economist.com/blogs/pomegranate/2014/06/protest-culture-morocco.

from pointing to the deep-rooted legitimacy of the King,[33] this statement refers to the relative lack of direct communication channels between the King and the people, and the relative absence of trade unions and other societal groups and actors who used to serve as intermediaries. Similarly, Interviewee 15 observed:

> citizens lost their trust in politicians and government institutions but they did not lose their trust in the King. In daily life everyone repeats 'they (politicians) are all thieves (*voleurs/chefarra*), *Sidna* (the King) is the only one working (in the people's interests).' You can observe this when a group of citizens protests about a specific problem. On their banners they ask the King to help them and find solutions and not anyone else.

He continued by saying that this distinction is in fact wanted by the *Makhzen*. 'The state propaganda is designed to push people to lose trust in all actors except the king.'[34] However, this trend is also reinforced by the repressive apparatus: 'People are aware that if they want to protect themselves they have to shout "long live the king" even if they are not convinced' (Interviewee 15).

Activists' Notions of Citizenship

In order to better understand the discursive linkages between various types of rights and the relationship with the state, it is useful to consider our findings on how the activists understand the notion of citizenship.

Many of our interviewees referred to a comprehensive notion of citizenship rights. For example, Interviewee 7 said, 'for me it does not include only political rights but also social and economic rights. Citizenship

[33] Unlike the protest movements in Tunisia, Egypt and Libya, Moroccan activists in the F20M could not raise the demand for the head of state (i.e. the king) to go. Benchemsi cites three reasons for this. First, its long history gives the Moroccan monarchy a deep legitimacy. Second, the current king is not perceived as a tyrannical dictator by most of the population. Third, he is seen as a symbol of national unity which holds the ethnically and culturally diverse population together, and his departure might mean the disintegration of the nation and violent conflicts. In short, 'Morocco's activists are well aware that calling for the monarchy's demise would alienate the great majority of their followers'. See, Benchemsi, 'Morocco's Makhzen', 224–5, quote on pp. 224–5. See also Cavatorta, 'Morocco: the Promise', 89ff.

[34] See also, Sater, 'Patronage', 159, 170–71, for the point that in the minds of the people, the King is juxtaposed with the perceived corrupt and ineffective bureaucracy, elected (sub-national) government(s), as well as established political parties.

means the right to work, housing, education . . . Dignity (*karama*) and social justice are the biggest citizenship problems in Morocco and the fight towards a real citizenship is still long.' The notion of dignity was also mentioned by Interviewee 21 (see also Interviewees 8 and 4): 'For me citizenship is dignity and it is a universal right to be respected as a human being with rights everywhere in this world. It is not related to the Moroccan flag or borders; those do not mean anything to me. It is also a rejection of *hogra* because the poor and the marginalised people have nothing but their dignity. This is why I like the slogan we used to shout in 2011: "We are citizens not subjects"' (*ehnna mouwatinin machi ra'aya*). This universal aspect of citizenship rights was also echoed by other respondents (Interviewees 10, 18, 23 and 24).

Some respondents only referred to the political dimension of citizenship. '[Citizenship] is the right to express our opinions, accept diversity and difference, to be able to live together in society where everyone has its own place. It is to live in a democratic society where each citizen has his/her voice and express[es] his/her opinions and concerns' (Interviewee 12, see also Interviewee 3).

Others viewed citizenship as having mainly to do with access to and participation (*moucharaka*) in public decision-making. Interviewee 7 (similar to Interviewees 9 and 16) stated: '[Citizenship means] to have access to the state to decide about what the state should or should not do in terms of laws and policies . . . That the citizen can decide on the matters that affects his/her daily life . . .'[35]

The notion of accountability (*redevabilité/moussaala*) was also mentioned, e.g. by Interviewee 15: 'What is important for me in that concept is my right to ask for the political and economic accountability of the people in power and my right to live with dignity, our right to be protected by the state.'

---

[35] Interestingly, a World Bank-funded nano-survey with almost 20,000 responses conducted during March–April 2014 revealed that 71 per cent of those surveyed want to have access to public sector information, and 58 per cent want to participate in decision-making; however, 71 per cent also indicated that public information is relatively hard to access, and 84 per cent had no prior experience in public engagement. Less than half were aware of the right of citizens to present petitions or legislative motions. RIWI, 'RDIT™ measures citizen thoughts in Morocco for the World Bank's project on Open Data', 28 July 2014, accessed 7 June 2017, https://riwi.com/rdit-measures-citizen-thoughts-in-morocco-for-the-world-banks-project-on-open-data/. The dataset is available at https://finances.worldbank.org/Other/World-Bank-Morocco-Citizen-Engagement-Nano-Survey-/tg37–mj88/data). Note that the organic laws on motions and petitions were only adopted in July 2016.

On the other hand, for some activists, citizenship does not have much resonance at all. Interviewee 13 (active in UEX) said, 'we do not have an internal debate on that in our group. We do not question the concept itself. And I do not think that normal citizens in Morocco care about that, they are busy with their daily life. I am sure if you ask them they will say "the state belongs to it owners" (*dawla dial maliha* in Moroccan Arabic; or *al-dawla li-l-ashabihim* in standard Arabic). It means that the state is not theirs. For me it is an empty concept that does not mean much.' Later on he added, 'I think not even the state stopped one minute to think about what makes someone a full citizen in this country.'

This sentiment is also dominant in the responses we got to the question about the state's definition of citizenship.

THE STATE

Citizens and Subjects

Some interviewees went back to the distinction between citizens and subjects:

> The state looks at us as subjects (*sujets, ra'aya*), not as people who have rights. In one protest I heard a representative of the Ministry of the Interior saying to protesters 'those human rights are spoiling you, if I was in charge I would starve all of you. You had enough bread [i.e. you are not hungry anymore] and now you think that you can rule [and ask for more rights]!' (Interviewee 12)

Similarly, according to Interviewee 24, 'the state focuses a lot in its discourse on the duty part, because in its opinion the citizens are not fulfilling their duties (*responsabilités, mass'ouliates*). And of course it is less focusing on the rights part because it means more problems to resolve.' Instead of rights, subjects are granted privileges, according to Interviewee 17; 'the state talks about your rights as if they are privileges (*privilèges, imtiyazat*) that institutions are giving you'.

Along with the notion of 'subjects', interviewees also mentioned other ways in which they believe the state is perceiving them which hint at a more neoliberal governmentality. According to Interviewee 8, 'I do not think that the state itself in its practice sees us as citizens, [but rather] it sees us as consumers and as people to be managed in a territory . . . It does not expect anything from us except to go to work, accept our conditions without claiming anything, and consume everything that it provides, such as political discourses or material goods.' To this, Interviewee 7 added, 'the state wants us to respects the traffic rules, keep the beaches clean, and not use plastic bags, without giving us any rights'.

Elections

However, the dominant view among our interviewees was that the state's discourse emphasises the duty to vote in elections. As Interviewee 16 said, 'the state institutions are limited in their definition; citizenship is [limited to voting in] elections'. This is confirmed by Interviewee 15 (see also Interviewees 9, 10 and 23): 'If you do not vote you are not citizen, this is what the state thinks and what the king said in one of his speeches.'[36] He continued by saying, 'this is itself depriving you from one of your rights as a citizen, namely to boycott the elections. This is dangerous, this is a definition based on the interest of the state in you as a voter . . . It is dangerous because citizenship is reduced to a vote and this disregards all the other universal values that can make you a citizen.'

Our findings are confirmed by Moroccan scholar Maati Monjib, who argues that 'citizenship is mainly focused on elections and parties. In the official discourse, the right to vote and run for office remains the most important feature of citizenship, whereas political freedoms, social change, equality, dignity and economic justice – the main demands of the people in 2011 – tend to be marginalised.'[37]

Values and 'Civic Behaviour'

Interviewee 16 also highlighted the current debate between secular and religious notions of citizenship in Morocco:

---

[36] See the King's speech on the 54th anniversary of the 'King's and People's Revolution' in 2007, where he states, 'le vote est l'un des éléments clés de la citoyenneté responsable' ('voting is a key element of responsible citizenship'). Accessed 19 April 2017, http://www.maroc.ma/fr/discours-royaux/discours-de-sm-le-roi-mohammed-vi-à-la-nation-à-loccasion-du-54–ème-anniversaire-de. Similarly, the *Makhzen* presented the participation in the July 2011 referendum on the new Constitution as a civic and democratic duty (Srhir, 'Le Mouvement', no page number). In the throne speech of 2016, held just before the parliamentary elections, the King said, '[le] citoyen . . . doit assumer ses responsabilités pour ce qui est de choisir les élus et de leur demander des comptes' ('the citizen must take his responsibilities and choose the elected politicians and ask accountability from them'). Accessed 19 April 2017, http://www.maroc.ma/fr/discours-royaux/texte-integral-du-discours-royal-loccasion-de-la-fete-du-trone.

[37] Monjib, 'Morocco's Illiberal Regime', no page number; see also Srhir, 'Le Mouvement', no page number.

> In schools the values of citizenship are not clear in our educational programs. There is the problem of [Arab and Berber] identity and a lot of confusion. For example: the values of modernity as democracy, rights and duties [which are different from] other values in the Islamic education such as subordination, respect of elders, etc. The state has no idea of the type of citizen that it wants. We give children contradictory values in the school. We want people to participate but with moderation and within the state's rules.

This statement is well illustrated by the notion of 'civic behaviour' (*comportement civique*) as defined in the High Council for Education's Strategic Vision for Reform 2015–2030. The definition emphasises attachment to religious and patriotic principles of the citizen's country, respect for the symbols of the nation, and his obligations towards the country (*patrie*) as well as his responsibilities towards himself, his family and his community. It ends in a rather neoliberal twist by saying that the citizen should be able to count on himself and show a real spirit of initiative.[38]

However, Interviewee 17 (similar to Interviewee 19) reminds us that 'the state' should not be seen as a monolithic or reified entity but that it consists of various parts, and that this in turn gives rise to various definitions of citizenship:

> I do not think that the state has a proper definition of citizenship, even if what we learn in school is 'duties and rights'. [It] also depends on which part of the state we are dealing with. The Ministry of the Interior is not the CNDH (*Le conseil national des droits de l'homme*, the National Human Rights Council). Each of them has its proper definition and conceptualisation of what are the Moroccans' rights and duties.

We can thus observe quite different understandings of citizenship on the part of the state, but all of them limited in terms of granting rights.

---

[38] Conseil supérieur de l'éducation, de la formation et de la recherche scientifique, 'Pour une école de l'équité, de la qualité et de la promotion: Vision stratégique de la reforme 2015–2030' (2015), 97, which in turn cites an extract of the royal letter addressed to the conference on 'civic behavior' (*le comportement civique*), organised in 2007 by the High Council for Education. Translated from French by the first author. As Muhammad Faour points out, 'teaching young students what it means to be citizens who participate in and contribute to their societies rather than subjects of the state who are taught what to think and how to behave is key to democratic progress'. See, Muhammad Faour, 'The Arab World's Education Report Card: School Climate and Citizenship Skills', Washington DC: Carnegie Middle East Center, Carnegie Endowment for International Peace, 3 (2012). According to Ennaji, however, 'since Morocco's independence until very recently, citizenship education has not been a central purpose of public education'. See, Moha Ennaji, 'Multiculturalism, Citizenship, and Education in Morocco', *Mediterranean Journal of Educational Studies* 14 (2009) 1: 8.

Tactical Responses: 'The Makhzen Acts Like God'

We now turn to a discussion on the state's reaction to the activists' 'acts of citizenship'. Our interviewees confirmed the observations made in the Introduction, i.e. that the space for civil society and citizen mobilisation overall is rapidly shrinking. Most of them characterised their interactions as a 'cat and mouse game' (Interviewee 21), in which the state apparatus deploys seemingly unpredictable and random strategies, which are nevertheless following a certain internal logic. As Interviewee 17 put it, 'in our case [i.e. One Hour of Reading], they wanted to know who is behind us and . . . let us know that the space is not 100 per cent ours. They are just letting you use it for a reason, they will take it back when they want to.'

Interviewee 21 illustrated this point by saying:

> when it is in the state's interests, they can let it go, for example in a period when [Minister of the Interior] Hassad was in conflict with [Prime Minister] Benkirane, they were not stopping our activities in the public space [i.e. the Philosophy in the Street], because our discourse has progressive values which were annoying the Islamists. They needed us at that particular moment to send a message to the PJD. But when this period ended, they started to stop us from time to time.[39]

According to Interviewee 13, in UEX, they are involved in a 'war of attrition' with the state: '[The local authorities] will use all their resources till we stop showing up one day. The state is very patient in those things; they are annoying us till one day we get tired and disappear.' This dynamic is described very poignantly by Interviewee 19: 'The repression can come back any moment depending on the political situation. The *Makhzen* acts like God: It gives with one hand and takes with the other, never sleeps, never forgets and rarely forgives.'

However, as was the case with the state's definition of citizenship, Interviewee 21 pointed out that 'the state system itself is not homogen[e] ous, most of the times it depends on the people who are in charge of the city, for example in Casablanca the Philosophy in the Street activities were not always stopped while in Marrakech they were forbidden'.[40] He added

---

39 A similar dynamic seems to have taken place in Tangier between PAM and PJD deputies and councillors (according to Interviewee 8).

40 During the F20M protests, the police in the various cities also reacted differently – for example, it did not take any action in Casablanca and Rabat while in Marrakech, it violently cracked down on activists. See, Benchemsi, 'Morocco's Makhzen', 213. This could be because the activists in Marrakech were not backed by traditional political groups as was the case in Rabat and Casablanca.

that these are not only institutional decisions but personal ones as well, depending on who is the governor, their own interpretations of the orders from the central authorities, etc. In Marrakech, the local authorities mobilised so-called 'thugs' (*baltgayyiya*; a term borrowed from the Egyptian context) to organise protests against other citizens who are protesting. This allows the local authorities to say that it is other citizens who are against the protesters, and that they (i.e. the local authorities) are only there to ensure public order.[41] Indeed, our respondents (e.g. Interviewee 16) more generally mentioned the government's strategy to co-opt them into regime-friendly associations.

Carrots and Sticks

More generally, the state's strategy can be called one of 'carrots and sticks'. According to Interviewee 8, this 'is still and has been the strategy of the state since independence. And we can see it now from what is happening in Al Hoceima. The state keeps a low profile until people's anger comes out and then it starts the co-optation, and when the movement calms down the repression of the individual starts.' Interviewee 3 illustrates this for the case of the Amendis protests in Tangier:

> I think that the authorities were very smart as usual. They let the people get out their anger in the street, while trying to identify who were behind this protest, and at the same time trying to negotiate a solution with Amendis. The challenge for the authorities was to manage the protests so they would not get big and politicised, and find a solution that can partly make people satisfied so they can go back to their homes.

[41] This is a continuation of practices used in 2011. As Benchemsi points out, 'each time a Feb20 local group announced a protest venue, "resident associations" suddenly mushroomed there, pledging to "defend" their neighborhood against "extremists" and "troublemakers". These were in fact pro-Makhzen goons, largely manipulated by local authorities . . .' See, Benchemsi, 'Morocco's Makhzen', 220–1, quote on p. 221. Anti-F20M groups also spread rumors about the activists, making them out for 'anarchists' or 'homosexuals', or members of the Polisario, and 'Ramadan eaters', both in the social media as well as traditional media. See Brouwer and Bartels, 'Arab Spring in Morocco', 19; and Hannoum, 'Tangier', 276, 282. Hannoum reports vandalism and damage to shops and banks in Tangier on 20 February 2011 that were clearly the work of the *Makhzen* in an attempt to blame the movement for the violence and portray them as a group of destroyers and anti-royalists. See, Hannoum, 'Tangier', 277–80.

Avoiding Co-optation

Having reviewed the state's strategies, how do the groups we studied deal with them? Interviewee 15 from the Theatre of the Oppressed explained that:

> our relation with the state is based on respecting the law. We try to follow the law and try to change the law related to [the use of] public space. We are now involved in an advocacy initiative to change the law related to the public space. We do our best not to be in confrontation with the Ministry of the Interior, it's just a waste of energy.

Similarly, Interviewee 9 of the Prometheus Institute asserted that:

> we have a good relation as partners, they know we produce serious reports based on real facts and research. We collaborate with most institutions, but we are sure that they [intelligence services] are following us, [to find out] with whom we work, on what, etc. We limit ourselves so as not to be in confrontation with the state [i.e. not to cross certain red lines] and try to stay independent financially.

A similar statement was made by Interviewee 24 in relation to FMAS (*Le forum des alternatives Maroc*). A Berber activist, Interviewee 11, mentioned that '[w]e do not have any problems in organising our actions. They [state authorities] do not see us as a danger.' In short, for most of the groups it is important to learn 'how to negotiate with the political actors and the state without being captured' (Interviewee 9).

Indeed, this learning process started already in 2011 during the constitutional reform process, during which the royal-appointed Consultative Commission for the Constitutional Reform invited F20M members to participate in its consultations with civil society organisations and political parties. All of them refused, given that they considered the process undemocratic.[42] As Sater points out, most of 'Morocco's middle class and opinion makers, with their resources at universities, civil society, media, and the private sector, [had] already been absorbed into networks of patronage' by the time of the F20M protests (e.g. through their incorporation into the leadership of regime-friendly new political parties such as the Authenticity and Modernity Party – PAM, established in 2009).[43] Our respondents are thus acutely aware of this dynamic and are searching for

---

[42] Sater, 'Patronage', 170; Benchemsi, 'Morocco's Makhzen', 218; El Karmouni, 'Mouvement', footnote 23.

[43] Sater, 'Patronage', 168; Hannoum, 'Tangier', 286–7, confirms this point.

ways in which they can exploit the limited space for civic mobilisation without being co-opted.

'The Constitution Has Nothing to Do with Reality'

As for their views on the 2011 Constitution, most respondents dismissed it as being irrelevant to their struggles, mainly because they do not see its articles on popular petitions and other forms of protest being applied (Interviewees 2, 3, 5, 8, 11, 15, 18, 20, 21, 23). As Interviewee 19 put it, 'to be honest, we all know that the Constitution is not only far from being perfect but has nothing to do with the reality'. Instead, as Interviewee 12 observed:

> the practice is the real constitution in Morocco and this is what the monarchy does, namely to create rituals [such as the '*ba'ya*' or oath of allegiance ritual], boundaries [self-censorship and self-regulation by both elected politicians and civil society] and taboos. They are respected by everyone without any questioning. Now who has the political power in Morocco to say to the King that he is not respecting the Constitution and to mobilise people around it? No one, and we all know that including the King himself.

Rather, as has been observed by scholars as well but perhaps not been put in such crude terms, 'you have to understand that this Constitution was written for the international opinion and the intellectual masturbation of the Moroccan elite, not for the people themselves. People can talk to us on TV about it but no one cares' (Interviewee 13).

Others were less dismissive about the Constitution but still sceptical about its potential role in opening up spaces for 'acts of citizenship'. According to Interviewee 16 (see also Interviewee 14):

> the Constitution gave us some rights but with limits . . . The Constitution in my opinion was more interested in models of participation than the quality of this participation. We will create models that the state will implement without any ownership from the citizens, it means that we will participate as they want us to do. They win because they are more interested in numbers of people who participate . . . The challenge for us as activists now is to open the public space and this we did not yet succeed to do.

To end on a more hopeful note, Interviewee 24 said:

> I cannot say that the Constitution is perfect, but in this text there are Articles that we can use to create more participation opportunities for citizens. I think that we should stop seeing the change as a goal but as a process, and this process is not perfect . . . There are a lot of Articles like the one on participation at the

local level with the municipalities that civil society has to work and advocate for in terms of getting organic laws passed to make participation possible for citizens at the local level.

CONCLUSION

To conclude, our findings show that former F20M members have developed new forms of organising that claim the public space through 'acts of citizenship'. However, the object of such acts is often a certain (perceived or real) socio-economic right (e.g. access to affordable water services), rather than a specific political right (e.g. freedom of expression, or free and fair elections). In other words, mainly due to the strong popular legitimacy of the King and the *Makhzen*, social mobilisations in Morocco were – at least until recently – fragmented around professional or other social groupings, though former F20M activists sometimes managed to inject a more political citizenship dimension to such protests. We also found that the activists' understanding of citizenship is mostly a universalist one and linked to notions of dignity and participation in public decision-making processes (outside elections). This understanding stands in contrast to the state's discourses on citizenship, which focuses on citizens as subjects with duties (in particular, to vote in elections) who are occasionally granted privileges, not rights. However, it also became clear that the state is not monolithic, and that various entities within the state may convey different discourses. This tendency is mirrored by the various location- and person-dependent repressive practices by state agencies towards the activists. However, generally, the dominant tendency is for the state to try to wrong-foot the activists and co-opt them into regime-friendly associations, followed by the repression of individual activists. The activists in this study are thus continuously searching for ways to avoid (too much) co-optation while still claiming public spaces for their acts of citizenship. Given their mostly negative views on the potential of the new Constitution to formally open up such spaces, this dynamic will most likely continue, unless their more political definition of citizenship becomes more embedded in Moroccan society, as recent events may imply.[44] Our findings thus illustrate Étienne Balibar's

[44] A further dimension of 'acts of citizenship' which provides fertile ground for further research is that of 'cultural citizenship' in Morocco. See Mohamed El Marzouki, 'Citizens of the Margin: Citizenship and Youth Participation on the Moroccan Social Web', *Information, Communication and Society* 19 (2016) 1: 1–15, accessed 28 April 2017, http://dx.doi.org/10.1080/1369118X.2016.1266373, for a

observation that 'the birth of the citizen as *subject of power* [subversive *of* authority] does not mean the disappearance of the subject as a *subject to power* [submissive *to* authority]'.[45]

study of the production/consumption of user-generated video as articulations and critiques of conditions of marginality which constitute new political subjectivities committed to resistance and struggle (13–14). See also, Zakia Salime, '"I Vote I Sing": The Rise of Aesthetic Citizenship in Morocco', *International Journal of Middle East Studies* 47 (2015) 1: 136–9.

[45] Cited in Engin F. Isin, 'Citizenship Studies and the Middle East', in *The Crisis of Citizenship in the Arab World*, eds. Roel Meijer and Nils Butenschøn (Leiden: Brill, 2017), 515–16 (emphasis in original).

5. Enduring 'contested' citizenship in the Gulf Cooperation Council

Zahra Babar

Citizenship is an essential component of the modern nation state, providing the foundations for the relationship between a government and the governed. While citizenship is understood as a universal concept in a world of nation-states, the ways in which it is expressed and the rights it affords are contingent on its evolution within a local context, and particularly the processes of state formation as well as historical, and cultural traditions.[1] Over the course of the past 50 years or so, most of the ruling elites in the six Gulf Cooperation Council (GCC) countries have actively engaged in state-building processes that have included, among other things, articulating a collective identity to serve as the basis of national citizenship. Gulf monarchs prioritised the carving out of distinct, nation-based identities for the inhabitants of the Persian Gulf who, pre-dating the establishment of independent nation-states in the middle of the last century, had maintained close ties to each other based on their linguistic, religious, kinship and tribal affiliations.

Given the fact that many of the region's residents came from nomadic, tribal backgrounds and were used to moving over porous, loosely controlled borders, from the very beginning the rulers of the six Gulf monarchies considered the separation of populations along the newly established national territorial boundaries an essential component of building statehood. In order to have a modern state to rule over, it was imperative not only to delineate and control landmasses, but also to

[1] For a sample of this literature see, Ruth Lister, 'Inclusive Citizenship: Realizing the Potential', in *Citizenship Between Past and Future*, eds. Engin F. Isin, Peter Nyers, and Bryan S. Turner (New York: Routledge, 2008), 54; Andrea Cornwall, Steven Robins and Bettina Von Lieres, 'States of Citizenship: Contexts and Cultures of Public Engagement and Citizen Action', Institute of Development Studies Working Paper 363 (University of Sussex, 2011), 13; Jane Kinninmont, 'Citizenship in the Gulf', in *The Gulf States and the Arab Uprisings*, ed. Ana Echague (FRIDE and the Gulf Research Center, 2013), 50–51.

conclusively determine who would be the permanent, settled population of each state. Identifying with the nation now superseded pre-existing forms of traditional identification that were based on looser affiliations such as tribal belonging and/or place of birth or origin. In addition to strengthening sovereign control over borders and populations, the crafting of national identity projects was meant to ensure the long-term loyalty and allegiance of the now settled population of the newly established countries towards the monarchies that ruled them. While asserting sovereign dominion over land and people might have been critically important to the rulers, they were not able to unilaterally resolve all issues of territory and population immediately upon statehood. In fact, in many cases territory and population continued to serve as problematic arenas of competition and contestation which would resurface time and again either between countries and their neighbours or within the domestic realm of different states between the rulers and the ruled.

The chapter analyses how the legal, political, and economic construction of an 'exclusionary' Gulf citizenship, designed to ensure that citizens owe their allegiance and loyalty to their regime and nation, is coming under increasing strain since 2011. The fundamental principles of citizenship which provide strict criteria of who can or cannot be included are being manipulated once again in some of the authoritarian Gulf monarchies. In some cases, there are visible strains on the traditional rentier arrangements, and signs that the states' ability to 'buy' the loyalty of their citizens appears to be wearing thin.[2] While social and economic goods have served as the traditional cornerstone in the relationship between regimes and citizens within these rentier states, in reality the negotiations in these arrangements are far more complex and nuanced rather than mono-dimensional and transactional. Over the past few years there are increasing indications of a more demanding and politically expressive Gulf citizenry that is focused on a broader agenda than one limited to accessing resource rents.[3] The sudden surge in citizenship revocation cases seen in

---

[2] For more on rentier states in the GCC, see Mehran Kamrava, 'The Political Economy of Renterism', in *The Political Economy of the Persian Gulf*, ed. Mehran Kamrava (London: Hurst & Company, 2012), 39–68; Hazem Beblawi, 'The Rentier State in the Arab World', *Arab Studies Quarterly* 9 (Fall 1987) 4: 383–98; Abdulhadi Khalaf, 'The Politics of Migration', in *Transit States: Labour, Migration and Citizenship in the Gulf*, eds. Abdulhadi Khalaf, Omar Alshahabi, and Adam Hanieh (London: Pluto Press, 2015), 39–56.

[3] Kristin Smith Diwan, 'Gulf Societies in Transition: National Identity and National Projects in the Arab Gulf', Workshop Report (Arab Gulf States Institute in Washington, June 2016), 12.

the GCC since 2011 provides evidence of the states' ongoing politicisation of citizenship rights in the face of challenges (either perceived or real) to their authority.

This chapter builds on the body of work which has already established that citizenship has from its very evolution been a critical component of the state-building experience in the GCC, and has continued to remain closely linked to the advancement of particular political interests of the various regimes.[4] Issues of inclusion in terms of categorising which groups of inhabitants have the legal right to belong to and participate in the state, or exclusion in terms of those who are denied belonging and participation, continue to be animated by the particular political dynamics that have occurred at different historical junctures. Most recently, in light of the Arab Uprisings, new arenas of contestation have emerged, or perhaps more accurately, old arenas are being revitalised in new forms, once again highlighting the political nature of the citizenship domain. Since the 2011 uprisings, there have been changes to nationality and terrorism laws that have served to securitise citizenship by, on the one hand, allowing the states to engage in citizenship withdrawal, while on the other hand, expanding access of citizenship to previously excluded categories of residents. This presses against the framing of a Gulf citizenship provided through a benign yet autocratic leadership that is an irrevocable entitlement to all those who qualify through *jus sanguinis*. If citizenship is a privilege that can be withdrawn when certain political conditions are breached, or meted out when certain political conditions necessitate it, as recent events demonstrate, then surely citizenship itself is a site of political contestation for both regimes and residents.

This chapter draws on some of these unfolding dynamics in GCC states. It suggests that while some of what we are seeing may bear a resemblance to habitual responses by authoritarian regimes to address political challenges through further exclusion and marginalisation, it also underscores the fact that these state responses exacerbate the contestation between the state and the citizenry over the very meaning of citizenship.

---

4 For more information, please consult Gianluca Paolo Parolin, *Citizenship in the Arab World: Kin, Religion and Nation-State* (Amsterdam: Amsterdam University Press, 2009); Anh Nga Longva, 'Citizenship in the Gulf States: Conceptualization and Practice', in *Citizenship and the State in the Middle East: Approaches and Applications*, eds. Nils A. Butenschøn, Uri Daivs, and Manuel Hassassian (New York: Syracuse University Press, 2000).

AUTHENTICITY AND THE POLITICS OF BELONGING

At the broadest legal level, across all six GCC states, nationality laws have over time established stringent criteria for determining who can be considered as genuinely belonging to the national territory and deserving of citizenship rights.[5] The Gulf States' nationality laws as they exist today apply very strict interpretations of *jus sanguinis* when it comes to identifying who can legally claim nationality.[6] In most cases, citizenship is limited to those who can claim historical and territorial linkages via their male parentage to a particular state from the pre-independence era. Citizenship is mostly passed on via the male parent and his associated ancestral bloodline, and until fairly recently most female GCC citizens were unable to pass citizenship to their offspring if they married a foreigner.[7] Providing citizenship rights on the basis of this stringent criteria of eligibility has served to filter out those who are considered not to belong to the national fold. Over the past two decades, several of the GCC states have introduced naturalisation clauses, but the very strict criteria that must be met means that in reality very few of the millions of foreigners who are resident in the Gulf are able to seek citizenship via naturalisation processes.[8] Additionally, the nationality laws in the region are steeped in language which references loyalty and allegiance to the nation and frequently directly to the ruler himself. Despite the various legal means and measures in place around the awarding of citizenship, in essence citizenship, at least through the way in which it is legislated, continues to be subtly articulated as a privilege and 'gift' given by the Gulf monarchs to those whom they consider eligible. Much of the statutory framework around citizenship appears to be less focused on establishing a balanced set of rights and duties between the state and the citizen in a way that conforms to the norms and customs of citizenship within liberal democracies.

Not unlike other political phenomena, conceptions of citizenship are influenced by the larger contexts within which they take shape. In liberal democracies citizenship is generally associated with a host of political

---

5 Parolin, *Citizenship in the Arab World*, 95–111.

6 For explanation of *jus sanguinis* see James Brown Scott, 'Nationality: *Jus Soli* or *Jus Sanguinis*', *The American Journal of International Law* 24 (January 1930) 1: 58–64; William Rogers Brubaker, *Citizenship and Nationhood in France and Germany* (Cambridge, MA: Harvard University Press, 1992), 81–2.

7 Parolin, *Citizenship in the Arab World*, 98–100.

8 Ibid., 100–104.

rights. Applied to the GCC, such a 'Western'-defined conception of citizenship lends itself to the assumption that there is no *real* citizenship in this part of the world, but instead a structure that creates a bounded national membership of sorts that centres on the socio-economic dimensions of a relationship between rulers and their subjects. It is certainly true that social and economic rights have been dominant features in the framing of Gulf citizenship, while political rights have been far more limited within these authoritarian monarchies.[9] However, the presumption that this means there is somehow an absence of *real* citizenship in itself needs problematising.

The evolution and changes to Gulf citizenship over the recent past suggest that within its own context, GCC citizenship is just as political in essence as it is within any liberal state, and is an important political tool for both inhabitants and the authoritarian state. The very category of citizen remains a political one (just as does the category of the state), regardless of whether the shape of political arrangements and the context it operates within are authoritarian or liberal. Being a citizen has political meaning to the people who reside in the Gulf, to those who have access to categories of residency, to those who are excluded from these categories of residency altogether, and to those who design and police it. Contestations around who belongs to the nation, who has access to citizenship rights, and what these actual rights are in practice, have occurred ever since independence and at various stages of the development of the GCC countries.

As others have argued, even if political participatory rights are not the primary foundations of citizenship in the GCC (and elsewhere in the Middle East), citizenship remains a core domain from which to study political and social dynamics of different countries in the region.[10] Rather than studying Gulf citizenship through the lens of limited democratic possibilities, scholars need to be attentive to the new meanings and articulations of citizenship that are being demonstrated by the practices of both the state and citizens. Much of the broader literature on the Persian Gulf points to both the lack of authentic citizenship provided by the state, as well as an absence of the realisation of citizenship from Gulf nationals themselves.[11] Much of the underlying assumption has been that the state's

---

[9] Longva, 'Citizenship in the Gulf States: Conceptualization and Practice', 183.

[10] Rania Maktabi, 'The Politicization of the Demos in the Middle East: Citizenship between Membership and Participation in the State' (PhD Thesis, University of Oslo: 2012), 19.

[11] See for example Longva, 'Citizenship in the Gulf States', 179–97; Michael Ross, 'Does Oil Hinder Democracy?' *World Politics* 53 (2001) 3: 325–61; Abdulhadi

commitment to a citizenship based on exclusion, non-recognition of belonging, and repression of political action, has prompted Gulf nationals to a sort of voluntary surrendering of political rights that comes with being citizens. Recent events suggest that there is a need to move beyond the limitation of citizenship studies that are focused not only geographically on the experiences of liberal democracies, but are also embedded in their normative frame. The Gulf monarchies' context serves to situate the study of the evolution of citizenship practices as well as its meaning in a context that lacks both institutional structure and avenues for citizens' mobilisation, and also affords little official recognition of citizens' inherent rights to express their politics. Given the emerging global trends within liberal states that appear to be stimulating exclusionary rhetoric and practices around citizenship on the basis of ethnicity and authentic belonging, it is important to examine how such contestations over citizenship have developed within illiberal states.

As other observers of the Persian Gulf have pointed out, during the period immediately after independence, the GCC monarchies asserted their nascent statehood by establishing formal control over their territory through strictly crafted and managed borders, and clearly defining the permanent, settled population that could claim to belong to the country.[12] These efforts were not seamless, and in fact were highly charged by the political climate of the time. The rulers of these new states were conscious from the beginning of their mutual dependence on one another, and the need to ensure friendly and cooperative relationships with their new 'national' neighbours for the sake of long-term security and viability. However, these considerations were carefully balanced by each of the rulers against the equally important task of carving out individual political identities of each newly demarcated independent state.[13] The early period of independence of the GCC states brought to the forefront what would become lingering regional competition over both

Khalaf, 'The Politics of Migration', in *Transit States: Labour, Migration and Citizenship in the Gulf*, eds. Abdulhadi Khalaf, Omar Alshahabi, and Adam Hanieh (London: Pluto Press, 2015), 39–56; Donald Losman, 'The Rentier State and National Oil Companies: An Economic and Political Perspective', *The Middle East Journal* 64 (2010) 3: 427–45.

[12] Gwenn Okruhlik and Patrick J. Conge, 'The Politics of Border Disputes: On the Arabian Peninsula', *International Journal* 54 (1999) 2: 230–48; Claire Beaugrand, 'Nationality and Migration Control in the Gulf Countries', *INAMO* 46 (2006), 10–14.

[13] Okruhlik and Conge, 'The Politics of Border Disputes'; Dina Alqadi, 'The Door that Cannot be Closed: Bidoon Citizenship in the United Arab Emirates' (Unpublished Dissertation, Duke University, 2015), 52–9.

territorial boundaries and demography. Decades later these six states' founding monarchs' inherent suspicion of the true loyalty of the subjects over whom they were to rule has left its imprint on both the legislative apparatus as well as the social fabric that binds citizens to the GCC states and to each other.

While precise conditions and contexts do vary across the six monarchies, there has been an overall regional effort since independence to frame access to GCC citizenship along the lines of ethnic belonging, and to articulate a *Khaleeji* nationality that is embedded in the idea of an indigenous and uniform Arab heritage of sorts. However, this condensing down of a GCC nationality tied to a particular ethnic-linguistic authenticity did not take place naturally and suddenly, but deliberately, gradually, and with contestation. For example, during the 1960s, when Dubai, Sharjah, and Abu Dhabi were working towards the final stages of forming what would eventually be the federation of the United Arab Emirates (UAE), the issue of which residents would be eligible for federal citizenship and would hold an Emirati passport was a source of disagreement among the rulers of these three emirates.[14] The rulers of Abu Dhabi were much more anxious about retaining strict controls over which segments of the population would be eligible for federal citizenship, particularly when it came to the Persian-origin residents who made up a large proportion of Dubai's population.[15] Dubai had been much more open to expanding citizenship to Persians, and prior to the formation of the federation had provided citizenship to larger numbers of its Persian-origin residents.[16] These early tensions in determining access to the united federation's citizenship were more about political power-sharing struggles between the different Emirati rulers rather than disagreements over the actual 'authenticity' of the ethnic composition of the population itself.[17] Initial vulnerabilities around the challenges of statehood itself were compounded by the anxieties that the different Emirati sheikhs felt vis-à-vis each other, and national identity and citizenship served as one of the domains in which these tensions were manifested.

While the UAE serves as one example of a particular historical case that shaped ideas on populations with divided loyalty, similar dynamics have been visible across most other GCC states both during the

---

14 Alqadi, 'The Door that Cannot be Closed', 52.
15 Ibid., 53.
16 Ibid.
17 Ibid.

post-independence period and at various stages of state-building since. Claire Beaugrand has written extensively about the Kuwaiti experience, which initially fostered citizenship access to a plural mix of ethnicities and economic classes in the 1950s.[18] However, by the 1960s, increasing revenues from hydrocarbon rents, and intensification of rentier-based welfare benefits, compounded by ongoing competition and conflict between urban elites and the Kuwaiti tribes all combined to steadily erode the more inclusive pathway to citizenship that had existed up until that point.[19] The issue of providing Kuwaiti citizenship to the stateless Bidoon remains unresolved for the past 30 years because of the internal political competition and social divisions between different segments of Kuwaiti society today and how they view the issue. Different social groups in Kuwait either support or resist incorporating the Bidoon through citizenship as they feel doing so will either enhance or challenge their own political positions in the country. This marginalisation of the Bidoon is partially a result of Kuwait's historically exclusionary evolution of nationality law, but is also very much embedded in modern day political struggles in the country.[20]

Through their nationality laws, the GCC states have tried to ensure that they retain complete control over who has access to full citizenship. This has not gone uncontested, however, as evidenced by changes both in law and practice over time. Over the past decade, across the region there has been an increasing narrowing of access to citizenship. At the same time, GCC states have enacted laws that have differentiated tiers of citizenship rights. Such practices include: determining who is entitled to different economic benefits on the basis of ancestry; which citizens are entitled to participate in elections or vote; and whether or not women can pass citizenship on to their children. Especially in the aftermath of the 2011 Arab Uprisings, many GCC states have also resorted to the increasing use of nationality revocation as a tool of political control and discipline of those considered to be behaving outside the accepted norms. At the same time, we have seen instances of citizenship expansion, for example, to create greater inclusion of women's rights, and also to provide citizenship through naturalisation to inhabitants who would not otherwise qualify.

---

18 Claire Beaugrand, 'Statelessness and Administrative Violence: *Biduns*' Survival Strategies in Kuwait', *The Muslim World* 101 (2011) 2: 232–4.

19 Beaugrand, 'Statelessness and Administrative Violence', 234.

20 Ibid., 246–9.

THE POLITICS OF MEANING IN GULF 'ECONOMIC' CITIZENSHIP

From about the 1960s and the 1970s, each of the GCC states began building on conceptions of a unique and privileged national citizenship that would confer particular sets of rights, primarily of a socio-economic nature, to each citizen. As luck would have it, these nascent nationality laws were being established almost at the same time as the hydrocarbon-based economies were starting to deepen their roots. A strange marriage of sorts occurred as a result, one that would bind Gulf citizenship very closely to the rentier logics that would come to dominate almost all aspects of political, economic, and social relations within the region. The influence that the development of the hydrocarbon sectors of the modern states of the Gulf had on the state–citizen relationship from its very early stages cannot be discounted, nor can the ensuing impact of the state's ability to confer largesse on the people be minimised.[21] The oil-generated revenues that began to accrue to the state coffers from the middle of the last century gave rulers the unforeseen ability to share wealth with their populations at unprecedented levels, and provided these monarchies with the necessary financial ability to enhance their legitimacy and deepen their authority over the public.[22] The subsequent evolution of legal and political notions of citizenship, along with the increasingly high economic privileges tied to it, clearly served to provide not only incentives for nationals to support the existing regimes and their rulers, but, over time, also provided the regimes with an economic motive for limiting citizenship to only a select few.[23]

For the few scholars of the Gulf who have actively studied the evolution of citizenship, the relationship between nationals and the region's rulers is one presumed to be established along paternalistic and largely benevolent lines. The monarchs extend generosity towards their citizens in return for receiving loyalty and patronage.[24] As long as citizens behave according to the socially, politically, and economically established rules of the rentier relationship, they can presume to benefit from the goodwill of their rulers. The GCC states all exhibit different levels of classic 'rentier' state-society conditions. Rentier states, in the simplest and broadest definition of the term, are those whose patterns of economic and political development have been dominated by the extraction of natural resources and the

---

21 Longva, 'Citizenship in the Gulf States', 180.

22 Kinninmont, 'Citizenship in the Gulf', 51–2.

23 Zahra Babar, 'The Cost of Belonging: Citizenship Construction in the State of Qatar', *Middle East Journal* 68 (2014) 3: 420.

24 See, for example, Longva, 'Citizenship in the Gulf States', 180.

subsequent generation of wealth or 'rent' earned through the sale of those natural resources.[25] In the GCC states, domestic political arrangements have been shaped by the regimes' ability to generate vast quantities of rent from the hydrocarbon sector. Under classic rentier theory, state–citizen relationships are deeply affected by the fact that such regimes have an independent source of wealth not derived from their own citizenry (in the form of taxation). In rentier economies, it is argued, rulers disburse funds in order to build a stable state and also to buy themselves political peace and the consent of their people.

States disburse their rentier earnings to their citizenry through various mechanisms, sometimes as direct transfers, but more often through indirect benefits. GCC citizens as such may benefit not only from occasional government stipends, but also from guaranteed employment in the public sector, free education, training, health care, subsidized housing, free electricity and water, and a host of other benefits. Such largesse places continuous strain on the financial capacity of the state. As the GCC populations have expanded and the number of citizens with heightened expectations has grown, the regimes have struggled to continuously maintain such forms of financial generosity. Limiting state munificence is considered anathema to the rulers, as they fear losing their citizens' support and compliance should they fail to meet expectations. Regimes across the Gulf are locked into these long-standing arrangements, and hesitate to withdraw the financial benefits of citizenship as doing so could mean domestic instability and political tensions.

The various constraints that characterise Gulf citizenship have led to something of a consensus among most scholars of the region that there is in fact no tangible political meaning to citizenship in this particular context.[26] Citizenship is in a sense hollowed out, when all it really allows for is a heightened degree of financial and social well-being. This critical lack of access to political citizenship is seen as being directly tied to the exceptionalism of the political economies of the Persian Gulf monarchies, to the existing rentier bargains visible across the region, and to the regimes that have successfully 'bought' the political acquiescence of the subjects

---

[25] See for example, Kamrava, 'The Political Economy of Rentierism', 39–68; Hazem Beblawi, 'The Rentier State in the Arab World'; Khalaf, 'The Politics of Migration', 39–56.

[26] For more discussion on political meanings of citizenship in the GCC see, Parolin, *Citizenship in the Arab World*; Longva, 'Citizenship in the Gulf States'; Michael Herb, 'A Nation of Bureaucrats: Political Participation and Economic Diversification in Kuwait and the United Arab Emirates', *The Journal of Middle East Studies* 41 (August 2009) 3: 375–95.

over whom they govern. Citizenship can only be considered to be a gift that has been given to small, selective groups of those who inhabit the Arabian Peninsula, on the basis of *jus sanguinis*. These groups' rights are limited to the provision of a generous basket of financial and economic goods that is disbursed at the pleasure of the state, and provides little in the way of political membership. This argument follows on from the general assumption that unless there is a radical shift in the current pattern of the capacity of the GCC states to actively engage in rent distribution, the very idea of an authentically *political* GCC citizenship is doubtful.

Increasingly, there are signs across the Gulf states that there is in fact a politics of meaning when it comes to Gulf citizenship. These signs force us to question the somewhat reductive reasoning that when citizenship comes without conferring formal political rights it is by its very nature apolitical. Gulf experts have pointed out that there is a need to broaden our collective understanding of what political participation means in the context of authoritarian states, where we do not see signs of formal political participation nor institutional practices that mirror those we see occurring in liberal democracies.[27] In the absence of formal politics, there are still signs across the Gulf that various forms of political expression and participation take place, albeit independently of institutional development, reform, or the creation of mechanisms for organised forms of political engagement.[28] As existing ruling arrangements in the region are coming under increasing strain as a result of growing populations and decreasing hydrocarbon revenues, most of the GCC governments are engaging in (or considering) reforming their delivery of economic goods to their populations. This can be seen in, among other places, national development plans like the Saudi 2030 Vision. Among the stated goals to be achieved by 2030, the plan lists decreasing overall unemployment from 11.6 per cent to 7 per cent while also increasing women's work force participation from 22 per cent to 30 per cent in the same time frame.[29] With its emphasis on expanding private sector employment among citizens one sees how the Saudi government aims to change the terms of the classic 'rentier agreement' and decrease citizens' dependence on public sector employment. In this context, prevailing assumptions about the essence and meaning of citizenship are coming under growing strain.

---

27 Abdulhadi Khalaf and Giacomo Luciani (eds.), *Constitutional Reform and Political Participation in the Gulf* (Gulf Research Center, 2006), 12.

28 Ibid., 14–16.

29 Vision 2030, 'Thriving Economy Rewarding Opportunities', Vision 2030 Kingdom of Saudi Arabia.

EXPANDING AND CURTAILING CITIZENSHIP POST ARAB UPRISINGS

Beyond the Gulf region and at the international level, there exists no complete consistency between what different nationality laws offer in terms of gender equality. In particular, citizenship laws differ widely in regard to a woman's rights to pass her citizenship on to her children. There are over two dozen countries that still do not give female citizens the right to pass on their nationality to their children, and most of these countries are based in the Arab world.[30] This specific restriction on female Gulf citizens has brought glaring international and local condemnation to the GCC states. Not only have GCC regimes received their share of international criticism for supporting what is widely considered to be a gender-biased position relating to citizenship accrual, but the issue has also been one which has garnered a great deal of domestic attention as well. The issue of what rights to give to female citizens has been a socially important one, as increasingly GCC women marrying foreigners were placed in the predicament of not being able to pass on a host of important social and economic rights to their children. Over the past decade, most of the GCC states took measures to ensure that the children of female citizens were able to access a series of privileges usually reserved for citizens such as access to education, healthcare, and certain limited opportunities for employment in the labour market. In fact, over time one could argue that on many levels the actual privileges in the socio-economic sphere were provided to these non-citizen children of female citizens, while the actual granting of full citizenship was denied. Over the past few years there has been much discussion in the media and in the public sphere in relation to the issue of women's rights to pass on citizenship to their children.[31]

Citizenship across much of the region was traditionally considered to pass to a child through the father, so that female citizens who marry foreigners find themselves unable to pass citizenship rights to their

---

[30] 'Background Note on Gender Equality, Nationality Laws, and Statelessness' (United Nations High Commission for Refugees, 2014).

[31] Huda Sajwani, 'Citizenship Law for Emirati Women Sets Good Example', *The National*, 23 December 2011; Samir Salama, 'New UAE Citizenship Rule for Children Clarified', *Gulf News*, 9 January 2012; 'Resolution Issued to Set up Committee for UAE Citizenship Applications', *Gulf News*, 14 December 2011; 'Panel to Implement Citizenship Directive', *Gulf News*, 15 December 2011; Habib Toumie, 'Saudi Mothers Closer to Passing Citizenship to Their Children', *Gulf News*, 29 January 2017.

progeny.[32] However, there are differences among the six countries, and the laws currently differ when it comes to the conferral of nationality to the offspring of female citizens. Qatar and Kuwait have rigid nationality laws that do not permit female citizens who marry foreigners to pass on citizenship rights to their children. Qatar does not allow its female citizens to pass on citizenship rights to their children even if they are unable to access citizenship from their father, which means that potentially they could end up stateless. Kuwait follows an almost identical approach, allowing only Kuwaiti fathers to pass on citizenship. Both Kuwait and Qatar do, however, provide for means by which the children of Kuwaiti and Qatari mothers can, upon reaching the age of majority, apply for naturalised citizenship. However, the exact mechanism for how these children are able to obtain naturalised citizenship once they are adults remains obscure, as there is little information on how many cases of naturalised citizenship are awarded each year in each of these countries.

Saudi Arabia, Oman, the UAE, and Bahrain on the other hand have either already adopted changes to their nationality laws to expand the rights of women when it comes to passing on nationality, or over the past few years have taken steps to reform their nationality laws and address this inequality. In Bahrain and Oman, female citizens are able to pass on citizenship to their children (who can either be born within the country or outside of it) if their fathers are unknown or if their fathers are stateless.[33] Bahrain and Saudi Arabia are both considering draft legislation which would permit Bahraini and Saudi mothers to confer their nationality to their children in a wider range of circumstances.[34] The UAE amended its nationality law in December 2011 to expand citizenship rights to the children of female Emiratis. However, the new law only allows these children to apply for their Emirati citizenship after they have reached the legal age of maturity, which is 18 years old. The changes to the law mean that Emirati women who marry foreigners are able to ensure that their children can access the labour market at adulthood, which must have been a key motivating factor in pressing the state on this issue. Within the first few years that the new law was implemented in the UAE, a relatively large number of people applied for their citizenship – in 2015 a total of 152 people with Emirati mothers and foreign fathers obtained their citizenship, and in 2016 another 97 cases of citizenship were granted

32 Wanda Krause, 'Gender and Participation in the Arab Gulf' (Research Paper, Kuwait Programme on Development, Governance and Globalisation in the Gulf States, 2009), 12.

33 'Background Note on Gender Equality, Nationality Laws, and Statelessness'.

34 'Background Note on Gender Equality, Nationality Laws, and Statelessness'.

under this law.[35] These figures appear to highlight the fact that there are an increasing number of Emirati citizens who are marrying foreigners, a phenomenon that is often seen by Gulf leaders as being problematic and threatening. Interestingly enough, after the establishment of the new law in the Emirates, news media appeared to suggest that by increasing the access of citizenship rights to the children of Emirati women the UAE might have a better means of combating another heavily discussed social problem, namely the increasing demographic imbalance in several of the GCC states which has seen citizen populations dwindle in comparison to an ever increasing flow of foreign migrants.[36]

This access of citizenship to the children of Gulf women who marry foreigners has evolved slowly, and clearly is a result of contestation around not only women's rights, but also questions of national identity and belonging. Clearly the phenomenon of women marrying outside their country of citizenship is widespread across the region, with the Saudi Ministry of Labour releasing public data in 2011 which showed that that year 1,988 Saudi women had married foreigners, out of which the large majority had married citizens of neighbouring GCC states.[37] However, a Saudi Ministry of Justice report from 2012 produced far higher numbers, stated that about 700,000 Saudi women in total were married to foreigners, and that in 2012 alone 13,117 Saudi women had married non-Saudis.[38] The consequences of such a large number of marriages, potentially resulting in many thousands of children who would be unable to access Saudi citizenship, has no doubt animated policymaking circles in the Kingdom. In response, in 2013 Saudi Arabia enacted a major policy change in relation to the status of the children of Saudi mothers and non-Saudi fathers, allowing them to access the same economic and social benefits as Saudi citizens, particularly in terms of accessing educational benefits as well as public health care. Additionally, Saudi female citizens were able to sponsor their children as well as their non-Saudi husbands so that they could access jobs in the private sector.[39] Concerns persisted, however, when it came to

---

35 'UAE: 97 Children of Emirati Mothers, Expatriate Fathers Get Citizenship', *The Great Middle East*, 1 December 2016.

36 Huda Sajwani, 'Citizenship Law for Emirati Women Sets Good Example', *The National*, 23 December 2011.

37 'Breakthrough: Saudi Women Can Pass Citizenship Rights to their Children', *Al Arabiya*, February 2013.

38 'Saudi Women Married to Foreigners Urge Govt to Solve their Problems', *Arab News*, Jeddah, 6 March 2015; Nadia Al-Fawaz, 'Saudi Women Prefer to Marry Foreigners', *Arab News*, 7 November 2014.

39 Habib Toumi, 'Saudi Mothers Closer to Passing Citizenship to their Children', *Gulf News*, 29 January 2017.

entering the labour market without the same access as full Saudi citizens, particularly because over the past few years the Kingdom has adopted much more strenuous efforts to nationalise the labour market through its *Nitaqat* policies. The *Nitaqat* programme heavily privileges the hiring of Saudi nationals over foreigners, and rewards private sector companies that adopt policies of actively hiring Saudi citizens.[40] Subsequent clarifications were made by the Saudi government, stating that the newly granted rights to children of Saudi mothers included them being considered as Saudi citizens in relation to the *Nitaqat* programme, thereby ensuring their greater chances of employment in the private sector.[41]

The children of Saudi mothers and other Gulf women who have a foreign father have often existed in a sort of blurry, grey zone. While they have enjoyed some socio-economic rights, they have been restricted from accessing all of the economic benefits provided to citizens. Through its process of reforming policies to create better conditions for the children of Saudi mothers, the Kingdom has been very careful in articulating the nuanced distinction between 'citizenship rights' and 'citizenship' itself. The path of reform appears to acknowledge that in principle the children of Saudi women have a moral right to social and economic equality to their cousins and peers, and thus policies and laws have been amended to address this disparity. However, currently the children of Saudi mothers cannot press the same claim when it comes to acquiring citizenship and nationality itself.[42] This very articulation of a distinction and separation between the two – citizenship rights versus citizenship – underscores the fact that for the state and for people, citizenship is a lofty, politically salient notion which holds a lot more meaning than mere economic well-being.

Based on the publicly available data, the vast majority of Saudi women have been marrying men from Yemen, Qatar, and the UAE, which one would assume would be considered socially and politically acceptable to the Saudi regime. However, in fact the effect is the opposite, and the reluctance on the part of the state to provide full rights of political belonging to the children of mixed-*Khaleeji* parentage is partially driven by primordial concerns regarding future challenges that the rulers might face when governing over populations that have dual citizenship rights, split allegiances and dubious loyalties.

---

40 Francoise De Bel-Air, 'The Socio-Political Background and Stakes of "Saudizing" the Workforce in Saudi Arabia: the Nitaqat Policy', *Gulf Labour Markets and Migration Research Note*, 2015.

41 'Breakthrough: Saudi Women Can Pass Citizenship Rights to their Children'.

42 'Children of Non-Saudi Fathers to be Counted as Citizens: MoL', *The Saudi Gazette*, 30 December 2015.

Another area that is seeing a social response from citizens is the expansion of citizenship by GCC governments to select groups of migrants or foreigners. GCC nationals are not predisposed towards adding new citizens to their demography, particularly if they are considered not to share the same language or heritage, and most of all if they are seen as serving a political objective of a repressive regime. The most obvious recent arena where this issue emerged as a critical focal point of contestation was in Bahraini both during and after the 2011 uprisings. One of the core demands made by Bahrain protestors in 2011 centred on the issue that the government was granting naturalised citizenship and a host of financial benefits to foreigners for its own political reasons and in a non-transparent manner.[43] While there is no public data on citizenship naturalisation in Bahrain, and no concrete numbers as to the extent of the practice by the government, this issue did and continues to animate grievances among members of the Bahrain public and especially the political opposition.[44] Within Bahrain, there have been increasing statements from scholars, activists, and average citizens suggesting that the Bahraini government has been providing citizenship to foreigners, mainly Sunnis, and doing so to 'buy foreign loyalty.'[45] The assertion by the opposition is that the regime is engaged in an active and aggressive effort to 'Sunnify' the small country by importing Sunnis and providing them with fast-tracked citizenship.

The Bahrain case is interesting as, despite the fact that Bahraini society has historically maintained a reputation for being one of the most tolerant and inclusive in the region, much of the anger and resentment that had been articulated seems to frame the case as that of a local, beleaguered citizenry being stripped of its rights to jobs and financial support by unscrupulous migrant workers who are taking advantage of the political climate and benefiting at the expense of citizens. Bahraini activists have suggested that the government is attempting to ignore the real issues at hand by bypassing its own social base, and purchasing loyalty from outside, much as they would import construction or domestic workers. The undertone of the conversation is that the migrants in question are serving in some ways as 'scabs,' disrupting the social norms around citizens' expectations much as scabs would disrupt the effectiveness of a labour strike. Many of the demonstrators who have been calling for change believe they are being discriminated against, while in contrast newly naturalised citizens

---

43 Zoi Constantine, 'Protests over Citizenship for Sunnis from Abroad Shake Bahrain', *The National*, 20 March 2011.

44 Ary Baker, 'What Lies Beneath: Bahrain's New Citizens Fuel Unrest', *TIME*, 11 March 2012; Kinninmont, 'Citizenship in the Gulf', 53.

45 Baker, 'What Lies Beneath'.

are accessing benefits that they should not be able to access. That this phenomenon is said to be occurring simultaneously as other Bahrainis are being stripped of their citizenship has even further fuelled the fire. Since 2012, the state has stripped many Bahrainis of their citizenship, many of them being Shiʿa.

Over the past five years, Bahrain, Oman, the UAE and Kuwait have all adopted amendments to their laws on nationality and terrorism that serve to expand the basis upon which these states can revoke citizenship. Many of the changes in law reflect an increasing concern with loyalty and allegiance on the part of individuals. By adopting ambiguous definitions of what constitutes a crime that would warrant the loss of citizenship, the states are left with considerable discretion in terms of applying the law. Citizenship stripping has been a strategic tool used by several countries in the region to curtail pressures for political change.[46] Bahrain has not been alone in its use of citizenship revocation to discipline citizens' bargaining with the state, as several other GCC states have been using this extreme tool against their people. While Bahrain in 2012 revoked the citizenship of 31 individuals who were deemed to be threats to national security, in 2013, Sheikh Khalifa bin Zayed, the ruler of the UAE, did the same thing to seven Emiratis. The Emirati citizens who lost their citizenship rights had been accused of belonging to the Muslim Brotherhood organisation. In 2014, Kuwait followed suit when it revoked the citizenship of 18 people, including the spokesman of a major opposition group. Ever since 2012, Kuwait has been engaged actively in stripping citizenship from people, mostly on claims that they only received their citizenship based on fraudulent grounds. In actual fact, however, the citizenships revoked have been largely political. Following on from the initial acts of citizenship revocation carried out in 2012, many other Bahrainis have also had their citizenship stripped over the past five years. While the state has justified these revocations on the basis of sedition or anti-state activities, activists and opposition members in Bahrain have suggested that the motivation remains sectarian in nature, that the core issue is the suspicions of the ruling Al Khalifah in terms of the allegiance of Shiʿi Bahrainis, and that they are somehow considered to be working closely with Iran. Some of the other GCC states, like Qatar and the Kingdom of Saudi Arabia, have not overtly engaged in citizenship stripping, but have relied on other means to ensure social order since the Arab revolts. Saudi Arabia has issued a number of decrees in response to protests in the eastern regions of the Kingdom, and one authorised the withdrawal of citizenship from every

---

46 Kinninmont, 'Citizenship in the Gulf', 52.

Saudi involved in the protests, without the possibility of a royal pardon in the future. Social media sites in Saudi Arabia reported that the authorities had mentioned 300 activists in these decrees, all of whom could potentially lose their citizenship under the new law. However, there have to date not been any actual incidents of citizenship stripping reported in the press in the Kingdom.

CONCLUSION

In conclusion, this chapter suggests that just as the meaning, practices, and legislative framework of citizenship evolve based on a country's particular geography, history, political economy, and culture, so do different patterns of social contestation and competition around the rights of citizenship reflect their context. While citizens in the six GCC countries have historically contended with the confines of restrictive authoritarian structures, and in many ways lack both the legal and institutional support necessary for full political expression, they continue to challenge the state in asserting full authority over the citizenship domain. The GCC states and regimes for their part have also, at different time periods, engaged in the politicisation of citizenship in reaction to particular threats from the external and internal domain. Since the 2011 Arab Uprisings, across the Gulf we have seen a revitalised struggle between people attempting to claim greater access to their rights, and states attempting to reassert their authority and repress any public politics that appear to undermine it. This has been particularly visible in the domain of citizenship, with an increasing political use of nationality revocation as well as nationality expansion, both of which have served as sites of contestation between states and the public.

6. Bahrain's citizenship policy of inclusion and exclusion

Zeineb Alsabeehg

> The Bahraini citizenship represents a charter of rights. Even when I had the Bahraini citizenship, I did not enjoy my rights. Now the picture is clear: We are taking your citizenship and accordingly your rights.
>
> Author interview with a Bahraini whose citizenship has been revoked.[1]

INTRODUCTION

The public dissatisfaction with the Bahraini regime was evident when masses of people protested in the tiny Gulf country as part of the Arab Uprisings in 2011. The Al Khalifa monarchy had promised political reforms at the beginning of the millennium, but these promises were to a great extent perceived as unfulfilled. The new Constitution in 2002 did not transit the country into a democracy, although it theoretically stated fundamental rights to citizens. The restoration of the parliament, which is only partially elected by popular vote, did not give people real access to political decision-making. Supreme power remains in the hands of King Hamad bin Isa Al Khalifa and his royal family, who occupy most high-ranking positions in the state. The repression of dissidents continued and became more severe before the outbreak of the 2011 uprising.

The protestors gathered in the Pearl Roundabout in the capital Manama shortly after they took to the street on 14 February 2011. Both Sunni and Shiʿi protestors stressed national unity. 'We are brothers, Sunni and Shiʿi – we will not sell this country', they chanted. They called for democracy and an end to suppression of dissidents. They longed for equal citizenship in light of systematic discrimination which the Shiʿi majority population had experienced for a long time. The protestors demanded a political system in which everyone had equal access to political participation and

1 Ebrahim Al-Aradi, a Bahraini doctor exiled in Lebanon.

where the government was elected by popular vote. Furthermore, they demanded equal rights to public employment and other public services. Discriminatory patterns in the political system and the job market, among other spheres, had made Shiʿi Bahrainis worse off than their Sunni fellow citizens.

The protests in the Pearl Roundabout lasted only one month. In mid-March 2011, the Bahraini government sought support from troops from the Gulf Cooperation Council (GCC) in order to 'maintain order and security'. A harsh crackdown on dissidents followed. People who had participated in the protests were fired from their jobs or banned from continuing their education in universities. Thousands were arrested, while several were killed – some of them as a result of torture in custody. Oppositional figures were sentenced to long imprisonment for 'plotting a coup'. In addition, hundreds had their citizenship revoked, the majority of whom became stateless. Several protestors were sentenced to death, three of whom were executed in January 2017. The crackdown especially targeted members of the Shiʿi community.

Since the suppression of the uprising, sectarian politics have become more severe. In the pro-governmental media, the Bahraini uprising was framed as a Shiʿi revolt against the Sunni rulers. The protestors were accused of being supported by Iran. The government used the accusation of Iranian involvement in domestic affairs as a justification for the intervention of GCC troops.[2] In this way, the Bahraini protestors' aspirations for democracy and respect of human rights were crushed on the suspicion of having ties with Iran and being part of transnational Shiʿism. The Shiʿi protestors were portrayed as the tools of foreign agents. Accordingly, they were seen as disloyal citizens.

The state has manipulated the politics of citizenship of inclusion and exclusion to its advantage. This chapter examines the citizenship policies. It assesses who the people were whose citizenship was revoked, why their citizenship was revoked, and what consequences these measures have had on individuals and families. Special attention is given to cases in which people have been stripped of their citizenship and sentenced to death. Moreover, the chapter examines the naturalisation policy of the state. Because at the same time as predominantly Shiʿi Bahrainis are having their citizenship revoked, the authorities are naturalising foreigners from

---

[2] Mahmoud Cherif Bassiouni, Nigel Rodley, Badria Al-Awadhi, Philippe Kirsch, and Mahnoush H. Arsanjani, *Report of the Bahrain Independent Commission of Inquiry* (2011), 383–5, http://www.bici.org.bh/BICIreportEN.pdf (accessed 8 March 2017).

Sunni-dominated countries on politically motivated grounds. The chapter shows the sectarian nature of Bahrain's politics of citizenship of inclusion and exclusion. Furthermore, it highlights how the authorities' understanding of citizenship is centred on the idea of personal loyalty to the ruler. This in contrast to a rights-based definition expressed by protestors.[3] This chapter was finished in mid-June 2017 and all data are earlier than that date.

CITIZENSHIP REVOCATIONS

Bahraini authorities have within a period of less than five years, between November 2012 and June 2017, withdrawn citizenship from more than 450 Bahraini citizens. The number of citizenship revocations is on the rise; only during the first half-year of 2017 the number rose from 350 to at least 450, representing an increase of almost 30 per cent. The number is massive when taking into consideration the small population of Bahrain. The resident population is 1.4 million, of which less than half holds Bahraini citizenship. Approximately 600,000 are Bahraini citizens, whereas the rest are mostly migrant workers. The citizenship revocations shed light on the exclusionary policies of the state. Individuals who have their citizenship revoked are transmitted from the status or position of 'citizen' to 'non-citizen'. They are deprived of the rights and duties they had once enjoyed. The citizenship revocations target dissidents the authorities no longer regard as members of the political community. These individuals are predominately Shiʿi.

The Citizenship Act of 1963 states that citizenship can be revoked only 'by order of His Majesty the Governor', i.e., the King. However, over the past years, similar powers have been given to other authorities. In a 2014 amendment to the Citizenship Act the power to revoke citizenship was extended to the Ministry of Interior. Furthermore, in 2013, the Law of Protecting Society from Terrorist Acts of 2006 was amended. The law now permits the judiciary to revoke citizenship of individuals accused of terrorist acts after the approval of the King. As a result, three authorities have the power to revoke citizenship: the King, the Ministry of Interior, and the courts. The King has revoked the citizenship in

---

[3] The chapter is based on my MA thesis *From Citizen to Non-Existent: A Study of Bahrain's Politics of Citizenship* (2017), MA, University of Oslo, submitted in May 2017. Data were collected from two sources; my own interviews with Bahraini activists in exile whose citizenship had been revoked and official Bahraini documents, reports by human rights groups, UN documents, and mass media inputs.

four cases, while the Ministry of Interior is responsible for 104 citizenship revocations.[4] Bahraini courts have issued the remaining – around 350 – revocations.

The opportunities to re-obtain Bahraini citizenship are minimal. The Citizenship Act stipulates that re-obtainment can only happen by a decree from the King. There have been attempts of legal appeals against decisions of citizenship revocation since 2012, but none have succeeded.

Who Are Excluded?

On 6 November 2012, 31 individuals had their citizenship revoked by a decree from the Ministry of Interior.[5] These revocations were the first of their kind since the outset of the 14 February Movement in 2011. However, revocations of citizenship have also taken place in the past, but to a lesser extent compared with the present rate. Among those who had their citizenship revoked in 2012 were former parliamentarians, human rights defenders, and Shiʿi clerics. One of them was Abdulhadi Khalaf, a member of the Bahraini parliament from 1973 to 1975, and a professor of sociology in Lund University, Sweden, since 1990. UN Special Rapporteurs note that '[t]he majority of the published names are reportedly Shiite political activists'. They write that the revocations 'may be directly related to these persons' work for the defence and promotion of human rights in Bahrain'.[6] One woman had her citizenship revoked in 2012. After 2012, all those excluded through the mechanism of citizenship revocation were men.

After a break in 2013, a total of 21 individuals had their citizenship revoked in 2014 by three separate court orders. However, the instrument

---

4 However, an assessment of the original legal documents of the revocation decrees (as found at http://www.legalaffairs.gov.bh/ (accessed 16 March 2017)) that are reportedly issued by the Ministry (according to Bahrain News Agency), shows that the documents are signed by the King, the Prime Minister and the Minister of Interior. Thus, perhaps, in practice the King approves the revocations by the Ministry, similarly what the law requires in cases of revocations by court orders.

5 Critics highlight that the 2012 revocations by the Ministry of Interior were themselves unlawful because the Ministry was granted the power to revoke citizenship for the first time in the 2014 amendment of the Citizenship Act.

6 UN OHCHR, 'Mandates of the Special Rapporteur on the Promotion and Protection of the Right to Freedom of Opinion and Expression; the Special Rapporteur on the Rights to Freedom of Peaceful Assembly and of Association; the Special Rapporteur on Freedom of Religion or Belief; and the Special Rapporteur on the Situation of Human Rights Defenders', Statement No. BHR 12/2012, 29 November 2012, https://spdb.ohchr.org/hrdb/22nd/public_-_AL_Bahrain_29.11.12_(12.2012).pdf (accessed 20 November 2017).

of citizenship revocation was most extensively applied in 2015 and 2016 – with 2017 as a third year.[7] Two hundred and eight and 90 revocations took place in 2015 and 2016, respectively. Most of these (221) were a result of trials and were issued by Bahraini courts based on charges of terrorism. Most of the people stripped of their citizenship are not prominent members of the opposition; often they are ordinary individuals or protestors. For example, on 11 June 2015, 56 Bahraini nationals were stripped of their citizenship in the same court case. Twenty-seven of them were students, and nine were below the age of 18. Furthermore, 41 of them were from Bani Jamra, an exclusively Shiʿi village.[8]

The most extensive incident of citizenship revocation happened on 31 January 2015. On that day, 72 individuals had their citizenship revoked by a single decree by the Ministry of Interior. One of these individuals, doctor Ebrahim Al-Aradi, said:

> I found my name on the list of 72 Bahrainis stripped of their citizenship. They had mixed our names – among us were authors, journalists, and religious scholars – with names of individuals fighting for Daesh [ISIS]. [This was] to deceive the international community into believing the government revoked the citizenship of all these people because they are terrorists.[9]

Some of the ISIS affiliates on the list had appeared on videos and officially declared their affiliation to ISIS and threatened Bahraini authorities. For example, one – identified as Salman Turki, who was number 35 on the list – said in a video that 'we will return to Bahrain not with our passports, but with our weapons'.[10] Another – Abdulaziz Al-Jowder, number 41 on the list – carried out a suicide attack in Iraq on ISIS' behalf, as proclaimed by the terrorist organisation the same month the revocations were issued.[11] The names of 20 ISIS and Al-Qaida members were inserted on the same list with around 50 peaceful Shiʿi activists. One of the activists

---

7 As proof of the increased use of citizenship revocations, 21 individuals had their citizenship revoked during a single week in March in 2017, while the same number of revocations was issued throughout 2014.

8 Bahrain Institute for Rights and Democracy (BIRD), 'Full Documentation (Cases) [Revoked Nationalities 2012–2015]', 2016, http://birdbh.org/wp-content/uploads/2016/02/Revoked-Nationalities2012–15.pdf (accessed 20 November 2017), 6.

9 Author interview with Ebrahim Al-Aradi, 28 February 2017.

10 Bahrain Mirror, 'Bahraini Isis Members Respond to Stripping their Nationalities: We Will Enter Bahrain by Arms Not Passports, and We Will Behead the King', *Bahrain Mirror,* 5 February 2015, http://bahrainmirror.com/news/22065.html (accessed 20 November 2017).

11 Bahrain Mirror, 'داعش 'تعلن عن قيام عبدالعزيز الجودر' أبوهاجر البحريني 'بتنفيذ عملية انتحارية بالعراق [ISIS Announce that Abdulaziz Al-Jowder'Abo Hajar Al-Bahraini'

is Sayed Ahmed Alwadaei, director of advocacy for the Bahrain Institute for Rights and Democracy (BIRD), a UK-based human rights group. Alwadaei writes, '[t]he message has never been clearer: the government of Bahrain views us, who advocate for democracy, human rights and change in Bahrain, as equals to the Jihadi-terrorists of ISIS'.[12]

Besides the decrees of September 2012 and January 2015, the third – and so far last – instance of citizenship revocation by the Ministry of Interior took place on 20 June 2016. Then Sheikh Issa Qassim, Bahrain's most prominent Shiʿi cleric, was stripped of his citizenship. The European Parliament, protesting the citizenship revocations of Sheikh Qassim and others, called on the Bahraini authorities 'to end any discrimination against the Shia population'.[13] As noted by several sources, the overwhelming majority of the approximately 450 individuals stripped of their citizenship are Shiʿis. According to a human rights report, '[a]s many as 292 of those [more than 330 who were reported as of January 2017] who have had their citizenship revoked are members of the country's marginalized Shia majority'.[14] That is almost nine out of ten. Moreover, revocations are still issued. For example, the courts revoked the citizenship of at least 100 individuals during the first six months of 2017. All were Shiʿi protestors except for one who was charged with joining ISIS.

Few of those who have their citizenship revoked have a citizenship other than the Bahraini one. The majority, both those in exile and almost all those still inside Bahrain, therefore end up stateless.

Carried out a Suicide Attack in Iraq], *Bahrain Mirror,* 27 January 2015, http://bahrainmirror.com/news/21890.html (accessed 20 November 2017).

12 Sayed Ahmed Alwadaei, 'We Are Human Rights Defenders, but Bahrain Says We're Terrorists', *The Guardian*, 9 February 2015, https://www.theguardian.com/commentisfree/2015/feb/09/human-rights-defenders-bahrain-says-terrorists (accessed 20 November 2017).

13 European Parliament, 'European Parliament Resolution on Bahrain (2016/2808, Rsp)', 6 July 2016, http://www.europarl.europa.eu/sides/getDoc.do?pubRef=-//EP//TEXT+MOTION+P8–RC-2016–0900+0+DOC+XML+V0//EN (accessed 20 November 2017).

14 Americans for Democracy and Human Rights in Bahrain (ADHRB), Bahrain Institute for Rights and Democracy (BIRD), and Bahrain Center for Human Rights (BCHR), 'Bahrain's Third Cycle UPR: A Record of Repression', 2017, http://www.adhrb.org/wp-content/uploads/2017/03/2017.2.28_Web-Version_ADHRB_BCHR_BIRD_Bahrain-3rd-Cycle-UPR-Assessment.pdf (accessed 8 March 2017), 56.

Why Are They Excluded?

The Constitution of Bahrain (Article 17) states: 'A person inherently enjoying his Bahraini nationality cannot be stripped of his nationality except in case of treason, and such other cases as prescribed by law'. *Treason* is thus the declared reason of citizenship revocation according to the Constitution. However, in the last years, other laws which regulate this issue have been expanded. In each of the decrees by the Ministry of Interior and the King, the Citizenship Act of 1963 is mentioned. More concretely, reference is made to Article 10 (c), which was amended in 2014. It states that citizenship can be revoked of a Bahraini national 'if he causes damage to the interest of the state or takes action contrary to the duty of loyalty to it'. In some decrees, there is only a reference to the regulation in the Citizenship Act, followed by the names of those stripped of their citizenship. This was the case, for example, with the 31 revocations in 2012.

In the statement concerning 72 individuals who had their citizenship revoked in 2015, the Ministry of Interior had made reference to Article 10 (c) in the Citizenship Act and had listed ten accusations against the named. Among these accusations were: (1) Defaming the image of the regime, inciting against the regime and spreading false news to hinder the rules of the Constitution; (2) Carrying out a series of explosions so as to subvert homeland security and terrorise citizens; (3) Inciting and advocating regime change through illegal means; and (4) Belonging to terrorist groups fighting abroad.[15] Which of these accusations were directed to which of the 72 individuals remained unclear. Ali Abdulemam, a well-known Bahraini blogger who was named on the list, commented on this lack of information as follows:

> They provided a list of what they call 'the acts' (*al-af'al*) that we did so our citizenship deserved to be revoked. But it does not say that I as Ali Abdulemam did this and this. No, '72 did this'. It is a general statement that 'you are acting against the national security, you are involved in an armed movement'. I do not know which of these allegations applies to me.[16]

For Abdulemam, it is clear that the real reason is that he is 'active in exile for the pro-democracy movement'. He believes the government uses citizenship

---

[15] Ministry of Interior, 'MOI Statement: 72 Individuals Stripped of Citizenship', *Bahrain News Agency*, 31 January 2015, http://bna.bh/portal/en/news/651916 (accessed 20 November 2017).

[16] Author interview with Ali Abdulemam, a Bahraini blogger and activist exiled in the UK, 22 February 2017.

revocation 'as a weapon to punish the opposition'. The government wants to 'send a message to others to not call or go against the government loudly because it might have the same consequences as Ali got or others got', he explained.[17] Al-Aradi agrees with this view. He believes his citizenship was revoked because he practised his duty to save injured protestors during the 2011 uprising and because he spoke to the international media about the human rights situation in Bahrain.[18] Al-Aradi, like the others on the list, never received a formal personal letter concerning the decision to revoke his citizenship. He just heard the decision through official news agencies.

In the case of stripping Sheikh Issa Qassim of his citizenship in June 2016, the Ministry of Interior justified the decision with the statement that Sheikh Qassim 'encouraged sectarianism and violence'. They claimed that he had 'established organizations that follow an external religious political authority' and contributed to undermine 'the rights of the people and the rule of law'.[19] These accusations are refuted by Professor Emile Nakhleh, who has followed the situation in Bahrain for a long time. He writes:

> Reading the charges in the government's citizenship revocation statement is baffling to those who have followed Sheikh Isa Qassim's peaceful activism on behalf of human rights, democracy, and inclusion. He has always promoted reconciliation between the Shia majority and the Sunni minority under the al-Khalifa rule.[20]

The citizenship revocations by Bahraini courts have also been criticised. The courts, which have issued around 350 citizenship revocations until June 2017, base their decisions on the Law of Protecting Society from Terrorist Acts of 2006. This anti-terrorism legislation has been internationally criticised for its vague definition of 'terrorism'. For example, according to Article 1, terrorism has the purpose to 'obstruct public authorities . . . from doing their work' and to 'harm national unity'. This has enabled the state to prosecute dissidents and to restrict people's freedom of expression.[21] Moreover, the wide-scale application of the anti-terrorism law is alarming – which signifies that something is abnormal. In 2013, there was

---

17 Ibid.

18 Author interview with Al-Aradi.

19 Ministry of Interior, 'Citizenship Revoked for Creating Extremist Sectarian Environment', *Bahrain News Agency*, 20 June 2016, http://www.bna.bh/portal/en/news/733106 (accessed 20 November 2017).

20 Emile Nakhleh, 'Bahrain's Unending Repression: Enough Already!' *LobeLog*, 2016, https://lobelog.com/bahrains-unending-repression-enough-already/ (accessed 20 November 2017).

21 Bahrain Center for Human Rights, 'The Terrorism Law in Bahrain: A Tool to Silence Dissidents', 2014, http://www.bahrainrights.org/sites/default/files/

on average one terrorism case every ten days.[22] This is a very high number for a country with such a small population as Bahrain. Among those tried under this law are human rights defenders, political leaders, peaceful protestors, and even children. According to the Bahrain Center for Human Rights, there is a pattern 'which clearly shows the targeting of a specific religious sect and political orientation' under the banner of 'terrorism'.[23]

Furthermore, where the anti-terrorism legislation is applied, suspects are often subjected to torture and other ill-treatment under interrogation. In all terrorism cases Amnesty International examined, the 'detainees were never allowed access to their lawyer when interrogated at the CID [Criminal Investigations Directorate] and later their lawyers faced restrictions defending them'.[24] The confessions obtained under such circumstances are often the only 'evidence' to sentence the suspects, including revoking their citizenship and/or sentencing them to death.[25] Amnesty International emphasises that the law itself empowers the police and Public Prosecution 'to act without any restrictions when investigating terrorist acts, putting detainees held in connection with terrorism-related investigations at a high risk of torture and other ill-treatment'.[26]

These examples show that the authorities thus exclude and revoke citizenship of Bahraini nationals on pretence of terrorism. The accusations of terrorism are clearly expressed in the court cases, in which defendants are often forced to sign prepared confessions under the threat of torture. The Ministry of Interior also bases its decrees on similar accusations. This is evident in the ten-point list published in connection with 72 revocations in January 2015, where human rights defenders were named along with ISIS suspects.

The foregoing signifies that any political threat or challenge directed against the ruler is interpreted as something which 'causes damage to the interest of the state'. In this way, the state is understood to be synonymous with the ruler, and accordingly, criticism of the ruler is interpreted as 'tak[ing] action contrary to the duty of loyalty to [the state]'. Shiʿi citizens appear as the greatest victims of the exclusionary policies by being

---

Terrorism%20Laws%20in%20Bahrain%20–%20FINAL.pdf (accessed 20 November 2017), 3–4.

22 Ibid, 5.

23 Ibid, 3.

24 Amnesty International, 'Bahrain: New Anti-Terrorism Amendments Pave the Way to Further Abuses', 16 December 2014, https://www.amnesty.org/en/documents/mde11/051/2014/en/ (accessed 20 November 2017).

25 Bahrain Center for Human Rights, 'The Terrorism Law in Bahrain', 6.

26 Amnesty International, 'Bahrain: New Anti-Terrorism Amendments'.

particularly suspected of disloyalty. That reflects a concept of citizenship that frequently excludes members of a certain sect.

What Are They Excluded from?

Citizenship defines an individual's legal status in a state. As a non-citizen, the individual is not entitled to many, if not most, rights and resources available to Bahraini citizens. Among those rights is, firstly, the right to education. Primary and secondary education are free and compulsory for all citizens. When the individual is no longer recognised as a citizen, he is not legally entitled to the education provided by the state. This includes state-sponsored scholarships and grants to pursue higher education. The consequences for those stripped of their rights to education are not fully visible yet because the youths who are stripped of their citizenship are imprisoned. Most of them, if not all, will be grown men when they complete their sentences. Therefore, Bahrain will likely get a number of stateless men with a low level of education as a result of the citizenship revocations.

Secondly, people stripped of their citizenship face problems in the job market. Since they are no longer citizens, they have to apply for a job licence as migrant workers. To get a job licence in Bahrain, you need an employer who can sponsor you.[27] Accordingly, many were dismissed right after the revocation of their citizenship. They face problems of re-employment because few employers are inclined to sponsor stateless individuals. Furthermore, they cannot apply for a job licence because they have to hand in their identification papers such as passports and national ID-cards to the Immigration Office after the revocation of their citizenship.[28] Those serving sentences inside prison will probably face the same difficulties in finding employment after they are released.

Thirdly, those who have had their citizenship revoked face issues as residents in Bahrain. As non-citizens, they have to apply for a residence permit in their own homeland. However, they cannot complete such an application because they cannot identify themselves. They therefore end up as 'illegal residents' in Bahrain. As a result, many have been forcibly deported, while others risk the same fate. For example, at least six

---

27 Bahrain Center for Human Rights, 'Statelessness in Bahrain' (2014), http://bahrainrights.org/sites/default/files/Stateless%20in%20Bahrain%20-%20Final.pdf?_ga=2.150010486.1371990683.1511192594-1090663098.1502055609 (accessed 20 November 2017), 6.

28 Amnesty International, 'Harassment of Bahrainis Rendered Stateless', 30 October 2014, https://www.amnesty.org/en/documents/mde11/042/2014/en/ (accessed 20 November 2017).

individuals, including lawyer Taymour Karimi, were deported during the first half-year of 2016 after receiving summons from Public Prosecution that they had violated Bahrain's immigration and residency law.[29] Those currently serving in Bahraini prisons will probably face deportation after completing their sentences. Bahrainis who have already been deported had the choice between three destinations: Iraq, Lebanon and Turkey.[30]

Fourthly, the right to movement and travel are restricted for those who are stripped of their citizenship. Those who reside inside Bahrain (although 'illegally', according to the authorities) have to avoid checkpoints because they lack identification documents. The increased number of checkpoints in the aftermath of the 2011 uprising exacerbates the situation for this group. People have been arrested at checkpoints because they lack identification papers.[31] Moreover, the opportunities to legally travel abroad are absent without a passport. Other opportunities to leave the country are highly restricted as Bahrain is an island state with only one causeway linking it to neighbouring Saudi Arabia. The only (legal) way for an individual revoked of his citizenship to leave the country is by being deported by the authorities – though it will be a one-way ticket without any prospect of returning.

Those deprived of their Bahraini citizenship in exile also experience difficulties in movement and travel. As most of them end up stateless, the country they live in must provide them with identification and travel documents. Even then, however, they would still not able to travel to Bahrain and are thus kept away from their families. For example, Abdulhadi Khalaf, even though he holds Swedish citizenship, notes:

> I cannot visit my family in Bahrain including my 94 years old mother. [Like other Bahrainis whose citizenship have been revoked], I became a foreigner in the eyes of Bahraini authorities.[32]

In addition, he and others whose Bahraini citizenship has been revoked are often not able to travel to other countries in the GCC. This has implications for Khalaf's academic work. He is now unable to conduct fieldwork in the region. He cannot participate in regional conferences nor

---

[29] Human Rights Watch, 'Bahrain: Stop Deportations of Nationals', 20 March 2016, https://www.hrw.org/news/2016/03/20/bahrain-stop-deportations-nationals (accessed 20 November 2017).

[30] Bahrain Mirror, 'Dr. Masoud Jahromi in Interview with Bahrain Mirror: I Waved Goodbye to the One Who Deported Me', *Bahrain Mirror*, 1 May 2016, http://bahrainmirror.com/en/news/30834.html (accessed 20 November 2017).

[31] Amnesty International, 'Harassment of Bahrainis Rendered Stateless'.

[32] Author interview with Abdulhadi Khalaf, 2 March 2017.

have direct contacts with colleagues in the GCC region and perhaps in other countries in the Middle East.[33]

Fifthly, those who lose their citizenship tend to lose the right to control real estate and other assets they own.[34] They are not allowed to buy land or sell their property. Furthermore, their bank accounts have been frozen. In this regard, Ali Abdulemam said:

> My retirement package is stolen by the government since my citizenship was revoked. Under my son's bank account, I had put an amount of money for him; I cannot move it or do anything with it because my citizenship is revoked.[35]

Khalaf had a similar experience. 'Our family house, where my mother lives, is in my name. It is considered, now, a "house of a foreigner". Accordingly, Khalaf cannot enjoy subsidies which citizens are entitled to. 'This means that my mother's bills for electricity and water supplies and other municipal services have been increased following the lifting of government subsidies on non-citizens', Khalaf explained.[36]

Sixthly, the loss of the Bahraini citizenship impacts the right to health care for individuals residing in Bahrain. Public hospitals offer free health services to citizens. For those stripped of their citizenship, even visiting private clinics may be difficult because they lack identification documents and may not be able to cover the expenses.

Finally, they also lose the right to receive state-subsidised social benefits.[37] The Bahraini government offers financial support to low-income inhabitants who have Bahraini citizenship. Those who lose their citizenship can no longer receive such benefits. This degrades the economic situation of an already disadvantaged group. An important social benefit is subsidised state housing. Bahrainis – the Shiʿis in particular – wait sometimes for decades to be granted a house. Currently, more than 50,000 Bahrainis wait for housing, while the available units are distributed disproportionally, with Shiʿi citizens under-prioritised.[38] When their citizenship is revoked, Bahrainis have to give up their housing aspirations once and for all.

---

33 Committee on Academic Freedom, 'Letter Concerning Revocation of Citizenship of 31 Bahraini Nationals', *Jadaliyya,* 11 December 2012, http://www.jadaliyya.com/Details/27599/Letter-Concerning-Revocation-of-Citizenship-of-31-Bahraini-Nationals (accessed 18 March 2018).

34 Bahrain Center for Human Rights, 'Statelessness in Bahrain', 6.

35 Author interview with Abdulemam.

36 Author interview with Khalaf.

37 Bahrain Center for Human Rights, 'Statelessness in Bahrain', 6.

38 Americans for Democracy and Human Rights in Bahrain (ADHRB), Bahrain Institute for Rights and Democracy (BIRD) and Bahrain Center for

The seven points above illustrate the rights citizens have and of which they are deprived in case of citizenship revocation. Human rights defender Sayed Ahmed Alwadaei summarises the situation:

> If someone got his citizenship revoked, it means he no longer exists within any system. They are no longer treated as citizens. Their bank accounts will be closed. They have no access to public health. They will be dismissed from their jobs. They will be treated as someone who is illegally residing in the country. If they have a state house given by the council, this will be taken away from them as well.[39]

Alwadaei stressed that Bahrainis whose citizenship has been revoked are 'treated as non-existing persons in the state'. Ebrahim Al-Aradi called the citizenship revocation a 'civil execution' of an individual. 'You [the state] made no existence for him in the country he is in', he stressed. 'It is like you [the state] have executed him civilly.'[40]

Implications for Families

Alwadaei furthermore stressed the fact that 'the implications are not only for the individuals. It goes far beyond, to their entire family, because any benefits your family receives from the state will be immediately stopped.'[41] The impact is also on citizenship rights of new-borns. They have no right to obtain Bahraini citizenship because their fathers do not have it anymore. The Bahraini citizenship is given to children through descent, in which the father must be a Bahraini citizen, according to the Citizenship Act (Article 4). Alwadaei emphasised the fact that 'mothers cannot forward the citizenship to her children – it can only happen through the father. This is in itself a discrimination within the law.'[42] So for people who have had their citizenship revoked, even though they are married to Bahraini women, it still means that their new-borns are deprived of Bahraini citizenship.

Alwadaei, who was stripped of his citizenship in 2015, said, 'that same year I had my first child and he has no right to obtain the Bahraini citizenship'. Alwadaei stressed that the case is the same for others in exile as well

---

Human Rights (BCHR), 'Apart in their Own Land', Volume 2, 2015, http://birdbh.org/wp-content/uploads/2015/09/ADHRB_ApartLand_Vol2_Web.pdf (accessed 20 November 2017), 32–4.

39 Author interview with Sayed Ahmed Alwadaei, 21 February 2017.

40 Author interview with Al-Aradi.

41 Author interview with Alwadaei.

42 Ibid.

as those inside Bahrain. Their children end up stateless unless 'the state which they live in provides citizenship for the stateless or for new-born children'. He points out that the Bahraini government is performing a 'collective punishment on the entire family' for the individual stripped of his citizenship.[43] Ali Abdulemam, who like Alwadaei is a political refugee in the UK, agreed on this point. In February 2017, he said:

> The revoking of citizenship will not stop at me as a person. It will go up after my kids and my family. My wife, for example, is pregnant and is supposed to deliver within one month. The baby will not have his citizenship as a Bahraini and he will not have a citizenship here in the UK. So this will cause some problems for us.[44]

The case is the same for Ebrahim Al-Aradi, who has a daughter who is not entitled to the Bahraini citizenship. He said, 'It is very sad when you see your daughter grows up and it is her right to own a citizenship. It is her right to be in her country.' He wondered, 'What is the fault of this little girl so she has to be punished?' From Al-Aradi's point of view, the biggest problem is this coming generation without the Bahraini citizenship. 'Those are the greatest victims', Al-Aradi stressed, 'our children who are born stateless, without a Bahraini citizenship.'[45] This generation without the Bahraini citizenship signifies that the number of excluded individuals as a result of citizenship revocations is higher than the approximately 450 who have been stripped of their citizenship since 2012.

For the stateless children inside Bahrain, the implications are similar to those of their fathers who live as non-citizens in the country. The parents report difficulties getting identification documents for their children. This even includes birth certificates. Furthermore, they do not have free access to health care. This has resulted in new-borns not receiving the ordinary vaccinations provided to others. Without identification documents, they additionally cannot apply for public schools.[46] Simply, their children suffer the same deprivations individuals stripped of citizenship suffer from. Alwadaei stressed the fact that 'this is a very early generation. You talk about 2012 when this began, but the consequences will last for many longer years.'[47]

---

43 Ibid.

44 Author interview with Abdulemam.

45 Author interview with Al-Aradi.

46 Bahrain Center for Human Rights, 'Bahrain: Children without Citizenship', 2017, http://bahrainrights.org/sites/default/files/BCHR Children Without Citizenship – March 2017.pdf (accessed 20 November 2017), 8–11.

47 Author interview with Alwadaei.

For individuals who were deported or who managed to flee the country beforehand, their families often go into self-imposed exile to live with their husbands or fathers. However, to travel out of Bahrain may be problematic for those family members. There have been incidents where family members of political activists have been subjected to reprisals by Bahraini authorities for the activities of their relatives. Wives have been held at airports, interrogated and threatened due to their husbands' activities.[48] Alwadaei, whose wife was subjected to such reprisals in October 2016, said, 'Usually, if they cannot get to you, they go after your family.'[49] For others, simply to travel out of the country in order to reunite with their husbands and fathers is impossible. That is the case of families with stateless children inside Bahrain. Without identification documents, the children and usually their mothers must remain in Bahrain.[50] In such cases, the families are forced to live separately.

DEATH SENTENCING STATELESS INDIVIDUALS

In some cases in which the courts have issued citizenship revocations, the defendants were also sentenced to death. At least 13 individuals, all of them Shiʿi, were made stateless and simultaneously sentenced to death between February 2015 and June 2017. Three stateless individuals were executed on 15 January 2017, which were the first executions of Bahrainis since 1996.[51] Of the remaining 10 defendants, eight were sentenced during the six months after the executions in January 2017. This signifies a massive increase in the use of citizenship revocations along with death sentences lately. In these cases, Bahraini authorities exclude these individuals *de jure* by depriving them of citizenship rights, and they proceed to exclude them *de facto* from the fundamental right to life.

Like others who have been stripped of their citizenship by court orders, the three executed by firing squad in January 2017 were convicted of terrorism. One of them was reportedly illiterate, another was a schoolteacher, and the third was a 21 year-old youth. They were accused of attacking and

---

[48] Human Rights Watch, 'Bahrain: Activist's Family Targeted', 6 March 2017, https://www.hrw.org/news/2017/03/06/bahrain-activists-family-targeted (accessed 20 November 2017).

[49] Author interview with Alwadaei.

[50] Bahrain Center for Human Rights, 'Bahrain: Children without Citizenship', 8–11.

[51] One execution took place in 2010 in which a Bangladeshi was executed in Bahrain.

killing three police officers by planting a bomb in the village of al-Daih in 2014.[52] One of the police officers was an Emirati, reflecting the continued presence of riot police from neighbouring countries in Bahraini streets after GCC troops were invited to help to crush the 2011 uprising. The suspects were found guilty of bombing the officers and were sentenced on 26 February 2015. On 9 January 2017, the sentences were upheld. Less than a week later, the three stateless individuals were executed.[53]

Amnesty International reports that the suspects claimed they were tortured to make confessions.[54] One of the defendants, schoolteacher Abbas Al-Samea, had before the execution made public statements through leaked videos from prison, protesting his and the others' innocence. He stated that he and his family had been targeted for a long time, and that he was charged with terrorism in retaliation for coming from a well-known oppositional family and a village that is in the forefront of the protests. Al-Samea spoke indignantly about the treatment he was subjected to in what he called the 'torture centres'. He said:

> The brutal physical and psychological torture was unbearable. My family were threatened, and the situation escalated to a level that even my lawyers were threatened with dismissals and revoking of their [job] licence if they withdraw from the court hearings.[55]

As a result of the torture, Al-Samea told his mother in 2015 that 'I am dying. I am being executed every day.'[56] The case of Al-Samea and the other convicted in the same case exemplifies the fact that ordinary individuals belonging to the Shiʿi community in Bahrain are subjected to harsh sentences by being revoked of their citizenship and

---

[52] Americans for Democracy and Human Rights in Bahrain (ADHRB), Bahrain Institute for Rights and Democracy (BIRD), Bahrain Center for Human Rights (BCHR) and European Centre for Democracy and Human Rights (ECDHR), 'Bahrain Executes Stateless Torture Victims Following King Hamad's Authorization', 15 January 2017, http://www.adhrb.org/2017/01/bahrain-executes-stateless-torture-victims-following-king-hamads-authorisation/ (accessed 20 November 2017).

[53] Ibid.

[54] Amnesty International, 'Bahrain: New Anti-Terrorism Amendments'.

[55] Abbas Al-Samea, 'مترجم: رسالة المحكوم بالاعدام المعتقل عباس السميع للشعب من سجنه [Translated: Statement by Death Sentenced Inmate Abbas Al-Samea to the People from His Prison]' *Bahrainalyoum3 YouTube Channel*, 2 June 2016, https://youtu.be/ItNfDt3lgSY (accessed 20 November 2017).

[56] Bahrain Mirror, "بلا أسنان أمامية وأنف مكسور وأذن تنزف.. عباس السميع: أنا أعدم كل يوم" [Without Front Teeth, A Broken Nose and a Bleeding Ear. Abbas Al-Samea: I am Being Executed Every Day]", *Bahrain Mirror*, 13 April 2015, http://bahrainmirror.com/news/23383.html (accessed 20 November 2017).

sentenced to death. In fact, human rights groups state that Al-Samea was at the school he worked at as a teacher when the bombing he was convicted of took place.[57] This case furthermore illustrates how court sentences are based on confessions extracted by torture. The others on death row in Bahrain have similar stories. For example, two young Shiʿi men (20 and 21 years old), accused of killing a policeman in the village of Karbabad, were sentenced to death and had their citizenship revoked on 6 June 2017. They also claim they made confessions after being beaten in the head, face and groin, which caused severe pain in the ear canal of one defendant, while the other had his nose broken. None of them have received medical treatment in the aftermath of their torture.[58]

The cases of stateless individuals who have been sentenced to death further illustrate the severity of Bahrain's policy of exclusion. In these cases, the authorities proceed to physically exclude Shiʿi Bahrainis by means of execution.

NATURALISATIONS

At the same time as Bahraini nationals are having their citizenship revoked – and, in certain cases, being executed – naturalisation of foreigners is taking place. The practice, like the revocation of citizenship, is not a new phenomenon. What is new is that during the past few years it has increased. The Citizenship Act of 1963 (Article 6) stipulates certain residency and language requirements for foreigners to become eligible for Bahraini citizenship. However, it also declares that citizenship can be granted to anyone 'by order of His Majesty the Governor', i.e., the King. On account of this royal prerogative, foreigners have been naturalised in Bahrain without having fulfilled the necessary residency and language requirements.[59]

---

57 ADHRB, BIRD, BCHR and ECDHR, 'Bahrain Executes Stateless Torture Victims'.

58 Bahrain Institute for Rights and Democracy (BIRD), 'Bahraini Court Issues Two New Death Sentences amid Torture Allegations', 8 June 2017, http://birdbh.org/2017/06/bahraini-court-issues-two-new-death-sentences-amid-torture-allegations/ (accessed 20 November 2017).

59 Jane Kinninmont, 'Bahrain: Beyond the Impasse', *Chatham House (The Royal Institute of International Affairs)*, 2012, https://www.chathamhouse.org/sites/files/chathamhouse/public/Research/Middle East/pr0612kinninmont.pdf (accessed 20 November 2017), 18.

Who Are Included?

The naturalisations are commonly linked to the mass-recruitment of foreign Sunnis to serve in Bahrain's security sector. The Ministry of Defence and Ministry of Interior are hiring security forces and police staff from abroad, while almost totally excluding Shi'i citizens from the national security apparatus. The total percentage of Shi'i Bahrainis in the security services is believed to be about 2–5 per cent, while they constitute up to 70 per cent of the population.[60] It is estimated that at least 95 per cent of the military personnel in the Bahrain Defense Force belong to the Sunni creed, while the same is 90 per cent or more among the police forces.[61] Many of them are native Sunni Bahrainis. For example, a recent study shows that 17 per cent of native Sunni men work in the military or police.[62] However, foreign-born Sunnis form an even larger proportion. They are recruited to serve in the security services and in exchange are often granted the Bahraini citizenship.

In 1998, it was estimated that around 8,000 to 10,000 Sunni families from Jordan, Syria, Pakistan and Yemen had been given the Bahraini citizenship. The men were reportedly working in the security services. In total, the families were estimated to represent 40,000 to 50,000 new citizens, which in 1998 were equal to around 13 per cent of the native population.[63] In 2002, in the run-up to Bahrain's first parliamentary election in decades, 20,000 individuals from the al-Dawasir tribe in Saudi Arabia were reportedly naturalised. Furthermore, they were brought to Bahrain in order to cast votes in the election, according to interviews made with members of the al-Dawasir tribe in June 2002.[64] Thus, in addition to being included through gaining access to citizenship and gaining access to state services such as state houses, they rapidly obtained political rights. Therefore, these naturalisations are criticised for being a deliberate attempt by the state to diminish the voice of the Shi'i majority.

In 2007 a census revealed that the resident population was 42 per

---

[60] Ian Siperco, 'Bahrain's Sectarian Challenge', *Middle East Policy Council*, 2010, http://www.mepc.org/articles-commentary/commentary/bahrain-s-sectarian-challenge (accessed 20 November 2017).

[61] ADHRB, BIRD and BCHR, 'Bahrain's Third Cycle UPR: A Record of Repression', 174–5.

[62] Justin Gengler, *Group Conflict and Political Mobilization in Bahrain and the Arab Gulf: Rethinking the Rentier State* (Bloomington: Indiana University Press, 2015), 114.

[63] Mansoor Al-Jamri, 'State and Civil Society in Bahrain', *Middle East Studies Association*, 6 December 1998, http://bahrain.wikia.com/wiki/State_and_Civil_Society_in_Bahrain (accessed 20 November 2017).

[64] Gengler, *Group Conflict and Political Mobilization*, 45.

cent higher than expected. Although the number of migrant workers in the country had probably increased, the increase is also ascribed to the 70,000 persons who had been granted Bahraini citizenship between 2001 and 2007.[65] Nevertheless, among those 70,000 were also native Bahrainis and their families who had returned to Bahrain from exile in 2001 after the King issued a royal amnesty to political opponents. However, in 2011, it was estimated that Bahraini citizens with a foreign origin could constitute up to 200,000 persons or one-third of the total citizenry.[66] All these numbers remain, however, scholarly estimations because of lack of transparency of the Bahraini government.

The exact naturalisation rate is unknown, but it is probably increasing as a consequence of hiring new security personnel after the 2011 uprising. All recruits tend to come from Sunni-majority countries and are Sunnis. For example, 2,500 Pakistani recruits joined the Bahraini military during a few months in 2011.[67] In 2014, 2,500 former retired officers from Jordan were serving in Bahrain's security apparatus.[68] Observers note that Bahraini authorities are practising 'demographic engineering' through mass naturalisation. They believe the on-going policy is intended to change the demographic balance between Shiʿis and Sunnis to transform the Shiʿi majority into a minority.[69] One of the critics of the naturalisation policy is Nabeel Rajab, president of the Bahrain Center for Human Rights.[70] Back in 2014, he had the following comment on citizenship revocations of nine individuals:

> [The authorities] are bringing thousands and thousands of people from abroad and naturalising them, while the indigenous populations' passports are revoked by the minister of the interior or the court.[71]

---

[65] Kinninmont, 'Bahrain: Beyond the Impasse', 18.

[66] Omar Al-Shehabi, 'Demography and Bahrain's Unrest', *Carnegie Endowment for International Peace*, 16 March 2011, http://carnegieendowment.org/sada/?fa=43079 (accessed 20 November 2017).

[67] Mujib Mashal, 'Pakistani Troops Aid Bahrain's Crackdown', *Al Jazeera English*, 30 July 2011, http://www.aljazeera.com/indepth/features/2011/07/2011725145048574888.html (accessed 20 November 2017).

[68] Nazgol Kafai and Ala'a Shehabi, 'The Struggle for Information: Revelations on Mercenaries, Sectarian Agitation and Demographic Engineering in Bahrain', *Jadaliyya*, 29 May 2014, http://www.jadaliyya.com/Details/30741/The-Struggle-for-Information-Revelations-on-Mercenaries,-Sectarian-Agitation,-and-Demographic-Engineering-in-Bahrain (accessed 18 March 2018).

[69] Ibid.

[70] Nabeel Rajab has been arrested since June 2016. He risks long-term imprisonment on charges related to freedom of expression.

[71] Alex MacDonald, 'Bahrain Strips Nine Nationals of Citizenship for Alleged Iran Ties', *Middle East Eye*, 7 August 2014, http://www.middleeasteye.net/news/bahrain-strips-nine-nationals-citizenship-466606651(accessed 20 November 2017).

As it appears, the inclusion of new citizens follows the same sectarian lines as Bahrain's politics of exclusion. While foreign Sunnis are welcomed as new citizens of the state, access of native Shiʿis to Bahraini citizenship is being restricted. The former are hired in the security sector from which Shiʿis have for a long time been largely excluded. 'The government has made concerted efforts to erode Bahrain's Shiite majority, mostly by recruiting foreign-born Sunnis to become citizens and serve in the country's security forces', as Freedom House describes it.[72]

RATIONALES BEHIND THE POLICY OF INCLUSION AND EXCLUSION

The examination of Bahrain's citizenship policy of inclusion and exclusion signifies the state's sectarian motives. 'Shias are clearly being targeted on the basis of their religion', several UN rights experts pointed out in 2016. They mentioned the revocations of citizenship of many Shiʿis, including the senior Shiʿi cleric Sheikh Isa Qassim, as an example of 'the systematic harassment of the Shia population by the authorities in Bahrain'.[73] In fact, already in 2006, the 'Bandargate' report – named after the author Saleh al-Bandar, a British citizen who worked as an adviser to the Bahraini government at that time – revealed that the authorities deliberately aimed to exclude Shiʿis in order to 'improve the general situation of Sunnis'.[74] Observers note, Bahrain – along with Saudi Arabia – 'is the most often-cited example of state-sponsored anti-Shiism throughout history'.[75]

The regional setting enhances the perception of Bahraini Shiʿis as an out-group. Since the Islamic Revolution in Iran in 1979, the suspicion of Shiʿis has reportedly become more severe. They have repeatedly been accused of working as agents of Iran with the aim of establishing a Shiʿi

---

[72] Freedom House, 'Freedom in the World 2017: Bahrain', 2017, https://freedomhouse.org/report/freedom-world/2017/bahrain (accessed 20 November 2017).

[73] UN OHCHR, 'UN Rights Experts Urge Bahrain to End the Persecution of Shias', 16 August 2016, http://www.ohchr.org/EN/NewsEvents/Pages/DisplayNews.aspx?NewsID=20375&LangID=E – sthash.VhWQgfLj.dpuf (accessed 20 November 2017).

[74] Laurence Louër, *Shiism and Politics in the Middle East* (London: Hurst, 2012), 100–101.

[75] Laurence Louër, 'The State and Sectarian Identities in the Persian Gulf Monarchies: Bahrain, Saudi Arabia, and Kuwait in Comparative Perspective', in *Sectarian Politics in the Persian Gulf*, ed. Lawrence G. Potter (London: Hurst, 2013), 118.

government in Bahrain. This accusation was expressed in pro-governmental media during the 2011 uprising.[76] In addition, from time to time, Bahraini authorities claim they have caught terrorist groups with links to Iran and Shiʿi militant groups such as Hezbollah. Such claims have been voiced regularly since 1981. In that year, a group of Bahraini exiles from Iran was caught in Dubai airport, accused of planning a coup in Bahrain.[77] The credibility of such claims has been criticised, in particular the allegation of Iran's involvement in the 2011 uprising.[78] However, in light of the geopolitical rivalries in the region – predominantly between Saudi Arabia and Iran, which themselves overlap with the sectarian divide – the Bahraini government seems to suppose that Shiʿis cannot be trusted.

The propaganda of Shiʿis as traitors and a security threat feeds the view of the regime as a protector of Sunni interests. It manipulates the Sunni minority to seek regime protection from what is supposedly awaiting them in case of regime change: Shiʿi domination and Sunni degradation.[79] In this way, Bahraini authorities have invested in a divide and rule approach based on sectarianism in order to maintain their own power and rule.

CITIZENSHIP AS A LOYALTY-BASED GIFT VERSUS A RIGHT

The policies of inclusion and exclusion in Bahrain signify that the authorities' understanding of citizenship is centred on the idea of citizens as loyal subjects to the ruler. As a result, foreigners are hired from abroad and granted citizenship in (advance) reward for loyalty. The authorities perhaps believe that foreign-born Sunnis are more loyal and are easier to control than the native population, which from time to time has mobilised against the government – most recently during the Arab Uprisings in 2011. Contrastingly, native – predominantly Shiʿi – Bahrainis are having

---

76 Justin Gengler, 'Understanding Sectarianism in the Persian Gulf', in *Sectarian Politics in the Persian Gulf*, ed. Lawrence G. Potter (London: Hurst, 2013), 68–74; Kristin Smith Diwan, 'Royal Factions, Ruling Strategies and Sectarianism in Bahrain', in *Sectarian Politics in the Persian Gulf*, ed. Lawrence G. Potter (London: Hurst, 2013), 162–5.

77 Louër, 'The State and Sectarian Identities in the Persian Gulf Monarchies', 124.

78 Kinninmont, 'Bahrain: Beyond the Impasse', 20–2; Louër, *Shiism and Politics in the Middle East*, 95.

79 Kylie Moore-Gilbert, 'From Protected State to Protection Racket: Contextualising Divide and Rule in Bahrain', *Journal of Arabian Studies* 6(2) (2016): 163–81.

their citizenship revoked if they do not fulfil this expectation of the role of citizen as an obedient and loyal subject of the state. Oppositional activism, which is perceived as a threat to the ruler's grip on power, appears to be evidence of 'disloyalty'. In this way, the authorities target even ordinary individuals who are associated with a family, a village or a sect (read: Shi'i) that is known as being oppositional.

The deprivation of citizenship rights from people indicates that the authorities perceive these rights as privileges, which they can bestow on those who are loyal according to their perspective, while depriving them of those who they perceive as disloyal. Abdulhadi Khalaf stressed that the public policies signify that the Bahraini authorities treat citizenship as a 'gift' (*makrama*) which they can bestow upon loyal subjects and rescind from them at will. He states:

> [The] incidents of collective naturalization, along with cases of collective revocation of citizenship, resemble an official declaration of the idea that the ruling [family does] not consider citizenship to be a right for citizens . . .; rather they consider it a gift that they bestow upon the people. The ruling family reserves the right to grant or revoke this gift at any time.[80]

Khalaf points out that the authorities 'consider revocation of citizenship or passports as one of their tools to control their subjects'. According to him, '[c]itizenship, whether seen as a formal identification instrument, as a marker of political belonging, or a social identity, is contingent on the discretion of the ruler'. In this way, citizenship functions as a mechanism of differentiation between people. Ebrahim Al-Aradi emphasised that 'the 14 February uprising occurred precisely to return citizenship rights to [their] owners', i.e. the citizens rather than the rulers.[81] Thus, from the perspective of many (former) citizens, Bahraini citizenship does not live up to their expectation of citizenship as a provider of the rights based on a social contract. In this regard, Al-Aradi said:

> The Bahraini citizenship represents a charter of rights. Even when I had the Bahraini citizenship, I did not enjoy my rights. Now the picture is clear: We are taking your citizenship and accordingly your rights.[82]

The increased use of citizenship revocations is in this way adding to the long-running presence of differentiated citizenship in Bahrain, in which

---

80 Abdulhadi Khalaf, 'GCC Rulers and the Politics of Citizenship', *Al-Monitor*, 26 December 2012, http://www.al-monitor.com/pulse/politics/2012/12/gcc-rulers-use-citizenship.html (accessed 20 November 2017).
81 Author interview with Al-Aradi.
82 Ibid.

citizens have different access to public employment, state housing and high-ranking positions in the state. The demand for equal citizenship was precisely a main cause for the eruption of the uprising in 2011. The response from the authorities has been an extensive use of citizenship as a political tool to control the inhabitants under their jurisdiction. The ruling elite employ the 'gift' of citizenship to honour supporters and punish dissidents. According to Human Rights Watch, 'Bahrainis who dare speak out for change now risk not only arbitrary detention and torture but statelessness and deportation to an uncertain future.'[83,84]

CONCLUSION

In the hands of the Bahraini authorities the politics of citizenship have become a specific manipulative instrument of inclusion and exclusion by revoking people of their citizenship on the one hand and giving citizenship to loyal subjects on the other hand. The citizenship revocations are based on the suspicion that certain individuals are damaging the state's interests. These people are perceived as 'tak[ing] action contrary to the duty of loyalty to [the state]' (the Citizenship Act, Article 10c). The cases of citizenship revocations show that 'loyalty to the state' is understood to be synonymous with 'loyalty to the ruler'. It is not just activists as a whole who are targeted. Ordinary members of the Shiʿi community such as clerics, academics and even youth are suspected as a security threat due to their religious background, many of whom have already been deprived of their Bahraini citizenship.

At the same time as citizenship revocations take place, the Bahraini authorities are naturalising thousands from Sunni-majority countries, many of whom are recruited into the security services. In this way, Sunnis are included in spheres which Shiʿis are kept from. This signifies the sectarian nature of the politics of exclusionary and inclusionary citizenship.

This chapter furthermore examined what it implies to be deprived of citizenship rights. People who have their citizenship revoked lose the right to (1) education, (2) employment, (3) residency, (4) movement, (5)

---

83 Human Rights Watch, 'Bahrain: Citizenship Rights Stripped Away', 21 August 2014, https://www.hrw.org/news/2014/08/21/bahrain-citizenship-rights-stripped-away (accessed 20 November 2017).

84 Before this book was printed, the number of citizenship revocations had increased from 450 in June 2017 to 578 in mid-February 2018. The number of stateless Bahrainis in death row had become 18. At least eight individuals were deported during the first five weeks of 2018.

property, (6) health care, and (7) social benefits. These rights and services are given with an expectation of loyalty in exchange. When an individual is regarded as disloyal, he is accordingly deprived of these rights. Even his children born after the decision of citizenship revocation are deprived of these rights. Moreover, the citizenship revocations are sometimes followed by death sentences, of which some have already been carried out on stateless individuals.

The authorities' concept of citizenship appears thus to be centred on the idea of citizenship as a gift. The state – which, in many cases, is understood as synonymous with the ruler – gives citizenship and the related rights in exchange for loyalty. In this way, citizenship is used as a political tool to honour supporters and punish dissidents who are perceived as disloyal by the authorities. On a more general level, Bahrain's citizenship policy of inclusion and exclusion reflects a perception among rulers of the Gulf monarchies of the state as being the possession of the ruling dynasty, not of the citizens.

7. Citizenship in the 2014 Egyptian Constitution

Nathalie Bernard-Maugiron

The Egyptian Constitution of 2014 was praised as a secular document that enshrined greater rights for Egyptian citizens. The Constitution of 2012, by contrast, was labelled as that of an authoritarian Islamist state, at odds with standards of human rights.[1]

A thorough comparison of the 2014 and 2012 texts, however, challenges this binary narrative: the Constitution of 2014 is structurally very similar to those of 2012 and 1971, and there are more similarities than differences between the two documents, even though the religious provisions in the Constitution of 2012 received much attention. There are fewer references to religion in the Constitution of 2014, but the powers of the military and of the president were expanded, military trial of civilians was allowed, citizens were discriminated against on a religious basis, and the judiciary was entrenched without any accountability mechanism being provided. Furthermore, human rights provisions were relegated to the implementing legislation and come second to the protection of national security and the fight against terrorism.

---

[1] See, for instance, Mohamad Elmasri, 'Unpacking Anti-Muslim Brotherhood Discourse', *Jadaliyya*, 28 June 2013, accessed 20 September 2015, http://www.jadaliyya.com/pages/index/12466/unpacking-anti-muslim-brotherhood-discourse and 'Morsi myths: Re-examining justifications for Egypt's coup', *Middle East Eye*, 3 July 2013, accessed 20 September 2015, http://www.middleeasteye.net/fr/node/44836; L. Lavi, 'An Examination of Egypt's Draft Constitution Part I: Religion and State – The Most Islamic Constitution in Egypt's History', *MEMRI*, 3 December 2012, accessed 20 September 2015, http://www.memri.org/report/en/0/0/0/0/0/0/6846.htm; D. Serodio and C. Hulsman, *The 2014 Egyptian Constitution in Context: Perspectives from Egypt*, July 2015, accessed 20 September 2015, http://www.academia.edu/14738019/The_2014_Egyptian_Constitution_in_Context_Perspectives_from_Egypt_D._Serodio_and_C._Hulsman. See, however, H. Albrecht, 'Egypt's 2012 Constitution: Devil in the Details, not in Religion' (United States Institute of Peace, *Peace Brief*, 25 January 2013), accessed 23 September 2015, http://www.usip.org/sites/default/files/PB139–Egypt%E2%80%99s%202012%20Constitution.pdf.

A number of new human rights provisions were added, but lengthening the list of rights guaranteed by the Constitution will make little difference if there is no correlation with the political reality and if no enforcement and accountability mechanisms are provided. The implementation of the Constitution of 2014 has so far been very problematic from a human rights perspective.

This chapter will analyse the status of the citizen in the Constitution of 2014 by studying its drafting process to assess whether it was inclusive and allowed representation for a large number of citizens. An analysis of citizens' rights and implementation mechanisms established by the Constitution will then follow. If the Constitution of 2014 enshrined greater rights for citizens than previous texts, they have so far remained as theoretical as they were under the 1971 and 2012 documents.

A NON-INCLUSIVE DRAFTING PROCESS

Neither the 2012 nor the 2014 constitution-drafting processes were inclusive and participatory. In both cases, a major faction of society was ignored and the process was used by the most powerful groups to extend their advantage over their rivals and reinforce their position within the state.

An instrument of national unity, a constitution should be a consensual document, a product of negotiations that reflects the interests and powers of the different categories of citizens. However, both the 2012 Constituent Assembly and the 2014 Committee of 50 conceived constitution building as a short-term victory that involved only the dominant groups. Both drafting processes deepened political divides and exacerbated the political crisis by turning the Constitution into an instrument of power for one dominant faction rather than a social contract binding all citizens together.

The Constituent Assembly and the Constitution of 2012

The March 2011 Constitutional Declaration adopted by the Supreme Council of the Armed Forces (SCAF) after the removal of President Hosni Mubarak stipulated that a new constitution would be drafted by 100 members chosen by the Parliament. This document would be the first constitution to be drafted by an elected body. Previous basic laws had all been written by unrepresentative committees appointed by the executive. The newly elected Parliament, dominated by Islamists, nominated the members of the Constituent Assembly in March 2012. One month later, however, the Constituent Assembly was declared unconstitutional by the State Council (*Majlis al-Dawla*)[2] because half its members had been chosen from within the legislative Assembly. A second Constituent Assembly was elected in June, after SCAF threatened to appoint itself a body if the Parliament did not succeed in electing a new one. This new Constituent Assembly was assigned seats according to a deal between the representatives of 22 parties and the head of SCAF,[3] even though the elections resulted in a majority of more than 60 per cent for the Islamists. Seven women were elected, of whom five were members of the Muslim Brotherhood. Most non-Islamist members withdrew from the Assembly during the drafting process, complaining of the hastiness with which the process was conducted and the way preparatory works were carried out.[4] The Constitution was adopted by a referendum in December 2012 by a majority of 63.8 per cent but with a low turnout of 32.9 per cent. Six months after the adoption of the Constitution, the law organising the Constituent Assembly was declared unconstitutional by the Supreme Constitutional Court (SCC).[5] However, the Court confirmed the validity of the Constitution since it had been approved by the people in the referendum.

This was the first time Islamist parties were offered the opportunity to participate in the drafting of a constitutional text and to set down their vision of society. Their acceptance of the supremacy of a higher state norm, binding on all legal and political bodies, is significant, since classical Islamic law does not allow for the concept of a constitution written by the people's representatives: law can only be the expression of the will of God and norms are established by religious scholars, not by elected representatives of the people. The mere fact that Islamist groups agreed to become political parties and run in elections to sit in an elected legislative/constitutional assembly demonstrates their readiness to make concessions and accept – at least verbally – the rules of the game of democracy. While the 2012 Constitution included new provisions referring to Islam and religion, it granted ultimate sovereignty to the people (art. 5):

---

2 The State Council is a court in charge of controlling administrative action with regard to laws and regulations.

3 For the content of the deal, see, for instance, 'Egypt Parties End Deadlock over Constitutional Panel', *BBC News*, 8 June 2012, accessed 20 September 2015, http://www.bbc.com/news/world-middle-east-18360403.

4 '30 Members of Egypt's Constituent Assembly Threaten Walkout', *Ahram Online*, 8 November 2012, accessed 20 September 2015, http://english.ahram.org.eg/NewsContent/1/0/57537/Egypt/0/-members-of-Egypts-Constituent-Assembly-threaten-w.aspx.

5 Supreme Constitutional Court, No. 166/34, 2 June 2013.

'Sovereignty belongs to the people alone who shall practice and protect it, preserve its national unity and be the source of authority as stipulated in the Constitution'. It also grounded the political system on the principles of democracy and consultation (art. 6).[6] Participation of Islamic parties in democratic processes could, therefore, contribute to moderating their ideologies and behaviour.[7]

The Committee of 50 and the Constitution of 2014

The 2014 drafting process also failed to build political consensus. After the suspension of the 2012 Constitution in July 2013 following the removal of President Mohamed Morsi by the army, a very innovative but unsuccessful two-step process was established to draft a new constitution. A committee of 10 legal experts was nominated by Interim President Adly Mansour, and was given one month to prepare amendments to the 2012 Constitution, before passing them on to a committee of 50 members, the 'Committee of 50'. These 10 experts were six judges and four constitutional law professors from Egyptian universities. The Committee of 50 was supposed to reflect the major components of society.[8] In practice, its members were selected by the interim president on the basis of uncertain criteria. More than two-thirds of the seats were allocated to representatives of various institutions within the state apparatus – the army, the police, al-Azhar University, national councils – or were otherwise close to the state, and all had been in direct confrontation with the Muslim Brotherhood. Leftist and Nasserist groups were represented by more than 10 members, while only two seats were allocated to Islamists: one for a Salafist from the Nour Party and the other for a former member of the Muslim Brotherhood who had resigned from the group the year before. The prejudice against the representation of Islamists in that committee echoed the bias against secularists, liberals,

---

6 The translation of the 2012 and 2014 Constitutions is based on the Arabic official documents published in the *Egyptian Official Gazette*. An English translation, not always fully accurate, is available on Egypt's State Information Service website, http://www.sis.gov.eg/newvr/theconistitution.pdf (2012 Constitution) and http://www.sis.gov.eg/Newvr/Dustor-en001.pdf (2014 Constitution).

7 See, for example, Olivier Roy, *Democracy and Political Islam after the Arab Revolutions* (European Council on Foreign Relations, 14 December 2012), accessed 20 September 2015, http://www.ecfr.eu/article/commentary_democracy_and_political_islam_after_the_arab_revolutions.

8 Political parties, intellectuals, workers, farmers, unions and syndicates, national councils, al-Azhar University, the churches, armed forces and the police, the youth, etc. For a full list of the members of the Committee of 50, see Serodio and Hulsman, *The 2014 Egyptian Constitution in Context*.

and leftists during the drafting process of the 2012 Constitution: 'Just as secularists were side-lined from the 2012 constitution-drafting process, Islamists were almost entirely excluded from the Committee of 50. The drafting process thus served to deepen political divides among Egyptians rather than as a means to achieve consensus.'[9] Five women were appointed to that committee.

The Committee of 50 was given only 60 days to prepare the final draft of the Constitution. The members managed to extend the deadline by insisting that the 60-day limit meant 60 working days, and did not include official holidays. However, such a short deadline implied that the Constitution had to be written in a rush with little time to engage in serious discussions; a six-month timeframe had previously been imposed by the March 2011 Constitutional Declaration for the drafting of the 2012 Constitution, which had been widely regarded as too short. During their discussions, the Committee of 50 paid little attention to the work of the 10 experts and disregarded their recommendations. They decided to meet in closed sessions, limited to the core members, and the 10 experts were not even allowed to attend. Members were banned from giving public statements to the press, the only communication being by the official spokesperson, who gave updates on the debates in daily press conferences. With the absence of media coverage, the majority of Egyptians lost interest and no longer followed the constitution-drafting process. By comparison, the debates in the 2012 Constituent Assembly had been widely publicised in the media, most plenary sessions of the Assembly were broadcast on television,[10] and people within wider society, such as youth groups, had launched constitution-writing and awareness-raising campaigns.[11] In both drafting processes, Egypt refused international legal support and civil society played a very limited role.

---

[9] *Carter Center Urges Dialogue and Constitutional Change to Strengthen Democratic Governance in Egypt* (Carter Center, 12 March 2014), accessed 24 February 2015, http://www.cartercenter.org/resources/pdfs/news/pr/egypt-constitution-031214.pdf.

[10] For a comparison between the two drafting processes, see Fattouh El Chazli, 'Egyptian Constitutional Drafting: A Comparative Review', *Jadaliyya*, 27 January 2014, accessed 20 September 2015, http://www.jadaliyya.com/pages/index/16060/egyptian-constitutional-drafting_a-comparative-rev.

[11] Yasmine Farouk, 'Writing the Constitution of the Egyptian Revolution: Between Social Contract and Political Contracting (March 2011–July 2013)', *Arab Reform Initiative*, November 2013, accessed 24 February 2015, http://www.arab-reform.net/sites/default/files/Cons_Egyptian%20Constitution_Y.Farouk_Nov13_Final_Layout_En.pdf.

The Army Controlled the Constitution Transition Process

The army exerted control over the whole transition process and several times altered the timeline to suit its own interests.[12] While ruling the country from February 2011 to June 2012, SCAF decided on the sequencing for the election processes and the drafting of the Constitution. The Muslim Brotherhood and other Islamist groups wished to have elections first while leftist and liberals pushed hard for a new constitution in advance of elections. In the end, it was decided to hold parliamentary elections before the convening of a Constituent Assembly, and the presidential elections were organised in June 2012. This was considered by liberals as the confirmation of a secret alliance between the army and the Muslim Brothers: SCAF would guarantee them a favoured place on the political scene in exchange for a commitment to respect the privileges of the army and to avoid confrontation on the street.

At this critical stage, the army acted twice as a constituent body. Two days after Mubarak's fall, SCAF suspended the 1971 Constitution, thus creating a legal vacuum. They then appointed a committee tasked with amending the Constitution. Its deliberations were closed and provided no public accountability. Less than three weeks after the completion of its work, a dozen amendments to the Constitution of 1971 were submitted to a referendum. They were adopted on 19 March 2011 by an overwhelming majority of 77.2 per cent with a level of participation of 41 per cent. The Islamist groups gave SCAF's amendments unconditional support and shifted the debate onto the terrain of religion to convince the people to vote in their favour. Their main preoccupation was actually that the amendments be adopted so that the process of reform would move on to next stage: the legislative elections which they knew they could win. On the other hand, the majority of the liberal groups and the forces of the left – young revolutionaries and Copts included – called for a vote against the amendments, questioning either the procedure by which they had been drawn up or their limited nature and the questionable content of certain provisions.[13]

---

[12] Tamir Moustafa, 'Drafting Egypt's Constitution: Can a New Legal Framework Revive a Flawed Transition?' (Brooking Doha Center, Paper Series, 1 March 2012), accessed 24 February 2015, http://www.brookings.edu/~/media/research/files/papers/2012/3/12%20egypt%20constitution%20moustafa/new1%20drafting%20egypts%20new%20constitutionenr03.pdf.

[13] 'Amendments Betray the Spirit of Egypt's Revolution: "No" Campaigners', *Ahram Online*, 18 March 2011, accessed 20 September 2015, http://english.ahram.org.eg/News/8003.aspx.

A few days later the Constitution of 1971, suspended on 13 February and amended on 19 March, was replaced by the Constitutional Declaration of 30 March 2011 that was to serve as the interim Constitution. This document was drafted in secret by anonymous and unaccountable figures and was not submitted to a referendum, even though 10 days before, the constitutional amendments had been submitted to the people. The Constitutional Declaration was amended by SCAF in June 2012 to increase its authority before relinquishing the executive power to the newly elected president. This laborious administration of the transition by the army gave an impression of improvisation and the absence of an overall vision.

After the 2012 Constitution was suspended following Morsi's removal, Interim President Adly Mansour issued a new Constitutional Declaration on 8 July 2013, which established the rules of power for the new transitional period and designed a timeline for amending the 2012 Constitution and conducting elections. This document was also drafted in secret and not submitted to a referendum. The military command was represented by two members in the 2012 Constituent Assembly and one member in the Committee of 50.

The military establishment was also interested in shaping some provisions in the new Constitution to ensure their autonomy. A list of inviolable supra-constitutional principles to guide the constitution-writing process circulated in August 2011. A revised version proposed in November 2011 by the Deputy Prime Minister (the 'Selmi document') stated that Egypt was a 'democratic civil state', Islam its official religion and the *Shari'a* the main source of legislation. Non-Muslims were given the right to follow their own creeds in personal status and religious matters. But the supra-constitutional principles also made the army the guarantor of constitutional legitimacy and proposed shielding the military's budget from civilian oversight. SCAF was solely responsible for all matters regarding the armed forces and had the right to approve legislation pertaining to the armed forces before it came into effect. Moreover, the army was afforded very significant powers of intervention in the process of drafting the Constitution.

These provisions were rejected by Islamists, who resented the attempt by the military to impose guidelines on the forthcoming Constituent Assembly and constrain its power. Liberals and leftists also strongly objected to this set of principles, as it would perpetuate the political role of the armed forces in domestic governance by embedding fundamental constitutional provisions that preserved their institutional autonomy and financial interests.

The army managed to include within the Constitutions of 2012 and 2014 several of these principles that had been rejected earlier in the process. Thus, for the first time in Egyptian constitutional history, a privileged position was granted to the army at the constitutional level. The Constitution of 2012 gave the military a significant number of privileges, which were maintained and even strengthened in the Constitution of 2014.

The budget of the army is not to be made public and will not be subject to parliamentary scrutiny, appearing instead as a single figure in the annual state budget. In the past, the budget of the military and the economic activities of the army were already essentially outside democratic monitoring procedures, but this was stated explicitly for the first time in the 2012 Constitution. The Constitution of 2014 maintained this state of secrecy.

The Constitution of 2012 allowed for the trying of civilians in military courts for crimes that 'harm the Armed Forces'. This provision was criticised and, early in the drafting process, several members of the Committee of 50 supported a complete ban on subjecting civilians to military courts. In the end, though, the Constitution of 2014 kept the possibility of civilians being brought before military courts, even though the provision was made more explicit by defining crimes that harm the armed forces as those that 'represent a direct assault' against them and by restricting this jurisdiction to specific kinds of cases. However, the language is so broad that the military courts still enjoy wide jurisdiction, covering all places that belong to the armed forces, including clubs, hotels, and petrol stations.[14]

The Constitution of 2012 also stated for the first time that the Minister of Defence had to be drawn from the officer class. The Constitution of 2014 added that for two presidential terms, i.e. eight years, he would have to be approved by SCAF. This opaque and chaotic constitution making process, dominated by the military, was considered 'as a short-term political deal rather than a long-lasting social contract'.[15]

The Judiciary, an Active Participant in the Constitution Transition Process

The judiciary has emerged as a central political player on the Egyptian scene. By taking what were considered as explicitly political decisions against President Morsi, the courts have been considered as one of the main actors behind his removal. The State Council, alongside the SCC,

[14] In October 2014, the President expanded the capacity of military courts by subjecting to their jurisdiction a large number of public facilities such as roads, bridges, and railways.

[15] Farouk, 'Writing the Constitution'.

ruled on very sensitive political issues, most notably the composition of Egypt's first Constituent Assembly, which it declared unconstitutional in April 2012, a move that led to the dissolution of the Assembly and to the delaying of the formulation of the Constitution. A year later, the SCC delivered a similar ruling, declaring the law on the organisation of the second Constituent Assembly unconstitutional. The latter ruling came almost half a year after the new Constitution, drafted by that Assembly, had been adopted by popular referendum and entered into force.

Judges were also directly involved in the different phases of the constitution-drafting process: the Committee of eight experts appointed in March 2011 by SCAF to amend the 1971 Constitution included three judges; the November 2011 supra-constitutional principles established by SCAF gave the SCC the power to decide on conflicts between SCAF and the Constituent Assembly regarding the content of the draft constitution; the Constituent Assembly of 2012 included six judges; and six of the 10 seats in the Committee of Experts appointed by Interim President Adly Mansour in July 2013 to prepare amendments to the 2012 Constitution were held by members of the judiciary.

The drafting process also saw the rise of the judiciary as a self-interested body in wider political processes. Rather than simply acting as an arbiter for disputes between state institutions, it managed to enshrine considerable autonomy for itself in the Constitution of 2014. For example, the general prosecutor is to be selected by the Supreme Council of the Judiciary, a body run by senior judges in charge of supervising judicial affairs, including appointment processes and disciplinary sanctions, while the SCC will be able to appoint its own chief justice from among its members. As before, judges will be appointed on the basis of the recommendation of the Supreme Council of the Judiciary and will not be removable. The budget of the judiciary will be incorporated into the annual state budget as a single figure, meaning they will receive their budget in a lump sum and will be able to transfer funds from one line to another without having to acquire the approval of Parliament. Laws regulating the judiciary will need a majority of two-thirds of Parliament to be amended.

As a result of this process, judges were able to gain greater autonomy with little accountability and very few checks on their authority.[16] No mechanism for controlling the judiciary was established with the exception

[16] See the publication of Arab Reform Initiative by Karim El-Chazli, 'The Judiciary in the Constitution: Lost Opportunities for Reform and Enshrinement of the Judiciary's Impenetrability', *Daily News Egypt*, 25 March 2014, accessed 24 February 2015, http://www.dailynewsegypt.com/2014/03/25/2014-egyptian-constitution-without-accountability-checks-balances-part-ii/.

of the Supreme Council of the Judiciary, and no reform of the justice system was provided. 'Some observers have argued that increasing judicial independence is a positive development. However, in a country like Egypt where courts are generally seen (with notable exceptions) as failing the people, increasing judicial independence before operating wholesale reform means that the negative practices of the past will become much more difficult to change.'[17]

RIGHTS OF THE CITIZENS IN THE 2012 AND 2014 CONSTITUTIONS

The Constitution of 2014 mentioned citizenship and citizens in several of its provisions. Some citizens were granted a special status while others do not enjoy full citizenship rights.

Citizenship in the 2014 Constitution

The word 'citizenship' (*muwatana*) was added to the 1971 Constitution by an amendment of 2007: according to the revised Article 1, the Arab Republic of Egypt was a democratic state based on citizenship.[18] The same principle was featured in the 2012 Constitution, which stated the following: 'The political system is based on the principles of democracy, consultation, citizenship that confers on all citizens the same public rights and duties, political pluralism and a multi-party system, peaceful transfer of power, separation of powers and the balance between them, the rule of law, and respect for human rights and freedoms; all as elaborated in the Constitution' (art. 6). The Constitution of 2014 (art. 1) declared that 'the Arab Republic of Egypt is a sovereign state, united and indivisible, where no part may be given up and its system is a democratic republic based on citizenship and the rule of law . . .'. Furthermore, according to the preamble of the 2014 Constitution, the 1919 revolution that ended the British protectorate 'established the principle of citizenship and equality for all the people'.

---

[17] Zaid al-Ali, 'Egypt's Missed Constitutional Moment', *Foreign Policy*, 17 December 2013, accessed 24 February 2015, http://foreignpolicy.com/2013/12/17/egypts-missed-constitutional-moment/.

[18] For a study of the historical intellectual debate around citizenship in Egypt see Gianluca P. Parolin, 'Traditional Intellectuals and the "Citizenship" Debate in Egypt: A Gramscian Reading', in Asifa Quraishi-Landes and SherAli Tareen (eds.), Constitutions and Pluralism in Muslim States and Societies (Herndon: IIIT, 2018), pp.156–179 (forthcoming).

Article 6 grants nationality to children of Egyptian fathers or mothers. It also stipulates that the law will define the requirements for acquiring nationality. This provision did not introduce a new principle, since the right to transmit their nationality to their children had already been granted to Egyptian mothers by an amendment to the nationality law in 2004.[19] Moreover, it does not remove the continuing gender discrimination between male and female citizens, as Egyptian husbands can transmit their nationality to their wives while Egyptian wives cannot transmit their nationality to their foreign husbands.

The Constitution of 2014, like its predecessors, declares that all citizens are equal before the law and equal in rights, freedoms, and general duties (art. 38).[20] It gives a list of grounds on which discrimination is prohibited: religion, belief, sex, origin, race, colour, language, disability, social class, political or geographic affiliation, or any other reason.[21]

Some rights are limited to Egyptian citizens, many of which were included in previous constitutions. Social solidarity should ensure a decent life for all citizens (art. 8);[22] all citizens shall enjoy equal opportunity without discrimination (art. 9);[23] public offices are a right for citizens on the basis of merit (art. 14);[24] all citizens have the right to social security (art. 17),[25] to health and to healthcare (art. 18),[26] to education (art. 19),[27] to enjoy the Nile River (art. 44),[28] as well as the seas, beaches, lakes, mineral water, and natural reserves (art. 45),[29] to culture (art. 48), to use all forms of public means of communication (art. 57), to organise public meetings (art. 73),[30] to form political parties (art. 74),[31] to establish associations

---

19 For a study of the evolution of nationality law in Egypt and other Arab countries, see Gianluca Parolin, *Citizenship in the Arab World: Kin, Religion and Nation-State* (Amsterdam: Amsterdam University Press, 2009).

20 Art. 40 (1971) and art. 33 (2012).

21 The Constitution of 1971 forbade discrimination on the basis of origin, language, religion, or belief while the Constitution of 2012 declared that citizens were equal before the law, without giving a specific list of grounds.

22 Art. 7 (1971) stated that 'Social solidarity is the basis of the society' and art. 8 (2012) that 'The state works toward securing a sufficient level of life for all citizens'.

23 Art. 9 (2012) and art. 8 (1971).

24 Art. 64 (2012) and art. 14 (1971).

25 Art. 66 (2012) and art. 17 (1971).

26 Art. 62 (2012) and art. 16 (1971).

27 Art. 58 (2012) and art. 18 (1971).

28 Art. 19 (2012) declared that the Nile River was a national wealth that had to be protected by the state.

29 Art. 20 (2012) stated that they had to be protected by the state.

30 Art. 50 (2012) and art. 54 (1971).

31 Art. 51 (2012) and art. 5 (1971, amended in 2007).

(art. 75),[32] to housing (art. 78),[33] to food and clean water (art. 79);[34] every citizen has the right to vote, run in elections, and express his opinion in referendums, with the participation of citizens in public life a national duty (art. 87);[35] while the state commits to developing a comprehensive plan to eradicate illiteracy among citizens of all ages (art. 25);[36] and no citizen should be expelled from the state's territory or prevented from leaving it (art. 62).[37]

The right to run in presidential elections is only available to Egyptian citizens and is denied to those who also hold another nationality, or whose parents or spouse do. A similar requirement exists for the position of prime minister (art. 164): he shall be an Egyptian citizen born to Egyptian parents, and neither he nor his spouse may hold the nationality of any other country. The Constitution does not require that the president or prime minister be Muslims. Only Egyptian citizens who hold a certificate of basic education will be allowed to run for membership of Parliament (art. 102).

The Constitution also provided special protection for certain categories of citizens, considered as particularly vulnerable, like the elderly (art. 83) and people with disabilities (arts. 80 and 81),[38] who shall also be allocated 'proper representation' in local councils (art. 180).

Stronger protection for women's rights[39]

The Constitution of 2014 also strengthened the status of women's rights compared with previous constitutions. The state commits itself to achieving equality between men and women in all civil, political, economic, social, and cultural rights in accordance with the provisions of the Constitution (art. 11), and it shall guarantee women the right to hold public and senior management offices in the state and to be appointed to judicial bodies and entities without discrimination.

The Constitution added that the state ensures female empowerment in order to reconcile women's duties towards their family with the requirements of the workplace. The Constitution thus maintained the

---

32 Art. 51 (2012) and art. 55 (1971).
33 Art. 68 (2012).
34 Art. 68 (2012).
35 Art. 55 (2012) and art. 62 (1971).
36 Art. 61 (2012) and art. 21 (1971).
37 Art. 42 (2012) and arts. 50 to 52 (1971).
38 Art. 70 (2012).
39 For a study of the status of gender and citizenship in the Arab world, see Suad Joseph (ed.), *Gender and Citizenship in the Middle East* (Syracuse University Press, 2000).

gender-based stereotypes that had been included in the 1971[40] and 2012[41] Constitutions, with the belief that a woman's place is at home. Domestic responsibilities are to be the sole burden of women, since there is no similar reference to the role of men in the raising of children. The 2014 Constitution also declared that the state shall provide care to and protection for motherhood and childhood.[42] This provision had been criticised when it was included in the Constitution of 2012 as it was considered emblematic of the emphasis given by Islamists to family values, even though it replicated an article from the Constitution of 1971.

The political participation of women is also mentioned in the Constitution: the state must ensure their 'adequate representation' in the Parliament (art. 11). Moreover, 25 per cent of the seats in local councils shall be allocated to women (art. 180).[43] Additionally, for the first time the state makes a commitment to protect women against all forms of violence (art. 12). A law against sexual harassment was also adopted in June 2014.

Special status of religious minorities

Article 3 of the 2012 Constitution provided for the religious autonomy of the Christian and Jewish minorities. Their own religious laws would be the main source of legislation for regulating their personal status, religious affairs, and the selection of their spiritual leaders. This legal plurality in the field of religious affairs had already been established in Egyptian legislation but this was the first time it was stated at the constitutional level, probably in order to compensate Christians and Jews for the increased emphasis on the *Shariʿa*. Other non-Muslims citizens remained subject to the general Egyptian legislation as it was codified for Muslims.

---

40 Art. 11 (1971): 'The State shall guarantee to women the compatibility between their duties towards the family and their work in the society, their equality with men in the political, social, cultural, and economic fields without violating the rules of Islamic shari'a'.

41 The 2012 Constituent Assembly intended first to keep art. 11 (1971) but this provision, which had remained almost unnoticed in the previous Constitution, aroused such strong opposition within women's rights NGOs that the final version of the Constitution left out the reference to Islamic *Shariʿa* in that regard, while still entrusting the state with enabling the reconciliation between the duties of a woman towards her family and her work (art. 10).

42 Art. 10 (2012).

43 The Constitution of 1971 had been amended in 2007 to authorise the legislator to provide a quota for the representation of women in the Parliament. The electoral law had ensured that 64 seats (14 per cent of the seats in the 454-member People's Assembly) would be allocated to women. The Constitution of 2012 provided no special measures for political participation of women.

At the request of the various Christian denominations this provision was not removed from the 2014 Constitution. At an early stage in the discussion process several members of the Committee of 50 had declared their readiness to amend the Constitution to extend religious autonomy to all non-Muslims. However, committee members representing al-Azhar and the Salafi group al-Nour expressed their strong opposition to the proposed amendment, arguing that it would lead to disturbances in the social order and the pillars of Egyptian society being undermined.[44] As a result of this pressure, the Committee of 50 agreed not to amend that provision.

This article can be considered as undermining the rights of non-Muslims as citizens, since all citizens should be equal before the law and follow the same rules in all aspects of life. The Constitution of 2012 had been criticised for including this provision: 'Egypt's current rulers conceive of Copts not so much as equal citizens but as a distinctly sectarian constituency that is best left in the hands of the Church. For instance, Article 3 of the Constitution vouchsafes control of the personal status affairs of the Coptic Orthodox to the Coptic Orthodox Patriarch, regardless of whether particular Copts are, in fact, believers or not.[45] This criticism can also be applied to the similar provision found in the Constitution of 2014, even though the latter document was not drafted by an Islamist Constituent Assembly. Some Coptic activists called for its removal, arguing that it allowed the church too much control over its followers,[46] and claimed that they would rather submit to the general Egyptian law, which they considered more open to divorce than Christian religious law.[47] The fact that, as before, Article 2 of the 2014 Constitution declares that Islam is the religion of the state and that the principles of the Islamic *Shariʿa* are

---

[44] Manar Mohsen, 'The Grand Mufti and Al-Nour Party Oppose Proposed Amendments to Sharia-related Articles in the Constitution', *Daily News Egypt*, 18 September 2013, accessed 20 September 2015, https://www.dailynewsegypt.com/2013/09/18/the-grand-mufti-and-al-nour-party-oppose-proposed-amendments-to-sharia-related-articles-in-the-constitution/.

[45] Paul Sedra, 'Has Citizenship Got a Future in Egypt?', *Jadaliyya*, 8 April 2013, accessed 24 February 2015, http://www.jadaliyya.com/pages/index/11111/has-citizenship-got-a-future-in-egypt.

[46] In practice, such autonomy means the Coptic Orthodox Church can refuse to give a licence for a new marriage to Copts divorced before Egyptian national courts. It also allows Churches to refuse recognition of the conversion of one of their followers to another religion.

[47] Since the amendment in 2008 of the 1938 personal status regulations for Coptic Orthodox, divorce is only allowed in cases of adultery or apostasy, while Muslim women can file for divorce on several grounds.

the main source of legislation also generates difference in status between Muslim and non-Muslim citizens.

Article 43 of the 2012 Constitution stated that freedom of belief was inviolable, but went on to say that freedom to practise religious rituals and establish places of worship was only allowed for the followers of revealed religions, i.e. Muslims, Christians, and Jews; other religions could not practise their rituals in public. This had already been the case in Egyptian law but it was expressed at the constitutional level for the first time.[48] The Constitution of 2014 (art. 64) declared that freedom of religion is absolute, but, again, only followers of the revealed religions are given the right to practise religious rituals and establish houses of worship. Egyptian citizens who follow other religions or beliefs, and even those who have no belief, are excluded from these freedoms. There is no mention of the right to change one's religion.

Christians, like youth, shall be granted 'appropriate representation' in the first Parliament elected after the promulgation of the Constitution, with the meaning of 'appropriate representation' being specified by the law (art. 244). In the 2015 parliamentary elections, 24 seats were allocated to Christians.

The Constitution of 2014 did ensure broader social and cultural rights than previous Constitutions, granting more protection to vulnerable groups like women, children, and the disabled. While the Constitution was supposedly committed to implement Egyptian citizens' lives, many provisions, however, are vague and contain insufficient protection mechanisms.

INSUFFICIENT PROTECTION MECHANISMS

The language of constitutional provisions is important but procedural and substantive safeguard mechanisms to enforce them even more so. The Constitution of 2014, like those of 2012 and 1971, left much up to the implementing legislation. Many provisions, particularly in the field of human rights, call on laws for regulation and implementation. While legislating, the House of Representatives may restrict these rights and freedoms or even deny them altogether.

The Constitution tried to prevent possible abuse by the Parliament through the requirement of a majority of two-thirds of its members passing legislation that implemented the rights and duties stipulated in the Constitution (art. 121). This requirement was introduced to strengthen

---

48 Art. 46 (1971) only stated: 'The State shall guarantee the freedom of belief and the freedom of practice of religious rites.'

their protection and prevent the adoption of restrictive laws. A two-thirds majority, however, may be difficult to reach on controversial issues and may also make it more difficult to amend authoritarian laws already in force.

The Constitution of 2014 also tried to limit the discretionary power of the legislator by preventing ordinary legislation from restricting the 'core and essence' of rights and freedoms (art. 92). That article restricts the scope of limitation of human rights provisions that the legislator may adopt. However, it does not establish a set of criteria to determine the core and essence of a particular right and against which laws it should be measured. A law considered to restrict the core and essence of a right would have to be challenged for unconstitutionality before the SCC. This Court, in turn, would determine what the essence and core of the particular right were. This provision has been considered as too vague to prevent possible abuses.[49]

The power of the constituent legislator has also been limited to protect human rights: provisions pertaining to the principles of freedom and equality stipulated in the Constitution may not be amended, unless to bring more guarantees (art. 226). The Constitution, therefore, bans constitutional amendments that would decrease the protection of citizens' freedom or equality, considered as supra-constitutional.

According to Article 93 of the Constitution, the state is bound by international human rights treaties that are ratified by Egypt and consequently given the force of law. This provision incorporates international law as part of its domestic law, but fails to ensure its supremacy over national legislation, since treaties will be treated as statutory law. According to the legal principle that holds that if two laws have the same legal value, the most recent one shall prevail, the domestic law may be enforced even if it contradicts a treaty obligation, as long as it was adopted more recently. The 2014 Constitution, therefore, does not recognise the supremacy of international law over domestic law.

Given that the 2014 Constitution devoted more attention to second and third generation rights than previous texts, their implementation will put pressure on the budget. Fulfilling these socio-economic entitlements will have financial implications. The Constitution mandated for the first time that minimum shares of the gross domestic product (GDP) be spent by the state on four sectors every year: health care (3 per cent, art. 18), primary and secondary education (4 per cent, art. 19), higher education (2 per cent, art. 21), and scientific research (1 per cent, art. 22). These stipulations

---

[49] Zaid al-Ali, 'Egypt's Missed Constitutional Moment'.

were to be enforced gradually and the rates were to be met in full in the state budget of the 2016/2017 financial year. However, the 2016/2017 state budget was adopted without including these spendings.[50] Besides, 'allocating rates for government spending in the Constitution suggests that reform rests on how much is spent, while the most important economic challenge remains how it is spent'.[51]

Citizens' rights may turn out not to be worth the paper they are written on if they fail to be implemented. Non-governmental organisation (NGO) reports show that the implementation of the 2014 human rights provisions has been very problematic.[52] The constitutional referendum itself took place in a political environment where there was no real opportunity for dissent. According to Transparency International, an international NGO that monitored the referendum, the government 'harassed, arrested, and prosecuted peaceful critics, closing democratic space to promote views and debate before the referendum'.[53] Amnesty International stated in a January 2014 report that 'three years on, wide-scale repression continues unabated'.[54] According to the Arabic

---

[50] Rania Rabeaa Elabd, 'What Makes Egypt's Budget So Controversial?' *Al-Monitor*, 6 July 2016, accessed 28 February 2017, http://www.al-monitor.com/pulse/en/originals/2016/07/egypt-budget-constitution-controversy-sisi-requirements.html.

[51] Yussef Auf, 'The New Draft Constitution Part IV: Social and Economic Rights', *Atlantic Council*, 14 January 2014, accessed 24 February 2015, http://www.atlanticcouncil.org/blogs/egyptsource/the-new-draft-constitution-part-iv-social-and-economic-rights.

[52] See for instance, *4th Revolution Anniversary Marks Alarming Decline of Egypt's Human Rights* (FIDH, 23 January 2015), accessed 24 February 2015, https://www.fidh.org/IMG/pdf/egypt23012015.final.pdf. See also European Parliament, *Resolution on the Situation in Egypt* (12 January 2015), accessed 24 February 2015, http://www.marietjeschaake.eu/wp-content/uploads/2015/01/B8–0026–2015–Motion-for-a-resolution-on-the-situation-in-Egypt.pdf; *World Report 2015, Egypt* (Human Rights Watch, 2015), available: http://www.hrw.org/world-report/2015/country-chapters/egypt, accessed 24 February 2015; *Report 2014/2015, Egypt* (Amnesty International, 2015), accessed 24 February 2015, https://www.amnesty.org/en/countries/middle-east-and-north-africa/egypt/report-egypt/, and the *Violations of a Constitution before the Ink is Dry* (Arabic Network for Human Rights Information, 18 November 2014), accessed 2 March 2015, http://anhri.net/?p=137609&lang=en.

[53] *Egypt Constitutional Referendum Preliminary Report* (Transparency International Observation Mission, 16 January 2014), accessed 24 February 2015, http://www.transparency.org/files/content/pressrelease/Preliminary_Statement_Egypt.pdf.

[54] 'Egypt Three Years on, Wide-scale Repression Continues Unabated' (Amnesty International, 23 January 2014), accessed 24 February 2015, http://www.amnesty.org/en/news/egypt-three-years-wide-scale-repression-continues-unabated-2014–01–23.

Network for Human Rights Information (ANHRI), the Constitution was violated before the ink was dry.[55] The Egyptian Initiative for Personal Rights also lamented that 'most of the protections and safeguards enshrined in the constitution were ignored while some were flagrantly violated by the government'.[56] According to a report of the International Federation for Human Rights (FIDH) published in January 2015:

> In fact, the human rights situation in Egypt has deteriorated at an exceptional speed. The current political climate does not permit any form of dissent or criticism of the government, whether by protest, independent journalism, or even social media postings. Human rights defenders, journalists, and political opponents continue to be targeted and imprisoned. Independent media outlets continue to be censored. The rights enshrined in Egypt's 2014 Constitution remain ink on paper, and the judicial authorities entrusted to uphold the rule of law have become the primary arm of state-repression.[57]

Even some of the most emblematic provisions of the 2014 Constitution, such as Article 11 that guaranteed the right of women to hold high positions in the judiciary, have not been implemented. In January 2014, the State Council rejected women candidates' applications for membership. When the Head of the National Council for Women wrote a protest letter to the State Council, she was accused of violating 'appropriateness and manners' and threatened with criminal action by the State Council. There has been no investigation into this violation of the Constitution, and the judiciary has not been held accountable for failing to enforce a constitutional provision. The absolute power over their internal affairs granted by the Constitution protects judges from possible sanction or reform. The provision providing for the adoption of a transitional justice law during the first meeting of the Assembly (art. 241) has not been implemented either.

---

[55] *Violations of a Constitution before the Ink Is Dry* (Arabic Network for Human Rights Information).

[56] *Egypt: Where Impunity is Entrenched and Accountability is Absent* (Egyptian Initiative for Personal Rights, 31 December 2014), accessed 11 March 2015, http://eipr.org/en/pressrelease/2014/12/31/2320.

[57] *4th Revolution Anniversary Marks Alarming Decline of Egypt's Human Rights* (FIDH). See also European Parliament, *Resolution on the Situation in Egypt; World Report 2015* (Human Rights Watch) and *Report 2014/2015, Egypt* (Amnesty International).

CONCLUSION

The Constitution of 2014 has improved the protection of citizens' rights, but these improvements are undermined by the way the Constitution was written and shortcomings in the implementation provisions. They are also undermined by the special status and powers given to the military, the judiciary, and even the police, as well as by the lack of political will to enforce them. In practice, the position of Egyptian citizens has not fundamentally changed after the 2011 uprising and the adoption of the 2014 Constitution.

The constitution-drafting processes were neither inclusive nor participatory. In 2012 and 2014 a major section of society was left out and the two constitution-building processes were used by the most powerful groups to extend their advantage over their rivals and reinforce their own position in the state: 'it was designed to serve the needs of a particular moment and of specific players, above all the military and the judiciary'.[58] Consensus was lacking even among the members of the Committee of 50, who failed to agree on important issues such as the sequencing of the upcoming parliamentary and presidential elections, and which voting system to employ. All these issues were referred by the Constitution to the legislature and, in the absence of a Parliament, they were decided by the President.

In the current political context and the absence of efficient accountability mechanisms, the human rights provisions have not managed to improve citizens' rights. Moreover, in Article 86 the Constitution stated that 'the preservation of national security is a duty, and the commitment of all to uphold it is a national responsibility ensured by law', and Article 237 requires the state to fight all types and forms of terrorism. In Nathan Brown's words, this Constitution 'provides for a security state with a democratic face'.[59] The war against terrorism has led to the suspension of human rights provisions and the adoption of several repressive measures that curtailed citizens' rights and freedoms, such as the protest law adopted in November 2013 by then acting-president Adly Mansour, or the decree adopted in October 2014 that expanded the scope of military

---

[58] Marina Ottaway, 'Constitutional Models vs Political Reality: The Making of Arab Constitutions after the Uprisings', (*IEMed Yearbook 2014*), accessed 24 February 2015, http://www.iemed.org/observatori/arees-danalisi/arxius-adjunts/anuari/anuari-2014/Ottaway_Constitutions_Arab_Uprising_Models_international_standards_IEMed_yearbook_2014_EN.pdf.

[59] Nathan Brown, 'Egypt's Constitutional Cul-de-sac', (CMI INSIGHT, No. 1, March 2014), accessed 14 February 2015, http://www.cmi.no/publications/file/5108-egypts-constitutional-cul-de-sac.pdf.

jurisdiction. 'By invoking nebulous concepts such as public order and the interests of society, these laws and proposals all allow for immense prosecutorial discretion. At the same time, their language empowers state institutions like local security offices, universities, and various ministries to regulate individuals' actions, such as prohibiting protests or other public gatherings.'[60]

The President himself declared that in the current exceptional circumstances Egypt is facing, ensuring stability is the top priority and some violations of human rights are inevitable.[61] He added a few months later that the 2014 Constitution was written with good intentions, in particular the provisions giving broad powers to the Parliament, but that this was not enough to govern a state.[62] Draft laws have been submitted to the Parliament to amend the Constitution and enable the President to stay longer in power. In the absence of any political will, the prospect of establishing democracy and respect for citizens' rights may, therefore, be becoming more and more distant.

---

[60] Nathan J. Brown and Katie Bentivoglio, *Egypt's Resurgent Authoritarianism: It's a Way of Life* (Carnegie Endowment for International Peace, 9 October 2014), accessed 24 February 2015, http://carnegieendowment.org/2014/10/09/egypt-s-resurgent-authoritarianism-it-s-way-of-life.

[61] 'Sisi Defends Egypt Police, Recognizes Rights Abuses', *Al-Arabiya News*, 20 January 2015, accessed 24 February 2015, http://english.alarabiya.net/en/News/middle-east/2015/01/20/Sisi-defends-Egypt-police-but-acknowledges-rights-abuses-.html; 'Egypt's Sisi Says Protests not Priority under Current Circumstances', *Ahram Online*, 20 January 2015, accessed 24 February 2015, http://english.ahram.org.eg/NewsContent/1/64/120777/Egypt/Politics-/Egypts-Sisi-says-protests-not-priority-under-curre.aspx. This statement raised criticisms by Nour Farahat, a prominent law scholar (http://albedaiah.com/news/2015/09/13/96697, accessed 20 September 2015), and by the novelist Alaa al-Aswani, (http://www.egyptindependent.com/news/novelist-slams-president-over-constitution-remarks, accessed 20 September 2015), for whom the Constitution should represent an obligation on all citizens, especially the President. It sparked questions around possible amendments of the Constitution to reduce the powers of the Parliament and increase those of the President.

[62] Khaled Dawoud, 'The Debate over Egypt's Constitution' (Atlantic Council, 24 November 2015), accessed 19 March 2018, http://www.atlanticcouncil.org/blogs/menasource/the-debate-over-egypt-s-constitution.

PART II

Islam and the issue of citizenship

8. The political, politics, and political citizenship in modern Islam

Roel Meijer

INTRODUCTION

Much has been written on political Islam as a movement and on its ideology but very little from the perspective of political philosophy. In this chapter I will analyse three aspects of political Islam which I believe are essential for understanding its content. The first is 'the political', the second is politics, and the third is political citizenship. I will argue that the three are closely entwined. If political citizenship means political participation and recognition of individual rights, it can only come about when politics is based on some idea of the sovereignty of the people and has the function to reach a compromise between conflicting interests, while the political is the philosophical foundation of the other two.

I have borrowed the term 'the political' from a selection of political philosophers (Claude Lefort, Chantal Mouffe, Sheldon Wolin, Michael Walzer and Alan Ryan) who argue that politics has a logic and rationality of its own and is based on the recognition of conflict and its containment.[1] Lefort makes a distinction between 'politics' (*la politique*) and 'the political' (*le politique*). The first applies to daily political travails, institutions and daily practices, the stuff political science deals with, while the latter is transcendental, symbolic and foundational and is the focus of political philosophy. The political sets the goals of society, regulates power relations. It is concerned with establishing a political order that can resolve conflicts inherent to society. It is directly related to legitimacy and identity. The second common element is the notion that the political, although it is foundational, is indeterminate. Lefort argues that

[1] For an excellent introduction to the concept of the political, see James Wiley, *Politics and the Concept of the Political: The Political Imagination* (New York: Routledge, 2016).

modernity is characterised by the 'radical indeterminacy' of the political.[2] This leaves a void, an 'empty place' which can only be temporarily filled by politics. The third element is that in the transition to modernity power, law and knowledge have become permanently separated. Attempts to eliminate this instability, suppress conflict, and impose harmony and unity lead to totalitarianism.[3] This view not only accepts secularisation but also regards it as a necessity and a means of ending totalising attempts to bring these fields of activities under an overarching ideology; it accepts that there is no absolute truth and that pluralism is the norm of modernity.

To accept that there is no absolute truth has far-reaching consequences for politics and ultimately for political citizenship and the content, forms and extent of political participation. Michael Walzer argues that politics is human, temporal, contingent, inconclusive, indefinite, provisional, pragmatic – based on arguments, positions, and alliances, always subject to reconstruction and conflict, and as such opposed to 'finality'.[4] Chantal Mouffe argues that in the absence of an absolute truth the political enemy becomes a political opponent. Following Lefort, she argues that the political 'requires that, within the context of the political community, the opponent should be considered not as an enemy to be destroyed, but as an adversary whose existence is legitimate and must be tolerated'.[5] This means that a certain consensus about the rules of the game in the service of the 'common good' is absolutely necessary. She calls this 'agonistic pluralism'. However, all these thinkers are careful not to crush the room for politics and the peaceful resolution of conflict by an excess of consensus and harmony. According to Mouffe, the 'agonistic dynamic is hindered by an apparent excess of consensus'.[6] Likewise, Sheldon Wolin regards 'political space' as essential for resolving conflict; 'the plans, ambitions, and actions of individuals and groups incessantly jar against each other – colliding, blocking, coalescing, separating . . .'.[7] Society is held together by the 'political art' to deal with antagonism and conflict and 'to make it

---

[2] Claude Lefort, 'La logique totalitaire', in Claude Lefort, *L'invention démocratique* (Paris: Librarie Artheme Fayard, 1981), 85–106.

[3] Claude Lefort, *The Political Forms of Modern Society* (Oxford: Oxford University Press, 1986), 305.

[4] Michael Walzer, 'Drawing the Line: Religion and Politics', in Michael Walzer, *Thinking Politically: Essays in Political Theory.* Edited and with Introduction by David Miller (New Haven: Yale University Press, 2007), 147–67.

[5] Chantal Mouffe, *The Return of the Political* (New York: Verso, 1993), 4.

[6] Ibid., 4–6.

[7] Sheldon S. Wolin, *Politics and Vision: Continuity and Innovation in Western Political Thought* (Princeton: Princeton University Press, 2004), 16.

possible for competing forces to compromise in order to avoid harsher remedies'.[8]

The threat to the political and politics and political citizenship is not just located in an overemphasis on consensus and harmony. It is also constituted by modern social, economic, religious and ideological interests, which 'colonise' the political and politics. Carl Schmitt, for example, opposed the 'politicization of society', or the 'sociologization of politics', which he believed occurred after the 'democratization and massification of politics'.[9] Sheldon Wolin has the same critique but from a democratic perspective.[10] He complains that throughout European history the political has been 'absorbed' by, 'displaced' in, and 'diffused' into ethics, technocracy, or, in the case of Marxism, class struggle.[11] Alan Ryan, referring to Plato, calls this process 'antipolitical'.[12] Others, referring to the French existentialists, who denied the relevance of the political, 'politicide'.[13] In the past, religion has been the most important factor to absorb the political into doctrine and diffuse it into church and ritual, a process Ryan calls confusing 'state craft' with 'soul craft'.[14] In contemporary bureaucratised society, it is especially technocracy that has taken over the function of the political and turned politics into 'policy'. This has led Michael Walzer to argue that the 'walls of separation' between economics, society, religion and politics must be maintained if the trinity of the political, politics and citizenship is to be upheld.[15] Political citizenship dissolves if the political and politics are absorbed by other disciplines and sectors in society in their struggle for hegemony and their denial of the role of politics as a way to allow existing problems to emerge and be resolved. Indeterminacy, recognition of conflict, and agonistic relations are essential for political citizenship.

This struggle is also reflected in academic disciplines that deal with politics. As economics and technocracy have gained a dominant say in neoliberalism, politics and the room for political participation have been

---

[8] Wolin, *Politics and Vision*, 40.

[9] Wiley, *Politics and the Concept of the Political*, 4.

[10] Wolin, *Politics and Vision*, 190–91;

[11] Wolin, *Politics and Vision*.

[12] Alan Ryan, *On Politics: A History of Political Thought from Herodotus to the Present* (London: Penguin Books, 2012), 31.

[13] Luuk van Middelaar, *Politicide: De moord op de politiek in de Franse filosofie* (*Politicide: The Assassination of Politics in French Philosophy*) (Brussels: Historische Uitgeverij, 2011).

[14] Ryan, *On Politics*, 70.

[15] Michael Walzer, *Thinking Politically: Essays in Political Theory*. Edited and with Introduction by David Miller (New Haven: Yale University Press, 2007).

side-lined by bureaucracy or the market. The political and politics have had an even harder time in Middle Eastern studies, where the focus is on Islam. From the perspective of political philosophy, cultural anthropology focuses on the diluted, diffused and fragmented political in Islamic rituals, values, symbols, dress codes, comportment and associations;[16] Islamic studies seeks the political in Islamic injunctions and the *shari'a*; political science reduces the political to the resilience of authoritarian states; while civil society theory has located the political in voluntary associations, which are supposed to promote 'civility', pluralism and democracy.[17]

For the same reason it is not surprising that citizenship has hardly figured in Middle Eastern studies. In so far as recent studies have focused on citizenship, they mostly focus on the equality between Muslims and non-Muslims,[18] and hardly include politics or the political. In this chapter, I want to bring all three together. Recognition of the political as an independent indeterminate field, opens up 'space' for politics and recognises the political rights of citizens.

Locating the political in modern Islamic political thought is important for several reasons. First, it shows how it is absorbed and displaced by and diffused over Islamic doctrine, identity politics and Islamic law. Second, it explains the pervasive and deeply rooted ambiguity in 'political' Islam or Islamism. Although many researchers have pointed out the fundamental ambivalence of Islamism, they often regard its contradictions and vagueness as intentional, whereas its foundation lies in the absorption and displacement of the political.[19] Third, it can explain the responses of different Islamist groups during the Arab Uprisings. Only those movements which recognised the political and accept equal citizenship, such as the Tunisian Ennahda Party, were able to make cross-ideological coalitions with secular nationalists and the left and establish a new more democratic citizenship regime. Retrieving the political is therefore a crucial element in establishing a new, more democratic citizenship regime, as increasingly more Islamic thinkers realise.

In this chapter I will analyse how Islamic thinkers have struggled with concepts of the political, politics and citizenship, how they have absorbed, displaced and diffused the political, and what consequences that has had

---

16 Dale F. Eickelman and James Piscatori, *Muslim Politics* (Princeton: Princeton University Press, 1996).

17 For more on this debate, see 'Introduction', in *The Crisis of Citizenship in the Arab World*, eds. Roel Meijer and Nils Butenschøn (Leiden: Brill, 2017) 1–37.

18 Rachel Scott, *The Challenge of Political: Non-Muslims and the Egyptian State* (Stanford: Stanford: University Press, 2010).

19 Olivier Roy, *The Failure of Political Islam* (London: IB Tauris, 2004).

for politics and citizenship. After a brief introduction to 'classical Islam', I will discuss ideas of Muhammad ʿAbduh, Hasan al-Banna, Sayyid Qutb, Yusuf al-Qaradawi, Abdelwahhab El-Affendi, Abu al-ʿAla Madi, and Jasser Auda. I have chosen these authors because I believe they illustrate crucial developments over the past hundred years in Islamic political thought on the political, politics and political citizenship.

The Political in Classic Islam

As in all religions in the pre-modernity the political is a difficult concept to locate and isolate. It is enmeshed with and diffused in other concepts and usually is subsumed under an ethical dimension that replaces it. The difference with Christianity is that Islam did not deny it was based on power. It was also more this worldly; life was not a 'valley of tears'. It was worth living as long as it was lived according to the precepts of the Qur'an. But it was not at first theorised and fully subsumed under Islamic precepts. Much was decided by a power struggle between rulers and ʿulama. During the Umayyads the political reigned supreme in the sense that the caliph was a political figure who decided doctrine and also continued the prophecy. Politics trumped religion, also in theory. The other challenge was the role of rationalism and the political space the ruler could claim. This struggle was decided during caliph Ma'mun (786–833 AD) with the defeat of the Muʿtazila, Greek philosophy and independent inquiry. Although in the tenth century ʿulama lost the political struggle with the ruler, they gained control over doctrine. The legacy of the struggle, however, left the ʿulama with a deep suspicion of politics and the political. Although Islam became the official state religion and politics and the ruler was legitimated in Islamic terms, especially the Hanbali ʿulama distrusted political rulers whom they regarded as unjust. Politics and power were regarded as necessary to defend the Dar al-Islam and secure the implementation of the *shariʿa*. Its function was to maintain unity and combat partisanship and divisiveness (*fitna*), which would lead to chaos (*fawda*). In practice, this meant that politics was restricted. Political participation was limited to consultation (*shura*) by the ʿulama, and in practice meant discrete advice (*nasiha*) to the ruler. ʿUlama did have power, especially during revolts when the population pushed them to the forefront to voice their grievances, but this was never formalised. Other groups in society, such as tribes, guilds, and the Jewish and Christian *millets*, enjoyed a considerable amount of independence as long as they paid taxes. As in all empires, they were dispersed and diverse. In the meantime, the state developed its own laws, the *qanun*, which referred to the *shariʿa* but did not fall under *shariʿa*. The *mazalim* courts fell under the state and *siyasa al-shariʿa* was largely independent.[20] This changed with the introduction of the nation-state and a new citizenship regime that required a new intensive relation between citizen and state and a unified, homogeneous, educated population.

The Natural Order as the Political

Muhammad ʿAbduh's (1849–1905) *Risalat al-Tawhid*,[21] first published in 1897, is a synthesis of Western influences and Islam at the end of the nineteenth century. ʿAbduh was a modernist who would have great influence on Islamic reformist thought. His book combines classic Islamic terms, Ashʿarism, liberal ideology, British utilitarianism, notions of self-help, and French sociology to convey a liberal content. Although ʿAbduh never uses the terms 'politics' (*al-siyasa*) or 'citizenship' (*al-muwatana*), he diffuses their meaning in religion, society, and a general concept of order and harmony. This eclecticism is evident in the many categories he uses to convey the meaning of citizen: 'humanity' (*al-insan*), 'people' (*al-nas*) or the classic Islamic 'subjects/human being' (*ʿabd*/*ʿabid*), or 'soul' (*nafs*), but also the more modern term 'individuals' (*afrad*). One of the techniques to bring Islam to a more modern, abstract level of thought is to bring out the 'purposes of Islamic law' (*maqasid al-sharʿiyya*). These are represented by such terms as the 'general good' (*al-maslaha al-ʿamma*), 'reform' (*islah*), and 'well-being/happiness' (*saʿada*). The common good is obtained through 'rational proof' (*al-dalil al-ʿaqli*),[22] 'reason' (*ʿaql*), 'man's capacity to power' (*qudra*), 'choice' (*ikhtiyar*), 'free choice' (*al-istiqlal al-insan bi-iradatihi*), and individual interpretation (*ijtihad*) of the original sources. The basic struggle, according to ʿAbduh, is between 'obscurantism/ignorance' (*juhhal*), 'traditionalism' (*taqlid*) on the one side, and rationalism and 'progress of science' (*taqaddum al-ʿilm*) on the other.[23] To demonstrate his modern stance, *ʿilm* in ʿAbduh's interpretation is no longer Islamic knowledge but modern science.

Despite ʿAbduh's awareness of change, development, and imbalance under the impact of British colonialism, or what Lefort would call 'radical indeterminacy', the key notion of the political in his work is the concept

---

20 Knut Vikør, *Between God and the Sultan: A History of Islamic Law* (London: Hurst, 2005).

21 In the following section, I will refer to both the Arabic version of Muhammad ʿAbduh's main work, Al-Imam Muhammad ʿAbduh, *Risalat al-Tawhid* (Cairo: Dar al-Maʿarif, 2003), as well as the English translation by Ishaq Musaʿad and Kenneth Cragg, *The Theology of Unity* (Kuala Lumpur: Islamic Book Trust, 1966).

22 ʿAbduh, *Risalat al-Tawhid*, 22/ *Theology*, 30.

23 Ibid., 24–33/29–40.

of 'order' (*nizam*).[24] God provides for a divine 'perfect order' and social 'harmony',[25] and man can discern this deist cosmology[26] through his rationality. God's omnipotence is apparent from ʿAbduh's section on will (*irada*), knowledge (*ʿilm*), freedom of choice (*ikhtiyar*), which deal less with human faculties and agency than with the attributes of God. In that sense, they are intended to instil humility and awe for the perfect order God has created.[27] The '[general] good' (*al-maslaha*)[28] and '[general] well-being' (*al-saʿada*) are given and derive from natural law and are not created and adjusted by the people, as in the theory of John Locke.[29] ʿAbduh's use of sociology is put at the service of this divine order. Along the liberal lines of civil society, he uses the Western term of 'society' (*mujtamaʿ*), which consists of individuals (*afrad*),[30] who form 'relationships and associations (*jamaʿat*) that are distinctively their own'.[31] But they are not autonomous. Rather they are subject to divine law/guidelines (*sharʿ*).This order is threatened by such irrational elements as 'passions' (*shahawat*), 'imbalance' and 'corruption' (*fasad*)[32] and not by a clash of political interests based on legitimate differences of opinion and interests. In that respect, ʿAbduh follows the traditional Islamic view of conflict (*fitna*),[33] and the Oneness of God (*tawhid*), which has both a religious and a political connotation, unifying the believers. Divine law (*sharʿ*) has the purpose to protect man/society from deviation, divisions (*fitan*), fanaticism (*taʿassub*), unify them, and establish a divine order.[34]

Although ʿAbduh does not use the word citizen (*muwatin*), it is clear he does have a concept of its meaning. In his programme of reform, citizens are called upon to become active, take responsibility, contribute to public debate and promote the progress of society. Citizenship is influenced by his concept of order (*nizam*) and his call for agency along rational lines. It is based on his concept of human nature and its attributes, 'acquisition' (*kasb*),[35] consisting of memory, imagination, and reflective 'thought' (*fikra*). A balance between these leads to 'moderateness' (*iʿtidal*), which

---

24 Ibid., 42/46

25 Ibid., 42–6/46–9.

26 He calls it the 'civilized human order' (*nizam al-ʿumran al-bishri*), 72/ 70.

27 Ibid., 48–9, 63–8/50–1, 62–6.

28 Ibid., 59/57.

29 Ibid., 78–80/76–7.

30 Ibid., 90–2/85–6.

31 Ibid., 91/86.

32 Ibid., 71/ 69.

33 Ibid., 34/39. For his analysis of passions, see also 71, 89, 114/69, 84, 105.

34 Ibid., 79–80/76–7.

35 Ibid., 67/65.

can be put in the service of the 'general good' (*maslaha*) and which, in turn, leads to 'well-being/happiness' (*sa'ada*). Typical for the rising Egyptian middle class, the ideal of citizenship is based on individual virtue, 'science' (*'ilm*), 'wisdom' (*hikma*), 'honesty' (*sidq*), 'fidelity' (*imana*), 'integrity' (*wafa' bi-l-'uqud*) 'steadfastness to pledges', and empathy with the weak are mentioned as the foundations of civility.[36] 'Abduh, however, does not uphold an inclusive, democratic notion of citizenship. In his view, only the elite can discover the rational truth through *ijtihad*: 'the prophets are to the corporate and the social what reason is to the personal'.[37] Prophecy and revelation are meant for the masses. Citizenship does, however, extend to Jews and Christians, who as part of the elite enjoy equal rights.

Guidance as the Political

The great difference between Muhammad 'Abduh and Hasan al-Banna (1906–1949), the founder of the Muslim Brotherhood in 1928, is that the latter turns Islam into a communitarian ideology. Like 'Abduh, al-Banna claims that Islam is an order, but it is an authoritarian, and, in the sense of Lefort, even a totalitarian order. This danger is located in its ideological overstretch and 'absorption' of the political. Islam is called a 'comprehensive order' (*nizam kamil*) that covers *all* aspects of life (*al-islam ma'na shamil*).[38] It provides for a '*perfect* social order (*nizam ijtama'i kamil*) in all aspects of life'.[39] And by having the 'complete and all-encompassing program' (*al-manhaj tamm shamil*) and creed (*'aqida*) it can produce the 'best systems for practical and spiritual life'.[40] Absorption of the political, however, is most apparent in the slogan 'Islam, religion and state' (*Islam, din wa-dawla*). At the same time the political is diffused in such pronouncements as 'Islam is faith and worship, a state, nationality and religion, a spirit and deed, a holy text and a sword . . .'.[41] The finality of the political, in Walzer's words, is achieved by equating faith and power. Faith (*iman*)

---

36 Ibid., 109/102.
37 Ibid., 114/106.
38 Hasan al-Banna, '*Da'watuna*', in *Majmu'at rasa'il al-imam al-shahid Hasan al-Banna* (n.p.: Dar al-Shihab, n.d), 16. Hasan a-Banna, 'Our Mission', in *Five Tracts* Translated by Charles Wendell (Berkeley: University of California Press, 1978).
39 Hasan al-Banna, '*Bayna al-ams wa-l-yawm*', in *Majmu'at rasa'il*, 140. Hasan al-Banna, 'Between Yesterday and Today', in *Five Tracts*, 18.
40 Hasan al-Banna, '*Nahwa al-Nur*', in *Majmu'at rasa'il*, 59. Hasan al-Banna, 'Towards the Light', in *Five Tracts*, 104–5.
41 Khalil al-Anani, 'The Power of the Jama'a: The Role of Hasan al-Banna in Constructing the Muslim Brotherhood's Collective Identity', *Sociology of Islam* 1 (2013) 1: 50.

is the foundation of power, agency and activity, and the basis of the movement is the 'principle' (*mabda'*), or even simpler, the 'truth' (*al-haqq*).[42]

The political in Hasan al-Banna's writings is replaced and represented by the concept of 'guidance' (*irshad, tawjih*)[43] and 'rule' (*amr*).[44] This is also reflected in its top-down organisation. The leader of the movement is called the General Guide (*murshid al-'amm*), the politburo, the Guidance Council (*maktab al-irshad*). While 'Abduh's reform programme was based on rationalism, al-Banna's is mostly focused on organisation, hierarchy and the socialisation and disciplining of its members in the Tanzim (the Organisation). Ideologically, it is reflected in the negative connotation 'politics' (*al-siyasa*) usually has, and its association with 'shackles', 'differences', 'kinship' (*'asabiyya*) and foreign occupation.[45] Throughout his work he complains of 'partisanship' (*hizbiyya*), 'division' (*firqa*), 'dissension' (*fitna*), 'dispersion' (*shatat*), which undermine the unity (*wahda*) of the *umma*. Politics is condemned as 'chaos' (*fawda*), 'deviation' (*muruq*), and 'apostasy' (*ilhad*).[46] Like 'Abduh, al-Banna considers 'desires/passions' (*ahwa'*) as well as 'personal interests' threatening.[47] In this manner he denies the political dimension of problems and transplants the political to the religious domain where it is inoculated as religious 'differences of opinion' (*ikhtilaf*), which are acceptable and even 'inevitable' as long as they are restricted to the 'branches' (*furu'*) of *fiqh* and do not endanger its 'foundations' (*usul*).[48] Within this context, al-Banna's call for popular oversight (*muraqaba*) of the ruler has little meaning,[49] because in the end political differences are overcome not by debate and political compromise but by 'bonding of the hearts, mutual love, and cooperation for "the common good" (*al-khair*)'.[50]

Given the threat Hasan al-Banna discerns to the nation, his concept of the citizenship is less universal and inclusive and much stronger and substantive and 'thick' than 'Abduh's. It is also less rational, and, due to the depth of the

---

42 al-Banna, '*Da'watuna*', 22/'Our Mission', 56.

43 Ibid.,18/49; Hasan al-Banna, '*Nahwa al-Nur*', 57/'Towards the Light', 103.

44 See Roel Meijer, 'The Muslim Brotherhood and the Political: An Exercise in Ambiguity', in *The Muslim Brotherhood in Europe*, ed. Roel Meijer (London: Hurst, 2012), 295–320.

45 al-Banna, '*Nahwa al-Nur*', 58/'Towards the Light',104; Hasan al-Banna, *Bayna al-ams wa-l-yawm*',131/'Between Yesterday and Today', 18; and Hasan al-Banna, '*Nizam al-hukm*', in *Majmu'at rasa'il*, 211–27.

46 al-Banna, *'Bayna al-ams wa-l-yawm*', 137/'Between Yesterday and Today', 26.

47 al-Banna, '*Da'watuna*', 18/'Our Mission', 50.

48 Ibid., 23–4/59.

49 al-Banna, '*Nizam al-hukm*', 213.

50 al-Banna, '*Da'watuna*', 24/'Our Mission', 58.

crisis in interbellum Egypt, more emotionally charged and populist. His use of the term citizen (*muwatin*) is rare and does not have a modern meaning.[51] Rights (*huquq*) are restricted to nations and do not extend to individuals.[52] In his communitarian view individuals can only fully realise their potential by becoming members of the Muslim Brotherhood. One becomes a 'citizen' in joining the movement and submission to unity (*wahda*), the 'whole' (*jami'*), and ascribing to the 'credal bond' (*rabitat al- 'aqida*)[53] that holds the community together. The highly activist concept of the citizen is expressed in the term 'believing activists' (*al-'amilun al-mu'minun*), or the struggler (*mujahid*), who demonstrates his commitment (*iltizam*) through loyalty to the Brotherhood. This step is a rite of passage. Becoming a member is a fundamental personal transformation through the ritual of repentance (*tawba*) and acceptance of a set of ideological prepositions. Through this act one does not only leave the world of materialism, dissidence, corruption and treachery behind, but also the society of half- and non-citizens, the weaklings, hypocrites and waverers, those who pursue their personal interests and live in the domain of 'doubt in God'.[54] The internal unity was maintained by organisation which was based on the principles of 'listening and obeying' (*al-sam'a wa-l-ta'a*) and promoting the regeneration of Islam. Obedience, discipline and sacrifice also occur in words that replace citizenship, such as 'soldier' (*jund*) and associations with the army, physical health, and jihad.[55] The allegiance is to the leader through the *bay'a* and is unconditional. Internal unity was stressed, debate discouraged and opposition suppressed as dissidence (*fitna*).[56]

Although the ambiguity that the absorption by and displacement of the political in Islamic moral guidance (*irshad*) produces is probably not intentional it also had tactical advantages. It gave Hasan al-Banna the room to play the political game both ways as an apolitical *da'wa* social movement aimed at moral revival as well as a political organisation that could claim not to seek political power but exerted it anyway because it left it undefined.[57] Other branches of the Muslim Brotherhood would use this ambivalence to

---

51 See, for instance, Hasan al-Banna, '*Risalat al-mu'tamar khamis*' (Address to the Fifth Congress), in *Majmu'at rasa'il*, 158.

52 al-Banna, '*Bayna al-ams wa-l-yawm*',135/'Between Yesterday and Today', 24.

53 al-Banna, '*Da'watuna*', 21– 2/'Our Mission', 53–5.

54 Ibid.

55 al-Banna', *Nahwa al-Nur*', 63–5/'Towards the Light', 110–14.

56 See also Khalil al-Anani, 'The Power of the Jama'a', 51.

57 Much has been written especially in French on speaking with a forked tongue, or *le double langage*, as a conscious strategy of the Brotherhood. See, for instance, Caroline Fourest, *Frère Tariq: Le double discours de Tariq Ramadan* (Paris Grasset, 2010[2004]).

their advantage. The Jordanian Muslim Brotherhood escaped suppression as a charity organisation and became the prop of the Jordanian monarchy against the left and pan-Arabism, which did have an overt political goal.[58] At some point, the movement would, however, pay the price, especially when it also developed a violent, jihadist strain. Hasan al-Banna himself was assassinated and the Brotherhood was banned after the Secret Apparatus had assassinated Prime Minister Mahmud Fahmi al-Nuqrashi in 1948. The Brotherhood was legalised again under his conservative successor Hasan al-Hudaybi, but unsurprisingly, during the 'March Crisis' of 1954 its deep political ambiguity was confirmed when it withdrew its support to the democratic/political opposition to Nasser and helped the military to power. The Algerian Front Islamique du Salut (FIS) made the same mistake some 40 years later. The contradictory statements of its leaders gave the military the opportunity to cancel the elections in 1992 and stage a coup. Three years earlier this ambiguity allowed the National Islamic Front (NIF) in the Sudan to ally itself with the military and come to power, with disastrous results for the country, for it, like the Brotherhood in Egypt after the more recent Uprisings, had no political programme when it came to power.

Jihad as Politicide

Before the realisation that the totalising claims of the Islamist movement did not work to its advantage, the Brotherhood would first have to go through a radical phase. Sayyid Qutb (1906–1966) took the contradictions of the 'comprehensive system' to its radical conclusion. He eliminated the vagueness and ambiguity of diffusion of the political of Hasan al-Banna by heightening the sense of crisis and seeking the solution in an even greater individual commitment and self-sacrifice in waging jihad. This, however, would expose the basic contradictions of the project. Qutb's world is a dichotomous one and the struggle a zero-sum game. 'Everything around us expresses *jahiliyya*:[59] people's ideas, their beliefs, habits, traditions, culture, art, literature, rules and laws.'[60] Ironically, Qutb as a novelist and

---

[58] The Egyptian branch also pursued the tactic of being registered as welfare, an Islamic charity organisation, and playing politics from there. See Gudrun Krämer, *Hasan al-Banna* (Oxford: One World, 2010), 30 and 48.

[59] The term *jahiliyya* is usually used to connote the pre-Islamic period, but Qutb has radicalised it by using it to refer to imperfect Muslim society after the revelation of Islam.

[60] Roxanne L. Euben, *Enemy in the Mirror: Islamic Fundamentalism and the Limits of Modern Rationalism. A Work of Comparative Political Theory* (Princeton: Princeton University Press, 1999), 57.

intellectual (*muthaqqaf*) was aware of the afflictions of modernity and its fragmentation, indeterminacy and conflict. His solution, however, was the total submission to God's sovereignty (*hakimiyya*). In his totalitarian suppression of the political, power, knowledge and law were incorporated in the religious, which has become the transparent, absolute truth. As a result, Walzer's 'walls of separation' between politics and economics and religion and politics, and Lefort's separation between power, law and knowledge, are brought down by presenting the world as a cosmic struggle of belief (*al-iman*) and truth (*al-haqq*) against unbelief (*kufr*).[61] Consequently, all sources of knowledge other than Islam are rejected because they are 'corrosive', 'limited', and 'fallible'.[62] As such, they threaten the unity of religious knowledge and *tawhid* (Oneness of God). [63]

Qutb's solution is the expression of the ultimate paradox: 'Pure' Islam, the antipolitical, becomes the ultimate political; total freedom is found in complete submission; and harmony and peace is achieved through violence.[64] Like a black hole, faith has absorbed the political: 'First, belief ought to be imprinted on hearts and rule over consciences – that belief which demands that people should not bow before anyone except God or derive laws from any other source'.[65] Freedom is not liberty to decide over a range of possibilities and fulfil one's life creatively; rather, human agency and rationality consist of choosing for God and working according to his plan. It is as if only one solution is available in economics, politics and legislation. Social justice, equality, and freedom follow from this submission.[66] The totalitarian dimension is further underlined in his fatalism that life is 'foreordained, destined, his path planned, his existence designed with purpose'.[67]

In Qutb's cosmology Hannah Arendt's dictum that citizenship is the right to have rights is an absurdity: in a perfect order and complete submission to the sovereignty of God (*hakimiyya*) believers have no need for rights; faith and piety are the yardstick of happiness; and conflict and strife are regarded as a zero-sum game of absolutes with outsiders. The real, actual Egyptian citizen, already suspect in al-Banna's view, is in Qutb's opinion a member of *jahili* society, subject of a *jahili* regime, and a such a partner to the 'authoritarian bargain' and the social contract that

---

61 Ibid., 62.
62 Ibid., 70.
63 Seyyid Qutb, *Milestones* (Damascus: Dar Al-Ilm, n.d.), 72.
64 Ibid., 34.
65 Ibid., 35.
66 Ibid., 63.
67 Ibid., 72.

it entails.[68] Qutb's ideal citizen is a totally different person. Qutb discerns three phases in Islamic history. The first occurred in the golden period of Islam, when faith was absolute and life was perfect and even God's laws did apply. In this period 'there was no occasion to enforce the limits and punishments which God has prescribed; for now conscience was the law-enforcer, and the pleasure of God, the hope of the Divine reward, and the fear of God's anger took the place of police and punishments'.[69] Then, only pure believers existed, whose hearts were 'free from pride of lineage, of nationality, of country, of tribe, of household – in short, when God Most High saw them to be morally pure – then he granted the great trust, the conscious assumption of being God's representative on earth'.[70] The second phase occurred in the period of decline and what he calls *jahiliyya*. In *jahiliyya* society, unbelief (*kufr*) and laxity of norms and laws are associated with politicisation of Islam and its banalisation, and secularisation, when 'people became dehumanized and beasts'.[71] The third period is that of building the ideal society of liberation of complete submission to Islam. It is here, however, that crucial elements associated with citizenship occur, in the sense that it supports agency and empowers the believer. First, joining Qutb's project is a totally individual decision of taking personal responsibility and awareness of the necessary religious obligations and commitments. Like the first Muslim community in Medina, one can only become a true believer when one is free from personal, clan and tribal relations, and the customs and laws that they follow,[72] and thus obtain 'dignity and honor'.[73] All believers are equal in this pristine, pre-political community, where one becomes a 'trustee' (*khilafa*) of God through 'moral purity and spiritual fortitude'.[74] However, at this stage Qutb takes a more radical step, for vice-regency in his vision means performing the armed jihad, not *jihad al-nafs* (struggle for personal improvement). The crisis of *jahiliyya* is so dire that jihad is called for. Jihad is not simply a means of attaining the good life, as two researchers concluded, 'it *is* the good life'.[75] With his emphasis

---

68 It is interesting that Al Qaeda uses the same reasoning for justifying attacks on non-Muslim foreign citizens. They are not innocent because as citizens they vote for the government that attacks Muslims.

69 Qutb, *Milestones*, 30.

70 Ibid., 31.

71 Euben, *Enemy*, 59.

72 Qutb, *Milestones*, 33.

73 Ibid., 26.

74 Ibid., 29, 72.

75 Hendrik Hansen and Peter Kainz, 'Radical Islamism and Totalitarian Ideology: A Comparison of Sayyid Qutb's Islamism with Marxism and National

on absolute submission, obedience to the higher ideal, and radical self-sacrifice of the martyr for utopian ideals, together with harmony, peace and paradise Qutb radically undercuts the reformist project to accept the political and develop an Islamic concept of the citizenship.[76] The ultimate consequences of the absolute denial of the political is the abnegation of legal, formal citizenship through the categorical *takfir* of all Muslims who accept the *jahiliyya* state they are living in. One can only be a citizen in the City of God where the laws of the *jahili* state do not apply. Not surprisingly this ultimate rejection of the unbelieving state and society has the greatest appeal on the discriminated, marginalised and alienated Muslim semi-citizens in Europe.[77]

Community, Exclusion and Violence

Qutb's radical drawing of lines between insiders and outsiders had severe consequences for Salafism. Although Salafism has many different strands, they share more in common than what separates them. The difference between so-called 'quietists', 'politicos', or 'jihadis' is totally subordinated to their common foundation to create a pure community devoted to the Oneness of God (*tawhid*). Their internal discipline is maintained through the principle of 'promoting the good and rejecting the bad' (*al-amr bi-l-ma'ruf was nahi 'an al-munkar*), while the boundaries with the outside, hostile world of unbelief are secured through the practice of 'loyalty to Muslims and disavowal of the unbelievers' (*al-wala' wa-l-bara'*). And while Salafism is supposed to end the ambiguity and wishy-washiness of the Muslim Brotherhood, it has not done so. Instead, it has deepened the problem by the complete denial of the political as an independent space, as is apparent in the politicisation of religious concepts and techniques which have been turned into instruments of exclusion.[78] In this process *takfir*, the radical drawing of boundaries, has absorbed politics; jihad is just one of its expressions.

Socialism', *Totalitarian Movements and Religions* 8 (2007)1: 61 (emphasis in original).

[76] Euben, *Enemy*, 81–2.

[77] Roy, *The Failure*. See also Zoltan Pall, Chapter 9 in this volume.

[78] See Emin Poljarevic, 'The Ambiguity of Citizenship in Contemporary Salafism', in *The Crisis of Citizenship in the Arab World*, eds. Roel Meijer and Nils Butenschøn (Leiden: Brill, 2017), 338–74.

POST-ISLAMISM: RE-INSTATING THE POLITICAL AND CITIZENSHIP

The Qutbian turn has encountered strong opposition for theoretical and practical reasons. Theoretically, it had boxed Islamism into a corner. *Takfir* enhanced sectarianism and led to an endless regression of accusing Muslims of deviation, while jihad proved ineffective as a means of toppling authoritarian states in the 1990s. Islam in the subsequent period had to become domesticated again and a religion for the middle classes, which had totally different ideas of life, aspirations, interests and career plans than the activists who were focused on self-sacrifice and jihad. One way to find a solution is to recognise the political, open space for politics, and accept the notion of citizenship. This turn coincided with the unravelling of the authoritarian bargain and the search for a new social contract in the 1980s.[79] It was done in small steps, but basically was achieved by developing ʿAbduh's concept of the 'common good' (*al-maslaha al-ʿamma*).

Hasan al-Hudaybi's Opening

The first to launch an attack on Qutb's totalitarian claims was Hasan al-Hudaybi (1891–1973) in his *Preachers not Judges* (*Duʿat la qudat*), written in 1969 and published in 1977. Though never mentioning Sayyid Qutb or many of his themes such as *takfir* directly, and himself in many ways a conservative thinker, al-Hudaybi laid the foundation for revisionism within the Brotherhood without addressing the political directly. He accepted the idea of God's sovereignty and rejected people's sovereignty. But he limited the extent of submission by denying that *hakimiyya* covered all acts of man and was absolute and not subject to interpretation.[80] He also denied the central doctrine of *jahiliyya* and the notion that Muslims were sinful if they did not strive for an Islamic state. Islam was an inclusive and tolerant religion and deviation from the *shariʿa* was a sin (*maʿsiya*) instead of an act of unbelief (*kufr*). Taking part in jihad, according to al-Hudaybi, was not the ultimate fulfilment of Muslims. No less important, *Preachers not Judges* provided room for human agency and human responsibility in a broader sense than the stark choice between unbelief and jihad. Following ʿAbduh, al-Hudaybi

[79] See, Roel Meijer, 'Citizenship, Social Pacts, Authoritarian Bargains, and the Arab Uprisings', in *The Crisis of Citizenship in the Arab World*, 67–104.

[80] Barbara Zollner, *The Muslim Brotherhood: Hasan al-Hudaybi and Ideology* (London: Routledge), 102.

also reintroduced a measure of reason and challenged the necessity of the Islamic state. Likewise, he did not regard the first Islamic period as a golden age. Muhammad was not perfect and infallible, but exemplary.[81] He opened space for politics by first making a distinction between what belonged to religious observance and obedience (*ʿibadat*), and necessary to follow, and what was not and not mentioned but liable to human interpretation and discretion: 'The truth is that God (praise him and let him come) left many worldly matters to us in order to regulate these in line with our reasoning'.[82] All these matters of human interchange, the so-called (*muʿamalat*), including politics, could be covered with a social contract and should be negotiated between citizens.[83] This allowed for the election of the ruler, sanctioned by an oath of loyalty (*bayʿa*).[84] In this way al-Hudaybi expanded the extent of human freedom and self-determination. He also allowed the right to revolt but embedded it within the rule of 'promoting the good and forbidding the wrong' (*al-amr bi-l-maʿruf wa al-nahi ʿan al-munkar*) by accepting passive resistance with the heart (*bi-l-qalb*) rather than a violent action with the hand (*bi-l-yad*). His acceptance of the notion of a fundamentally different concept of citizenship from Qutb, however, was based on the acceptance of dispute and the acceptance of argumentative contestation 'by means of the tongue' (*bi-l-lisan*). This fell within responsibility and collective duty (*fard al-kifayya*) rather than a personal duty (*fard al-ʿayn*). Hudaybi considered learning rather than jihad a personal duty.

Al-Hudaybi is not a revolutionary thinker. In finding a 'balance between obedience and resistance',[85] he was conservative. The room for *muʿamalat* is restricted and therefore also the 'space' for politics. He accepts the idea of the caliphate and the Islamic state and the figure of the righteous ruler as the lynchpin of the Islamic state. He warns against *fitna* if the concept of the sovereignty of the people would be introduced, and limits the right to choose the ruler to an elite (*ahl al-ʿaqd wa-l-hall*).[86] However, he has prepared the way for his successors to accept the political by accepting *hizbiyya*[87] and acquire an interest in a rights discourse and constitutions

---

[81] Ibid., 80–81.
[82] Quoted in Zollner, *The Muslim Brotherhood*, 103.
[83] Ibid., 104, 110.
[84] Ibid., 121.
[85] Ibid., 136.
[86] Ibid., 122.
[87] Roel Meijer, 'The Muslim Brotherhood and the Political: An Exercise in Ambiguity', in *The Muslim Brotherhood in Europe*, eds. Roel Meijer and Edwin Bakker (London: Hurst, 2012), 295–320.

as means of restricting the power of the authoritarian rulers in what some called post-Islamism.

Yusuf al-Qaradawi's Fiqh of Balances

Yusuf al-Qaradawi (1928–)[88] is an exponent of a trend that arose in the 1980s, which has been called the New Islamists or Wasatiyya (the middle way).[89] This trend is aware that Islam must come up with an answer to the challenges of the new citizen regime that was emerging after the unravelling of the authoritarian bargain and the opportunity to develop notions of the political and citizenship. He calls *wasatiyya* a 'balance between the general goals and the details of the text (*nusus*)'. It especially deals with 'reality'.[90] In this, he is more 'progressive' than the conservative wing of the Brotherhood that grabbed power in the Tanzim before the Arab Uprisings and largely was inspired by Qutb's denial of the political. He is one of the first who explicitly uses terms as 'democracy' (*al-dimuqratiyya*), 'citizenship', 'political participation' (*musharaka*), 'equality' (*musawa'*) 'freedom of opinion', and 'rights' and even 'human rights', and does not shy away from 'partyism' (*hizbiyya*). He openly investigates the concept of 'politics' (*al-siyasa*) in one of his many books. On the other hand, his goal is not to acknowledge the worth of these concepts but to encapsulate them in the 'comprehensive system'[91] which provides a 'complete method for life' (*manhaj mutakamil li-l-haya*).[92] A good example is his critique of Western political science that focuses on what he calls the 'truth of power' (*haqq al-quwa*), whereas Islamic politics is based on the 'power of truth' (*quwa al-haqq*).[93] This demonstrates that he analyses what politics should be (ethics) rather than what it is. Politics, in his opinion, is immoral and is related to passions (*ahwa'*). It must always be subordinated to religion and its *only* function is to 'empower (*tamkin*) religion on earth'.[94] In this sense, al-Qaradawi can be regarded as a 'liberalised authoritarian' update

---

88 Jakob Skovgaard-Petersen and Bettina Gräf, *Global Mufti: The Phenomenon of Yusuf al-Qaradawi* (London: Hurst, 2009), 8.

89 Raymond W. Baker, *Islam without Fear: Egypt and the New Islamists* (Cambridge, MA: Harvard University Press, 2003).

90 Yusuf al-Qaradawi, *al-Din wa-l-siyasa: ta'sil wa radd shubahat* (*Religion and Politics: Certainty and Repulsion of Doubt*) (Cairo: Dar al-Shuruq, 2007), 107–108.

91 al-Qaradawi, *al-Din wa-l-siyasa*, 71.

92 al-Qaradawi, *Sahwa al-islamiyya bayna al-jumud wa-l-tataturruf* (Cairo: Dar al-Shuruq, 1990), 104.

93 al-Qaradawi, *al-Din wa-l-siyasa*, 60.

94 Ibid., 135–6.

of Hasan al-Banna.[95] He modernises the slogan 'Islam is religion and state' and turns the state into a modern bureaucratic instrument of supervision that imposes its views concerning creed, thought, values, feelings, tastes and conduct on its population. In this, the state has a mission (*risala*).[96] Sovereignty of the people is restricted, because he assumes that it is always based on *shari'a*. Likewise, the common good (*maslaha*) is adaptable and flexible, but within the confines of the religious 'texts' (*nusus*).

Despite his attempts at absorption of the political in the religious and putting it under heavy control, he does try to find ways to deal with modernity. Al-Qaradawi comes closest to a notion of politics in what he calls the '*fiqh* (jurisprudence) of balances'. The *fiqh* of balances accepts the indeterminacy of modernity – or what he calls 'reality' (*al-waqi'*) – and provides a way to deal with it. He realises that modern life changes (*taghyir*) and he even encourages people to change with it. The challenge is to keep a balance between general principles and details, goals and means.[97] Al-Qaradawi states that 'If we apply the *fiqh* of balances, we will find a way to compare one situation to another and weigh the profits against losses in the short and the long runs and then choose what we judge as leading to the realisation of interest and the avoidance of evil in the best way possible.'[98] According to this principle Muslims are even allowed to participate politically under non-Islamic rule and ally with non-Muslims as long as it is in the interest of the Muslim community.[99] The same *fiqh* applies to Islamic politics in Muslim majority countries and there al-Qaradawi opens up a large degree of 'political space' to politics and the agency of the people. He calls for a civil state (*al-dawla al-madaniyya*) because it is run by the people not by the 'ulama, who are inflexible, think in absolute terms, and in which case it would be a religious state (*al-dawla al-islamiyya*).[100] He believes it should be based on debate of current affairs in order to adjust to modern challenges and lead to the common good. In order for this debate to be open, constitutions must stipulate that Islamic parties can lay no claims to the truth and they must draw up programmes that explain their views on modern topics such as economics, culture and politics. In this system rulers are held accountable by the *umma*, the

---

95 Brumberger, 'The Trap of Liberalized Autocracy', *Journal of Democracy* 13 (2002) 4: 56–68.

96 al-Qaradawi, *al-Din wa-l-siyasa*, 146–7.

97 Ibid., 126–8.

98 al-Qaradawi, *Priorities of the Islamic Movement in the Coming Phase* (Cairo: Dar al Nashr for Egyptian Universities, 1992), 42–3.

99 Ibid., 38.

100 al-Qaradawi, *al-Din wa-l-siyasa*, 158.

people. These programmes are based on *ijtihad*, *tajdid*, and the *fiqh* of general purposes (*al-maqasid*) and balances (*al-muwazanat*) and principles (*al-awliyyat*).[101] In the end, however, the political/religious system is based on consensus, and the settling of differences, such an important aspect of the political, falls within Islamic 'reference' (*marja'iyya*) of correct behaviour (*adab al-khilaf*)[102] and possibilities (agency) are highly restricted by religious texts (*nusus*).[103]

Although Yusuf al-Qaradawi only wrote on citizenship in a later phase of his life,[104] his concept of citizenship is central to his *fiqh* of balances. It seems he has taken several steps to come to his book on citizenship and notions of citizenship were developed as a strategy to counter extremism (*ghuluw*), which he associates with violence and *takfir* and Qutb's '*fiqh* of rejection'. Unsurprisingly, his concept of citizenship is couched in terms of the ethics (*akhlaq*) of the middle way (*wasatiyya*) and moderateness (*i'tidal*). His emphasis is on active participation, and taking responsibility for the common good: 'Islam solves the problems of people through people themselves'.[105] Compared to his predecessors, al-Qaradawi differs from 'Abduh in that *ijtihad* has become democratised and seems to suggest that the real citizen is an average person who through education and social and individual responsibility can practise the *fiqh* of balances, or practical reason.[106] On the other hand, *ijtihad* is restricted by 'ulama who have real knowledge and have the final authority to bring text and reality in balance. From Qutb, al-Qaradawi differs in the sense that the ideal is not the *mujahid* (jihadi) but the *mujtahid* (the interpreter), while he differs from Hasan al-Banna in that he is more open and addresses himself to a broad, open social movement, not to a closed Tanzim. In many ways, however, al-Qaradawi adds to the internal contradictions and ambiguity of the Brotherhood's ideology by absorbing these new terms within its paradigm without resolving their tensions. These contradictions caught up with al-Qaradawi when he first supported the fall of Mubarak but refused to acknowledge the end of the unpopularity of the Morsi presidency in July 2013.[107]

---

101 Ibid., 153.

102 al-Qaradawi, *Sahwa*, 124.

103 al-Qaradawi, *al-Din wa-l-siyasa*, 169.

104 Yusuf al-Qaradawi, *al-Watan wa-l-muwatana fi daw' al-usul al-'aqdiyya wa-l-maqasid al-shar'iyya* (*the Nation and Citizenship in the Light of the Contract and the Goals of Islamic Law*) (Cairo: Dar al-Shuruq, 2010).

105 al-Qaradawi, *Priorities*, 71.

106 Ibid., 111, 145.

107 David H. Warren and Christine Gilmore, 'One Nation under God? Yusuf al-Qaradawi's Changing Fiqh of Citizenship in the Light of the Islamic Legal Tradition', *Contemporary Islam* 8 (2014) 3: 217–37.

MAQASID AL-SHARI'A AS THE POLITICAL

Later generations after al-Qaradawi extended the notion of politics further. They have several common characteristics. Firstly, they are not bound by the concept of the comprehensive system, and secondly, they are more open to Western concepts of the political, politics and citizenship. This has resulted in a major shift in the conception of the political, the room for politics and the concept of citizenship.

Abu al-'Ala Madi's Civil Politics

A good example is Abu al-'Ala Madi, who is not a thinker per se but was the political leader of the Wasat Party. In 2007 Madi published a book on the legal equality of the Coptic minority in Egypt, *The Issue of the Copts, Islamic Law, and the Islamic Awakening*.[108] Refreshingly, he explicitly states that his book is basically about politics and religion is subordinated to that goal and that the solution to the problems in Egypt is not a return to Islam but the introduction of democracy – which is in itself a revolutionary position for a leader of the Islamist movement. Nowhere, he argues, do the Islamic sources say anything about a state; it only provides for 'norms and values' (*qiyam*).[109] He states that the Wasat Party is not a 'religious party' (*hizb dini*) but a 'civil party' (*hizb madani*). It is pursuing a 'political project' with 'modern' views on the state, which should be a civil state (*al-dawla al-madaniyya*), where 'the people are the source of all powers (*al-sha'b masdar al-sulutat*), where [judiciary, legislative and the executive] must be separated from each other and be independent from each other in a general balance'.[110] He goes on to state that 'this principle will guarantee the people the right to legislate themselves through laws it agrees upon what are its interest'.[111] Politics is based on a 'human constitution' that guarantees respect for the law, equality and freedom of belief.[112] This inclusiveness is enhanced by shifting the focus from *shari'a* to 'Arab Islamic civilisation' (*hadara al-'arabiyya al-islamiyya*), 'with everything that it entails' of a 'human civilisation'. Membership of this state is based on 'partners in this culture' (*shuraka' fi hadhihi al-hadara*), 'complete

---

108 Abu al-'Ala Madi, *Mas'ala al-qibtiyya, wa-l-shari'a, wa-l-al-sahwa al-islamiyya* (*The Issue of the Copts, Islamic Law and the Islamic Awakening*) (Cairo: Safir al-Duwwaliyya li-l-Nashr, 2007).

109 Ibid., 96.

110 Ibid., 97.

111 Ibid.

112 Ibid., 95.

equality', and 'full citizenship' (*muwatana kamila*) without regard for religion. Despite these giant strides towards accepting both politics and citizenship, several researchers have expressed their reservations about the extent of inclusion.[113] Madi still talks about an 'Islamic political system' (*al-nizam al-islami al-siyasi*), 'which organises the values (*qiyam*) of this system but does not determine its specific form'.[114]

Abdelwahhab El-Affendi and Politics as a Separate Field

Abdelwahhab El-Affendi goes furthest in the awareness of the undemocratic element in modern Islamic political thinking by absorption of the political. He is one of the few who criticises the Islamic harmony model by stating that Islamism has 'idealized the Muslim *umma* too much, and made too many assumptions about its unity and its moral credentials'.[115] The problem, he argues, is that Muslims have made Islamic politics 'sacred' with the result that it has become apologetic and totalitarian. 'The debate on political authority was plagued by many other problems from early on, particularly expressing opinions in normative terms, thus camouflaging the key political questions as theological arguments.'[116] El-Affendi advocates a more realistic stance on politics. He argues that Muslims must acknowledge that 'power creates its own rules, which were sometimes outside conventional morality and religion'.[117] This means that Muslims should give up the search for a virtuous ruler who in practice is often a 'pious dictator'. The state should be in the service of society not the other way round, and echoing the liberalism of Michael Walzer, power should be 'limited, divided, revocable and open to challenge'.[118] Citizens should be free from coercion, enjoying rights to privacy, to develop their own conscience, and become active participants who have responsibilities for the welfare of the community and hold rulers accountable.[119]

---

113 Ibid., 97.
114 Ibid., 101–2.
115 Abdelwahhab El-Affendi, *Who Needs an Islamic State?* (London: Malaysia Think Tank, 2008, 2nd print), 27.
116 Ibid., 76.
117 Ibid., 47.
118 Ibid., 50.
119 Ibid., 130–31.

Jasser Auda and the Purposes of the Shariʿa as the Political

Jasser Auda in his theory of the *maqasid al-shariʿa* (purposes of Islamic law) goes even further. Although Auda works well within the idea of a comprehensive system, in the sense that he believes that *shariʿa* covers all facets of life, he also embraces modernism and therefore starts from different principles.[120] He is especially interested in arriving at an ethical system of higher values (*maqasid*). He also argues that Islamic law must be adaptive and flexible. Only then can it be 'a drive for a just, productive, developed, humane, spiritual, clean, cohesive, friendly, and highly democratic society'.[121] This is brought about by finding the purposes, intent, principles, goals, and objectives of Islamic law. These are justice, human dignity, free will, magnanimity, facilitation, and social cooperation, civility and human rights.[122] He builds upon the works of, among others, the medieval thinker Abu Ishaq al-Shatibi (1320–1388), and the modernist Tunisian Muhammad al-Tahir Ibn ʿAshur (1879–1973). Although Auda mentions neither citizenship nor politics in his theoretical work, he makes important steps to turn *maqasid* into the Islamic equivalent of the political and *maslaha* as the foundation for citizenship. He does this in several steps. First, he separates the divine text from human interpretation. While the *shariʿa* is divine, the *maqasid*, like *fiqh*, are human, changeable, fallible, debatable, and based on *ijtihad*, which is inherently democratic in the sense that everyone has the right to apply *ijtihad* on all issues of *muʿamalat*. As a result, there is not one but 'multiple truths'. Second, as a human activity, *fiqh* depends on cultural, local, and historical circumstances. This leaves no room for absolute claims and accusations of heresy,[123] leading to sectarian conflicts.[124] Third, he embraces the rapid tempo of modernity and argues for the 'contemporalisation' of the interpretations of the texts, and adjustment to 'reality through the jurisprudence of reality (*fiqh al-waqiʿ*)'. The new trends are open to modern values, human rights and rationality. Fourth, Auda regards Islam as a holistic system that hangs logically together, instead of a book of literal truths. Islamic law does not provide a fixed law, as literalist Salafis believe, but 'a way of life', a 'world view' (*Weltanschauung*).[125]

---

120 Ibid., 169–180.

121 Jasser Auda, *Maqasid al-Shariah as Philosophy of Islamic Law* (London: The International Institute of Islamic Thought, 2008), xxii–xxiii.

122 Ibid., 1, 175.

123 Ibid., 59, 193–5

124 Ibid., 61.

125 Ibid., 104.

If the indeterminacy of the political is accepted through recognising the openness and flexibility of the *maqasid*, and the space for politics and resolving conflicts is broadened, Auda bases the concept of the citizen on equal rights and political empowerment. The room for politics is expanded by de-sanctifying daily life and loosening the bond between text and reality, broadening the range of *mu'amalat* at the expense of the area of rituals (*'ibadat*). A way of increasing the range for human interpretation and action is to make a distinction between Muhammad as prophet and as human being. The last Auda calls 'policies' and these are changeable and adaptable even if they are acts of Muhammad.[126] In the end, Auda states, 'there are no "politics" in Islam without wisdom, *maqasid* and higher purposes upon which they are built'. Politics in its indeterminacy therefore cannot be against the *shari'a*.[127] Citizenship is based on the *maqasid* of *shari'a* to preserve and foster faith, life, mind, offspring, honour and property.

Given these ideas, it is unsurprising that Jasser Auda wholeheartedly supported the Arab Uprisings. In his *Sharia and Politics* he emphasises the right to revolt, and the need for justice. Politics should be based on the preponderance of the 'benefits of the nation' (*masalih al-watan*) and 'public interest' over individual interests.[128] He argues that the main priority of the revolution is 'character building'. But it is clear that this character building is the creation of the citizen.

CONCLUSION

The chapter has demonstrated that in one way or another Islamic thinkers have grappled with the political, politics and citizenship since the confrontation with the West and the introduction of the nation-state. While Muhammad 'Abduh tried to accommodate them through reason and the common good, Hasan al-Banna tried to absorb them theoretically in the 'comprehensive system' and organisationally in the Tanzim of the Brotherhood. This process was deepened by Sayyid Qutb, but after his project was proven unable to resolve the contradiction between total freedom and total submission, thinkers such as Yusuf al-Qaradawi tried to find a 'middle way' between the extremes of Qutb and the apoliticism

---

126 Jasser Auda, *Sharia and Politics: Questions for Post-Revolutionary Phase*, https://cscsebook.files.wordpress.com/2016/12/sharia-and-politics.pdf, accessed 4 December 2017, 25–8.

127 Ibid., 34.

128 Ibid., 22–3.

of Salafism. It is only a newer generation of thinkers such as Abu al-ʿAla Madi, Abdelwahhab El Affendi and especially Jasser Auda who allow for the political, politics and citizenship to fully emerge and become compatible with a democratic notion of modernity. In their case the main opponent is not Western imperialism, or Western ideas and lifestyles, or even secularisation, but Islamic literalism as expressed in Salafism. They regard it as a symptom of the general political and religious malaise of the region. Like Muhammad ʿAbduh, they believe that Islam is compatible with modernity and supports universal norms. This does not mean that they have accepted the secularism of Claude Lefort, Chantal Mouffe, Sheldon Wolin, Michael Walzer and their radical indeterminacy, agonistic opponents, and 'walls of separation', but they have come a long way to redefining the political, accepting politics as a separate space, and embracing political citizenship which provides the right to independent political participation.

9. Can the *umma* replace the nation? Salafism and deterritorialised citizenship in Lebanon and Kuwait

Zoltan Pall

INTRODUCTION

This chapter examines how participating in the Salafi movement might influence the individual's relationship to the state and his/her belonging to a political community defined by the modern concept of 'nation'. Salafism on the discursive level offers a deterritorialised version of citizenship in the global *umma* where membership is based on the purity of one's adherence to Islam rather than territorial and/or ethnic belonging. This chapter looks at how this idea of deterritorialisation translates in two localities where Salafism has gained significant foothold.

In this chapter I examine the relationship between Salafis and citizenship that is defined by belonging to nation states. For Salafis, the modern nation state as a form of political organisation lacks legitimacy because it bounds the loyalty of citizens to the nation instead of religion and the *umma*. Yet, the majority of Salafis do not attempt to violently overthrow the nation state, but rather coexist with it. Salafis participate in parliamentary elections in a number of states such as Kuwait, Egypt, Tunisia and Yemen. Despite the pragmatism of Salafis, the participants of the movement are actively looking for ways to bypass the boundaries of the nation state and recreate the circumstances in which the Salafi concept of deterritorialised citizenship can be lived. This chapter inquires how this happens in the case of Salafi groups that reject violence as a means to change reality.

The first section of the chapter discusses the Salafi notion of citizenship and explains how this notion is based on the utopian outlook of the members of the movement. My discussion here is based on quotes from the most renowned religious authorities of Salafism and personal observations. The second and third sections present two case studies from Lebanon and Kuwait. In Lebanon, Salafis claim to be the vanguard of the

Sunni community. Therefore, they need to negotiate how they envision the place of Sunni Muslims as constituents of a multi-sectarian state and as parts of the deterritorialised umma. Kuwaiti Salafis regard their country as a centre of Islam whose material wealth can be used to unify the *umma* through spreading the uncorrupted form of Islam. A faction of Salafis here allies with the ruler in an attempt to 'Salafise' the official practice of Islam in Kuwait. Furthermore, Salafis also emphasise the need of allegiance to the Emir rather than a modern Kuwaiti nation.

SALAFISM AND TRANSNATIONAL CITIZENSHIP

Salafism is best known as a proselytisation movement that intends to change the religious identity of other Muslims. Salafis intend to imitate the religious practices and morality of the first three generations of Islam (*al-salaf al-salih* – righteous ancestors), and to do so they adopt a literal understanding of the scripture. The ultimate aim of Salafism is to make other Muslims accept that their version of Islam is the orthodox one and leave other interpretations that are seen as distorted from the pure form of religion.[1]

Salafis claim that all aspects of life are codified in the foundational texts of Islam, the Qur'an and the Sunna (prophetic tradition). Literal reading of these texts, without 'distorting' their meaning by logical and metaphorical interpretations provides guidance for all aspects of human life. This means that by careful reading of the Qur'an and the Sunna, it is possible to discern clear instructions not only about practising religion but also mundane aspects of life such as how to behave, speak or dress.[2] By this, Salafis detach Islam from the local cultural context. In other words, believers should not

---

1 Salafi doctrines and practices have been discussed extensively. See for example, Bernard Haykel, 'On the Nature of Salafi Thought and Action', in *Global Salafism: Islam's New Religious Movement*, ed. Roel Meijer (New York: Columbia University Press, 2009); Quintan Wiktorowicz, 'Anatomy of the Salafi Movement', *Studies in Conflict and Terrorism* 29 (2006) 2: 216–34; Richard Gauvain, *Salafi Ritual Purity: In the Presence of God* (London and New York: Routledge, 2013).

2 As a young Salafi *shaykh*, whom I interviewed in Lebanon, explained to me, the *shari'a* fulfils a similar role for humans as the 'operating instructions' for an electronic device. As he said, 'when you follow what is written in the instructions your device functions perfectly, when you do not do that then it might break. When people follow the rules of Islam exactly as God has revealed them they are always happy, their life goes well and they are pure in both their soul and their body. When someone disregards the *shari'a* things often go wrong for him and he feels anxiety because his soul is not clear.' Interview, Tripoli, Lebanon, 13 October 2009.

act or live according to the cultural codes of a given locality, but rather should go back to the scripture that supposedly replaces the former.[3]

By this, Salafis intend to recreate the ideal community of Muslims as, according to their belief it used to be during the time of the *Salaf*. In many respects, Salafism resembles what Price et al. call 'grounded utopian movements' (GUMs).[4] GUMs create strong utopias in order to counter different types of oppression and injustice (real and perceived). In other words, the followers of such a movement create a parallel reality to escape from the conditions present in the surrounding world. 'Grounded' here means 'that the identities, values, and imaginative dimensions of utopia are culturally focused on real places, embodied by living people, informed by past lifeways, and constructed and maintained through quotidian interactions and valued practices that connect the members of a community'.[5] For Salafis, these practices try to imitate the Prophet and his companions in most aspects of life: praying exactly like the Prophet as informed by the Hadith, dressing accordingly, interacting with others based on Hadith narrations about how the first Muslims interacted with each other and also with non-Muslims.[6]

Salafis differ from most other GUMs, such as the Rastafari movement, in one crucial aspect. While the main goal of the former is to maintain an autonomous, alternative lifestyle for their participants, it is equally important for Salafis to convince others to adopt their worldview and practices. In other words, their end-goal is to export their utopian vision to the larger society. Doing so they follow different methodologies (sing. *manhaj*/pl. *manahij*). Most of the Salafis actively engage in various preaching activities such as holding religious lessons in mosques. Salafis are extremely active on the web and maintain thousands of websites and Internet forums in order to spread their ideas on how the Muslim should act, behave and what his/her rights and obligations are towards others. Yet, some go further than that and participate in institutions and public debates, or intend to impose the utopia on the wider society by launching armed jihad.

Understanding this utopian aspect is crucial in order to discuss the

---

3 Olivier Roy, *Globalised Islam: The Search for a New Ummah* (London: Hurst, 2004).

4 Charles Price, Donald Nonini and Erich Fox Tree, 'Grounded Utopian Movements: Subjects or Neglect', *Anthropological Quarterly* 81 (2008) 1: 130–35.

5 Ibid., 128. The authors give examples of GUMs such as the Rastafari movement, or Mexico's Zapatistas.

6 According to Salafis, acts and deeds of the Prophet should not be interpreted in the given historical context, but most of the time should be imitated exactly regardless of time.

Salafis' concept of 'citizenship'. For Salafis, only this utopian community can be fully legitimate as this is the one which is described in the scripture. The existence of nation states leads to the fragmentation of the community of Muslims (*juz'iyya*) as it defines the individual's identity as Algerians, Kuwaitis, and other nationalities, not chiefly as Muslims. The modern nation state derives its legitimacy from the electoral participation of citizens and/or a social contract between rulers and ruled (such as the case of Kuwait). Therefore, according to Salafis, the state demands the individual to be loyal to something else other than God.

This concern is voiced by many mainstream Salafi authorities such as the former Grand Mufti of Saudi Arabia 'Abd al-'Aziz bin Baz (1910–1999), often in subtle ways. He issued a *fatwa* explaining that if a country is an Islamic one but some of the fellow citizens disobey the rulings of Islam (*mukhalif li-l-din*), then the Muslim individual cannot show loyalty towards him/her as he/she should be regarded as an enemy.[7] Another contemporary Salafi authority Salih bin 'Uthaymin (1925–2001) remarked that 'the Muslim's homeland is where his religion is practised (*watan al-muslim ma huwwa yastaqim bihi dinuhu*)'.[8] Therefore, there is no reason for a believer to distinguish himself according to nationality.

Yet, the majority of Salafis in one way or another coexist with the nation state and even cooperate with it. Most Salafis in many respects live a normal life just like anyone else. They pay taxes (where taxation exists) and carry a passport and identity documents issued by the authorities of the nation state. Some Salafis actively engage in public debates and participate in institutional politics by voting and standing as candidates in parliamentary elections. This has become increasingly apparent during the Arab Uprisings when Salafi political parties emerged in Egypt, Tunisia and Yemen. In Kuwait, Salafis have been part of the political process since 1981. While all Kuwaiti Salafis justify their political participation arguing that they use state institutions to spread the *da'wa*, Salafi MPs often engage in debates over mundane issues such as the distribution of social benefits by the state, or even the question of who is included or excluded as a Kuwaiti citizen.[9]

However, for Salafis, at least in theory, the nation state is always a temporary solution. Here I have to note that for most Salafis, the existence of terri-

---

[7] http://www.binbaz.org.sa/fatawa/2071, accessed 25 May 2017.

[8] Salafis widely regard the Saudi scholar Muhammad bin 'Uthaymin as one of the greatest specialists in jurisprudence and his website is widely consulted. See: http://binothaimeen.net, accessed 12 June 2017.

[9] Kuwaiti Salafis are divided over the issue whether to grant citizenship to the over 100 thousand stateless people in Kuwait commonly called *bidun* (the Arabic word means without).

torial states is not a problem per se. Very few Salafi groups pursue an agenda of unifying Muslims in one political entity in the same way as Hizb al-Tahrir does, for example.[10] Perhaps the only noteworthy Salafi exception is the Islamic State in Iraq and Syria (ISIS). Most Salafis have no problem with the existence of a territorial state ruled by a Muslim ruler in a way the *shariʿa* legitimises it. In this respect, however, Salafis differ. A faction of Salafis calls for acceptance of and obedience to a ruler (*hakim*) who is Muslim and has been able to secure his rule over a territory either through the choice of his subjects or by force (*hakim mutaghallib*). Others accept the ruler only if Muslim inhabitants of the territory pledge allegiance (*bayʿa)* to him.[11]

What Salafis generally do not accept is the kind of citizenship that the modern nation states offer based on equality and sovereignty of the people. As I already indicated above, for participants of the movement the loyalty of Muslims can only be towards God. For this reason, many of the Salafis reject citizenship that is granted due to birth within the boundaries of a given nation state. Instead, the citizenship should be granted according to religious belonging, and Muslims and non-Muslims living in the same territory should have different rights and obligations as described in the scripture. For example, the Egyptian Shaykh Yasir Burhami, the spokesperson of the country's largest Salafi organisation, al-Daʿwa al-Salafiyya (Salafi Call) from which the Salafi political party Hizb al-Nur (Nour Party) has emerged, called for the reformulation of the citizenship law in Egypt according to the example of the Prophet's contract with the Jews in Medina. This, according to the Shaykh, would prevent the country's Coptic minority holding jobs that would grant them authority over Muslims (such as politicians, army officers, etc.).[12] Others, such as the Kuwaiti ʿAbd al-Rahman ʿAbd al-Khaliq argue that granting national citizenship regardless of religious belonging is acceptable since Islamic states that implement the *shariʿa* do not exist yet. Yet, according to the Shaykh, this citizenship circumscribed by man-made law should

---

10 *Hizb al-Tahrir al-Islami* (Islamic Liberation Party). ILP was founded by Taqi al-Din al-Nabhani (1910–1973) in 1952 in East Jerusalem. The party's main message is the necessity of the unification of the Muslim world through the re-establishment of the Caliphate. It spreads its message mostly through publications, lectures, conferences and reading groups.

11 On the typologies of Salafism see Zoltan Pall, *Lebanese Salafism between the Gulf and Europe: Development, Fractionalization and Transnational Networks of Salafism in Lebanon* (Amsterdam: Amsterdam University Press, 2013), 22–8.

12 Emin Poljarevic, 'The Ambiguity of Citizenship in Contemporary Salafism', in *The Crisis of Citizenship in the Arab World*, eds. Roel Meijer and Nils Butenschøn (Leiden: Brill, 2017), 353. See also: http://www.anasalafy.com/play.php?catsmktba=71984, accessed 19 June 2017.

not enjoy preference over the system of rights and obligations of Muslims towards each other that are codified in the scripture.[13]

Most Salafis intend to recreate the utopia of the first Muslims not by dissolving nation states but rather by *bypassing* them. In this deterritorialised community regardless of geographical location, the same standards, codified in the scripture, would organise the life of Salafis. It means that regardless of whether they live in Egypt, Indonesia, or Germany, Muslims should follow the same rules and enjoy the same rights in the realm of interaction with other Muslims, non-Muslims or relationships between men and women. Wherever they can, Salafis make an effort to create spaces in order to live such a deterritorialised citizenship.

Salafis put this in practice where they are able to dominate a neighbourhood or establish a separate village. For example, after the end of the conflict in the Moluccas in Indonesia in 2002, members of the Salafi militia Laskar Jihad took over an entire neighbourhood in the middle of the city of Ambon, called *Kampung Muhajirin*. When I visited the area in 2014, it stood in sharp contrast with other parts of the city. Men, almost without exception sported untrimmed beards, dressed either in Gulf-style *dishdasha's* or trousers that do not reach beyond the ankle, and wore shirts that covered the arm until the elbow. Instead of wearing the usually colourful dresses women wear in the Moluccas, most women were covered in black clothes and *niqab*s covered their faces. Restaurants and shops of the district were prohibited to play music, and in the grocery shops photos of human faces on the boxes of consumer products were covered with black adhesive tapes. Secular education is banned and most children of this neighbourhood go to local Salafi schools that only teach Islamic subjects. Encounters with the Indonesian justice system are avoided, and intercommunity disputes are internally resolved through mediation (*sulh*).

What is especially interesting is the district's inhabitants' relationship with outsiders. Most of the Salafis of *Kampung Muhajirin* usually behave in a rather reserved and formal way with non-Salafis who enter the area. Non-Salafis are not allowed to buy property, rent houses and settle in the neighbourhood, while Salafis who come from abroad are welcomed. This was the case with participants of the Salafi movement in Yemen, Egypt and Europe, who were able to rent houses and as full members of *Kampung Muhajirin* were allowed to stay as long as they wanted.[14]

This practice is encouraged by Salafis in the Gulf, who aim to unite

---

13 Interview, Kuwait, 11 March 2012.

14 Interview with a leader of the community, Ustaz Abdussalam, 2 November 2014.

the *umma* under one utopian community whose members share the Salafi concept of deterritorialised citizenship. Saudi, Kuwaiti and Qatari charities try to achieve these goals by setting up networks of schools in various Middle Eastern and Asian countries where the curriculum is based on the same Salafi books and interpretations of Islam. Redirecting the Muslim individual's sense of belonging from the nation state to a universal understanding of Islam is another way to unify the Islamic Nation. The following two case studies will elaborate on this.

LEBANON

In this small, multi-confessional Mediterranean country, Salafis strive to transform the symbols of the evolving Lebanese Sunni sectarian identity. Often, highly popular Salafi shaykhs intend to connect 'Sunniness' (or the notion of Sunnism) to the Salafis' understanding of Islam. They also try to divest Lebanese Sunnis from their sense of belonging to the Lebanese nation state which is based on a political compromise to share power between the three largest confessions: Maronites, Sunnis and Shiʿis. This is done by emphasising the Sunnis' belonging to the wider *umma* on the basis of their doctrinal belief (*ʿaqida*).

Salafism in Lebanon appeared at the end of the 1980s in the country's Sunni majority areas after dozens of graduates of the Islamic University of Medina returned home and engaged in proselytisation activities. In the course of the 1990s, a vast network of Salafi religious colleges (*maʿahid sharaʿiyya*), charity endowments and mosques emerged in the north, the southern city of Sidon and the Western Biqaʿ Valley. Despite the multiple security crackdowns by the Lebanese authorities and the occupying Syrians, the movement preserved its influence.[15] When the Syrian army, due to international pressure following the murder of the former Prime Minister Rafiq al-Hariri in 2005 withdrew, the ensuing vacuum was filled by Salafis who took the opportunity to increase their influence on Lebanese Sunnis.

Salafism in Lebanon has been multi-faceted and diverse and reflects the global fragmentation of the movement.[16] Many Lebanese Salafis, whom I call purists, exclusively focus on preaching and performing rituals in a

---

[15] For a detailed account on the historical development of Lebanese Salafism, see Zoltan Pall, *Salafism in Lebanon: Local and Transnational Resources* (Cambridge: Cambridge University Press, 2018).

[16] Ibid.

correct manner and neglect public affairs. Others, however, believe that Islam extends its rulings to every domain of life. It is therefore a duty for Salafis to reflect and respond to issues that concern the vagaries of the *umma*. In the post-2005 Lebanese religious and political landscape, this *haraki* or activist faction of Salafis became more visible. The influence of prominent *haraki* shaykhs based in the North Lebanese city of Tripoli, such as Salim al-Rafaʿi, Zakariyya al-Masri and Daʿi al-Islam al-Shahhal, rapidly expanded in the decade following the assassination of Hariri.[17] Al-Rafaʿi and al-Masri attracted thousands of followers to their Friday sermons and slowly became among the most prominent religious authorities in Lebanon's Sunni community.

The political context explains why a lot of *haraki* Salafis managed to extend their popularity. After the withdrawal of the Syrians, the main power-brokers of Lebanon's sectarian politics, tensions emerged between the country's Shiʿi and Sunni communities. The former started to demand a larger share of the political decision-making.[18] In turn, Sunnis became frustrated with the military might and political influence of Hizbullah, the Shiʿi militia and political party. Under the pretext of resistance to Israel, Hizbullah maintained stronger armed forces than the Lebanese Army and controlled large areas in the Biqaʿ, Southern Lebanon, and Beirut. The movement even managed to enforce its will on the Lebanese government. This situation led to a continuous political crisis, which culminated in the 2008 military takeover of Beirut by Hizbullah.[19]

The political turbulences translated into a Sunni–Shiʿi sectarian rift. A strong sense of marginalisation and victimhood developed among the Sunnis, with many of my respondents commenting that the Shiʿis were imposing their will on the rest of the country by relying on Hizbullah's superior military force. Many Sunnis suspected that Hizbullah had its hand in the Hariri murder, which made them feel as if the whole Sunni

---

[17] Shaykh Salim al-Rafiʿi, the imam of Tripoli's Taqwa mosque is one of the most popular Sunni preachers in Lebanon with also a significant transnational audience (especially in Germany where he lived until 2006 when he was expelled). Zakariyya al-Masri is a renowned Salafi scholar and the imam of the Hamza mosque of Tripoli, who wrote dozens of books most of which contain conspiracy theories common among Salafis, such as a global conspiracy involving Iran and the West against Sunnis. Shaykh Daʿi al-Islam al-Shahhal established the institutional infrastructure of Salafism in Lebanon in the 1990s using his access to Gulf funds. See Pall, *Salafism in Lebanon*.

[18] Amal Hamdan, 'The Limits of Corporate Consociation: Taif and the Crisis of Power-Sharing in Lebanon Since 2005', in *Lebanon: After the Cedar Revolution*, eds. A. Knudsen and M. Kerr (London: Hurst, 2012), 46–50.

[19] Ibid, 53.

community was being targeted by the Shiʿis. Against this backdrop, conspiracy theories, claiming that Shiʿis intended to dominate the whole Middle East, starting with Lebanon, became widespread. The dire socio-economic conditions of several Sunni areas and the weakness of the Sunni political leadership added to the frustration of many in the community.[20]

The current Syrian conflict has greatly amplified the Sunni–Shiʿi sectarian tensions in Lebanon. Hizbullah was formerly supported by the Syrian regime, so the militia has provided military support to help Syria fight its own opposition. Sunnis, however, tend to generally be sympathetic to the predominantly Sunni Syrian rebels and believe that the fall of the Assad regime would lead to the weakening of Hizbullah and the Shiʿis. On several occasions, Sunni militants from Lebanon have found themselves opposing Hizbullah's fighters on the Syrian battlefields.[21]

In this socio-political context, Salafi discourse resonated well. Prominent Salafi shaykhs, such as Shaykh Salim al-Rafaʿi or Zakariyya al-Masri framed the current inter-communal tensions in Lebanon into a cosmic struggle between good and evil. Salafis see the world as a place of struggle between good and evil, or truth and falsehood (*siraʿ bayn al-haqq wa-l-batil*). The good side is represented by Sunni Islam. Those who follow whatever is codified in the scripture belong to this side (*muʿaskar al-iman* – the side of belief).

According to the rhetoric of Tripoli's Salafi shaykhs, Sunnis represent *muʿaskar al-iman* in Lebanon. Therefore, they are targeted and oppressed by those who belong to the realm of *taghut* (unbelief, anything that opposes Islam). Salafis identify the Shiʿi community and Hizbullah as the most dangerous enemies of the Sunnis. Shiʿis are outside of the realm of *al-iman* because of their deviations from the right tenets of Islam and their conspiracy against Sunnis throughout history.[22]

However, Salafi shaykhs, especially after the Arab Uprisings often point out that this Manichean struggle transcends the borders of Lebanon and encompasses the globe. Shaykh Salim al-Rafaʿi reminded his followers in one of his postings on Twitter that it is not possible to deal separately with

---

20 Pall, *Salafism in Lebanon*.

21 https://now.mmedia.me/lb/en/archive/two-lebanese-men-die-in-al-qusayr-battles, accessed 21 December 2014.

22 Shaykh Zakariyya al-Masri published dozens of polemical writings where he articulates (mostly unfounded) criticism on Shiʿi theology. Among his most severe accusations is that the Shiʿis believe that the Qurʾan was altered (*muharraf*) by the first three caliphs and that part of it is missing. Al-Masri also regards the Shiʿi belief in the infallible imamate as major *shirk* (*shirk akbar*), Zakariyya al-Masri, *Dawr al-Imbaraturiyya al-shiʿiyya al-shuyuʿiyya* (Tripoli: Markaz Hamza, 2007), 67–9.

the bomb attacks against Tripoli's Salafi mosques in 2013 and the siege of Aleppo between 2012 and 2016.[23] As the Shaykh argued, the 'perpetrator is the same . . . and [both events are parts of the] same project'.[24] In the Shaykh's worldview, this project aims to subdue the Sunnis. In another tweet in which he discusses the dire socio-economic conditions of Tripoli, he tells that it is happening because Tripoli is a Sunni majority city, and 'East and West [are] conspiring against it'.[25]

Shaykh Salim, as do the majority of the Lebanese *haraki* Salafis, sees the solution against this anti-Sunni global conspiracy in the unification of the *umma*. However, unlike other Islamic movements such as Hizb al-Tahrir or the Islamic State, this unity, at least initially, should not be based on abolishing the borders of the nation states. Instead, it should be achieved through creating uniformity in Sunni theology and religious practices. According to Shaykh Salim, the *taqlid* of the *madhahib*, speculative theology (*kalam*) and Ash'ari creed[26] should be erased from Sunni orthodoxy. The same applies to Sufi practices such as the visiting of the graves of saints and asking them for mediation to God (*tawassul*), and *dhikrs* in which Sufi shaykhs use 'sorcery (*sahr*)'.[27]

This kind of religious uniformity would create a transnational solidarity among Sunnis with the aim of facing the common enemy, the *taghut*, represented by the alliance of Shi'is, the West and Russia.[28] To stand strong against this danger, Sunnis should feel a new solidarity based on a common creed. As Shaykh Khalid, an associate of Salim al-Rafa'i told me, Sunnis should stop regarding themselves as members of a confes-

---

23 Fernande van Tets, 'Lebanon: Death Toll in Twin Mosques Bombings in Tripoli Rises to 47', *Independent*, 24 August 2013, http://www.independent.co.uk/news/world/middle-east/lebanon-death-toll-in-twin-mosques-bombings-in-tripoli-rises-to-47–8782812.html, accessed 13 November 2016. Syrian government forces with Russian help besieged Aleppo for four years until they captured most of the city from the rebels by December 2016. David Sim, 'The Fall of Aleppo Timeline: How Assad Captured Syria's Biggest City', *International Business Times*, 16 December 2016, http://www.ibtimes.co.uk/fall-aleppo-timeline-how-assad-captured-syrias-biggest-city-1596504, accessed 7 January 2017.

24 Tweet of Shaykh Salim al-Rafa'i, 23 August 2016.

25 Ibid.

26 Ash'arism, named after its founder Abu al-Hasan al-Ash'ari (874–936), one of the major theological schools of thought, gave space to metaphorical interpretation of certain attributes and features of God.

27 Salafis often accuse Sufi orders for practising sorcery during *dhikrs*, which is strictly prohibited by most schools of thought in Islam. Remke Kruk, 'Harry Potter in the Gulf: Contemporary Islam and the Occult', *British Journal of Middle Eastern Studies* 32 (2005) 1: 47–74.

28 *Khutba* of Shaykh Salim al-Rafa'i, 10 February 2012.

sion (*ta'ifa*). 'No, we aren't a *ta'ifa* in the same way as the Maronites or the Druze. We are *umma* with "legs and arms" across the globe . . . from China to Morocco and America.'[29] In a public lecture in al-Taqwa mosque in Tripoli's Bab al-Tabbana district Shaykh Salim al-Rafa'i called Sunni institutions, organisations and movements across the globe to overcome their differences and cooperate on the basis of shared religious principles.[30] He advised young people to socialise with fellow Sunnis and study *fiqh* together, instead of spending time with non-Muslims who adopt Western lifestyle.[31]

Haraki Salafis also stress that the rights and obligations of Muslims towards each other should not just exist in theory but also in practice. Obviously, it could not be expected from the secular state to uphold the rights of Muslims as it is codified in the *shari'a*. Muslims should make use of the current political crisis and create new forms of solidarity. Prominent Salafi shaykhs often call upon Sunni Muslims in the North of Lebanon not to consider the Syrian refugees as foreigners. They are fellow Sunnis who fled from the very same enemy that is trying to crush the Sunnis in Lebanon.[32] In the first half of 2012, *haraki* shaykhs under the leadership of Salim al-Rafi'i and Zakariyya al-Masri initiated a weekly *shura* (council)[33] in the Taqwa mosque in which shaykhs, leading figures of local families and a number of young committed Salafis participated. The event provided a forum to discuss the affairs of the communities in different city districts, solve disputes between families and even make decisions in matters of security.[34] In the absence of state institutions, the *shura* council decided to take matters into their own hands. As part of this new transnational solidarity, I saw, among the participants, a number of

---

29 Casual conversation, 7 July 2012.

30 Public lecture, Tripoli, 7 February 2016. See tweet of Shaykh Salim ar-Rafi'i on 7 February 2016.

31 Ibid.

32 *Khutba* of Zakariyya al-Masri.

33 The *shura* (consultation in Arabic) is rooted in Arab tribal traditions and refers to a consultation body. In early Islamic history it was the advisory body of the Rashidun Caliphs. Later it was reinterpreted several times. In the Arab Gulf, the advisory bodies of the rulers are also called *shura*, as are the different decision-making councils of Islamic movements such as the Muslim Brotherhood or Hezbollah. See, 'Shura', in Bossworth, *Encyclopaedia of Islam* (Leiden: Brill, 1960–2005); Ahmad Nizar Hamzeh, *In the Path of Hizbullah* (Syracuse and New York: Syracuse University Press, 2004), 45–8.

34 Security matters could include whether Sunnis should fight the Alawites in Jabal Muhsin and organise a militia against them, or whether they should instead rely on the Lebanese Army and the government's other security forces.

Syrians who had fled to Tripoli. They were granted the same opportunity to voice their concerns and vote on the basis that they were Muslims and local residents who rented properties in Tripoli. Therefore, Salafi shaykhs no longer considered them as guests but as citizens of the Sunni community.[35]

The above shows that Salafis intend to redirect the Lebanese Sunni community's sense of belonging to the Sunni transnational *umma* rather than to the Lebanese nation state. In this narrative, Sunnis cease to be a confession or religious community among others in a sectarian state. Instead, they are parts of the *umma* that is not defined by territory. They distance themselves from the non-Sunni Lebanese, as the latter belong to the realm of *taghut*. My observations during my fieldwork in Lebanon demonstrate that such discourses appeal to many of the Sunni Muslims of Lebanon. The reason is that Lebanon never developed a unified national ideology.

Rather, there have been competing concepts of national identity. Maronite Catholics, who constituted the dominant community in Lebanon until the end of the 1975–1990 civil war, were the main proponents of a narrative that stressed the existence of a unique Lebanese identity that sets the country apart from the rest of the Arab world.[36] The majority of the Sunnis, however, considered themselves as part of the Arab world. Historically, Lebanese Sunnis have always been attracted to Pan-Arab movements that proposed the reunification of Lebanon in some form with their Arab brethren either as parts of a larger Arab nation or an Islamic Nation.[37] As in the course of the twentieth century Arab Nationalism and Muslim Brotherhood type Islamism lost much of their credibility in the eyes of Lebanese Sunnis, Salafism has become an alternative form of transnational solidarity.[38]

---

35 Personal observation, July–August 2012.

36 Roshanack Shaery-Eisenlohr, *Shi'ite Lebanon: Transnational Religion and the Making of National Identities* (New York: Columbia University Press, 2008), 20–21.

37 Samir Khalaf, *Civil and Uncivil Violence in Lebanon* (New York: Columbia University Press, 2002), 113–14; Sune Haugbolle, *War and Memory in Lebanon* (New York: Cambridge University Press, 2010), 35.

38 Arab Nationalists were militarily defeated during the Lebanese civil war, and scattered into multiple small groups. The Brotherhood experienced resurgence in the 1990s but they could not translate this into political capital due to the oppression they experienced from the occupying Syrian forces, internal secessions and the personal ambitions of the movement's cadres. Pall. *Salafism in Lebanon*.

KUWAIT

In Kuwait Salafis gained prominence starting from the 1970s as a result of the proselytisation of a number of preachers who arrived in the country from abroad. Due to the relatively wide margins of freedom as compared to other Gulf countries, Salafis quickly extended their activities beyond organising religious lessons and delivering the Friday sermon. The movement appeared and took important positions in the country's public sphere. Salafis gained seats in Kuwait's professional syndicates and won the elections of several of the so-called cooperative societies (*jamaʿiyyat taʿawuniyya*) that have been the backbones of Kuwait's civil society since the 1960s.[39] Furthermore, Salafis also established media presence by getting a weekly column in the country's largest daily paper *al-Watan*. The Salafis' main religious authority, Shaykh ʿAbd al-Rahman ʿAbd al-Khaliq[40] justified the movements in Kuwait's institutional system by arguing that this way they could reach a wider audience for their *daʿwa* and could also prevent corruption in the syndicates and cooperative societies.[41]

Since 1981 Kuwaiti Salafis participate in parliamentary politics as well, usually forming rather significant blocs in the legislature. Unlike most other Gulf monarchies, Kuwait has a constitution and a functioning and rather influential Parliament.[42] ʿAbd al-Rahman ʿAbd al-Khaliq urged Salafis to participate in the elections in order to have the ability to stand up against the powerful Arab Nationalist and Leftist movements in the country.[43] Since then Salafis have been among the main constituents of Kuwait's political map often delegating ministers to cabinet. Yet, long term political participation has led to serious disagreements among the participants of Salafism in Kuwait.

The purist and *haraki* factions that I mentioned above appeared in

---

39 Kuwait's cooperative societies comprise retail stores and board members are elected by the shareholders. Board members are usually affiliated to one of the political groups in Kuwait, therefore an election in the *jamaʿiyyat* often foretells the expected results of the next elections.

40 ʿAbd al-Rahman ʿAbd al-Khaliq (b. 1939), and Egyptian, is regarded as one of the most important founders and leaders of Kuwaiti Salafism. He is one of the most influential ideologues of *haraki* Salafism alive.

41 Interview, Kuwait, 11 March 2012.

42 On the Kuwaiti Parliament see, Jane Kinninmont, 'Kuwait's Parliament: An Experiment in Semi-democracy', Chatham House Briefing Paper, August 2012.

43 Michael Herb. *All in the Family: Absolutism, Revolution, and Democracy in the Middle Eastern Monarchies* (Albany: SUNY Press, 1999), 162–5.

the 1990s and tore apart the, until then, quite united movement.[44] Purist Salafis, who are the focus of this case study, continued their participation in the political process, and most of the time in the 1990s and 2000s they constituted the most influential Salafi political groups.

Unlike the *haraki*s, purists emphasise the necessity of unconditional obedience to the ruler (*hakim, wali al-amr*) of a Muslim country provided he is not openly apostate. This means forbidding all kind of demonstrations, public criticism and political opposition.[45] While most of the time purist Salafis refrain from political participation, in Kuwait they justified continuing their presence in the legislature and the government by 'defending the ruler' against his opposition.[46] Furthermore, Kuwaiti purists also wanted to preserve their positions in the state institutions in order to keep political support for their transnational charity activism.

The purist Salafi faction in Kuwait is centred around one of the largest Islamic charities of the world, the Society for the Revival of Islamic Heritage (*Jamaʿiyyat Ihyaʾ al-Turath al-Islami* – SRIH). SRIH has presence in more than 50 countries from Europe to Southeast Asia, and counts as one of the major bankrollers of Salafism worldwide. The sources of the charity's funds are not only individual donors, but Islamic banks, members of the ruling family, sponsorship of the Ministry of Awqaf and Religious Affairs and *Bayt al-Zakat* (House of Zakat).[47] Therefore, it is no wonder that purist Salafis intend to strengthen their presence in the state institutions. Their political grouping, the Salafi Islamic Group (*al-Tajammuʿ al-Salafi al-Islami* – SIG), an officially independent entity but in reality intrinsically linked to SRIH, most of the time sided with the government against other political factions that took an oppositional stance.[48]

The unity of purists fell apart in the wake of the Arab Uprisings. The

---

44 I have discussed this in several publications in length. See, for example, Zoltan Pall, 'Salafi Dynamics in Kuwait: Politics, Fragmentation and Change', in *Salafism after the Arab Awakening: Contending with People's Power*, eds. Francesco Cavatorta and Fabio Merone (London and New York: Hurst, 2017), 171–80.

45 In forming this argument purist Salafis refer to a number of Hadith narrations. See, Pall, *Salafism in Lebanon*.

46 Pall, 'Salafi Dynamics', 177.

47 Bayt al-Zakat was established in 1985 by the Kuwaiti government to collect religious taxes (voluntarily) and donations. It works as a charity launching humanitarian projects across the globe.

48 Purist Salafis often face internal criticism due to maintaining a secret organisational structure that in many ways is similar to the Muslim Brotherhood. See, Zoltan Pall, 'The Development and Fragmentation of Kuwait's al-Jamaʿa al-Salafiyya: Purity over Pragmatism', Unpublished working paper.

latter also affected Kuwait and prompted mass demonstrations that led to the resignation of Prime Minister Nasir Muhammad al-Sabah in the summer of 2011.[49] These events led to the emergence of a broad opposition movement encompassing both secular and Islamic forces, which demanded major reforms in the political system.[50] A number of MPs and leading politicians of SIG sided with the opposition, arguing that such a move does not count as a disobedience to the ruler, as the latter permits political opposition.[51]

Those who remained within the ranks of SIG stood with the government and opposed the demonstrations. This rift mirrored the existing ideological differences within SRIH. Similarly to the case of SIG, many of the charity's employees resigned and some of the prominent ʿulama such as Nasir Shams al-Din left it, leaving SRIH under the control of a conservative purist faction.[52] The time for the conservative purist faction of Salafis to exert more influence on the state and state–society relations than before came after the Emir dissolved the Parliament in December 2012. Those purists who left SIG, along with other members of the opposition boycotted the next elections. As a result, SIG's conservative members became the only Sunni Islamic force in the Kuwaiti legislature between 2013 and 2016.[53]

The members of the conservative faction of the purists were rewarded by the government for their loyalty. SIG member ʿAli al-ʿUmayr received ministerial positions, and others became high ranking officials in other ministries.[54] Furthermore, Salafis close to SRIH were allowed to gain more influence and take over the Muslim Brotherhood's dominant position in Kuwait's Islamic institutions, such as the Ministry of Religious Affairs, the Bayt al-Zakat, Kuwait's main authority for the handling of religious taxes, and formerly Muslim Brotherhood dominated think tank,

---

49 Christian Coates Ulrichsen, 'Politics and Opposition in Kuwait: Continuity and Change', *Journal of Arabian Studies* 4 (2014) 2: 214–30.

50 Mohammad Alwuhaib, 'Kuwait: The Crisis and its Future', *Arab Reform Bulletin*, 2012, No. 63.

51 Interview with former MP ʿAbd al-Latif al-ʿUmayri, Kuwait, 11 November 2013.

52 See Pall, 'Salafi Dynamics'.

53 After the November 2016 elections the situation changed. All purists lost their seats while the *harakis* and the Muslim Brothers returned to the Parliament. Khalid al-Khalidi. '*Mufajaʾat intikhabat al-Kuwait: al-ikhwan wa-l-shabab ala hisab al-salafiyyin wa-l-sabaʾil*', *al-ʿArabi*, 27 November 2016, https://www.alaraby.co.uk/politics/2016/11/27/مفاجآت-انتخابات-الكويت-الإخوان-والشباب-على-حساب-السلفيين-والقبائل, accessed 28 November 2016.

54 First he became oil minister, then minister of public work.

al-Wasatiyya Centre. SRIH used its increased influence in the state institutions to 'salafise' the official religious discourse of the state, and gain more resources to extend its transnational networks. The ruling family gave its blessing, as the purist Salafis' stress on the obligation of Muslims to be loyal to the ruler provided additional legitimacy to Al Sabah.

After capturing positions in the state's institutions SRIH put forward its vision on the state–society relationship and the Muslim individual's relations to politics and the ruler. The Ministry of Religious Affairs became perhaps the most important vehicle for purist Salafis to do this. The ministry since the 1970s has been dominated by the Muslim Brotherhood. Most of the ministers and the majority of the staff were linked to the movement. After the political organisation of the Brotherhood, the Islamic Constitutional Movement (al-Haraka al-Dusturiyya al-Islamiyya – ICM) boycotted the political process along with other opposition parties, the government fired many of its cadres from the ministry and replaced them with members of SRIH.[55] Between 2012 and 2013 the Minister of Religious Affairs was a leading Salafi figure from SRIH's conservative faction, Sharayda al-Mu'sharji.[56]

Since 2013 the ministry has been publishing books and letters that very often focus on the role of the *hakim* and the obligations of his subject to him.[57] These publications largely mirror the purist Salafis' concept of state–society relationships. An international conference, organised by the ministry in January 2013 on *Shari'a* Politics (*al-siyasa al-shara'iyya*), and in which most of the participants were purist Salafis shows clearly this turn. The conference statement was published in the Kuwaiti press, and summarised the main points of the discussion.[58] First, the participants criticised the contemporary political systems of the world because they build on the individual as the main component of the state, instead of a group of people. The too wide margins of individual freedoms lead to

---

55 Series of interviews and informal talks with officials from the Ministry of Religious Affairs and Bayt al-Zakat between January and June 2016. Interview with Muhammad al-'Umar, a retired chief of department at the Ministry of Religious Affairs, Kuwait, 29 March 2016 and Interview with 'Abdullah Haydar, former head of the international projects' department at Bayt al-Zakat, Kuwait, 5 May 2016.

56 Later he was replaced by Yaqub al-Sani', who is not affiliated to any Islamic movement, but close to the ruling family.

57 See, for example, Bandar bin Nayif al-Mihyani al-'Utaybi, *Wa jadaluhum bi-ma hiyya ahsan: Munaqasha 'ilmiya hadiyal-18 shubha muta'allaqa bi-hukkam al-muslimin* (Kuwait: Sada al-Khayr li-l-Khadamat al-Islamiyya, 2013).

58 *al-Awqaf ikhtatamat fi 'aliyyat mustajiddat al-fikr al-islami*, *al-An*, 27 November 2013, http://www.alaan.cc/pagedetails.asp?cid=33&nid=161359, accessed 7 January 2014.

'selfishness' and 'chaos in criticism'. As a result, people might criticise the 'high ethics' (*akhlaqiyyat 'aliya*) of society that might lead to violent reactions from others.

To avoid these shortcomings, according to the conference's statement, Islam provided an alternative concept of state–society relations. In an ideal society the centre of the state is the Muslim ruler, who provides security for his subjects. In turn, the latter obey him. The conference statement elaborates on the conditions of criticism towards the ruler. According to this, only religious scholars can raise any kind of criticism towards the ruler. If this criticism is direct, i.e. targets specific actions of the ruler, it needs to be articulated in secret and only in person. Indirect criticism can be voiced openly but it should not mention the ruler or any of his specific actions. The statement also mentions that those who are not well versed in religious sciences should stay away from criticising the ruler, even if the latter is unjust and oppressive. Instead they should be patient and practice their religion.

One of the main ideologues of the purist Salafis, Dr. 'Abdullah al-Shurayka, the current head of al-Wasatiyya Centre, told me that he considers even criticising the members of the government forbidden as they are appointed by the Emir. Therefore, such questioning of the actions of ministers is equal to disobeying the ruler.[59] He also thinks that the Kuwaiti Parliament should be a purely advisory body that proposes and discusses policies, but does not launch attacks on high ranking government officials.

The purist Salafis' views completely negate what the Kuwaiti nation state as a quasi-constitutional monarchy has been built on. Unlike the other Gulf countries, in Kuwait the ruling system gains its legitimacy from power sharing between the ruling family and ordinary Kuwaiti citizens. Even the foundational myth of the country reflects that Kuwait's rulers are not supposed to have absolute power. According to this myth, Al Sabah was appointed to administer the affairs of the state by stronger and richer clans. In this way the latter could focus on trade. However, decisions are supposed to be made by consulting the heads of the most important families of the country.[60]

According to purist Salafis, Kuwait's political system gives a relatively wide platform to debate, and its relatively free media leads to the waste of the possibilities and riches of the country. According to a leading opinion

---

59 Interview, Kuwait, 27 April 2016.

60 Mary Ann Tétreault, *Stories of Democracy: Politics and Society in Contemporary Kuwait* (New York: Columbia University Press, 2000), 33.

maker of SRIH's conservative faction, Dr. Khalid Sultan al-Sultan (not identical to the Salafi politician Khalid Sultan bin 'Issa), the Kuwaiti government focuses its energies on defending itself from attacks coming from the opposition. According to him, due to the wide margins of freedom, 'whenever Kuwaitis are bored, [they] write an opinion piece, curse their leaders and launch demonstrations'.[61] Furthermore, the wide margins of freedom allow ideologies that oppose Islamic values to spread, such as liberalism. As he told me, ideally Kuwait should be a state which is controlled by the Emir, who is advised by the *'ulama* and the country's material resources could be used to expand the Salafi *da'wa* to Asia and Europe. In this way instead of being an 'insignificant country (*duwayla tafiha*)' which makes the news whenever the opposition is making demonstrations crippling the government, Kuwait could be an international centre of Islamic charity and proselytisation and could work in order to reconnect the *umma*.

In fact, purist Salafis utilised their increased influence in the state institutions to bring Kuwait a step forward to becoming such a global centre of Salafi activities. For example, the director of Bayt al-Zakat, 'Abd al-Qadir al-'Ajil retired in 2014, and his successor became an SRIH member, Ibrahim Salih. Salih hired a number of purist Salafi employees who utilised their access to the funds of Bayt al-Zakat to build their transnational networks. As one of the employees of the institution told me, Salafis from Europe and Southeast Asia made visits more frequently to Bayt al-Zakat when they knew what changes had occurred in it. Most often they managed to secure funds to their charity and proselytisation projects due to their personal connections with the new Salafi employees.[62]

SRIH also could exploit its presence in the Ministry of Religious Affairs to strengthen its already very extensive transnational links. In 2013 the ministry held another international conference in which Salafis played a dominant role. Similarly to the one I mentioned above, the main discussion of the meeting revolved around the role of the ruler and the speakers voiced very similar arguments.[63] The more interesting aspect of this conference is that the organisers received a huge budget from the ministry which they used to invite dozens of Salafi scholars and preachers from Europe, Australia and North Africa, who seemed to have similar lines of thinking as SRIH, but who had not been connected to the organisation previously. As one employee of SRIH told me, they used the opportunity

---

61 Interview, Kuwait, 29 April 2016.
62 Interview, Kuwait, 5 May 2016.
63 https://www.youtube.com/watch?v=HodznN8pEEI, accessed 7 May 2016.

to become familiar with these people, and if they appear to have the 'right mindset' SRIH would discuss future cooperation with them.[64]

CONCLUSION

In this chapter I have shown that Salafis strive to recreate a utopia that is based on the perceivably ideal community of Muslims during the lifetime of the Prophet and the first three generations of Muslims. They intend to imitate the practices of the first Muslims by the archaeology and literal interpretation of the scripture. By this, the Qur'an verses and Hadith narrations become a system of codes that cover all aspects of human life, including the relationship of Muslims to each other, to non-Muslims and to the state with often clear-cut rights and obligations. According to Salafis, for Muslims only one community exists, which is the *umma*, in which inclusion and exclusion are defined by religious belonging.

This line of thinking conflicts with the concept of the nation state and citizenship defined by belonging to a territorial nation state. Yet, Salafis, unlike some other movements, like Hizb al-Tahrir, generally do not want to abolish territorial states. Rather, they intend to unify the *umma*, bypass state borders, and reorient the Muslim individual's loyalty towards the transnational community of Muslims. At the same time, as I have especially shown in the case of Kuwait, Salafis observe national identities and characteristics of political systems. For Kuwaiti purists, the ideal political system is centred around a Muslim ruler obeyed by his subjects. Lebanese *haraki*s do not share these views, but they also question the legitimacy of the nation state based on a social contract between different religious communities, and instead stress the Lebanese Sunnis' belonging to the *umma*.

At the moment it is hard to tell the extent in which Salafis might influence the sense of belonging of Sunni Muslims both in Lebanon and in Kuwait. In the former, Salafism has dramatically grown in the past decade, and as I have shown elsewhere, the impact of the movement is traceable in the discourse of ordinary Muslims.[65] Yet, it remains to be seen how this might influence the attitudes of ordinary Sunnis towards the Lebanese nation state. In Kuwait it is not certain whether the current influence of purist Salafis in the state is a sign of a long term relationship with the ruling family or whether eventually SRIH will be dropped as happened with the Muslim Brotherhood. At the moment, purist Salafis could

64 Interview, Kuwait, 5 May 2016.
65 Pall, *Salafism in Lebanon*.

preserve their positions in the Islamic institutions of the state despite the electoral failure of SIG in November 2016. Yet, this might eventually lead to the decrease of their constituency as popular sentiments seem to favour the opposition, at least according to the result of the polls.

10. Iran's Hezbollah and citizenship politics: the surprises of religious legislation in a hybrid regime

Shirin Saeidi

This chapter argues that religious legislation on the ideal citizen in a hybrid regime can stabilise a state in crisis, without necessarily moving towards democratisation or upholding the state's authoritarian preferences. The study of subjectivities in hybrid regimes advances the field of citizenship studies by demonstrating how citizenship develops in different variants of non-democratic and non-authoritarian regimes.[1] Expanding our examinations of how citizenship evolves in different political regimes is a particularly urgent task given the rise of authoritarian practices in democratic regimes.[2] The chapter shows that hybrid regimes can also centre on self-governance and value loyal yet critical citizens to establish rule and manage populations.[3] Indeed, similar to liberal democratic and Western experiences,[4] self-governance in non-Western hybrid regimes can entail a multitude of potentials, forms and limits as these states seek to create 'conscious citizens' that willingly, but also creatively and collectively, participate in state-building.[5] Investigations into the workings of citizenship in hybrid regimes offer insights into what the contradictions

---

1 There are few studies that look at citizenship in hybrid regimes. See for instance: Shirin Saeidi, 'Creating the Islamic Republic of Iran: Wives and Daughters of Martyrs, and Acts of Citizenship', *Citizenship Studies* 14 (2010) 2: 113–26.

2 Ozan O. Varol, 'Stealth Authoritarianism', *Iowa Law Review* 100 (2015): 1673–742.

3 On hybrid regimes, see: Leah Gilbert and Payam Mohseni, 'Beyond Authoritarianism: The Conceptualization of Hybrid Regimes', *Studies in Comparative International Development* 46 (2011): 270–97.

4 Corey Brettschneider, *Democratic Rights* (Princeton: Princeton University Press, 2007).

5 Anna Krylova, 'The Tenacious Liberal Subject in Soviet Studies', *Kritika: Explorations in Russian and Eurasian History* 1 (2000) 1: 119–46.

which undergird these systems of governance[6] mean when it comes to coping with political change.

The post-revolutionary Iranian state is constructed through a peculiar variant of the hybrid regime. There are competitive elections for the legislative assembly and presidency. However, the Supreme Leader and Guardian Council are not popularly elected, yet these domains of power exercise significant political influence. Civil liberties are regularly violated in Iran. Loyal supporters of the Supreme Leader in Iran are members of the transnational Hezbollah movement. Hezbollah activists in Iran are part of a pious social group that acts as state agents in various security, political and social capacities. They believe state sovereignty belongs only to God, are not interested in democratisation and are the Islamic Republic's dominant support base. The term *Hezbollahi* (followers of the Party of God) was first associated with supporters of Ayatollah Khomeini and vigilantes who were willing to violently confront secular and leftist supporters during the 1979 Revolution.[7] Hezbollah's cultural affiliates today strongly oppose violence as a means of garnering political power. A good *Hezbollahi* citizen in Iran, similar to his or her counterparts in Lebanon, is most recognisable through an unwavering support of the Palestinian struggle and piety in everyday life.[8]

In post-2009 Iran, Hezbollah activists are relied upon to implement the Islamic Republic's new ideal citizen within society. The invocation of religious legislation and informal religious norms is particularly relevant to explorations of citizenship in hybrid regimes. This is because the use of religious legislation rarely creates the obedient, self-governing religious citizen that it intends to reproduce, although it is often called upon by political elites as an ideal. As such, it raises the following question: what work does citizenship do through the use of religious legislation and what does this reveal about a hybrid system's capacity to cope with political change? Hoodfar and Assadpour have argued that lively public debates, efficient governmental and societal communication networks, realistic expectations, and a belief in expertise resulted in a dramatic overturn of Iran's conservative post-revolutionary family planning agenda during the

---

6 Marc M. Howard and Philip G. Roessler, 'Liberalizing Electoral Outcomes in Competitive Authoritarian Regimes', *American Journal of Political Science* 50 (2006) 2: 365–81.

7 Ali Gheissari and Vali Nasr, *Democracy in Iran: History and the Quest for Liberty* (Oxford: Oxford University Press, 2006).

8 Roschanack Shaery-Eisenlohr, *Shiite Lebanon: Transnational Religion and the Making of National Identity* (New York: Columbia University Press, 2008).

1990s.[9] As such, the post-1988 female citizen was imagined as one that not only has rights, but as a person whose overall health should be of the utmost importance to the state. Relying on the Pakistani experience, Iqtidar highlighted the state's inability to enforce a specific type of Muslim citizen subjectivity through state management of religion by stressing the lack of societal consensus on who counts as a Muslim.[10] Lastly, Lehmann has argued that the Israeli state has been able to effectively undermine the state's original secular characteristic, but it has had limited success in creating its ideal Jewish citizen.[11]

In this chapter, I move into the ambit of citizenship and politics among pro-state Hezbollah affiliates in post-2009 Iran to make the counterintuitive argument that the legislation of religion is not necessarily a fruitless effort for the state even when it fails to uniformly produce its ideal religious citizen. Indeed, the contradictions and ambiguities of hybrid regimes work in different ways to produce particular types of citizens. In the Iranian case, there exists a disconnection between how autonomy and equality of Muslim citizens are legislated in Hezbollah's cultural institutions, how autonomy and equality are theorised by the Islamic Republic's founding fathers, and how the Muslim citizen emerged from the post-1979 constitution. Within Hezbollah's cultural institutions, there are contentions over the level of autonomy that activists can exercise, although it is generally agreed that this population is more pious than the rest of Iranian society. Conversely, the formal theorisation of citizenship by Iran's revolutionary leaders entails an interdependence between individual autonomy and obedience. Finally, the post-1979 constitution engenders even more independence through vague references to Islam and the attribution of sovereignty to God alone. The interaction between these three different centres of power results in unpredictable citizens in quotidian life.

Through the renewal of Hezbollah's cultural institutions, the state has been able to tap into society to create a socially and financially effective approach for promoting its cultural preferences during a particularly fractured moment in its post-revolutionary history. This is because the ambiguities and contradictions which surround the social contract in post-revolutionary Iran leave much room for politics, faith and imagination to intermingle. In the long term, however, the inconsistencies that underpin

---

[9] Homa Hoodfar and Samad Assadpour, 'The Politics of Population Policy in the Islamic Republic of Iran', *Studies in Family Planning* 31 (2000) 1: 9–34.

[10] Humeira Iqtidar, 'State Management of Religion in Pakistan and Dilemmas of Citizenship', *Citizenship Studies* 16 (2012) 8: 1013–28.

[11] David Lehmann, 'Israel: State Management of Religion or Religious Management of the State?' *Citizenship Studies* 16 (2012) 8: 1029–43.

this process work to produce unpredictable citizens among a population that is especially close to the Islamic Republic's security forces. Through their activism in cultural institutions, Hezbollah affiliates become empowered citizens of the Islamic Republic and the omnipresent sovereign God that rests above the state. The citizenry interventions that emerge from this elevated status may not necessarily move the state towards democratisation or reproduce the vigilant citizens for which the Islamic Republic had hoped.

Post-2009 Renewal of Hezbollah Cultural Institutions

This section discusses the revitalisation of Hezbollah's cultural institutions in post-2009 Iran. I argue that the Islamic Republic, similar to other states in the region after 2011, intended to redraw the boundaries of the nation after the 2009 unrest. It did so through a more aggressive promotion of its citizenship framework from within society. Importantly, this is a framework which refuses to acknowledge a discourse of rights or critical thought. This is despite the fact that a legal framework for rights and a politicised population are central to how citizenship is formally conceptualised by the founding fathers of the post-revolutionary state, such as Ali Shariati and Ayatollah Khomeini. Instead, a depoliticised, obedient form of citizenship is inculcated within Hezbollah's cultural institutions, which are more aligned with pious Muslim subjectivities and quite distant from the independent character of Hezbollah which these political elites also promote. Nevertheless, entering into Hezbollah's cultural institutions, and striving towards ideal Muslim subjectivities, affiliates are identified by the state as more pious than the rest of the population.

The 2009 presidential election conflict was initially based on the belief among segments of the population that Mir-Hussein Mousavi, not Mahmood Ahmadinejad (2005–2013), had won. However, the protests erupted into a movement demanding a revised citizenry framework. Against this backdrop of depleting authority, the Islamic Republic's leaders sought both to reassure their support base and redraw the boundaries of the nation through various Islamisation projects. Newly reconfigured cultural institutions in post-2009 Tehran were funded aggressively by the Revolutionary Guards (*sepah-e pasdaran*), Office of the Leader (*beyt-e rahbari*) and the Intelligence Ministry (*vezarat-e etelaat*). The creation of new institutions has been a survival tactic for elite leaders in the Middle East amidst social unrest.[12]

---

[12] Ellen Lust and Stephen N. Ndegwa, 'Governance Challenges in the Face of Transformation', *Middle East Law and Governance* 2 (2010) 2: 113–23.

For segments of the Islamic Republic's elite, the activism that they prefer inside and outside Hezbollah's cultural institutions is similar to what O'Neill has termed 'Christian Citizenship' in his study of post-war Guatemala.[13] O'Neill has argued that this form of religious citizenship centres on prayer, weeping, fasting, self-discipline and other traditions of neo-Pentecostal Christianity. O'Neill found that his interviewees work to construct the *City of God* through their volunteer activism and struggle to establish peace and 'save' Guatemala by means of 'spiritual warfare'.[14] Segments of the security faction that fund Hezbollah's cultural institutions rely on this understanding of religion to engender 'good citizens' that are obedient and focused on duties, and the state's delineation of the 'true' path to prosperity in this world and the next. Similar to other religious movements, they broadly promote the notion of citizenship as self-governance to better society through a Muslim framework. However, in addition to their daily acts of devotion, ideal citizens of the Islamic Republic should be prepared to follow political instructions handed down from above when revolutionary leaders dictate them. The denial of individual autonomy in the creation of cultural artefacts often becomes the first point of explicit and implicit contention between Hezbollah's cultural affiliates and those organs which fund the cultural institutions.

My three years of work with affiliates of post-2009 Hezbollah's cultural institutions illustrates that many interlocutors were consciously and at times unintentionally regarding themselves as an extension of God's will on earth. A self-governing citizen, as reformulated by my interlocutors, was not a citizen that only espouses Muslim subjectivities geared towards establishing a utopian city on earth through Islamic ritual practices, the miraculous, divine encounters, proselytising, and a return to self (although it certainly included all of these). Instead, such a citizen also viewed themselves to be *special* and closer to God than others due to his/her efforts at achieving higher levels of piety. This perspective of the self, which is bolstered by the state's support of Hezbollah affiliates through the distribution of resources, unintentionally fuses God's sovereignty with the people's sovereignty. Hezbollah's cultural institutions create an atmosphere conducive to the exchange of ideas, offer access to resources, and bring young men and women from religious backgrounds into the public sphere. Through this social process, the distinction between God's

---

[13] Kevin Lewis O'Neill, *City of God: Christian Citizenship in Postwar Guatemala* (London and Berkeley: University of California Press, 2010).

[14] Ibid., 88.

sovereignty and the people's sovereignty, which is central to politics in the Islamic Republic, becomes less of an obstacle for change. At the same time, it also makes that change more unpredictable. It is this political consciousness and social positionality that conditions citizenship for Hezbollah affiliates and intersects with the Islamic Republic's state-building efforts after 2009.

THE CONTOURS OF CITIZENSHIP IN THE ISLAMIC REPUBLIC'S FORMAL DISCOURSE

The aforementioned official citizenry framework, which is legislated in cultural institutions, is an incomplete one that only partially resonates with the state's own formal discourses on citizenship and constitutional text. This section delves into the political thought of the Islamic Republic's founders with the aim of understanding their perspective on citizenship in the post-revolutionary state. I argue that although thinkers such as Shariati and Khomeini do hold complex ideas on state–societal relations, they tend to favour obedient citizenship for the majority of the population and most of the time. Through the theorisation of Iran's founding fathers, obedience is not simply a blind following of leadership or pious Muslim behaviour. Instead, obedient citizenship has embedded within it autonomy, requires critical thought, demands self-control, and a dedication to the formal discourses of the 1979 Revolution. The closer that one becomes to this understanding of obedient citizenship, the higher levels of piety they are believed to embody. In turn, their citizenry status elevates them before the state and allows them more authority to delineate autonomy and equality.

The idea of individual and collective rights and responsibilities is extensively addressed by religious ideologues of the 1979 Iranian Revolution, but without utilisation of the term citizen (*shahrvand*). Ideal citizenry subjectivities were also legislated formally and informally. Anti-colonial and revolutionary movements have historically been sites for rethinking established frameworks for doing politics, and not simply reactionary responses to the international governing system.[15] However, it seems that Iran's Islamist leaders also saw no need to unify the people and their rights under the rubric of citizenship. This may in part be due to the fact that the nation-state, while sought after, did not alone determine how Islamist

---

[15] Mark T. Berger, 'After the Third World? History, Destiny, and the Fate of Third Worldism', *Third World Quarterly* 25 (2004) 1: 9–39.

revolutionaries imagined 'solidarities', 'political modernity' or their larger projects for freedom.[16]

In a series of pre-revolution lectures which would later be referenced extensively by the Islamic Republic with respect to its citizenship paradigm (particularly after 2009), Shariati argued that in Islam, it is not blood, national borders or kinship that is utilised to build a community. He discusses a borderless community through the concept of *ommat*. He describes this *ommat* as 'a human society where all the individuals who share a common goal come together under the same leadership, to move towards their ideal'.[17] He defines the life as a member of an *ommat* as an existence based on responsibility and self-cultivation: 'Therefore, the goal is not to be human (*bashar*), but to become a human being (*ensan*). Being a member of an *ommat* is not being free and happy. It is moving correctly and swiftly.'[18] According to Shariati, Islam is also a social revolution in the manner in which it undermines class and produces individuals who are 'conscious, free and responsible'.[19]

The *ommat* is led by a leader (*imam)* with insights that will result in the most efficient and direct development (*takamol*) of the people. The leader directs people from what they are to what they should be as revolutionary persons. From Shariati's point of view, the human being is inherently incomplete and unable to reach God through his or her own path. Whether he addresses the character of Shiʿi *imams*, debates on alienation, free-thinkers, freedom of choice, or the history of creation, Shariati insists that national unity and cultural authenticity produce healthy societies and content individuals.[20] He is a strong advocate of critical thinking. He encourages Iranians to question their own history and to break out of the 'prison of society'.[21] However, in this effort, submission to a leader becomes necessary to generate a genuine revolutionary process of self-actualisation.

As I am beginning to suggest, Shariati remains ambiguous with regard to the issue of rights. This is not because he refused to recognise individual

---

[16] Karuna Mantena, 'Popular Sovereignty and Anti-Colonialism', in *Popular Sovereignty in Historical Perspective*, eds. Richard Bourke and Quentin Skinner (Cambridge: Cambridge University Press, 2016), 297–319, quote from 301.

[17] *Ommat-o-Imammat* is a collection of speeches given at Hosseiniyeh-ye Ershad (a meeting hall in Tehran) by Ali Shariati in 1348/1969. Ali Shariati, 1391/2012, *Ommat-o-Imammat* (Tehran: Teribon, 1348/1969), 20.

[18] Ibid., 27.

[19] Ibid., 102.

[20] For online access to Shariati's work see: http://anti666.ir/forum/thread-4324.html, accessed 29 November 2017.

[21] See for instance: Shariati's *ensan va Islam*: http://anti666.ir/forum/thread-4324.html, accessed 29 November 2017.

autonomy. For example, he claimed that 'man is capable of working like God' because God's divine spirit rests within human beings and allows them to decide on their path and begin to resemble the divine power in their daily lives.[22] However, he does seem uninterested in discussing the law. Although he clearly believes in God-made laws, he also insists that responsibility is central to the human experience.[23] For instance, he argues that if an individual perceives a leader to be intellectually, morally, practically, or religiously unfit, he or she has the right to reject that leadership – even if it means opposing the rest of the community.[24] He states the following: 'Even if all the people agree with him, you can condemn the leader, and there is no obligation to commit. The reverse is also true: if all the people view the leader as an infidel (*kafar)*, it is the right of the individual to remain a devoted follower.'[25] In this sense, Shariati supports the notion of citizen as an independent subject who can make claims, even perhaps disruptive ones, against a passive concept of citizenship as a member of a collective obeying a leader who is well versed in Islamic thought. Either way, the individual cannot determine his or her own path to reach God and must obey a trusted leader. However, Shariati avoided a 'literalist reading of either *ummah* [religious community] or *imamat* [leadership]' in these early and significant lectures.[26] As such, it seems that further details regarding the interaction between these two notions should be decided upon in the context which they emerge, and by those who intend to construct this form of social order.

It can be argued, then, that through Shariati's formulation of community, there is an interdependence between individual autonomy and obedience. This individual is, however, bounded by the pre-defined path of an Islamic Revolution which he or she believes is most authentic for the people of Iran. The revolution, in other words, is a tool for establishing an Islamic order that guides individuals and collectives towards prosperity in this life and the eternal afterlife. As Motahhari stated:

> An Islamic Revolution is the path for Islam and Islamic values. Revolution and resistance are for establishing Islamic values. We revolt for Islamic values, and

---

[22] Fatollah Marjani, *Man and Islam: Dr. Ali Shariati*, (Houston, Texas: FILINC, 1981), 6.

[23] Hamid Algar, *On the Sociology of Islam: Lectures by Ali Shari'ati*, (Berkeley: Mizan Press, 1979).

[24] Ibid., 67.

[25] Ibid.

[26] Kingshuk Chatterjee, *Ali Shari'ati and the Shaping of Political Islam in Iran* (New York: Palgrave Macmillan, 2011), 102.

> we resist for Islamic values. Therefore, the goal for us is Islam. Resistance and revolution are our tools. However, some have mistaken an Islamic Revolution for revolutionary Islam. For them, resistance and revolution are the end goal . . . the outcome of this is that we select from Islam, that which places us on the path of resistance, and that which we think does not place us on the path, we reject from Islam.[27]

When Motahhari was challenged during an interview about the irrefutable place of resistance in Islam, he stated the following:

> The principle of *jihad* and commanding what is just and forbidding what is wrong (*amr-e be ma'ruf va nahy- e az monkar*) must be kept alive and should never be abandoned. But that which we oppose is an understanding of Islam solely through *jihad*, claiming that Islam means *jihad* and *jihad* means Islam. This understanding overlooks other Islamic values.[28]

That the revolution must be carried out in the name of Islam was a shared characteristic among many thinkers during this period in Iran.

Ayatollah Khomeini regarded Islam as the framework that guides the nation and determines its rights.[29] The people's priority is to serve Islam and there is no known instance of him using the term citizenship. This is probably because he understood laws in post-revolutionary Iran to be divine laws, not profane state laws.[30] Abiding by God's law imposes certain limits on individual and collective autonomy which under a secular legal framework would be negotiable. In this manner, Shariati's understanding of leadership and community resembles Khomeini's notions of state–societal relations as both seem to agree on a general framework of obedient citizenship.

Unlike Shariati, however, Khomeini does address rights in legal terms. For Khomeini, and other revolutionary leaders who supported him after the 1979 Revolution, autonomy beyond the boundaries of Islam was recognised as outside the boundaries of the nation-state. But the notion of legal rights belonging to the individual was central in their conceptualisation of the nation-state and the Islamic Republic.[31] They often espoused a democratic understanding of rights that legitimises

---

[27] Morteza Motahhari *Ayandeye Enghelabe Islami ye Iran* (Tehran: Sadra Publishers, 26th edition, 1386/2007), 92.

[28] Ibid., 103.

[29] Ruhollah Khomeini, *Sahefeye Imam*. Speech. 1358/1979. No. 6, 436.

[30] Ghasim Shahbani, *Hoghughe Asasi va Sakhtare Hokumate Jomhuri ye Islami ye Iran* (Tehran: Etelaat Publishers, 28th edition, 1386/2007).

[31] See for instance the writing of Morteza Motahhari on human rights in his book *Ayandeye Enghelabe Islami ye Iran*.

an independent citizenry that challenges state authority on the basis of self-governance in the name and path of Islam. Similar to other revolutionary factions at the time, Khomeini readily criticised the Pahlavi state for violating citizen rights, including the rights of political prisoners.[32] He seemed particularly concerned about minority rights. He, for instance, believed that Sunnis in Iran should have equal rights:

> First of all, our Sunni brothers are never a religious minority. We have said many times that our treatment of religious minorities will be very good. Islam views them [religious minorities] as respectable. We will give them all of their rights. They have the right to hold their ceremonies, and they have the freedom to take part in political activities.[33]

During a radio message in 1358/1979, broadcast from Qom, he stated that all religious minorities, and indeed all people, are equal in rights with one another.[34]

Khomeini's discussion of rights posits them as a force which advances national independence. For instance, while in Paris in 1978, he stated the following about the Pahlavi state: '[. . .] and it has destroyed all the rights of the Muslim nation, all the freedoms; even the rights of minorities have been violated. The nation's independence has been taken, and they have used the country to advance their own interests and that of their [foreign] masters'.[35] The term 'masters' suggests that he believed nations should have the right to self-determination and should counter international violation of their rights. In his will, Khomeini advises the people and *Hezbollahi* youth in particular, to take it upon themselves to individually stop media sources which they believe promote corruption. Khomeini stated that this level of individual initiative is permissible when formal state institutions are approached, but refrain from enforcing Islamic decree within the media.[36] In defence of Islamic edicts, a citizen's independence extends to the edge of unruliness.

Khomeini's views on rights were not only developed in relation to the Iranian case but included the international system as well. He was not opposed to human rights. Rather, he was critical of the double-standards in the way they were enforced. When criticising human rights

---

[32] Ruhollah Khomeini, *Sahefeye Imam*, message 1357/1978. No. 4: 157.

[33] Ruhollah Khomeini, *Sahefeye Imam*, interview 1357/1978. No. 5: 292; See also No. 7: 150 and No. 4: 364 for the rights of minorities.

[34] Ibid., Message 1358/1979. No. 6: 462.

[35] Ruhollah Khomeini, *Sahefeye Imam*, interview 1357/1978. No. 5: 185.

[36] See http://farsi.khamenei.ir/imam-content?id=9447, accessed 20 April 2017.

in a 1356/1977 speech in Najaf, he stated: 'And this is America that we see in Israel – they have created that place. Look at what they have done to Muslims and what they are doing to them.'[37] During an interview in 1357/1978 in Paris, he addressed the Palestinian struggle as a struggle for rights.[38] Decolonisation and independence included for Khomeini the right of citizens to have rights as well as to engage in the international support for human rights. It seems that for Khomeini, allegiance to the Islamic Republic is performed through independent and transnational activism. However, claim-making is placed within an undetermined Islamic framework and does not include activism that undermines Islamic edicts.

What is significant about Khomeini's engagement with rights is the following: religion prevails over citizenship. While citizens are to be equal before the law, this does not mean that everyone will be treated the same in the Islamic Republic. While people do have the right to dissent, it does not mean that this right is uniformly applied to all people, or in all contexts. The state representative (understood broadly) retains the right to intervene and decide how the rules will be applied *in situ*. This is because Khomeini viewed piety (*taghva)* to be the most significant source of distinction between believers, which is also reflected in their status as citizens.[39] Like Shariati, Khomeini understood independence as embedded within the obedient citizenship framework. Moreover, placing ad hoc limits on citizens that run counter to parts of the social contract is not unique to non-democratic regimes, Iran, Islam, or the Middle East.[40] The advantages of relational autonomy have been emphasised elsewhere as well, including the North American context.[41] What is interesting here is the connection between an individual's level of autonomy and an ambiguous parameter surrounding Islam. The ambiguity derives from two conflicting sources of legitimacy. While the one is based on rights of citizens to revolt, freedom, and equality, the other derives from belief and the distinction in belief. Ultimately,

---

37 Ruhollah Khomeini, *Sahefeye Imam*, speech 1356/1977. No. 3: 333. There are many instances where human rights are criticised because of Western foreign policy in the non-Western world. See for instance *Sahefeye Imam*, No. 4: 39, 399, 400, 401, 402, 403.

38 Ruhollah Khomeini, *Sahefeye Imam*, interview 1357/1978. No. 5: 306.

39 Ruhollah Khomeini, *Sahefeye Imam*, speech 1357/1978. No. 6: 314; Radio message 1358/1979. No. 6: 462.

40 Amory Starr, Luis Fernandez, and Christian Scholl, *Shutting Down the Streets: Political Violence and Social Control in the Global Era* (New York: New York University Press, 2011).

41 Martha Albertson Fineman, *The Autonomy Myth: A Theory of Dependency* (New York: The New Press, 2004).

the right to exercise autonomy and delineate equality in the Islamic Republic seems to expand as a person's level of piety increases and when Islamic edicts are being violated.

After the death of Khomeini in 1989 and the presidency of Akbar Hashemi Rafsanjani came a new era in post-revolutionary Iran. With the end of the revolutionary period and the exhausting Iran-Iraq War (1980–1988), notions of citizenship and rights expanded. The emergence of the reform movement at the end of the Iran-Iraq War meant that citizens, and not just the elite, acquired the right to participate in defining what is Islamic and what is not. Elements within the Islamic Republic's ruling elite began explicitly to refer to the Iranian people as citizens who have rights based on Iran's legal framework.[42] Much of this had to do with the new interpretations of Islam. Foody has argued that reformist thinkers such as Abdolkarim Soroush and Muhammad Mujtahid Shabestari introduced liberal interpretations of Islam in post-revolutionary Iran. Although they relied on different methods, both scholars point out that the interpretation of religion is an individual right and obligation, and should not be legislated by elites alone.[43] While Soroush's work highlights the multiple interpretations of Islam and the relevance of individual experience, Shabestari stresses the limits of religious knowledge to address many modern issues.[44] The work of Kadivar is also significant in that he relies on Islamic sources to question Khomeini's absolutist authority of the jurist, identifying it as one model of an Islamic state among many.[45] With the new assertion in the 1990s of the individual's right to interpret Islam, leaders of the early days of the Revolution lost their cultural monopoly.

[42] Said Amir Arjomand, 'The Reform Movement and the Debate on Modernity and Tradition in Contemporary Iran', *International Journal of Middle East Studies* 34 (2002) 4: 719–31.

[43] Kathleen Foody, 'Interiorizing Islam: Religious Experience and State Oversight in the Islamic Republic of Iran', *Journal of the American Academy of Religion* 83 (2015) 3: 599–623.

[44] Mahmoud Sadri, 'Sacral Defense of Secularism: The Political Theologies of Soroush, Shabestari, and Kadivar', *International Journal of Politics, Culture, and Society* 15 (2001) 2: 257–70.

[45] Ibid.

MAKING IT (IL)LEGAL: THE INDEPENDENT CITIZEN AND THE POST-1979 IRANIAN CONSTITUTION

In this section, I argue that while the Islamic Republic's founders preferred the state's citizens obedient, though not void of autonomy, the constitution tends to engender independent citizenry practices for those who believe that sovereignty belongs only to God. How has the post-revolutionary citizen been legally articulated in the post-1979 constitution? The previous section argued that the state's formal theorisation of citizenship leans more towards obedient citizenship. This section, in contrast, will illustrate that the post-1979 constitution engenders in the text independent citizenship through the centrality of God's sovereignty. The post-revolutionary Iranian constitution has been studied as a poorly constructed document that deliberately and/or implicitly works to suppress citizenship, despite the fact that it has a chapter entitled 'The Rights of the People'. This is indeed a common and somewhat persuasive reading of the post-revolutionary Iranian constitution when we consider how ambivalent revolutionary leaders were to utilise the term citizenship. As Brown has argued, constitutions in the Middle East often rely on 'techniques to limit freedoms, democracy, and pluralism (without publicly repudiating them)'.[46] I am nevertheless more interested in understanding what these constitutional inconsistencies reproduce and less in the sinister intent that may have rested behind the drafting process.

The constitution oscillates between an unequivocally independent citizen and an obedient member of the nation within a vague framework of Islam. For instance, Article 9 states:

> In the Islamic Republic of Iran, the freedom, independence, unity, and territorial integrity of the country are inseparable from one another, and their preservation is the duty of the government and all individual citizens. No individual, group, or authority, has the right to infringe in the slightest way upon the political, cultural, economic, and military independence or the territorial integrity of Iran under the pretext of exercising freedom. Similarly, no authority has the right to abrogate legitimate freedoms, not even by enacting laws and regulations for that purpose, under the pretext of preserving the independence and territorial integrity of the country.[47]

---

[46] Nathan J. Brown, *Constitutions in a Nonconstitutional World* (Albany, New York: State University of New York Press, 2002), 89.

[47] http://www.iranonline.com/iran/iran-info/government/constitution-1.html, accessed 16 March 2017; http://www.emdad.ir/central/asnad/files/ghanoonasasi.pdf, accessed 16 March 2017.

Here it can be seen that the participation of an independent citizen, with public awareness and ethical sensibilities is legally permitted. The law suggests that this citizen should intervene when leaders undermine individual rights in the name of security or sovereignty. Yet the spatial and temporal boundaries of this law remain unclear, and the precise moments for acting as an independent citizen are murky at best. Importantly, who is to determine when a freedom is legitimate (*mashru*) and Islamically sound, and the processes through which freedoms can be reclaimed by the people are left unmentioned. Indeed, the boundaries on rights are more tangible than the level of autonomy one can exert in exercising rights as a Muslim.

A similar movement between an independent citizen and subdued national can be noted in other parts of the constitution as well. Article 8, for example, begins by boldly stating:

> In the Islamic Republic of Iran, commanding what is just and forbidding what is wrong (*amr-e be ma'ruf va nahy- e az monkar*) is a universal and reciprocal duty that must be fulfilled by the people with respect to one another, by the government with respect to the people, and by the people with respect to the government.[48]

This first half of Article 8 seems to legitimise independent citizenship. It suggests that if citizens believe an official policy, an official's actions or local initiatives carry the potential to do harm or are unjust, they have not only the state-sanctioned right but also the religious responsibility to intervene. However, in its concluding sentence, the transformative and performative potentials of Article 8 become potentially criminal instead of inherently supportive of vigilant citizens:

> The conditions, limits, and nature of this duty will be specified by law (this is in accordance with the Qur'anic verse; 'The believers, men, and women, are guardians of one another; they enjoin the good and forbid the evil').[49]

What is meant by law, and what law outside the constitution will determine when it is time to mobilise as citizens against injustice (*zolm*) remains unknown.

---

[48] http://www.iranonline.com/iran/iran-info/government/constitution-1.html, accessed 16 March 2017; http://www.emdad.ir/central/asnad/files/ghanoonasasi.pdf, accessed 16 March 2017.

[49] http://www.iranonline.com/iran/iran-info/government/constitution-1.html, accessed 16 March 2017; http://www.emdad.ir/central/asnad/files/ghanoonasasi.pdf, accessed 16 March 2017.

Another illustration is Article 20. It was intended to enforce equality between all citizens and states:

> All citizens of the country, both men and women, equally enjoy the protection of the law and enjoy all human, political, economic, social, and cultural rights, in conformity with Islamic criteria.[50]

The vague reference to Islam has been interpreted as a deliberate effort to limit women's rights.[51] In her discussion of women's status in post-revolutionary Iran, Paidar has argued that the Iranian constitution identifies the state as responsible for adhering to and protecting Islamic law, but the constitution refers to Islamic law 'as an extra-constitutional criteria in many of its articles'.[52] For instance, Paidar points to Article 21, which addresses the protection of mothers and the family, and identifies the government as responsible for also protecting women's rights within an Islamic legal framework. However, there does not exist any clarification on what women's rights are or what qualifies as Islamic law. In sum, I concur with Paidar's assessment that this constitutional move 'resulted in the subjection of the constitution to a divine law outside and above it'.[53]

One way to interpret the constitution's vague prose and language with respect to Islam is to recognise how a 'subordination of law to the dictates of power politics' is encouraged through it.[54] However, an attempt to curtail popular power through constitutional prose has been noted in other experiences with constitutional writing, including the American, French and Polish.[55] What makes Iran exemplary is the centrality of God's sovereignty to the entire enterprise, which is explicitly recognised in Articles 2 and 56 of the constitution. Article 4 of the constitution does stipulate that the *fuqaha* (experts of Islamic jurisprudence) of the Guardian Council have the right to judge all facets of social and political

---

[50] http://www.iranonline.com/iran/iran-info/government/constitution-3.html, accessed 16 March 2017; http://www.emdad.ir/central/asnad/files/ghanoonasasi.pdf, accessed 16 March 2017.

[51] Homa Hoodfar and Shadi Sadr, 'Islamic Politics and Women's Quest for Gender Equality in Iran', *Third World Quarterly* 31 (2010) 6: 885–903.

[52] Parvin Paidar, *Women and the Political Process in Twentieth-Century Iran* (Cambridge: Cambridge University Press, 1995), 261.

[53] Ibid.

[54] Daniel Brumberg and Farideh Farhi, 'Introduction: Politics of Contention and Conciliation in Iran's Semiautocracy' in *Power and Change in Iran* eds. Daniel Brumberg and Farideh Farhi (Indianapolis: Indiana University Press, 2016), 1–33, quote from 14.

[55] Brown, *Constitutions in a Nonconstitutional World*, 98.

life to make certain that 'Islamic criteria' are upheld, thereby making the clergy God's representatives on earth. However, this does little to resolve the ambiguity surrounding what counts as Islamic. This is because the document also holds that the most constitutionally powerful person in the country, the Supreme Leader, 'is equal with the rest of the people of the country' before the law (Article 107).[56] This stipulation in the constitution formally recognises that the clerical leaders of the Islamic Republic are fallible, therefore it reasserts God's sovereignty once again through an inability to define Islamic.

The ambiguity that upholds the entrance and exit of Islam in the text can also be read as proof of God's sovereignty and the state as a location for slippage – a place where justice can be undermined. Moreover, the text's intended audience is in key moments the Muslim *Ummah* (*ommat* in Persian) and not only the Iranian nation, which points towards God's elusive sovereignty again. It follows that from a Hezbollah affiliate's vantage point, for instance, the ambiguity that surrounds Islam is enabling precisely because it recognises a modern state's limit to uphold the 'sovereignty of truth and Quranic justice'.[57] God's sovereignty escapes state jurisdiction, and has the unique capacity to redeem independent citizenships through its 'promise of space'.[58] This constitutional ethos of space-making ingrains a 'constant adaptation and change'[59] into everyday life which makes establishing a post-revolutionary Thermidor[60] challenging, though not impossible. Furthermore, during daily acts of worship the yearning for utopia may intersect with what the individual's heart has come to learn to construct: a revised emancipatory political framework. The heart is another site for knowledge and virtue in Islamic traditions.[61] The heart could generate political work that those following the state's 'good citizen' framework never intended to do. Hence, there are multiple ways to study the post-revolutionary Iranian constitution, and one

---

56 http://www.iranonline.com/iran/iran-info/government/constitution-8.html, accessed 31 March 2017; http://www.emdad.ir/central/asnad/files/ghanoonasasi.pdf, accessed 31 March 2017.

57 http://www.iranonline.com/iran/iran-info/government/constitution-1.html, accessed 17 March 2017; http://www.emdad.ir/central/asnad/files/ghanoonasasi.pdf, accessed 17 March 2017.

58 Davina Cooper, *Everyday Utopias: The Conceptual Life of Promising Space* (Durham and London: Duke University Press, 2014).

59 Ibid., 4.

60 Crane Brinton, *The Anatomy of Revolution* (New York: W.W. Norton, 1938).

61 Timothy J. Gianotti, 'Beyond Both Law and Theology: An Introduction to al-Ghazzali's "Science in the Way of the Afterlife", in *Reviving Religious Knowledge*', *The Muslim World* 101 (2011) 4: 597–613.

approach is to examine its relevance to social contentions through the lens of a sovereign God that rests within and above the text.

CASE STUDIES

Islamisation of the Social Sciences

The final sections of this chapter illustrate the erratic movement of Hezbollah affiliates as obedient citizenship post-2009. It does so through case studies which examine two different Islamisation projects: one having to do with the social sciences and the other with women's rights. Together, these case studies demonstrate that when citizenry categories are established through distinction in beliefs but sovereignty remains in the hands of God, those closest to the state can become its most unpredictable advocates. Ultimately, a hybrid regime's legislation of religion through citizenship moves the state in an unknown direction as agents on the ground continually remake the boundaries on autonomy and equality through different frames of reference.

Like his predecessor, Ayatollah Khamenei's call for Iran's independence from Western social influence also promotes securitisation. Khamenei first referred to a cultural invasion (*tahajome farhangi*) during the 1990s when discussing the influence of the West in Iran. Senior leaders in cultural institutions remember being encouraged by his lectures on a 'software movement' (*jombeshe narmafsari*), which began in 2001, to focus on the Islamisation of the social sciences.[62] During these lectures, the Supreme Leader argued that students should focus on developing the Islamic Republic's theoretical power and ideas in order to strengthen its structural framework. While both of these paradigms stressed that a foreign attack was underway through the social sciences, it was only after the 2009 presidential conflict that the phrase, 'soft war' (*jange narm)*, was used to refer to Western influence in Iran.[63] Through such terminology, the stage was set for a confrontation with the West. Unable to tackle the cultural transformations of the country, some Islamic Republic elites reached the conclusion that they not only needed the formation of new

---

[62] http://farsi.khamenei.ir/speech-content?id=3053, accessed 29 November 2017. This is the earliest lecture I could find on this topic, but more can be located here: http://farsi.khamenei.ir/tag-content?id=1014, accessed 29 November 2017.

[63] Payam Mohseni, 'The Islamic Awakening: Iran's Grand Narrative of the Arab Uprisings', *Middle East Brief* 71, Brandeis University: Crown Center for Middle East Studies (2013), 1–9.

organic paradigms, but they also had to unequivocally conceptualise this process as warfare.

Thus the Islamisation of the social sciences is partly dependent on and invested in the securitisation of society through a deliberate effort at preventing independent citizenship by monitoring and vetting educational institutions. Yet even in this most conservative context, Hezbollah affiliates incorporate unsanctioned, and potentially risky, criticism towards the Islamic Republic to remake the boundaries on rights and equality. In one project report shared with me, several activists were invited by the Iran Think Tank Network (ITAN) to write a report for the National Foundation for Distinguished Scholars (*Bonyad Melli Nokhbegan*). ITAN was created over 10 years before the 2009 presidential crisis, but many leading cultural activists interested in projects related to Islamisation are employed by the expanding network. The report intended to help the state find a way to manage the gifted as claimants in the public sphere. It would also put forth ideas on how to prevent their ultimate departure from the country.

The almost 200-page report begins by briefly mentioning that, without institutional reform, it will be difficult to meet the needs of the gifted – an obvious reference to state corruption, among other problems – through an intervention that goes against the state's effort at eliminating rights discourses. It also stresses that the state should refrain from imposing specific cultural directives on individuals, as it identifies the social engineering of individuals to be contrary to the human spirit. It references the scholarship of contemporary Shiʿi thinkers, such as Bagheri and Tabatabaʿi, to argue that within the Islamic tradition, humans are recognised as embodying agency and interact with the world through their senses. As such, the report establishes the people's right to intervene at the centre of the Islamisation debate.

While the authors delegitimise efforts towards an extensive social engineering project aimed at individuals, they do support cultural engineering by acknowledging the Islamic Republic's right to enforce cultural regimes on institutions. They argue that the Islamisation of cultural institutions does not mean that all aspects of culture have to be dictated by Islamic law or norms. Rather, some aspects should be directly influenced; and other elements of Iranian culture 'that are not in conflict with Islam' should be 'directed' more gradually. They suggest that the state should employ indirect approaches for promoting its cultural agenda, along with direct ones such as profiling teachers by their adherence to Islamic rituals and symbols (e.g. prayer and *hejab*).

However, what is written here is the edited version of how many in the cultural wing of Hezbollah think about and address these issues in other moments of their social lives in the education system. For instance, I visited a women's dormitory at the University of Tehran in the spring of 2013 to carry out interviews for this project. I arrived late in the evening, unaware that I would not be allowed to leave the dormitory after 10 pm because no woman can exit the premises after that time. In order to leave, I had to get permission from the head of the dormitory, who happened to be present that evening due to a conflict that had taken place. I found her in an auditorium filled with angry female students, and along with the male director of the University of Tehran's security (*herasat*), she stood front and centre. The female students claimed that, a few hours earlier, four men who had taken drugs, climbed over the fence and chased down a female student. Female students had gathered at the scene and refused to return to their rooms until the head of security met with them. All of the female students that filled the auditorium were shouting, but two had microphones and were directing their complaints to the head of security. I recognised both as Hezbollah affiliates that I had met and interacted with at several cultural institutions. One of the students holding the microphone stated:

> We are sick of being treated like children and lied to. The university should either provide better protection for us or tell us not to leave our homes in *shahrestan*. . . you are only here having this meeting because you are afraid of unrest (*shuresh*). . . you will do absolutely nothing about this problem again as you have ignored it in the past.[64]

In this instance, then, female Hezbollah affiliates understood public performances of religious piety to include forms of morality that escaped the security forces' preferences, but which did coincide with the sensibilities of others in Iranian society.

I witnessed similar performances throughout the years that I carried out fieldwork for this project and worked at the university. In the fall of 2012, I attended a conference at the sociology faculty of the University of Tehran which addressed the gender quota system that barred women from many fields of study and was aggressively pursued after 2009. In the summer of 2012, it was announced that some 36 universities in Iran were barring women from 77 fields of study.[65] While we sat in an auditorium filled with several hundred students, one female student stood up and spoke most

---

[64] 12 May 2013 University of Tehran women's dormitory.

[65] Nazanin Shahrokni and Parastou Dokouhaki, 'A Separation at Iranian Universities', *MERIP* 18 October 2012. http://www.merip.org/mero/mero101812, accessed 29 November 2017.

eloquently. She argued that although she had passed the national entrance exam with high marks and was accepted into a difficult field of research, she was ultimately not given permission to enter the programme that year. She argued that this was unfair to her and many women in her position, and that she was opposed to it. I had met the young woman several times at a cultural institute and even interviewed her. Although during our group interviews, she expressed her enthusiasm to participate in cultural projects having to do with the Islamisation of women's rights, she had made it clear before other female Hezbollah cultural activists and me that she was not convinced by the state's moral argumentation regarding gender rights. She discussed how, for example, she had to endure her father's excoriation just for attending activities at cultural institutions. She discussed how stressed she was that her brother-in-law had prevented her sister from pursuing a Ph.D. Her father and brother-in-law were both clergymen and generally opposed women's presence in the public sphere. In their Islamisation efforts, some affiliates give those that embody the ritualistic and symbolic components of religion more political space than others. Nevertheless, developing a normative standard for university administration does not prevent Hezbollah affiliates from pushing the boundaries of autonomy and equality in other spaces of the educational system.

Islamisation of Women's Rights and the Anti-Feminist Movement Post-2009

Following the 2009 presidential election, the state tried to integrate women with religious backgrounds into Hezbollah's cultural institutions, albeit in segregated spaces. Women affiliated with Hezbollah have been integrated into formal and informal state institutions since the 1979 Revolution in Iran.[66] Prior to the 2009 crisis, however, the limited Hezbollah cultural spaces that did exist were mostly occupied by men. It was only after 2012 that this trend was being actively contested by female and some male affiliates. The state believed that feminist ideology played a central role in politicising women against it in 2009. The mere presence of women in these institutes is viewed as an approach for keeping them away from organised women's rights movements. But the integration of women into Hezbollah's cultural institutions, which includes interactions with male colleagues that cross the boundaries of gendered spaces, is also a rather innovative form of governance. This is a new approach which relies on

---

[66] Hamideh Sedghi, *Women and Politics in Iran* (Cambridge: Cambridge University Press, 2007).

the creativity, time and energy of its most sympathetic citizens to better develop the state's legislation of religion.

Islamisation of women's rights in post-2009 Iran is also different in form and content from other periods in post-revolutionary history. As Paidar has argued, from 1979–1981, the Islamic Republic focused on pushing women back into the private sphere and transforming gender relations through Islamisation of family and sexual relations. The endeavour was rather explicit during that time, including the curtailment of women's public presence and emphasis on the political relevance of religious symbols such as the *hejab* in signifying a new political order in Iran.

Today, the process is more a co-option that is carried out through ambiguous politics which seem to legitimise *Hezbollahi* youth's competing and contradictory interests. During the 2013 Congress on 7,000 Female Martyrs at Tehran's Vahdat Hall, I watched as Major General Hassan Firouzabadi, Chief of Staff of the Iranian armed forces at the time, spoke to an audience of all-female Hezbollah affiliates. He brought together several political strands in order to persuade women to cooperate, albeit through much ambiguity. First, he stated that while some people within the state may want to negotiate with the international system due to sanctions and threats, the 7,000 female martyrs tell us that we have to be active in fully defending an 'Islamic Iran'. He then spoke for a few minutes on the 2009 *fitna* (sedition), arguing that while those who protested following the 2009 presidential election stated that they wanted freedom, in reality, they were backed by American and British media outlets. Furthermore, he identified Fatemeh al-Zahra, the daughter of the Prophet Mohammad and wife of Imam Ali, as a role model for Shi'i and Sunni women. He claimed that any Muslim woman, even if she lives in a small town, should confront anyone who spreads rumours that promote discourses contrary to the official ones promulgated by the Islamic Republic. Up to this point, he had made it clear that he was addressing the women who were opposed to reformists within the ruling elite and who wanted to negotiate with the West; women who resisted opposition movements within society that made demands on the state; and women who during their everyday lives, even at home and within the family, challenged those who criticised the establishment.

He concluded by arguing that there was no reason why women fulfilling all of these criteria could not participate at the highest levels of the state. He asked: 'Why don't we have women at the negotiating table for the nuclear crisis when we have female nuclear scientists? Why don't we have women in the highest levels of the military when we had female military leaders in the Iran-Iraq War?' If women police the nation, they will be given opportunities to climb the state's power structures because they have exerted a higher level of piety by simply siding with the state's preferred citizenry body.

Due to the historical teleologies which exist in the state's anti-feminist formulation above, female Hezbollah activists rely on their own moral imaginings to connect the spiritual and material in a way that relates to Iran's changing social context. Scholars agree that social militarisation through prolonged international conflict is one of the definitive outcomes of revolutions and this character of a post-revolutionary state enhances its survival capacities.[67] State-controlled memorialisation of the Iran-Iraq War has a social militarisation effect within this social group that results in the unification of the private sphere and the state-building process for many. For example, a female leader in this newly solidified social group told me that she decided to marry her husband when they went on an *ordu* (camping trip) together to the South of Iran to visit war sites from the Iran-Iraq War. During the trip, an accident occurred in which some students died in full view of the other travellers. When she witnessed his bravery at the scene and his ability to regroup others, she decided to marry him. During my 2008 field research in Tehran on the sociological elements of the Iran-Iraq War, I heard similar stories of love from wives of Iranian war martyrs. The message the state aims to generate by rehashing this narrative is the following: piety and a dedication to the post-revolutionary state mean that one gives less attention to a suitor's economic status. In effect, the state places the spiritual and the material in opposition to one another and encourages Hezbollah cultural activists to prioritise the spiritual. This narrative positions women that make marital decisions through a social militarisation framework as martyrs' wives-in-waiting, and since 1979, this subjectivity has been a noble and sought after one for many who associate with the post-revolutionary state. If my research had ended here, it would seem that political elites had achieved their goal of creating the ideal 'good citizen'.

As my relationships developed, however, I began to see that many *Hezbollahi* women switch to modes of statecraft that undermine state-sanctioned discourses on love, marriage and piety with an underlying motivation for women's rights. While performances of public piety are important for this social group, they intersect with other human achievements such as higher degrees, gender equality in marriage, wealth, and frequent travel abroad that are considered to be equally praiseworthy. It is commonly known that pious Shiʿi women view Zeinab, the sister of

---

[67] See for instance, Theda Skocpol, 'Social Revolutions and Mass Military Mobilization', *World Politics* 40 (1988) 2: 147–68.

Imam Hussein, as a role model and this is particularly so for women affiliated with Hezbollah.[68] During interactions with female cultural activists, however, it was Iran's female leaders in the public sphere, including Ph.D. students, female professors, politicians, parliament members, writers, athletes, and artists by whom they seemed most inspired. This was surprising because, during my fieldwork in 2008, young women affiliated with pro-state stances overwhelmingly identified their mothers as their role models.[69] Their mothers, on the other hand, viewed Zeinab as a source of inspiration. This transformation and contrast between different generations and factions of pious women affiliated with the Islamic Republic are indicative of the unpredictability of Islamisation projects, and how they can remake religious identities in ways that escape the state's citizenship-building efforts.

These young people are influenced by the materialist ambitions which are central to city life in Iran today. Hezbollah affiliates are dedicated to public expressions of piety through marriages based on values, but they also firmly believe in progress (*peshraft*), understood to mean material development. For instance, when I got married in 2014 in Tehran, several leading female members of this social group privately suggested that I demand the right to divorce and request a high *mehrieh* arguing that it would protect me from ill-treatment in the marriage – a protection they did not have and continued to regret. They argued that because I held a Ph.D. from a prestigious university such as Cambridge that this legal demand was my right. This was an interesting perspective as it reasserted a classification of the population devoid of equality. One Hezbollah affiliate even stopped me on the street one day and told me that she could no longer keep silent and wanted to talk. As we walked, she gently expressed that my marital decision was all wrong because my husband did not have a Ph.D. She went further to argue that my husband should not only hold a doctoral degree, but preferably one from Cambridge itself, otherwise, she believed I was 'selling myself short'. Another affiliate remained adamant that I should marry a state elite. She argued: 'You deserve someone that is high-ranking, you know, like a member of the nuclear negotiation team.'[70] Female Hezbollah affiliates strike their own balance between public expressions of piety and material progress, oscillate between individual and collective rights demands, and in the process undermine the state's good citizen framework.

---

[68] Lara Deeb, 'Emulating and/or Embodying the Ideal: The Gendering of Temporal Frameworks and Islamic Role Models in Shi'i Lebanon', *American Ethnologist* 36 (2009) 2: 242–57.

[69] Saeidi, 'Creating the Islamic Republic of Iran'.

[70] Personal conversations, February 2014.

Another point which I found significant was how the women's suggestions divert from an egalitarian agenda based on relationality and mutual respect which has historically been proposed by those committed to gender justice within and outside of an Islamic framework in Iran. Material development here is strikingly different from what Deeb articulated as an understanding on the progress that included the community, and the rights and needs of others among pious Shiʿi Hezbollah supporters in Lebanon.[71] For instance, the legal demands cultural activists suggested I insist upon, would in practice mean that I could both divorce my husband and demand a large sum of money from him. This in effect is a contract set on privatised domination and not equality or piety in statecraft. While this suggestion does not fall outside the boundaries of religion, it does challenge the mode of morality enforced by the state and most Shiʿi scholars where a low *mehrieh* and a decision not to include further stipulations of the marriage contract are encouraged. However, because religiously there is room for negotiation on this issue, women draw on their feminist sensibilities to establish a contract which they personally prefer, and their preferences do not necessarily feel obliged to engage with piety at all. When I asked one activist if it was just to create such a contract, she stated the following:

> Look, we cannot run a country based on personal preferences or individual theorisations of justice. Maybe you think this is unfair [referring to the contract suggestion which included both a high *mehrieh* and the right to divorce], maybe you think it is feminism . . . but none of this changes the reality that this is a right that Islam gives to women. Therefore, it is Islamic, I love the Supreme Leader, and I am Hezbollahi.[72]

The state's promotion of a heteronormative narrative of marriages during the 1980–1988 period, and its subsequent dramatisation in the post-war years does not prevent female Hezbollah affiliates from imagining alternative moral futures that include women as citizens who dominate male counterparts in marriage, or even reject the institution of marriage altogether. While Hezbollah affiliates are influenced by the state's rhetoric on the war and current nuclear conflict, they are also employing material lenses geared towards personal and collective development when interacting within their society. Importantly, this conceptualisation of rights is not grounded in equality, and may not view as equally significant the

---

[71] Lara Deeb, *An Enchanted Modern: Gender and Public Piety in Shiʿi Lebanon* (Princeton, New Jersey: Princeton University Press, 2006).

[72] Personal interview, November 2013.

interests of men or other women. It is within this matrix of ambiguity and unpredictability that the role of female and male Hezbollah affiliates should be analysed.

CONCLUSION

Post-2009, the state hoped that Islamisation projects would encourage citizens to practise self-governance as obedience through a depoliticised admiration of the Divine. However, this formulation of the 'good citizen' was suffused with ambiguities. These are due to the tensions which exist between the legislation of religion in post-2009 Hezbollah's cultural institutions, the state's formal theorisation of citizenship, and its constitutional framework. The conflict which emerges between these domains of power over who the ideal Muslim citizen is, duly informs the political acts of Hezbollah affiliates on the ground. Hezbollah affiliates are not as interested in creating the City of God as they are in being individual and collective extensions of God on earth because of their exceptional piety which is augmented through the confirmation of cultural institutions. An examination of two Islamisation projects invested in reforming the social sciences and women's rights illustrates that the boundaries on autonomy and equality are continually being remade through this empowering yet risky perspective on self-governance.

At the beginning of this chapter, I asked what modes of citizenship the legislation of religion produces and what this means for the evolution of hybrid regimes. The chapter has suggested that elite support of new societal actors and institutions during moments of revived religious legislation may move the state formation process towards an uncertain path, producing citizens that are continually 'on the edge rather than progressing into the mainstream'.[73] At the same time, the expansions of institutions and empowerment of new social actors may also support state survival, at least in the short-term, through the formation of independent citizenship with ambiguous outcomes. Given the convergences in political culture and governing techniques between democratic and hybrid regimes, not to mention the similar ways in which they envision self-discipline as central to freedom, the findings in this chapter may be relevant elsewhere.

---

[73] Janet Newman, '"But We Didn't Mean that": Feminist Projects and Governmental Appropriations', in *Beyond Citizenship? Feminism and the Transformation of Belonging*, ed. Sasha Roseneil (London: Palgrave Macmillan, 2013), 89–111, quote from 101.

Acknowledgement

I would like to thank Roel Meijer, Nils A. Butenschøn, Omid Azadibougar, Adham Saouli, Jordan Cohen, Humeira Iqtidar, Paola Rivetti, Sarah Marusek, Soraya Batmanghelichi, Salvador Santino Jr. Regilme, Frank Gadinger, and Faten Ghosn for offering valuable comments on earlier drafts of this chapter.

PART III

International dimensions of citizenship rights

11. The EU and its southern neighbours: a fuzzy model of citizenship promotion?

Ruth Hanau Santini

This chapter investigates the way in which conceptual models of state–society relations are formulated and translated into practice by the European Union (EU) in its bilateral relations with the southern Mediterranean countries. It does so by looking at the evolution of European foreign policy since the 2011 Arab Uprisings, analysing first the revised European Neighbourhood Policy, but also the new strategies adopted by other EU bodies and frameworks, such as the European Instrument for Democracy and Human Rights and the European Endowment for Democracy. The chapter will empirically attest the degree to which EU policies have been inspired by the new strategies, as well as how far formulations of democratic ideals can be extrapolated from these policies. Lastly, it will elaborate on the relationship between these conceptual models of democracy and different models of citizenship, thereby cross-fertilising two strands of literature often kept separated, i.e. studies on democracy promotion or democracy assistance, and citizenship studies.

Citizenship studies are a recent field of scholarly study, and have yet to demonstrate their full potential in being consistently applied not just to the Middle East and North Africa,[1] but still more to the external action of the European Union. Tackling EU foreign policy in North Africa and the Middle East through EU citizenship approaches can shed light on the way in which highly sensitive EU discourses are generated across different institutions. Moreover, it can uncover different philosophical underpinnings across EU institutions on notions, such as citizenship, which do

---

[1] Roel Meijer and Nils Butenschøn (eds.), *The Crisis of Citizenship in the Arab World* (Leiden: Brill, 2017). Roel Meijer, 'Political Citizenship and Social Movements in the Arab World', in *Handbook of Political Citizenship and Social Movements*, ed. Hein-Anton van der Heijden (London: Edward Elgar, 2014), 628–60.

not suffer from the high visibility that EU democracy talk falls prey to. Analysing the change in the elaboration, formulation and implementation of EU policies since 2011 enables us to scrutinise the way in which post-Arab Uprisings state–society relations have been interpreted, politically represented and acted upon in Brussels.

The analysis of EU citizenship practices vis-à-vis the southern Mediterranean can also be justified on the basis of the recent politicisation of North African societies. The increased sense of citizenship, which has manifested itself in numerous ways, and employed a multifaceted repertoire of contention (a significant change from the pre-2011 political context in this region),[2] has required a fresh take on how the EU has adjusted, transformed, or indeed failed to transform its policies in the region.

The EU has framed the bulk of its bilateral policies with the southern Mediterranean around the European Neighbourhood Policy (ENP), held as a transformative policy tool for the development and stabilisation of neighbouring countries. The ENP was inaugurated in 2004, and covers bilateral relations between the EU and 16 different countries in Eastern Europe and the Middle East and North Africa (MENA). The southern dimension of the ENP embodies European attempts to promote good governance and stability and establish cooperative relations both within the MENA region and between these countries and the EU. It has been regarded as the European manifesto devising the steps supposedly leading southern Mediterranean countries to modernise and develop according to Western-defined standards.

By linking the post-2011 ENP documents, discourses and policies to different and alternative theoretical notions of democracy and citizenship, this chapter aims at tracing these policies to broader EU conceptual reflections of democracy and democratic citizenship. The analysis will uncover the EU's fuzzy and contradictory set of approaches to its democracy and citizenship policies in its southern neighbourhood.[3]

---

[2] Roel Meijer and Nils Butenschøn, 'Introduction' in *The Crisis of Citizenship in the Arab World*, 1–37.

[3] For an elaborate account of the different models of liberal democracy exported by international actors and a reference to the notion of fuzzy model by the EU in its democracy promotion, see Milja Kurki, *Democratic Futures: Revisioning Democracy Promotion* (London: Routledge, 2013).

1 CONCEPTUAL MODELS OF DEMOCRACY AND CITIZENSHIP IN THE EU EXTERNAL ACTION

EU and Democracy

Democracy, unlike other forms of government, is not about a specific goal that can be attained once and for all, or the content of specific policies.[4] As has been remarked time and again, from de Tocqueville down to today's political theorists, what is special about democracy lies mostly in its self-correcting capacity. Democracies constantly navigate between expectations and reality, learning from their mistakes in order to prevent them from occurring again in the future.[5] As Nadia Urbinati observes, it is trust, or to be more precise, a certain reasonable lack of it, that produces the dynamism of democracies and the continuous tension between politicians and citizens. Legitimacy should never be fully taken for granted.[6] When it comes to the EU, while the democracy deficit claim has been a thorny issue for decades,[7] and the 'nature of the beast' – referring to the EU's complex political identity and a multi-governance nature that mixes supranational and inter-governmental elements – has been a source of debate among both scholars and policymakers, questioning the features of the kind of liberal democracy it has promoted abroad has hardly been a central object of inquiry.[8]

The status of democracy as guiding principle for the internal and external working of the European Union remains problematic, however. Despite references to democracy in Articles 2 and 7 of the Lisbon Treaty, for the EU, democracy is not a binding legal principle, and remains at best a political value.[9] Given the lack of a specific democratic model upon

---

4 Norberto Bobbio, *Il futuro della democrazia* (Torino: Einaudi, 1984).

5 For a recent analysis of the potential regenerative capacity of democracy, see Ivan Krastev, 'Democracy as Self-Correction', Occasional Paper, (Washington: Transatlantic Academy) 2012–2013, Paper series No.1, accessed 5 May 2017, at: http://www.transatlanticacademy.org/sites/default/files/publications/Krastev_DemocracySelfCorrection_Dec12_web.pdf.

6 Nadia Urbinati, *Democrazia in diretta* (Milano: Feltrinelli, 2013).

7 For a recent overview of the debate, see Thomas Jensen, 'The Democratic Deficit of the European Union', *Living Reviews in Democracy* 1 (2009), accessed 25 May 2017, at: https://www.lrd.ethz.ch/index.php/lrd/article/viewArticle/lrd-2009–2/9.

8 For key exceptions see Kurki, *Democratic Futures*; Christopher Hobson, 'Liberal Democracy and Beyond: Extending the Sequencing Debate', *International Political Science Review* 33 (2012) 4: 441– 54.

9 Andrew Williams, 'Taking Values Seriously: Towards a Philosophy of EU Law', *Oxford Journal of Legal Studies* 29 (2009) 3: 549–77. Grainne de Burca, 'The Role of Equality in European Community Law', in *The Principle of Equal Treatment in EC Law*, eds. A. Dashwood and S. O'Leary (London: Sweet and Maxwell, 1997), 13–34.

which consistent external action can be based, the EU's rhetorical appeals to democracy should be read as political, un-enforceable and conceptually vague. These considerations hardly make the EU a standard setter in this realm.[10] Milja Kurki, for instance, argues that the EU, as a politically pluralist entity, has left the conceptual meaning of democracy undefined on purpose, leaving liberal ideals to compete with social democratic, reformist liberal, participatory, and other political ideologies.[11] Since there have been several different democratic experiences in the course of European history, the EU has never attempted to formulate a single unified democracy model. At least implicitly, therefore, the EU has acknowledged the existence of multiple democratic trajectories.

On the other hand, in drawing up its democracy support policies, it has struggled to be explicit about the model of democracy it wants to promote abroad.[12] It has done so by juxtaposing elements derived from several models next to each other, without ordering them or identifying a clear hierarchy of goals. As a result, it has ended up formulating a shopping list of desired policy outcomes. This can be explained partly by the attempt to de-politicise its support programmes for democracy, and turn it into a technical and non-controversial matter. As a consequence of such conceptual indeterminacy, the EU discourse appears confused and inconsistent. Nevertheless, according to Kurki, the EU's heterogeneity, derived from different ideological visions mixed and implemented across several institutions, bodies and agencies, can represent a strategic asset. It might, for instance, increase the leeway of the EU without appearing to impose one specific democratic model over others when dealing with third countries.[13] For more critical observers, however, behind the façade of a culturally neutral and depoliticised democracy, the EU is in fact advocating a specifically low intensity democracy that is more suitable to its economic interests, based on economic liberalisation and the development of the private sector.[14]

---

10 Dimitri Kochenov, 'Law Perspective: Praise Undeserved? The EU as a Democracy Promoter: A Skeptical Account', in *The Substance of EU Democracy Promotion*, eds. Anne Wetzel and Jan Orbie (London: Palgrave, 2015), 32.

11 Milja Kurki, 'Political Economy Perspective: Fuzzy Liberalism and EU Democracy Promotion: Why Concepts Matter', *The Substance of EU Democracy Promotion*, eds. Anne Wetzel and Jan Orbie (London: Palgrave, 2015), 35–7.

12 Milja Kurki, 'How the EU Can Adopt a New Type of Democracy Support' (FRIDE Brief, 112, March 2012).

13 Milja Kurki, 'Democracy and Conceptual Contestability', *International Studies Review* 12 (2010) 3: 362–86.

14 Devin K. Joshi, 'The Protective and Developmental Varieties of Liberal Democracy: A Difference in Kind or Degree?' *Democratization* 20 (2013) 2: 187–214.

Protective and Developmental Democracy as Heuristic Concepts

Two understandings of democracy are particularly relevant when it comes to citizenship rights. These are Protective Liberal Democracy (PLD) and Developmental Liberal Democracy (DLD). The former, developed in the eighteenth century, is inspired by the 'republicanism' of ancient Rome and revolves around constraining political leaders rather than empowering citizens or promoting collective gains. State powers are legally circumscribed and clearly divided between the executive, legislature and judiciary. In this system, freedom of speech and association, the right to vote and freedom of belief, as well as regular elections, competition between political parties, and freedom from arbitrary treatment are all legally ensured. Scholars opposed to protest movements in the US and Europe in the 1960s and 1970s,[15] regarded these as 'excesses of demands' and detrimental to democracy.

The developmental version of liberal democracy emerged in the nineteenth and twentieth centuries to compensate for certain inequalities inherent in the protective model. It balanced freedom with rights, and promoted a redistributive policy based on the assumption that in the absence of minimal conditions of economic equality, civil and political rights would be deficient.[16] For supporters of DLD, participation is unlimited. According to Quentin Skinner, who studied republican forms of democracy, democracy can only be based on the active participation of citizens. Earlier, Raymond Aron defended the importance of pluralism within liberalism, and of conflict as instrumental in creating political freedom.[17] More recently, Étienne Balibar pointed out that artificial creation of consensus in a society can never suppress conflicts, as conflicts are inherent to societies.

PLD, as opposed to DLD, has a narrow perimeter of defining features, revolving around civil and political rights rather than the empowerment of the citizen.[18] It focuses more closely on negative freedoms and the restraint by state authorities to infringe upon citizens' freedoms. Developmental democracy is 'thick', considers political participation as an end in itself, foresees a virtuous circle of pro-social, pro-statist behaviour, and advocates an active role of the state in welfare policies so as to enable all citizens to enjoy civil and political rights. And while protective forms of

---

[15] Michel Crozier, Samuel Huntington and Joji Watakuni, *The Crisis of Democracy*, Trilateral Commission (New York: New York University Press, 1975).

[16] Thomas H. Marshall, *Citizenship and Social Class and Other Essays* (Cambridge: Cambridge University Press, 1950).

[17] Hobson, 'Liberal Democracy and Beyond'.

[18] David Held, *Models of Democracy* (Stanford University Press, 2006), 78.

democracy comprise a set of rights and features defined once and for all, developmental models are premised on an evolutionary understanding of open-ended evolution of rights and conceptions. Besides their distinctive contents, therefore, the main aspect distinguishing the two models on an analytical level is a static, limited, procedural understanding of the protective kind, as opposed to a dynamic and transformative understanding espoused by the developmental democratic model. This analytical distinction can be fruitfully applied not only to liberal democracy but to models of democracy in general.

Citizenship Models

In the following typology, I have distinguished the key citizenship approaches according to a refined understanding of Thomas H. Marshall's tripartite classification of rights as civil (freedom of opinion, expression, assembly, religion), political (standing for elections, voting) and socio-economic (the creation of a functioning welfare system, the fight against poverty, redistributive policies).[19] I have added a distinction within each of these categories between protective or developmental understandings, one traditionally applied to conceptions of liberal democracy.[20] From the combination of these dimensions I have extrapolated four conceptual models of democracy and citizenship (see Table 11.1). Citizenship, in this model, is to be understood as a field of political struggle. It is a dynamic analytical category, possessing the power to reinvent and transform itself depending on the historical era it finds itself in. Citizenship, like democracy, can be expansive and evolutionary,[21] which makes its study in post-revolutionary contexts all the more appealing for heuristic purposes. Citizenship encapsulates a tension between freedom and obedience on the one hand, and between universalism and particularism on the other.[22] Following Balibar's thought, citizens are both subject *of* power and subject *to* power, where the former requires disobedience and the latter obedience.[23] Citizenship practices, stem-

---

19 Thomas H. Marshall, *Citizenship and Social Class and Other Essays* (Cambridge: Cambridge University Press, 1950).

20 Held, *Models of Democracy*; Joshi, 'The Protective and Developmental Varieties of Liberal Democracy'.

21 Étienne Balibar, *Citizenship.* Translated by Thomas Scott-Railton (Oxford: Polity Press, 2015).

22 Engin F. Isin, 'Citizenship studies and the Middle East', in *The Crisis of Citizenship in the Arab World*, eds. Roel Meijer and Nils Butenschøn (Leiden, Boston: Brill, 2017), 514.

23 Étienne Balibar, 'Citizen Subject', in *Who Comes After the Subject*, eds. Eduardo Cadava, Peter Connor, and Jean-Luc Nancy (London: Routledge, 1991), 46.

Table 11.1 Six models of democracy and citizenship

	Civil rights	Political rights	Social and economic rights
Protective democracy	Liberal procedural democracy / Passive citizenship	Liberal electoral democracy / Thin liberal citizenship	Neoliberal democracy (minimal social rights) / Neoliberal citizenship
Developmental democracy	High intensity liberal democracy / Liberal citizenship	Participatory democracy / Active citizenship	Social democracy / Socio-economic citizenship

ming from this conception, oscillate between these two modalities and their analysis enables us to ascertain the tension between citizens and the state in a contingent way. From that standpoint, alongside traditional analyses of changes in the EU's democracy assistance discourses and policies towards its southern neighbours, a critical account of the EU's external action in the southern Mediterranean can be successfully extrapolated by looking at how, given new empirical realities and demands coming from the bottom up in the region, EU citizenship discourses and practices have or have not changed, and the shape they have taken.

While ideal-types of democratic models abound, three are liberal democratic models with different emphases, and the other three are neoliberal, participatory and social democratic. Each can be articulated in line with a Protective or a Developmental understanding of democracy.

When democracy stresses the civil rights component in a protective understanding, it is a liberal procedural conception and a passive understanding of citizenship. Of the four main models of democracy promotion, the liberal conception remains the prevailing one. It represents the lowest common denominator among the democratic options available and the least politicised one, and therefore, it is potentially easier to export. The liberal model is historically based upon two factors: a certain degree of responsiveness of politicians to citizen demands, and free and fair elections.[24] In its most widespread form, derived from Joseph Schumpeter and mediated by Robert Dahl, liberal democracy prioritises the delegation of power, defends individual freedoms and political equality, and promotes competition among political parties in free elections, as well

[24] Robert Dahl, *Polyarchy: Participation and Opposition* (New Haven: Yale University Press, 1971).

as accountability of public officials to citizens. Procedural democracy as popularised by empirical democratic theory has a narrowly sectoral political view of democracy and a passive take on citizens.[25] In its most standardised version, liberty, as argued by Hobson, tends to be defined and measured on the basis of the absence of restraints, typically exemplified by the non-interference of the state in individuals' private affairs, including private property.[26] Within such a concept of liberal democracy, the contradiction between participation and representation remains unresolved, with the former sacrificed on the altar of the latter. This procedural version of democracy is thin, minimalist, and libertarian: it is a 'protective model of democracy'.[27] The role of government is limited, and freedom is almost exclusively understood as negative freedom, i.e. absence of state-led violence. So, while liberal procedural democracy requires standard civil and political rights in a protective understanding, i.e. minimal and static, the same liberal democracy becomes upgraded to higher quality if civil rights are actively empowered, be it through political conditionality, EU membership perspective, sanctions if they are not respected, or other forms of punishment. Liberal procedural democracy corresponds to a passive conception of citizenship: the individual is at the receiving end of clearly defined rights to be enjoyed with defined limits and constraints. Liberal participatory democracy, on the other hand, corresponds to an active model of citizenship, where the notion of rights is never-ending, evolutionary and transformative, and the capacity of citizens to demand, fight and expand their rights can be activated and enacted upon at any moment. The demarcation between the two, while potentially blurred on a factual level, on an analytical level is embodied by the move Balibar encapsulated in the idea that being a subject *to* power requires obedience, while being a subject *of* power requires disobedience. The shift from a passive to an active citizenship model takes shape precisely in this analytical distinction, despite Isin's own acknowledgement that the citizen-subject can be obedient, submissive to authority and subversive of authority at the same time, carrying in himself the possibility and danger of the obedient subject of sovereign power.[28]

If democracy emphasises the empowerment of participation and political rights – as was demanded with the rise of the civil rights movement

---

25 Philippe Schmitter, 'More Liberal, Preliberal, or Postliberal', *Journal of Democracy*, 6 (1995) 1: 15–22.

26 Hobson, 'Liberal Democracy and Beyond'.

27 Held, *Models of Democracy*.

28 See for analysis of Balibar's ideas, Engin F. Isin, 'Citizenship Studies and the Middle East', in *The Crisis of Citizenship in the Arab World*, 516.

in the United States in the mid-1950s, and which gained traction with the 1960s protest movements in the United States and Europe – we have forms of participatory democracy. These movements rejected the conventional liberal wisdom of the pitfalls of excessive participation and regarded the principle of delegation as an instrument of oligarchic power. While not disavowing the main tenets of liberal democracy, participatory democracy theorists hold that while liberal interpretations of democracy support formal equality, this makes little sense if the conditions for real equality have not been created; something that can only be accomplished through the intensive political participation of citizens beyond elections.[29] Participatory democracy holds that only citizen empowerment can counter an elitist democracy; interestingly, it emphasises communitarian rather than individualistic notions of freedom and democracy. As such, it shares some elements with certain contemporary Islamic conceptions of democracy, which uphold the collective dimension of rights and consultation (*shura*) over individual freedom.[30] Citizenship is active, as all citizens participate in political life in various forms. When, on the other hand, political participation beyond elections is discouraged, and a protective understanding of political rights is predominant, democracy is of a liberal electoral kind, and citizenship is a thin liberal citizenship. When the EU re-affirms the importance of political rights without tying the extent of bilateral cooperation to their actual respect and full implementation of democratic conditions, it is promoting a liberal electoral democracy. The corresponding model of citizenship is a thin liberal citizenship, where minimal political rights are respected or promoted and their extension and empowerment are limited. When, on the other hand, the EU openly advocates the empowerment of political citizenship, engaging directly with local political actors both within and outside government, attempting to widen political participation, it promotes participatory democracy.

When socio-economic rights are at the heart of democratic processes understood in developmental terms, as has been the case in Scandinavian countries since the 1950s, democracy becomes social democracy, and citizenship is centred around the enhancement of socio-economic rights for all citizens. In this understanding, economic freedom revolves around Keynesian models of economic development and the extension

---

[29] Benjamin Barber, *Strong Democracy: Participatory Politics for a New Age, 20th Anniversary Edition* (Berkeley, CA: University of California Press, 2003); Carole Pateman, *Participation and Democratic Theory* (Cambridge: Cambridge University Press, 1970).

[30] Massimo Campanini, *Il Pensiero Islamico Contemporaneo* (Bologna: Il Mulino, 2005), 145.

of citizenship rights. One of the main scholars articulating a vision of socio-economic rights as complementary to civil and political rights was the British sociologist T.H. Marshall. He espoused the view that in the absence of socio-economic rights, a democratic regime is little more than an empty shell reinvigorating existing inequalities. The social democratic model is predicated upon the principle of social solidarity and democratic control over economic processes. Social citizenship is a mechanism of universal solidarity, associated with work: in this approach, work represents the foundation of society, rather than the family as the key constitutive institution. In this classical view, the state has an important role to play from a redistributive perspective, as opposed to liberal and, above all, neoliberal understandings of democracy. Sheri Berman further identifies social citizenship not just as a tool to redistribute wealth in order to avoid extreme poverty, but as a mechanism of universal solidarity, and sees the EU's post-1945 hegemonic ideology linked to social democracy rather than capitalism. In a significant reversal from a neoliberal model, the economy should be at the service of the political, and especially so in countries undergoing political transitions.[31] That social democracy may be considered a distinctive ideology is based upon two main premises: namely, the primacy of politics, and communitarianism. In Berman's reading, social democracy emphasises the political sphere and community cohesion: it is a communitarian version of democracy as opposed to the vision of liberal democracy based on Lockean, atomistic individualism.[32] When the EU in its external actions adopts a developmentalist vision of socio-economic rights, it pushes for redistributive policies, a strong welfare state, joining forces with other international organisations to assist these countries' development in a geographically and socially balanced way.

If, on the other hand, socio-economic rights are curtailed, as is the case among many Western countries, liberal democracy transforms into neoliberal democracy, and citizenship becomes neoliberal citizenship. Here the emphasis is on individual liberty, economic competition, the supposedly self-correcting nature of the market, and the prioritisation of the economic sphere over the political one. In a neoliberal elitist understanding of democracy, electoral participation is the only legitimate popular political expression. According to this vision, markets should be freed from any constraint and the state is a passive observer vis-à-vis the creation of inequalities, especially within the overall retrenchment of the

---

31 Sheri Berman, *The Primacy of Politics* (Cambridge: Cambridge University Press, 2006).

32 Hobson, 'Liberal Democracy and Beyond'.

welfare state. At the same time, a parallel shift takes place on a conceptual level from a classical welfare model, typical of Scandinavian countries and Sweden in particular until the 1990s, to a residual model of welfare, as hypothesised by Anthony Giddens.[33] In its external action, when the EU pushes for rule of law and good governance in the economic realm by supporting the fight against crony forms of capitalism, in favour of open markets, liberalisation and privatisation, it is exporting a neoliberal understanding of democracy. Accordingly, the role of the state is kept at a minimum and politics is subordinated to the market.

The rest of the chapter will briefly analyse some of the EU policies vis-à-vis its southern neighbours and their nature among the models of democracy and citizenship mentioned above.

2 EU CONCEPTS AND PRACTICES OF DEMOCRACY AND CITIZENSHIP IN THE SOUTHERN MEDITERRANEAN

The ENP as a Tool of Democratic Change

In light of the post-2011 turmoil, the ENP, like most policies focusing on the MENA region, has been the object of wide debate, rethinking and reformulation.[34] The ENP was conceived as an alternative to two competing geopolitical approaches the EU was confronted with at the end of the 1990s: enlargement and geopolitics. Enlargement went hand in hand with the extension of the EU's *acquis*, and the radical transformations undertaken by countries willing to join the 'EU club'. Traditional geopolitics, meanwhile, was characterised by a mix of policy tools revolving around security and trade agreements. The ENP was devised as an alternative to enlargement and a softer form of geopolitics by other means. The strategic rationale was avoiding potential negative spillover effects from countries on its periphery. Starting from 2004, the ENP problematically collected 16 countries from the EU's eastern and southern neighbourhood under one single policy. Its technocratic nature was made evident by the lack of reference to any geopolitical justification for lumping together countries

---

33 Kurki, *Democratic Futures*, 73.

34 Mattia Toaldo and Susi Dennison, 'Pretending nothing has changed: the ENP and 'inclusive growth' in Morocco and Tunisia', unpublished policy memo, ECFR; Stefan Lehne, 'Time to reset the ENP', Carnegie paper, 4/2/2014, accessed 3 January 2017, at: http://carnegieeurope.eu/2014/02/04/time-to-reset-european-neighborhood-policy/h02l#.

ranging from Algeria to Ukraine, with a standardisation of steps and measures to comply with in order to intensify bilateral relations. When the Arab Uprisings broke out in 2011, EU foreign policy in the Mediterranean and the modernisation assumptions it was based upon were put into question. Shortly after the toppling of Presidents Zine El Abidine Ben Ali of Tunisia and Husni Mubarak of Egypt in January and February 2011, respectively, Stefan Füle, Commissioner for Enlargement and ENP made an unprecedented *mea culpa* in EU foreign relations, acknowledging that the respect for human rights and local democratic forces had not been at the forefront of the EU's action, and that relying on apparently resilient authoritarian regimes had been a myopic foreign policy choice.[35]

The 2011 uprisings had little to do with the ENP or other EU policies, since these had been adjusted to collaborate with authoritarian regimes, rather than nurture grassroots social and political forces. The Arab Uprisings, however, led to a rethinking of the modalities and goals of the ENP, with EU policymakers acknowledging the inadequacy of existing instruments. All previous criticisms directed at the ENP – an inconsistent policy of conditionality, Eurocentric conceptions, and rigidity of application – were suddenly taken seriously.

Since then, the EU's fuzzy liberal democracy scheme has suffered increasing criticism and demands for change, which have spurred initial diplomatic steps to develop new strategies for supposedly democratic assistance policies.

The first of these documents was the *Partnership for Democracy and Shared Prosperity*, published in March 2011, which outlined the notion of 'deep democracy', a concept that supposedly indicated an EU commitment to reforms, to be rewarded with greater integration in the EU (either in its market or in terms of mobility).[36] In this Communication, the will to change course by promoting democratic citizenship promotion was clearly expressed in an ideologically mixed formulation of democratic goals:

> This new approach should be rooted unambiguously in a joint commitment to common values . . . The commitment to democracy, human rights, social justice, good governance and the rule of law must be shared. The Partnership

---

[35] Stefan Füle, *Speech on the Recent Events in North Africa*, 28 February 2011. http://europa.eu/rapid/press-release_SPEECH-11– 130_en.htm, accessed 3 April 2017.

[36] European Commission, *A Partnership for Democracy and Shared Prosperity with the Southern Mediterranean*, COM (2011) 200 final. http://eur-lex.europa.eu/legal-content/EN/TXT/PDF/?uri=CELEX:52011DC0200&qid=1493210550074&from=EN, accessed 3 April 2017.

> must be based on concrete progress in these areas. . . . A thriving civil society can help uphold human rights and contribute to democracy building and good governance, playing an important role in checking government excesses. A range of non-government (NGOs) and civil society organisations (CSOs) can provide much-needed support for the reforms and involvement in areas close to citizens' concerns such as human rights, the environment, social and economic development.

For the first time, the ENP was explicitly tasked with being closer to the society end of the spectrum, rather than being purely an intergovernmental policy dealing almost exclusively with third countries' governments. Local civil society was acknowledged as a watchdog of government action, in a 'negative freedom' inspired approach, corresponding to a classic Western liberal orientation of clearly separating state and society, with society patrolling potential infringements of citizens' rights by the state. In Arab Muslim countries, this approach risked imposing a straitjacket on organisations remaining outside such a typically Habermasian reading of public space. First and foremost, this concerned Islamic charities or private foundations engaging in crucial civil and social activities, which failed to gain recognition in such under- or over-regulated social and political space. It did, however, incorporate many of the elements of a civil rights centred high intensity liberal democracy and a corresponding notion of liberal citizenship, with the EU actively promoting especially human rights-based CSOs and their watchdog role.

This approach was further substantiated in the *New Response to a Changing Neighbourhood* in May 2011,[37] the core of the so-called revised ENP, designed as a multifaceted, multiregional, multi-sectoral umbrella policy framework,[38] allowing for greater differentiation in terms of depth and speed of engagement. The May 2011 *Joint Communication* outlined the desired nature of the EU's policy by positing that:

> A new approach is needed to strengthen the partnership between the EU and the countries and societies of the neighbourhood: to build and consolidate healthy democracies, pursue sustainable economic growth and manage cross-border links. . .
>
> The new approach aims to:

---

[37] European Commission, *A New Response to a Changing Neighbourhood*, COM (2011) 303 final. https://ec.europa.eu/research/iscp/pdf/policy/com_2011_303.pdf, accessed 3 April 2017.

[38] Dimitris Bouris and Tobias Schumacher (eds.), *The Revised European Neighbourhood Policy. Continuity and Change in EU Foreign Policy* (London: Palgrave Macmillan, 2017), 3.

> Provide greater support to partners engaged in building deep democracy – the kind that lasts, with the right to vote accompanied by rights to exercise free speech, form competing political parties, receive impartial justice from independent judges, security from accountable police and army forces, access to a competent and non-corrupt civil service – and those engaged in reinforcing other civil and human rights that many Europeans take for granted, such as the freedom of thought, conscience and religion;
>
> Support inclusive economic development, so that EU neighbours can trade, invest and grow in a sustainable way, reducing social and regional inequalities, creating jobs for their workers and higher standards of living for their people . . .

According to the document, the overarching goal of the ENP was to consolidate and strengthen an unspecified form of democracy. The juxtaposition of sustainable growth, rather than referring to its equal redistribution, and the reference to managing links, implying flows of goods and migration, illustrates the extent of conceptual confusion behind the much-trumpeted qualitatively new EU foreign policy approach. In the same document, the EU stated it would curtail relations with governments violating human rights and democracy, by making use of targeted sanctions and other policy measures, something which never materialised. However, the focus remained on liberal procedural elements (fairness of elections, civil liberties, rule of law, security sector reform and civilian control of the military), albeit in its high intensity version, given the readiness to punish states violating the respect of these rights. Reference was also made to some elements of a social democratic conception of democracy, stressing the need to promote inclusive growth. A revision of the standard liberal vision of democracy and citizenship does not emerge from these documents, which continued to adhere to a vague formulation of democratic aspirations supposedly 'close to European experiences', without identifying the key elements representing the key constitutive elements of a democratic polity or an acceptable range. The inclusion of a list of 'deep democracy indicators' in the *Implementation of the European Neighbourhood Policy in 2011; Statistical Annex*, which could have served as benchmarks for the quality of democracy, did not lead to any substantial policy adjustment, as half of them were removed less than a year later in the *Implementation of the European Neighbourhood Policy in 2012*.[39] As argued by Kurki, 'alternative models of democracy – for example participatory or social democratic ideals – are not *systematically* [my italics] argued for. There is no sign of a deepening of democracy towards a "dual track democracy" with wage earner representation and economic

[39] Ibid., 16.

democracy, or participatory democracy which would entail locally derived agendas over national and international policies'.[40]

The 2011 Arab Uprisings have posed a whole new set of challenges to Schumpeterian understandings of democracy and have forced the EU to re-question its assumptions.

Interestingly, key standard liberal democratic procedures – long considered the defining feature of a democracy, i.e. elections – have grown less relevant as several regimes across the region allowed for the emergence of multi-party systems as a divide and rule tactic, or as a way to co-opt different kinds of oppositional forces. Since 2011, political participation has shifted from formal to increasingly informal channels across North Africa.[41]

Discursively, the EU added reference to 'inclusive and sustainable growth', which became the new post-2011 mantra, while it stressed that elections are only the starting point for democratic transition. However, this was before the electoral victory of the Egyptian and Tunisian Islamist movements (in the case of Tunisia, EU policymakers quickly endorsed the approach and leadership style of Ennahda, the dominant moderate Islamist party), the descent into chaos in Libya, and the deterioration of the Syrian civil war. The possibility of broadening the conception of democracy and adapting it to locally acceptable understandings, possibly religious ones, became harder after the Muslim Brotherhood won the elections in Egypt in 2012 and started operating under a strongly majoritarian conception of (illiberal) democracy,[42] in which it limited the space for civil society, adopted exclusionary political tactics, and took hold of national media outlets and other institutions, replacing top personnel with members of its own Freedom and Justice party.

The ENP between Normative Goals and Empirical Reality

The ENP's *Egypt 2014 Progress Report*, the EU assessment of reforms introduced by Egypt since the adoption of the latest ENP Action Plan, limited itself in 2014 to giving a summary of the main political events of the previous year, with barely a reference to the dramatic coup against the

---

40 Kurki, 'How the EU Can Adopt a New Type of Democracy Support', 7.

41 Asef Bayat, *Life as Politics. How Ordinary People Change the Middle East* (Stanford: Stanford University Press, 2010); Charles Tripp, *Power and Resistance: Paths of Resistance in the Middle East* (Cambridge: Cambridge University Press, 2013).

42 Shadi Hamid, *Temptations of Power: Islamists and Illiberal Democracy in a New Middle East* (Oxford: Oxford University Press, 2014).

democratically elected Muslim Brotherhood government. The document barely mentions human rights violations, the violent repression of protests or the limits to political participation imposed by the military regime. Nor did these events affect EU policies towards Egypt. EU aid to Egypt was particularly significant in 2013, reaching €1 billion. The *Report* offered only a shopping list of 'challenges' for the recipient country, with no prioritisation or hierarchy between goals as different as 'products' rules of origin, torture, [and] limits to freedom of association'.[43] More recently, on 11 October 2016, despite the further deterioration of all citizenship rights in the country, the EU signed a €129 million package of financial assistance for Egypt, supporting socio-economic development. The Union failed to apply the 'deep democracy' indicators as benchmarks, or naming and shaming the regime of President El-Sisi for its abuse of citizenship rights. It neglected the principle 'Less for less', espoused by the European Parliament, advocating a curtailment of financial support given the evidence of backsliding citizens' rights.

The *Progress Report*, which embodies the empirical implementation of the Neighbourhood Policy, has remained devoid of broader geopolitical considerations, and remains limited to a stock taking exercise, unable or unwilling to question assumptions, revisit arguments and priorities, and provide in-depth political assessments of how the situation has changed and how this impacts EU interests. In an accompanying memo, former EU High Representative Catherine Ashton reaffirmed the goals of the ENP, re-stating potentially contradictory qualitative goals such as establishing democracy, strengthening sustainable and inclusive economic development, and building security.

Strikingly, even in the most normatively oriented phase of European foreign policy in the region (between 2011 and 2014), the framing of democracy-related goals remained fuzzy. The EU under-theorised how actively sustaining democracy and maintaining security could be jointly promoted. Since 2014, and even more so since 2015, the Union has not only acknowledged its limited impact, both in the region generally, and on specific countries' counter-revolutionary and authoritarian backsliding, but made a U-turn: in 2015's newly revised ENP, the democratic and citizenship discourse was dropped in favour of stabilising the neighbourhood.

This is not to say that European security concerns were absent in the wake of the 2011 revolts: the Union started negotiating counter-terrorism

[43] European Commission, *Implementation of the ENP in Egypt: Progress in 2013 and Recommendations for Action*, 17 March 2014, accessed 5 May 2017, at: http://eeas.europa.eu/enp/pdf/2014/country-reports/egypt_en.pdf.

Action Plans with Morocco and Algeria as early as 2013. However, from 2014, the normative framework identifying stability with sustainable regimes that respected their citizens was abandoned, and reference was only made to interests, which Europe should safeguard, without identifying its democracy assistance values – including the promotion of forms of active or socio-economic citizenship – with its interests.[44]

The unexpected turn of events in 2013 (the coup against President Morsi in Egypt and the legitimacy crisis of Ennahda in Tunisia, leading to the formation of a technocratic government in the latter case) brought about a further revision of the ENP. Between March and June 2015, consultations with stakeholders were held and eventually five priorities were singled out. The 18 November 2015 *Joint Communication* listed: differentiation (as already stated in the 2011 revised ENP), focus, flexibility, ownership and visibility, across five areas of intervention where the EU and southern partners share common interests: trade and economic development, connectivity, security, governance and migration. The *2015 Review* represented a paradigmatic shift from deep democracy to prioritising stability and security. A conservative understanding of stabilisation orients the new approach. In the document's opening statements, it is argued that:

> The EU's own stability is built on democracy, human rights and the rule of law and economic openness, and the new ENP will take stabilization as its main political priority in this mandate.[45]

In terms of democracy and citizenship approaches the EU more firmly adopted protective understandings of rights. From this moment on, the discourse on political and socio-economic rights empowerment becomes obfuscated by reference to universal rights and human rights. In the 2015 ENP, socio-economic challenges lie at the core of bilateral relations, and geographic proximity is no longer a unifying feature, but rather a source of insecurity in terms of export of soft insecurity (migrants) and hard (terrorists), in a highly securitised existential narrative of the Union struggling to defend itself from challenges coming from the MENA region. It is not by chance that the document states that all engagements with Europe's

---

[44] European Commission, 'Neighborhood at the Crossroads: Taking Stock of a Year of Challenges', Press release, 27 March 2014, accessed 5 April 2017, at: http://europa.eu/rapid/press-release_IP-14-315_en.htm.

[45] European Commission, 'Joint Communication to the European Parliament, the Council, the European Economic and Social Committee and the Committee of the Regions'. *Review of the European Neighborhood Policy*, 18 November 2015, 3.

neighbours should contribute to increasing security on the European continent, especially since the Paris terrorist attacks in November 2015.[46] The dilution of European efforts to promote developmental understandings of democracy and citizenship rights also suffered from the retreat of the EU vis-à-vis its member states, which demanded and obtained a much closer association with the ENP. Without attributing a more normative value to policies adopted at the supranational level, the risk in re-nationalising this specific tool of European foreign policy is enhancing the search for minimum common denominator approaches, rather than more ambitious ones vis-à-vis third countries.

3 EXPLORING VARIETIES OF EU DEMOCRACY AND CITIZENSHIP PRACTICES BEYOND THE ENP

In the past two decades, the debate about different ways to promote democracy has flourished, centring particularly on the experiences of the US and the EU, and their practices[47] and shortcomings. More recent literature has focused on emerging powers' conceptions and shapes of democracy support in their neighbourhoods.[48]

According to the nature and number of actors the EU engages with locally, democracy and democratic citizenship can either be a government-to-government approach or a flexible approach with a mix of state and non-state actors within civil and political societies (trade unions, political parties, associations, NGOs, religious groups, individuals, etc.). The European Instrument for Democracy and Human Rights (EIDHR) and the European Endowment for Democracy (EED) are smaller initiatives, can bypass national governments and directly support CSOs (the EIDHR) or even politically active small groups and individuals (the EED). The EED was created at the end of 2012 and became operational in 2013, and notwithstanding a limited budget (6 million euros from the European Commission in its first few years) has

---

46 Ibid., 4.

47 Michael Cox and Brian Stokes, *US Foreign Policy* (Oxford: Oxford University Press, 2012); Richard Youngs and Katerina Pischikova, 'A More Pluralist Approach to EU Democracy Support', Carnegie Paper, Carnegie Endowment for International Peace, October 2013.

48 Thomas Carothers and Richard Youngs, 'Non-Western Roots of International Democracy Support', Carnegie Paper, Carnegie Endowment for International Peace, June 2014.

been very active in several southern Mediterranean countries, encouraging political citizenship in a developmental way. Modelled along the lines of the US National Endowment for Democracy (NED), created to support Eastern European transitions after the fall of the Berlin wall, it aims at fostering democracy abroad by offering small grants to political parties or community leaders. If more significantly funded, it could provide a critical support to local non-governmental political forces, which, under-represented or repressed, could form key avenues for mobilisation, and possibly produce political leadership. This would strengthen the EU's claim to fostering more participatory forms of democracy and active citizenship. The EED namely defines its mission as follows:

> The EED builds citizens' capacities and strengthens independent voices. It supports initiatives that build foundations for more inclusive and participatory democracies and work to counter corruption.[49]

The small but flexible EED complements the more technocratic ENP approach. In 2014, the EED received 1,300 requests for support and provided help to 130 democracy interest groups in 15 countries, which illustrates the breadth of its intervention despite its relatively small financial allocation. The EED has supported 20 initiatives in Tunisia alone in 2015, mostly in rural areas and with women.[50]

Theoretically, the EIDHR could represent a key tool in paving the way for a developmental version of liberal democracy, something which might have materialised had the EU kept the full list of deep democracy indicators as benchmarks in assessing democratic progress from one year to the next. Providing laws do not forbid private associations from receiving funding from abroad, the EIDHR enables the Union to bypass local governments and directly channel democracy support to selected associations and NGOs (not, however, unions, religious-based groups, or political parties).

Lastly, in June 2016, the EU presented a Global Strategy (EUGS), which updated and replaced the 2003 European Security Strategy (ESS) and the 2008 ESS Implementation Report. Among the guiding goals of the EUGS, the following ones are particularly relevant: strengthening security and defence; investing in the resilience of states and societies to Europe's East and South; developing an integrated approach to conflicts and crises;

---

[49] European Endowment for Democracy, Annual Report 2016, 5, accessed 26 April 2017, at: https://www.democracyendowment.eu/annual-report-2016/.

[50] European Endowment for Democracy, Annual Report 2016.

promoting and supporting cooperative regional orders; and reinforcing a global governance.[51]

Significantly, the MENA region was not singled out specifically, but several themes touch upon it, especially with reference to the neighbourhood, which is widened as far as the Arab world is concerned and stretches to the Gulf. Thematically, the approach the EU has formulated, albeit vaguely, is based on resilience (intended as the ability of countries to reform, withstanding and recovering from internal and external crises), and distinguished from passive acceptance of authoritarian backlashes. The importance of resilience is linked to the fight against terrorism, corruption, and organised crime. The protection of human rights is added to the list almost as an afterthought. The focus on the EU's strategic priorities and security concerns is further strengthened by the vagueness with which reference is made to human rights, let alone other categories of citizenship rights. Human rights should be promoted during a long-term process requiring a long-term engagement by the EU, in the absence of a new framework clearly incentivising their respect by local governments. The document underlines the importance for the EU to adapt its policies to definitions of locally developed rights, even in fields such as justice, security and defence,[52] at a time when the region is experiencing a widespread pattern of authoritarian backlash across policy sectors, including the justice sector, and when prevailing security conceptions revolve around regime stability rather than state or societal security. The EU, under the banner of 'principled pragmatism' tries to avoid the unprincipled pragmatism of the period before the Arab Uprisings on the one hand, and principled idealism on the other, refraining from strengthening its role in the promotion of a political rights agenda, and contenting itself with supporting human rights and civil society, while sacrificing its democracy assistance aspirations.[53]

---

[51] Council Conclusions on the Global Strategy on the European Union's Foreign and Security Policy, Foreign Affairs Council, 17 October 2016, accessed 24 April 2017, at: https://europa.eu/globalstrategy/en/eu-foreign-ministers-adopted-common-conclusions-implementing-eu-global-strategy.

[52] Shared Vision, Common Action: A Stronger Europe. A Global Strategy for the European Union's Foreign and Security Policy, June 2016, 25–6, accessed 15 May 2017, at: https://europa.eu/globalstrategy/sites/globalstrategy/files/regions/files/eugs_review_web.pdf.

[53] Eduard Soler I. Lecha and Nathalie Tocci, 'Implications of the EU Global Strategy for the Middle East and North Africa', Future Notes, Menara project, no. 1, July 2016, accessed 15 May 2017, at: http://www.iai.it/sites/default/files/menara_fn_1.pdf.

4 CONCLUSIONS

By looking at European foreign policy in the southern Mediterranean from the vantage point of democracy and citizenship conceptions, one is struck by the variety of tools adopted responding to very different theoretical underpinnings of democratic tenets. From the EIDHR, which supports a developmental civil citizenship approach, to the EED, which stands for a developmental political citizenship, the bulk, in economic and continuity terms, of the EU's engagement with southern Mediterranean countries is represented by more technocratic policies such as the ENP, which despite reformulations and either supposedly normative (as in the 2011 revised ENP) or pragmatic leanings (as in the 2015 revised ENP), have continued to operate, with striking continuity, in support of protective forms of democracy and in favour of a minimum common denominator for the respect of civil, political and economic rights.

While the EU has openly advocated for more inclusive societies and polities in its southern neighbourhood, a claim further re-stated in the 2016 EUGS, the citizenship models it has supported on the ground have continued to be characterised by exclusionary dynamics towards specific groups of citizens, often backtracking on small post-2011 advances in civil and political rights. In other words, despite having grown more aware of the importance of sustainable political systems based on fully democratic citizenship models as pre-conditions for the stability both of these countries and that of the EU, this vision has been supported with the smallest diplomatic instruments and limited economic resources, while the bulk of the EU's action has failed to shift from a promotion of different kinds of protective democracy to developmental ones. The liberal democracy exported by the EU in its neighbourhood has continued to focus on elections, procedural democracy, rule of law, civil society, restraining the more egalitarian and participatory aspects of democracy, and sacrificing the empowerment of both political and socio-economic rights on the altar of minimum advances in its human rights and procedural democracy agenda.

12. Citizenship and migration diplomacy: Turkey and the EU

Peter Seeberg

INTRODUCTION

Protests and demonstrations against the Baʿath-regime in Damascus in early 2011 initiated an increasingly violent internal conflict in Syria, causing widespread devastation and humanitarian disaster. Furthermore, the crisis gradually resulted in major displacement of Syrians to neighbouring states, in particular Jordan, Lebanon and Turkey. Some of the Syrian refugees attempted to reach Europe, and together with refugees and migrants from Asia and sub-Saharan Africa created what in the international media, but also in scholarly research, has been referred to as the Mediterranean migration crisis.[1] The recent migration crisis is characterised by a high level of complexity. First of all, the huge numbers of Syrian refugees, which in connection with the armed confrontations in Syria have been displaced to most of the Levant region, constitute a social and humanitarian challenge with repercussions beyond the region. Secondly, the Levant is exposed to migratory movements, involving refugees from the region and from Asian and African countries, work migration in and out of the region, and irregular migration using the Levant as transit area primarily targeting Europe.[2] Thirdly, the crisis is characterised by politicisation and securitisation of refugees and migrants, which affect how citizenship rights are being interpreted and

[1] Stefania Panebianco, 'The Mediterranean Migration Crisis: Border Control Versus Humanitarian Approaches', *Global Affairs* 2 (2016) 4: 441–5. See also Julien Jeandesboz and Polly Pallister-Wilkins, 'Crisis, Routine, Consolidation: The Politics of the Mediterranean Migration Crisis', *Mediterranean Politics* 21 (2016) 2: 316–20.

[2] Peter Seeberg and Zaid Eyadat, 'Introduction: Migration, Security, and Citizenship in a Changing Middle East', in *Migration, Security, and Citizenship in the Middle East: New Perspectives*, eds. Peter Seeberg and Zaid Eyadat (New York: Palgrave Macmillan, 2013), 1–23.

dealt with in connection with legal and political practices. A significant example could be seen when President Recep Tayyip Erdoğan of Turkey on several occasions in 2016 stated that Syrian refugees would be offered Turkish citizenship – a statement aiming at influencing the ongoing negotiations between Turkey and the EU concerning refugees and migrants.

It is the idea of this chapter to analyse the challenges for Turkey and the EU in dealing with the migration crisis from a citizenship perspective. The chapter discusses the notion of migration diplomacy, arguing that the migration crisis has resulted in a higher level of interdependence between Turkey and the EU. As a signatory to the 1951 Convention Relating to the Status of Refugees, Turkey sustains a geographic limitation clause regarding the convention, not accepting legal responsibility for protecting non-European refugees.[3] This entails a specific situation for the Syrian refugees in Turkey characterised by restricted access to citizenship rights like education, conditions related to employment, health services, etc. – a reality for which Umut Korkut has suggested the term 'selective humanitarianism'.[4] The legal practices attached to the Turkish policies towards Syrian refugees are based on a framework known as 'temporary protection' and reflect how the given challenges are perceived and addressed by the Turkish authorities.[5] Due to the massive intake of refugees and migrants, the Turkish government has had to develop a policy based on a stronger legal foundation and at the same time deal with its relations to external actors. These include the EU, international

---

[3] Feyzi Baban, Suzan Ilcan, and Kim Rygiel, 'Syrian Refugees in Turkey: Pathways to Precarity, Differential Inclusion, and Negotiated Citizenship Rights', *Journal of Ethnic and Migration Studies* 43 (2017) 1: 41–57.

[4] Umut Korkut, 'Pragmatism, Moral Responsibility or Policy Change: The Syrian Refugee Crisis and Selective Humanitarianism in the Turkish Refugee Regime', *Comparative Migration Studies* 4 (2016) 2: 1–10.

[5] Deniz Eroğlu, 'The Making of Immigration Policies in Turkey: An Analysis of the Law on Foreigners and International Protection Drafting Process', in *Politics and Law in Turkish Migration*, ed. Ibrahim Sirkeci, Doğa Elçin, and Güven Şeker (London: Transnational Press London, 2015), 25–38; Ayselin Yıldız and Elif Uzgören, 'Limits to Temporary Protection: Non-Camp Syrian Refugees in İzmir, Turkey', *Southeast European and Black Sea Studies* 16 (2016) 2: 195–211; 3RP, 'Regional Refugee & Resilience Plan 2017–2018 in Response to the Syria Crisis: Regional Strategic Overview' (Amman: UNHCR and UNDP, 2017) http://www.3rpsyriacrisis.org/wp-content/uploads/2017/02/3RP-Regional-Strategic-Overview-2017–2018.pdf, accessed 1 May 2017; 3RP, 'Regional Refugee Resilience Plan 2017–2018 in Response to the Syrian Crisis. Turkey' (Amman: UNHCR and UNDP, 2017) TURKEY3PRRegionalRefugee&ResiliencePlan2017–2018pdf, accessed 1 May 2017.

organisations and non-governmental organisations (NGOs), together with which Turkey has established agreements on how to cooperate on meeting the needs related to the migration crisis.[6]

The scope and wide-ranging perspectives of the refugee crisis have attracted scholarly attention and resulted in a large quantity of case studies and reports – often in contexts relevant for specific political or humanitarian purposes. The different types of material form the basis for this chapter together with observations and interviews carried out by the author in Turkey in March 2017 with diplomatic staff at European embassies and Turkish and international organisations. Official documents from the EU and the Turkish government have also been used as important sources. The following is structured in three sections, the first of which develops an analytical framework for the chapter. The next section analyses the legal and institutional set-up in Turkey for refugees and migrants, discussing how the conditions regarding citizenship unfold. Hereafter follows a section which analyses the agreements between Turkey and the EU seen in a citizenship perspective and discusses how the notion of citizenship is being contested and utilised in connection with migration diplomacy – in the context of Turkish and European foreign and security policy interests.

CITIZENSHIP, MIGRATION DIPLOMACY AND INTERDEPENDENCE – AN ANALYTICAL FRAMEWORK

The chapter links the notions of citizenship and migration diplomacy, the latter to be understood as including formal and informal policies, legal agreements, and practices[7] – in this case related to Syrian refugees in the context of Turkey–EU cooperation. The notion of citizenship, based on the classical definition coined by Thomas H. Marshall, means enjoying negative rights (religious freedom, privacy) and political rights (participating in elections, freedom of association) that the state and its institutions protect and, in the case of positive rights (education, health care, conditions in the labour market, including possible minimum wages,

---

6 Ahmet İçduygu, *Syrian Refugees in Turkey: The Long Road Ahead* (Washington DC: Migration Policy Institute, 2015).

7 Helene Thiollet introduces the concept 'migration diplomacy' in an analysis of labour migrants in the Arab Gulf, see Thiollet, 'Migration as Diplomacy: Labor Migrants, Refugees, and Arab Regional Politics in the Oil-Rich Countries', *International Labor and Working-Class History* 79 (2011) 1: 103–21.

etc.), guarantee for its members.[8] The formal level of regulation when it comes to the Turkish labour market and the efficiency of the state in controlling that the rules are complied with determine the extent to which the inclusion of the refugees actually works.[9] The labour market represents an example of a context where the legal status of refugees and migrants in Turkey can be of importance for the cooperation between the EU and Turkey. If accepted by both, the migration diplomacy constitutes a trade-off: Turkey receives financial aid from the EU for financing education and health services, accepting the refugees and migrants becoming active in the Turkish labour market etc., while the EU via its financial aid to Turkey can reduce the inflow of refugees and migrants towards Europe.[10] In some cases, the EU makes the implementation of financial assistance conditional on compliance with agreements, as can be seen in a Communication from the European Commission: 'Implementation of assistance is conditional upon strict compliance by Turkey with undertakings reflected in the EU–Turkey Joint Action Plan.'[11]

The question of citizenship rights for the refugees and migrants in Turkey is important for the EU, which has a foreign policy ambition of promoting European norms and standards. For Turkey the question of citizenship plays an important role both in its actual dealing with the refugees and migrants and in its (potential) cooperation and negotiations with other states and international organisations, NGOs etc.[12] As shown

---

[8] Paraphrased by James N. Sater, 'Citizenship and Migration in Arab Gulf Monarchies', in *Migration, Security, and Citizenship in the Middle East: New Perspectives*, eds. Peter Seeberg and Zaid Eyadat (New York: Palgrave Macmillan, 2013), 27.

[9] James Sater demonstrates this point in an analysis of the similar situation in Lebanon, see 'Migrant Workers, Labor Rights, and Governance in Middle Income Countries: The Case of Migrants Domestic Workers in Lebanon', in *Migration, Security, and Citizenship in the Middle East: New Perspectives*, eds. Peter Seeberg and Zaid Eyadat (New York: Palgrave Macmillan, 2013), 115–36. The Turkish case is analysed in Bilge Pinar Yenigün, 'Syrian Refugees in Turkey: Employment and Trade Unions' Response', *International Union Rights* 23 (2016) 3: 8–9; Kemal Kirişci, *Syrian Refugees and Turkey's Challenges: Going Beyond Hospitality* (Washington DC: Brookings, 2014).

[10] Yıldız and Uzgören, 'Limits to Temporary Protection', 200.

[11] The document is a report on the so-called Facility for Refugees in Turkey; see European Commission, Communication from the Commission to the European Parliament and the Council. First Annual Report on the Facility for Refugees in Turkey (Brussels: European Commission, 2 March 2017).

[12] See, for instance, Baban, Ilcan, and Rygiel, 'Syrian Refugees in Turkey'; Korkut, 'Pragmatism, Moral Responsibility or Policy Change'; Fulya Memisoglu and Asli Ilgit, 'Syrian Refugees in Turkey: Multifaceted Challenges, Diverse

by Christian Joppke, among others, the notion of citizenship is indispensable when analysing migration, because it is a relevant analytical tool for understanding the negotiations of rights and general living conditions for refugees and migrants in their new host countries.[13] The notions of citizenship and citizenship rights can therefore, function as political tools in connection with migration diplomacy manoeuvres.

The development of the relations between Turkey and the EU indicates an increasing level of interdependence related to migration. A useful theoretical concept for the analysis of this is the concept of complex interdependence, invented by Robert O. Keohane and Joseph S. Nye, who tried to bring together realist and liberal analytical elements in order to grasp what they saw as an era of interdependence, a novelty compared to earlier phases of political development.[14] In this understanding of state-to-state relations, cooperation is established as a result of common interests, which ideally bring about progress and stability. The relationship will typically rely on more than one common interest. Keohane and Nye's notion of multiple channels was meant to capture the idea of increased probability of cooperation between states that have common interests within significant fields and a lack of hierarchy in their cooperation. The complex relations between Turkey and the EU with their multidimensional fields of activities and the involvement of international rights regimes, organisations, etc. underline the relevance of Keohane and Nye's notion of complex interdependence. Over the past years the conditions for cooperation between Turkey and the EU have changed from a situation just a decade ago with the main focus on Turkey's possible accession to the EU, to a complex reality where in particular the migration crisis adds new dimensions to the Turkey–EU relationship and lays the foundation of a higher level of interdependence.[15]

Players and Ambiguous Policies', *Mediterranean Politics*, online: DOI: 10.1080/13629395.2016.1189479 (2016); Burak Gümüş and Deniz Eroğlu, 'Partial Integration of Syrian "Escapees" under the Rule of Turkey's Justice and Development Party (JDP)', *Contemporary Arab Affairs* 8 (2015) 4: 469–87; Ahmet İçduygu and Evin Millet, 'Syrian Refugees in Turkey: Insecure Lives in an Environment of Pseudo-Integration', *Instituto Affari Internazionali. Global Turkey in Europe*, Working Papers 13 August 2016.

13 Christian Joppke, *Citizenship and Immigration* (Cambridge: Polity Press, 2010).

14 Robert O. Keohane and Joseph S. Nye, *Power and Interdependence: World Politics in Transition* (Boston: Little, Brown & Co., 1977).

15 This despite the many controversies related to the stalled accession process and several of the political conflicts in connection with European criticism of the Turkish anti-terror laws and the fierce criticism by Turkish President Recep

The relationship between Turkey and the EU regarding migration has been an important issue in connection with the increasingly closer cooperation between the two actors following the start of the Turkish accession process in October 2005. Turkey's relationship with the EU can hardly be characterised as well-functioning, but it seems obvious that the common interests related to migration and security constitute potentially strong driving forces for closer cooperation between the two parties. A well-functioning process of inclusion and integration of the many refugees and migrants in Turkey is becoming increasingly important for the EU, not least because of possible spillover effects beyond Turkey from the crisis in Syria. The EU and Turkey seem to develop a form of security partnership, in some ways similar to the development of the cooperation between the EU and Jordan.[16] This security partnership finds its logic in the common interest in solving problems related to the recent crisis in the Levant, of which the Syrian refugee situation is one of the most significant.

As a result of the migration crisis, Turkey has more to offer the EU than before the crisis. At the same time, as the migratory movements have become more unpredictable and uncontrollable, this has underlined the security dimension – not least after the entrance of Islamic State on the political and military scene in Iraq and Syria. Discussions related to this over recent years have taken their starting point in the notion of migration as an important non-traditional security issue.[17] In İçduygu and Üstübici's study of Turkey–EU relations, they analyse how Turkey has changed from a traditional migrant-sending country to a country with a much more complex role when it comes to migratory movements.[18] Turkey's

Tayyip Erdoğan of the Netherlands and Germany for not allowing Turkish political campaigning in the two EU countries before the Turkish referendum in April 2017.

16 Peter Seeberg, 'Jordan, the European Neighbourhood Policy, and Commonalities of Interest: Building a Security Partnership Rather Than a Security Community', in *External Governance as Security Community Building: The Limits and Potential of the European Neighbourhood Policy*, ed. Pernille Rieker (New York: Palgrave, 2016), 163–86.

17 See Barry Buzan, Ole Wæver, and Jaap de Wilde, *Security: A New Framework for Analysis* (Boulder: Lynne Rienner Publ., 1998). For an analysis taking this perspective, see Peter Seeberg, 'Migration into and from Syria and Nontraditional Security Issues in the MENA Region: Transnational Integration, Security, and National Interests', in *Migration, Security, and Citizenship in the Middle East: New Perspectives*, eds. Peter Seeberg and Zaid Eyadat (New York: Palgrave Macmillan, 2013), 167–93.

18 Ahmet İçduygu and Aysen Üstübici, 'Negotiating Mobility, Debating Borders: Migration Diplomacy in Turkey–EU Relations', in *New Border and*

geographical proximity to the Arab Levant, the political unrest following the Arab uprisings, the increasing transit migration passing through Turkey, and the high number of Syrian refugees in Turkey taken together are elements forming a new reality which the migration policies have to deal with. This new reality is complex and has wide-ranging perspectives, not least in a security context. The Syrian refugees have, as a significant expression of migration as a non-traditional security issue, become an important factor in the context of the ongoing migration diplomacy.

From the side of the EU, the question of migration diplomacy also relates to the level of coherence and political consensus among the EU member states concerning the recent increased migration pressure. As shown by Susan Fratzke, the EU has never reached the necessary level of efficiency regarding its 'internal' mechanisms of relevance for receiving refugees and migrants.[19] The existing EU Dublin system is not capable of tackling challenges like the ones we have seen over recent years with the high numbers of refugees and migrants reaching Greek and Italian borders. The challenges resulted in a partial suspension of the Dublin system in 2015, when the inflow of refugees peaked, underlining the necessity for the EU in cooperation with Turkey to find solutions to the migration crisis.

THE TURKISH LEGAL AND INSTITUTIONAL MIGRATION SET-UP AND CITIZENSHIP

Recent years have seen hundreds of thousands of desperate Syrians risk their lives in attempts at reaching Europe by crossing the Mediterranean and Aegean Seas.[20] The number of refugees reaching Greece has been reduced by the EU–Turkey statement of 18 March 2016 (see next section), but, as indicated by Ahmet İçduygu and Evin Millet, the arrangements with the EU only indirectly influence the number of Syrians in Turkey.[21]

Citizenship Politics, ed. Helen Schwenken and Sabine Ruß-Sattar (New York: Palgrave Macmillan, 2014), 49.

[19] Susan Fratzke, *Not Adding Up: The Fading Promise of Europe's Dublin System*, Migration Policy Institute March 2015 (2015).

[20] Kemal Kirişci and Elisabeth Ferris, *Not Likely to Go Home: Syrian Refugees and the Challenges to Turkey – and the International Community*, in Turkey Project Policy Paper (Washington DC: Brookings, 2015). See also Kim Rygiel, 'Dying to Live: Migrant Deaths and Citizenship Politics Along European Borders: Transgressions, Disruptions, and Mobilizations', *Citizenship Studies* 20 (2016) 5: 545–60.

[21] İçduygu and Millet, 'Negotiating Mobility, Debating Borders', 44–59.

Hosting 2,973,980 Syrian refugees, Turkey is the largest receiving country.[22] In addition to that, by 31 December 2016, '291,209 refugees and asylum seekers from Iraq, Afghanistan, Iran, Somalia and a number of other countries were registered with UNHCR'.[23] According to spokesperson Abby Dwommoh, International Organization for Migration (IOM), the sheer volume of refugees calls for extraordinary measures and has made it necessary for Turkey to attract funding to help cover the significant expenses. Pointing to an in many ways well-functioning cooperation between the Turkish authorities and international organisations, including the IOM, she argues that the integration process also has caused concern, for instance, related to competition between local workers and the Syrian refugees and regarding tendencies towards inflation in housing rents.[24]

This has been confirmed by Bilge Pinar Yenigün, stating that 'tensions between Syrian refugees and Turkish communities have been gradually increasing with regard to competition over jobs, rising rent prices, cultural differences, strains on municipal services, health services and infrastructure, especially after the recent discussions on conferring citizenship to Syrians'.[25] The existence of such problems has also been demonstrated by International Crisis Group (ICG), which points to a wide range of areas where the lack of integration seems to be worsened by difficulties for the refugees in gaining access to the Turkish labour market and by a growing general negative sentiment in the Turkish population against refugees.[26] With high unemployment rates among Turks, in particular within the low-skilled and unskilled labour market, the conditions are very difficult for Syrians who attempt to acquire a job in Turkey. Local incidents of wage-dumping have, according to ICG, led to negative attitudes towards refugees, arguing that they are an economic burden and a threat against well-established local practices

---

22 The figure is from 6 April 2017; see UNHCR, 'Syria Regional Refugee Response. Inter-Agency Information Sharing Portal. Turkey', (2017). http://data.unhcr.org/syrianrefugees/country.php?id=224, accessed 1 May 2017.

23 'Turkey. UNHCR Operational Update October–December 2016', (UNHCR, 2017); 3RP, 'Regional Refugee Resilience Plan 2017–2018 in Response to the Syrian Crisis. Turkey'.

24 Interview by the author with Abby Dwommoh, Spokesperson and Communications Officer, IOM, Ankara, March 2017. The problem with the increasing housing rents due to the presence of the Syrians was confirmed in anonymous and informal interviews by the author with Turkish real estate agents, March 2017.

25 Yenigün, 'Syrian Refugees in Turkey', 8–9.

26 International Crisis Group, *Turkey's Refugee Crisis: The Politics of Permanence*, in *Europe Report* (Brussels: International Crisis Group, 2016), 3.

when it comes to employment within the informal sector.[27] In addition, the generally very tense security situation in the Levant, reinforced by the presence of Islamic State (IS, or Daesh) in Syria and Iraq, tends to make many Turks perceive the refugees as a potential security risk. This has in some cases led to xenophobia and to reactivation of deeply rooted anti-Arab sentiments in Turkey.[28] In the internal Turkish discussion about this theme, very different opinions are represented. The government represents the positive position, while trade unions and workers in general represent the opposite.[29] The legal status of the refugees in Turkish society complicates the conditions for participation in the labour market, and the pressure on educational and health services – in short, positive citizenship rights.

Citizenship can be utilised in negotiating the issue of migration in a foreign policy context (as will be analysed in the next section), but obviously it is also contested and negotiated in the internal Turkish context. When it comes to the actual Turkish labour market, there is a discrepancy between the official Turkish 'open door' policy regarding Syrian refugees and the realities on the ground. ICG has demonstrated that similar mechanisms can be found in other areas where Syrian refugees are included in integration processes. For the Turkish government and administration, it is imperative both to maintain a coherent migration policy and to develop well-functioning practices concerning refugees, in particular regarding the socio-economic conditions for the refugees, their integration and their social acceptance in Turkish society. Overall, the system is based on the Law on Foreigners and International Protection in Turkey. This law was drafted and approved by the Parliament in April 2013 and is an interesting and important document in the sense that it covers both foreigners arriving in Turkey as economic migrants and people in need of protection, refugees.[30]

Later on, new legal elements were added to the Turkish open-border policy, emphasising the temporary character of the Turkish protection regime. This reality has been assessed differently by researchers within the field. A neutral viewpoint is presented by Ayselin Yıldız and Elif

---

27 Informal and anonymous interviews with officials from Turkish trade unions confirm the views by IOM; Yenigün, 'Syrian Refugees in Turkey', and International Crisis Group, *Turkey's Refugee Crisis*.

28 International Crisis Group, *Turkey's Refugee Crisis*, 13.

29 The official, positive view can be seen in an article written by the Turkish Foreign Minister, Mevlüt Çavuşoğlu, 'Turkey and the Syrian Refugee Crisis: An Example for Humanity', *Turkish Policy Quarterly* 15 (2016) 3: 17–26. The more critical view can be found, for instance, in Yenigün, 'Syrian Refugees in Turkey'.

30 Eroğlu, 'The Making of Immigration Policies in Turkey', 36.

Uzgören, who argue that the system 'does not violate international obligations since Turkey maintains its geographical limitation under the 1951 Convention and its practices are generally in line with the UNHCR's Guide on Temporary Protection'.[31] In contrast, Korkut claims that the temporary protection framework might rest on a legal foundation but basically should be seen as a 'discursively constructed mechanism with vague implications, particularly regarding settlement and integration'.[32] The point of this argument is that rather than being based on a strict and well-defined rights-based approach, the Turkish legal framework is founded on a humanitarian discourse, aiming – as stated by the Turkish Minister of Foreign Affairs Mevlüt Çavuşoğlu – at harmonising the relationship between the refugees and the Turkish population, thereby facilitating a successful integration of Syrians into Turkish society.[33]

The process has only partly worked out satisfactorily, as already shown in the case of the Turkish labour market. Over time, the actual situation in Turkey changed and refugees became permanent residents. This, of course, has policy implications and consequences for the refugees. It also has consequences for the degree to which their citizenship rights are dealt with by Turkey. Taking education as an example, the Turkish authorities are confronted with enormous challenges to live up to the UN Convention on the Rights of the Child (guaranteeing the right to free education). There is no doubt that Turkey is investing significant financial and human resources in attempting to provide the children of the Syrian refugees with education, but the task is huge, and according to ICG, in November 2016, out of 900,000 Syrian children 400,000 still did not attend any Turkish schools.[34] This is due to a shortage of teaching facilities, but another important reason for their non-attendance is that a large number of Syrian children are forced to work.[35] The enormous dispersion of refugees

---

31 Yıldız and Uzgören, 'Limits to Temporary Protection'. See for the UNHCR guidelines, 'Guidelines on Temporary Protection or Stay Arrangements' (Geneva: United Nations High Commissioner for Refugees, 2014).

32 Korkut, 'Pragmatism, Moral Responsibility or Policy Change', 2.

33 Çavuşoğlu, 'Turkey and the Syrian Refugee Crisis'.

34 International Crisis Group, *Turkey's Refugee Crisis*, 5. According to the 3RP Regional Strategic Review the number of Syrian children in Turkey is somewhat higher and numbers 845,364 children. At the same time the share of children not attending school is claimed to be a bit lower at 341,689 children. 3RP, 'Regional Refugee & Resilience Plan 2017–2018 in Response to the Syria Crisis. Regional Strategic Overview', 35.

35 Sezen Yalçın, 'Syrian Child Workers in Turkey', *Turkish Policy Quarterly* 15 (2016) 3: 89–98.

throughout the whole of Turkey[36] makes it more difficult to enforce school attendance. According to some of the respondents of Yıldız and Uzgören, participation of Syrians in the Turkish labour market often takes place on an illegal and short-term informal basis.[37] It has also been claimed that different forms of selective practices exist in Turkey, but it is difficult to show if or to what extent this actually takes place. Gümüş and Eroğlu argue that ethnic-religious discrimination for instance has occurred against Alevis from Iraq.[38] Similarly, examples of sectarian discrimination in the Turkish integration process have been confirmed by ICG, and if the analyses are correct, this obviously represents violations of international law.[39]

Baban, Ilcan and Rygiel characterise the ambiguous position of Syrian refugees in Turkey in this way: 'The Turkish government has granted Syrians some of the social rights available to Turkish citizens, thereby incorporating Syrians within its existing social welfare system, while, at the same time, refusing to grant them status that would lead to longer term residency or full citizenship.'[40] The point that the Syrians are discriminated against in Turkish inclusionary policies, yet at the same time are given specific advantages when compared to some other refugees who are excluded from the EU–Turkey statement (see next section), constitutes in other words a specific regime in the Turkish legal practices regarding refugees. A decision to allow Syrian students to enrol in Turkish public universities without official proof of previous student status, which has been criticised for privileging them above students from other countries,[41] points in the same direction. The Turkish refugee regime is unique and paradoxical in that the Syrian refugees are granted some positive citizenship rights, but at the same time are being kept as some kind of non-citizens. The specific character of the conditions for the refugees opens up for contesting and negotiating the citizenship regime for Syrian refugees. In this way internal Turkish citizenship practices influence the preconditions for the migration diplomacy between Turkey and the EU.

---

36 UNHCR, 'Turkey. Provincial Breakdown of Refugees and Asylum-Seekers in Turkey, 1 March 2017', (United Nations High Commissioner of Refugees, 2017). http://reliefweb.int/map/turkey/provincial-breakdown-all-refugees-and-asylum-seekers-turkey-01– march-2017, accessed 1 May 2017.

37 Yıldız and Uzgören, 'Limits to Temporary Protection', 203.

38 Gümüş and Eroğlu, 'Partial Integration of Syrian "Escapees"'.

39 International Crisis Group, *Turkey's Refugee Crisis*, 15–17. The report also mentions discrimination of Kurds attempting to enter Turkey.

40 Baban, Ilcan, and Rygiel, 'Syrian Refugees in Turkey', 46.

41 Memisoglu and Ilgit, 'Syrian refugees in Turkey', 11.

EU–TURKEY COOPERATION, THE 18 MARCH 2016 STATEMENT AND THE POLITICS OF MIGRATION DIPLOMACY

> The EU is working with Turkey to stem the flows of refugees trying to cross into the Greek Islands with dangerous journeys across the Aegean, offering at the same time safe and legal paths to resettle into the EU. The EU–Turkey Statement of 18 March 2016 is delivering results.[42]
>
> (European Union: EU Migration Policy at a Glance)

During 2015, the number of refugees and migrants arriving in Greece increased dramatically and the eastern Mediterranean migration route surpassed the central Mediterranean route in numbers: Greece overtook Italy as the most significant point of arrival. International organisations estimated that more than one million refugees and migrants arrived in Europe in 2015, 300–400 per cent more than in 2014. Starting from November 2015, the EU and Turkey held meetings where the lines of a possible new cooperation dealing with the crisis were discussed, and in March 2016 the EU–Turkey statement was presented.[43] As pointed out by Thomas Spijkerboer, it seems that the decline in numbers preceded the EU–Turkey statement.[44] Nevertheless the statement and the whole

---

[42] European Union, 'EU Migration Policy at a Glance', (Brussels: European Union, 2016). https://eeas.europa.eu/sites/eeas/files/1_eu_migration_policy_at_glance_-_fact_sheet_2016.pdf, accessed 1 May 2017.

[43] For analyses of the statement, see Peter Seeberg, 'The EU–Turkey March 2016 Agreement as a Model: New Refugee Regimes and Practices in the Arab Mediterranean and the Case of Libya', *Global Turkey in Europe*, Working Paper 16, December 2016; Elisabeth Collett, 'The Paradox of the EU–Turkey Refugee Deal', *Commentary*, (2016), www.migrationpolicy.org, accessed 1 May 2017; Gloria Fernández Arribas, 'The EU–Turkey Agreement: A Controversial Attempt at Patching up a Major Problem', European Forum, *European Papers* No. 17, October 2016; Thomas Spijkerboer, 'Fact Check: Did the EU–Turkey Deal Bring Down the Number of Migrants and of Border Deaths?' *Oxford University, Faculty of Law. Border Criminologies*, No. 28, September 2016; Bilge Yabancı, 'The Future of EU–Turkey Relations: Between Mutual Distrust and Interdependency', *FEUTURE* Online Paper, No. 1 (2016), http://www.iai.it/sites/default/files/feuture_3.pdf, accessed 1 May 2017. Laura Batall Adam, 'The Refugee Card in EU–Turkey Relations: A Necessary but Uncertain Deal', *Global Turkey in Europe*, Working Paper 14, September 2016.

[44] Spijkerboer, 'Fact Check: Did the EU–Turkey Deal Bring Down the Number of Migrants'. The numbers of average daily arrivals at the Greek islands in the year 2016 went down from 1,932 in January to 1,904 in February, to 1,148 in period 1–20 March, to 333 in the last 10 days of March, to 114 in April and 47 in May. For the figures, see Gerald Knaus, 'Keeping the Aegean Agreement Afloat', *Turkish Policy Quarterly* 15 (2016) 3, 44.

development related to it had a significant impact on refugee movements between Turkey and the EU. Whereas the number of crossings by sea to Greece in April to August 2015 was 225,505, in the same period in 2016 it fell to 12,210. And, as mentioned by Gerald Knaus, the number of people who drowned in the Aegean went down from 366 in the first three months of 2016 to seven in the following three months.[45]

Historically, negotiations related to migration have constituted an important aspect of the EU–Turkey accession talks, mainly with a focus on Turkish work migration to EU states. Despite the fact that for years it has been possible to detect tendencies towards 'post-modern' demographic patterns in Turkey (first of all ageing of the population due to a decreasing birth rate),[46] the issue is still relevant and has symbolic significance. Therefore the statement includes an element dealing with visa liberalisation for Turkish citizens wanting to visit Europe. The EU–Turkey statement, listed in headlines below, can be considered an instance of migration diplomacy, whereby the EU receives fewer irregular migrants crossing its south-eastern borders, while in return Turkey receives financial aid, a reinvigorated accession process to become a member of the EU, and other elements.[47] This tends at the same time to increase the interdependence between the two parties. The statement, presented to the European Council by President of the European Commission Jean-Claude Juncker in March 2016, contained six main elements which were to be implemented before the end of 2016:

1. Returning to Turkey all new irregular migrants (economic migrants and asylum seekers) crossing to the Greek islands;
2. For every Syrian readmitted by Turkey from the Greek islands, resettling another Syrian from Turkey to the EU;
3. Accelerating implementation of the EU–Turkey visa liberalisation roadmap;
4. Speeding up the disbursement of funds through the Facility for Refugees in Turkey and increasing its resources;
5. Expediting preparations for the opening of new chapters in Turkey's accession negotiations; and
6. Cooperating to improve humanitarian conditions inside Syria.[48]

---

45 Ibid.

46 Kemal Kirisci, 'Turkey: A Country of Transition from Emigration to Immigration', *Mediterranean Politics* 12 (2007) 1: 91–7.

47 Seeberg, 'The EU–Turkey March 2016 Agreement as a Model'.

48 European Commission, 'Fact Sheet. EU–Turkey Agreement: Questions and Answers, 19 March 2016', (Brussels: European Commission, 2016). http://europa.eu/rapid/press-release_MEMO-16-963_en.htm, accessed 1 May 2017.

A very important ambition of the statement was to reduce the inflow of irregular migrants, and it is unsurprising that the 28 EU member states were able to support the statement relatively quickly.[49] In addition to controlling the flow of refugees, the EU also wanted to promote the standards of the international refugee regime. As stated by a senior member of staff at the EU delegation in Ankara, when asked about the EU's interests inherent in the 18 March statement: 'The interest of the European Union is to channel the flow of refugees, to better manage the flow of refugees and make sure the people go where they have to go, and that people are treated in accordance with international law and do this in a more structured and organized way.'[50] As mentioned, the ambitions were fulfilled to some extent. It can be argued that the advantages of the statement have been reaped primarily by the EU. Visa liberalisation remains on hold, and there has been very limited progress regarding the opening of new chapters as part of Turkey's EU accession process. Important reasons for this can no doubt be found in the July 2016 coup in Turkey and the subsequent harsh crackdown by the government on suspected coup plotters and other coup sympathisers within the army and public administration. Scepticism in the EU about the future of democracy in Turkey was evident already before the coup, not least as a result of Turkey's anti-terror law, which the government refused to change in accordance with EU wishes, and the provisions of the EU–Turkey statement have thus far not been sufficient to overcome these constraints on visa liberalisation and the opening of new accession chapters.

There has been a political discussion in Turkey of the foreign policy manoeuvres by the government regarding international donors. The CHP[51] has criticised the government's migration policies, claiming that they 'focus on making use of the refugee population in Turkey as a threat and a tool for blackmail in domestic and foreign policy, drawing upon them to extend its domain of power, and using human dignity as a tool for bargaining instead of developing policies that aim to improve the living conditions of refugees'.[52] Other dimensions are added to the view by CHP in an assessment by Fulya Memisoglu and Asli Ilgit, who argue that the Turkish policies are ambiguous in the sense that Turkey in a recent

---

49 Collett, 'The Paradox of the EU–Turkey Refugee Deal'.

50 Interview by the author with senior staff at the EU delegation in Ankara, March 2017.

51 *Cumhuriyet Halk Partisi* (CHP), the Turkish (social-democratic and Kemalist) Republican People's Party.

52 Veli Ağbaba, 'CHP's Policy Recommendations for the Refugee Question in Turkey', *Turkish Policy Quarterly* 15 (2016) 3, 29.

context suffers from a deteriorating image on international platforms while still attempting to follow its overall foreign policy interest, namely to become a full member of the EU.[53] It is important in this context, because the difference between the two positions is a difference between a proactive approach, which on behalf of Turkey aims at reaching out for foreign policy goals, and a policy which is rights-based and, on behalf of the citizenship rights of the refugees, primarily focuses on the internal perspective. It should be mentioned that it is difficult to be very precise when it comes to the character of the recent public debate in Turkey. This is a result of a high level of censorship and control of the Turkish media and public sphere following the failed coup in July 2016. The control of all kinds of political opposition has become severely tightened, a state of emergency has been adopted, and a high number of imprisonments have taken place.[54]

The critical situation has also had consequences for refugees and migrants in the sense that Turkish border control has been intensified, one of the aims being to keep out members of radical organisations who might hide in groups of refugees and migrants as part of migratory movements towards Turkey. Over recent years, furthermore, Turkey has been building a fence or wall along the border – planned to be finalised in 2017. Data from the UN Office for the Coordination of Humanitarian Affairs (OCHA) indicates that the fence/wall has contributed to a decrease in the overall number of refugees passing the border.[55] Infiltration by radical elements from the outside constitutes an important aspect of migration as a non-traditional security issue, and there is no doubt that the high number of acts of terror in Turkey in 2015–2016 has caused some discrimination against refugees and migrants from Syria – with negative consequences regarding the citizenship perspective. The EU–Turkey statement also contains this dimension in the sense that by significantly diminishing the intake of refugees and irregular migrants, potentially the risk of receiving problematic persons is being reduced. Furthermore other security-related risks, like human smuggling and trafficking, are being reduced. As emphasised by the German Ambassador in Ankara, Martin Erdmann, 'the main aim of this migration pact was to cut and destroy the human trafficking in the Aegean Sea and the rationale was that this

---

53 Memisoglu and Ilgit, 'Syrian Refugees in Turkey', 16.

54 M. Hakan Yavuz and Rasim Koç, 'The Turkish Coup Attempt: The Gülen Movement vs. the State', *Middle East Policy* 23 (2016) 4: 136–48.

55 See OCHA, 'Turkey | Syria: Border Crossing Status (as of 7 February 2017)', (New York: United Nations Office for the Coordination of Humanitarian Affairs, 2017).

human trafficking leads to a lot of human pain and inhumane treatment of these migrants'.[56]

As early as 2014 – in connection with the local elections in Turkey – discussions arose regarding the question whether the Syrian refugees residing in Turkey could obtain citizenship, but the discussions disappeared as changes did not take place in actual practice. In July 2016, President Erdoğan reiterated that refugees in Turkey under temporary protection should be granted citizenship. Initially this raised reactions among nationalists, who criticised the government, but in the somewhat chaotic political environment following the attempted coup, the discussion again gradually lost momentum.[57] It therefore remains unclear what actually was the background for Erdoğan's remarks. As shown by ICG, the AKP (*Adalet ve Kalkınma Partisi*, The Justice and Development Party, founded by Erdoğan; the dominant political party in Turkey since it gained power in 2002) denied allegations that electoral calculations played a role and emphasised the humanitarian intentions.[58] As mentioned by an interviewee at the EU delegation office in Ankara: 'The Turkish success story at least in the last 10–15 years is because of the harmonisation process, is because of aligning European legislation with the Turkish legislation, is because of the customs union with a free flow of goods.'[59] Therefore, as stated by Gerald Knaus, keeping the Aegean agreement afloat is very important in the sense that a 'collapse of the Aegean agreement would be a terrible blow for already tense EU–Turkey relations'.[60] It could furthermore have negative consequences for the well-functioning cooperation at the operational level between Greece and Turkey, as underlined by diplomatic staff from the Greek embassy in Ankara.[61] Overall the complex situation regarding EU–Turkish cooperation in dealing with the migration crisis has far from found its final solution – and as long as this is the case, many significant problems related to citizenship rights for refugees and migrants in the eastern Mediterranean remain unsolved.

---

[56] Interview by the author with Martin Erdmann, German Ambassador to Turkey, March 2017.

[57] Interview by the author with senior staff at the Austrian Embassy to Turkey, March 2017.

[58] International Crisis Group, *Turkey's Refugee Crisis*, 23.

[59] Interview by the author with senior staff at the EU delegation in Ankara, March 2017.

[60] Knaus, 'Keeping the Aegean Agreement Afloat', 50.

[61] Interview by the author with diplomatic staff at the Greek Embassy in Ankara, March 2017.

CONCLUSIONS AND PERSPECTIVES

Analysing the cooperation between Turkey and the EU in the context of the Mediterranean migration crisis offers an important opportunity for discussing how the notion of citizenship can be contested and utilised in political conflicts, negotiations, and everyday operational practices. The chapter has illustrated how both Turkey and the EU pursue foreign policy interests in a complex and sometimes conflictual migration diplomacy and that, in connection with this, the notions of citizenship and citizenship rights are negotiated, contested and utilised for the political purposes discussed above.

It is part of the arrangements between Turkey and the EU that the financial aid from the EU is conditional upon compliance with the EU–Turkey Joint Action Plan and the statement of 18 March 2016. This means that the EU insists that all activities funded by the EU must take place in accordance with international law regarding refugees. Citizenship rights thus constitute an important element of the migration diplomacy between Turkey and the EU. The visa liberalisation for Turkish citizens wanting to go to Europe indirectly reflects this, first of all by representing an improvement regarding positive citizenship rights for the Turkish population. In the ongoing migration diplomacy, however, the visa liberalisation has been associated with the question of Turkish counterterror laws, including the question of the death penalty. By demanding that all conditions must be met before visa liberalisation can become a reality, the EU insists on citizenship rights for (political) prisoners. In opposition to this Turkey argues that 'We have the PKK, Daesh and other groups launching attacks so it would not be intelligent to make amendments in the terrorism law at this point.'[62]

In principle the legal status of the 18 March 2016 statement is problematic in itself when it comes to its possible implementation and the citizenship dimensions involved. The statement was issued by the European Council, and is not legally binding. Rather it is a kind of 'soft law framework', and this weakens the statement, since 'such instruments bypass the checks and balances mechanisms built into the EU polity to safeguard EU law and fundamental rights'.[63] The situation on several of the Greek islands, where the reception centres involved in the refugee transfer have been turned

[62] Laura Pitel and Jim Brunsden, 'Blow for Migrants Deal as Turkey Rejects EU Terror Law Demands', *Financial Times*, 9 August 2016.

[63] Nicole Koenig and Marie Walter-Franke, 'One Year On: What Lessons from the EU–Turkey "Deal"?', *Jacques Delors Institut*, blog post, No. 17 March (2017).

into detention facilities, violates the EU's own standards as stated in the EU Reception Condition Directive.[64] And furthermore, as mentioned, the possibility of resettlement only applies to Syrian refugees. In addition to that, the UN Refugee Agency has expressed its concern about the fate of those sent back to Turkey, where the conditions for some of the refugees are insufficient and where the practices seem to be lacking transparency.[65] A final aspect regarding citizenship related to the statement is the time factor. The implementation of the resettlement procedures inherent in the statement has proven to be very slow. Koenig and Walter-Franke have calculated that it will take 13 years to resettle the 54,000 Syrians, less than 2 per cent of the Syrian refugees living in Turkey initially promised by the EU.[66] Obviously this is problematic, in particular from a citizenship rights perspective. Concerning the citizenship dimensions of the 18 March 2016 statement, a number of negative aspects, as shown above, can be mentioned – both in a Turkish and an EU context. But from a political viewpoint, the statement has solved significant common problems for Turkey and for the EU.

Also when it comes to activities outside the realm of the statement, Turkey and the EU have common interests. Integration of the refugees into the Turkish labour market is an obvious example. Turkey carries out a broad range of activities within this field and many refugees have obtained jobs in Turkey. However, some problems are affiliated with this. Most of the refugees in Turkey are being exposed to what has been called selective humanitarianism, and Turkey sustains a principle of temporary protection in its approach to the refugees. This reality has been criticised by the EU and by international organisations and NGOs for being problematic when it comes to citizenship rights, and Turkey has furthermore received criticism for creating a limited citizenship regime, leaving non-Syrians out of the statement between Turkey and the EU. Being the by far largest group of refugees in Turkey the Syrians obviously attract attention by the authorities – also because significant security aspects are attached to the crisis in Syria, including the threat from members of radical organisations who might cross the border.

---

64 See 'Directive 2013/33/EU of the European Parliament and of the Council of 26 June 2013 laying down standards for the reception of applicants for international protection', http://eur-lex.europa.eu/legal-content/EN/TXT/PDF/?uri=CELEX:32013L0033&from=EN, accessed 1 May 2017.

65 İlke Toygür and Bianca Benvenuti, 'One Year On: An Assessment of the EU–Turkey Statement on Refugees', *ARI, Elcano Royal Institute and Instituto Affari Interzionale* 21, March (2017).

66 Koenig and Walter-Franke, 'One Year On', 5.

The question of refugees in the context of ethnic-religious minorities is another area where the Turkish policy has been problematic regarding cooperation with the EU. The phenomenon is interconnected with the foreign policy interests related to the situation in northern Syria, and some of the refugees from this region have a Kurdish background. Turkey and the EU are on a collision course when it comes to the Kurdish question, which has been one of the significant stumbling blocks in connection with the EU accession talks. The issue has been reignited following the crisis in Syria and the resulting migration crisis. This compromises the idea of a security partnership between Turkey and the EU, and affects the citizenship regime for the refugees.

As shown, the official discourse of the AKP government is founded in the concept of 'harmonisation' – based on an ambition of improving social relations between the Turkish population and the refugees. Obviously it is in the interest of Turkey that the refugees become part of the labour market, so that the financial and social challenges of hosting a large refugee population can be reduced. The main Turkish interests are to integrate the refugees into society in order to avoid social problems and conflicts with the Turkish population living with the consequences of the harmonisation approach, and to acquire funds from the EU to cover the expenses related to the work. The EU shares the Turkish interest in maintaining an inclusion strategy, since this ideally leads to a situation where the majority of the refugees stay in Turkey. Regarding how the migration diplomacy affects the citizenship status of the refugees, it seems relevant to distinguish between a short-term and a long-term perspective. In a short-term perspective, the internal Turkish conditions for the refugees seem to be in focus: The lack of a clear and well-defined status for the refugees in Turkey is seriously affecting the citizenship regime. In the long run, the external dimensions become more striking. The lack of consensus between the EU member states has consequences for the citizenship regime, for instance in that the Syrian refugees are waiting for years for resettlement in the EU. The same is the case when it comes to the citizenship aspects of visa liberalisation as part of the 18 March statement. However, despite controversies and often different agendas, an increasing level of interdependence between Turkey and the EU seems to be a reality when it comes to dealing with the migration crisis.

Acknowledgements

I would like to thank the Institute for History, University of Southern Denmark, for providing the funding that made it possible to visit Turkey and carry out interviews and observations. Furthermore, I thank Instituto

Affari Internazionali, Rome, for inviting me to write the opening paper for the seminar 'Does the EU–Turkey Deal Represent a Model to be Replicated in Other Contexts?' held in Catania, 16 December 2016.[67] The seminar inspired useful thoughts for this chapter.

[67] Published as Peter Seeberg, 'The EU–Turkey March 2016 Agreement as a Model: New Refugee Regimes and Practices in the Arab Mediterranean and the Case of Libya', *Global Turkey in Europe*, Working Paper 16, December 2016.

13. Syrian refugees and citizenship

Lillian C. Frost and Musa M. Shteiwi

INTRODUCTION

The Syrian conflict has dragged into its sixth year with devastating consequences for its people and neighbouring countries. There are 5,058,456 Syrian refugees, including 2 million Syrians registered by the Office of the United Nations High Commissioner for Refugees (UNHCR) in Egypt, Iraq, Jordan, and Lebanon, including 660,785 in Jordan and 1,011,366 in Lebanon.[1] However, both countries cite higher figures of Syrian refugees, with approximately 1.3 million in Jordan and 1.5 million in Lebanon.[2] These countries have played a tremendous role in supporting the refugee crisis, stretching their thin resources to accept far more refugees than donor countries.

As of June 2017,[3] Syrian refugees in Jordan and Lebanon became protracted refugees, which are groups of 25,000 or more refugees from the same nation living in the same developing host country for at least five years.[4] With no resolution to the Syrian crisis in sight, Jordan and Lebanon must determine the sets of duties and rights given to these large non-citizen populations. This decision is critical because protracted refugees with limited rights in their host country cannot develop their human and economic potential, which hurts the host economy and fosters illicit activities.

---

1 'Syria Regional Refugee Response', UNHCR Information Sharing Portal, accessed 20 June 2017, http://data.unhcr.org/syrianrefugees/regional.php.

2 Jordan Ministry of Planning and International Cooperation, 'Jordan Response Plan for the Syria Crisis, 2016–2018', 2015, 14. Government of Lebanon and the United Nations, 'Lebanon Crisis Response Plan 2015–2016', December 2014, 3.

3 Note that Jordan and Lebanon did not reach a total of at least 25,000 Syrian refugees until June 2012, though refugees started arriving in 2011.

4 Gil Loescher and James Milner, 'Protracted Refugee Situations: The Search for Practical Solutions', in *The State of the World's Refugees 2006: Human Displacement in the New Millennium*, ed. UNHCR (Oxford: Oxford University Press, 2006), 105–27. UNHCR, 'Protracted Refugee Situations', UNHCR Report EC/54/SC/CRP, 14 June 2004.

This chapter analyses Jordan's and Lebanon's citizenship policies, focusing on how Syrian refugees, not including Palestinian refugees from Syria (PRS), have been integrated and excluded from 2012–2016.[5] Applying the lens of citizenship to these crucial decisions helps to place them within the larger context of state–society relations as well as highlights the specific types of rights refugees can access legally and informally. The chapter starts by defining citizenship and non-citizenship as well as the content of these relationships. The next section examines Jordan's and Lebanon's citizenship regimes since independence, and then assesses their non-citizenship regimes toward Syrian refugees. The following sections dig into the content of Syrian non-citizenship in these countries by looking at their formal and informal civil, political, social, and economic rights. This chapter concludes by highlighting the similarities in how states treat citizen and non-citizen groups as well as the utility of engaging the concept of non-citizenship.

CITIZENSHIP AND NON-CITIZENSHIP REGIMES

There is a vast literature examining and defining citizenship. This literature focuses on different dimensions of citizenship, which include citizenship as *identity and beliefs*, particularly liberal beliefs,[6] as an *activity* or *participatory practice*,[7] and as *acts* that shift established practices and represent claims to new rights.[8] Others associate citizenship with certain *sets of rights*. T.H. Marshall is the seminal example here; he argues that states extend rights in a specific historical sequence, with civil rights provided first, followed by political, and finally social rights.[9] Others focus

---

[5] There are about 20,000 PRS in Jordan and 32,000 in Lebanon. They have faced more restrictive policies because of sensitivities in Jordan and Lebanon concerning an increase in their Palestinian populations; thus, they merit a separate analysis. 'PRS in Jordan', UNRWA, accessed 1 December 2017, https://www.unrwa.org/prs-jordan. 'PRS in Lebanon', UNRWA, accessed 1 December 2017, https://www.unrwa.org/prs-lebanon.

[6] Will Kymlicka, 'Multicultural Citizenship within Multination States', *Ethnicities* 11 (2011) 3: 281–302. Christian Joppke, 'How Immigration Is Changing Citizenship: A Comparative View', *Ethnic and Racial Studies* 22 (1999) 4: 629–52.

[7] James Tully, 'Introduction', in *Multinational Democracies*, eds. Alain G. Gagnon and James Tully (Cambridge: Cambridge University Press, 2001).

[8] Engin Isin and Greg Nielsen (eds.), *Acts of Citizenship* (London: Zed Press, 2008), 10.

[9] T.H. Marshall, 'Citizenship and Social Class', in *Citizenship and Social Class and Other Essays*, ed. T.H. Marshall (Cambridge: Cambridge University Press, 1950), 1–85.

on citizenship as a *legal status*.[10] Still others view citizenship as a *contract*, representing a form of resource distribution,[11] a certificate regulating state–society relations,[12] or social practice.[13]

Despite this proliferation of work on citizenship, few studies have explored the concept of non-citizenship, which can be understood in terms of citizenship but is not the mere negation of citizenship.[14] These studies emphasise that non-citizenship and citizenship are not mutually exclusive, but instead refer to different relationships between a polity and its residents. Non-citizenship captures different groups of non-citizens, including those who are stateless (making them non-citizens in any country) and those who are living outside of their country of citizenship. The latter category includes refugees without citizenship in their host state, such as Syrian refugees in Jordan and Lebanon.

We engage Isin and Nyers' definition in conceptualising citizenship and non-citizenship, where citizenship is an institution mediating rights between subjects and the polity to which they belong.[15] This definition evades the normative elements imbued in many descriptions of citizenship as solely a European invention or feature of democratic governments. In addition, this definition does not assume that citizenship bestows membership in a state on its citizens, or conversely, non-membership on its non-citizens. Further, it avoids defining citizenship only as a relationship between a state and its citizens, acknowledging that citizenship is relevant for residents who are not citizens.

---

[10] Marc Morjé Howard, 'Comparative Citizenship: An Agenda for Cross-National Research', *Perspectives on Politics* 4 (2006) 3: 443–55.

[11] Nils Butenschøn, 'State, Power, and Citizenship in the Middle East: A Theoretical Introduction', in *Citizenship and the State in the Middle East: Approaches and Applications*, eds. Nils Butenschøn, Uri Davis, and Manuel Hassassian (Syracuse, NY: Syracuse University Press, 2000), 3–27.

[12] Uri Davis, 'Conceptions of Citizenship in the Middle East: State, Nation, and People', in *Citizenship and the State in the Middle East: Approaches and Applications*, eds. Nils Butenschøn, Uri Davis, and Manuel Hassassian (Syracuse, NY: Syracuse University Press, 2000), 49–69.

[13] Aihwa Ong, 'Cultural Citizenship as Subject-Making: Immigrants Negotiate Racial and Cultural Boundaries in the United States', *Current Anthropology* 37 (1996) 5: 737–62.

[14] With notable exceptions: Katherine Tonkiss and Tendayi Bloom, 'Theorising Noncitizenship: Concepts, Debates and Challenges', *Citizenship Studies* 19 (2015) 8: 837–52. David Plotke, 'The Rights of Noncitizens: Introduction', *Politics and Society* 42 (2014) 3: 287–91.

[15] Engin Isin and Peter Nyers, 'Introduction: Globalizing Citizenship Studies', in *Routledge Handbook of Global Citizenship Studies*, eds. Engin Isin and Peter Nyers (New York: Routledge Press, 2014), 1–11.

We conceptualise non-citizenship as the relationship between a polity and its non-citizens. More specifically, non-citizenship is an institution mediating rights between non-citizen subjects and the polity in which they reside (e.g., a state). This chapter focuses on the content of non-citizenship regimes toward Syrian refugees in Jordan and Lebanon. These regimes derive from both international and regional conventions as well as domestic laws and citizenship regimes. The combination of these influences is important for understanding the content of these non-citizenship regimes, especially when international and domestic influences clash, fostering differences between laws and their enforcement.

To dig into citizenship and non-citizenship, we engage Faulks' distinction between the extent, content, and depth of citizenship in analysing Jordan's and Lebanon's citizenship and non-citizenship regimes.[16] Faulks defines *extent* as who should be regarded as a citizen and what criteria, if any, are legitimate in excluding some from the benefits of citizenship. *Content* is the rights, duties, and obligations that citizenship entails, and *depth* refers to how demanding or extensive a person's identity as a citizen should be compared to other sources of social identity.[17]

In this chapter, we focus primarily on the content of citizenship. In addition, we break down the term 'content' by focusing on sets of civil, political, social, and economic rights. Following Marshall's distinctions,[18] *civil rights* include freedom of expression and assembly, protection of property, right to a fair trial, access to free movement, and protection from arbitrary imprisonment. Next, *political rights* include the ability to vote and hold office, and *social rights* include access to education, health care, housing, and social assistance. Further, building on Davis' critique of Marshall,[19] we add *economic rights*, which include the ability to obtain legal work and own a business. Unlike Marshall, however, we recognise that political rights are no longer a prerequisite for social rights, and we acknowledge that in the Arab World social rights have tended to emerge alongside very limited civil and political rights.[20]

In addition, we examine differences in the legal citizen rights offered and the enforcement of these rights in practice. The rhetoric and practices of governments are important because governments may simultaneously

---

16 Keith Faulks, *Citizenship* (New York: Routledge, 2000), 1–28.

17 Ibid., 7.

18 Marshall, 'Citizenship and Social Class'.

19 Davis, 'Conceptions of Citizenship in the Middle East'.

20 Roel Meijer 'Citizenship, Social Pacts, Authoritarian Bargains, and the Arab Uprisings', in *The Crisis of Citizenship in the Arab World*, eds. Roel Meijer and Nils Butenschøn (Leiden: Brill, 2017), 67–104.

promote accommodating rights in their rhetoric, while enacting policies in practice that undermine the realisation of these rights. For instance, the state could grant a group the right to obtain work permits, but in practice, the group may be unable to realise this right because the permit applications require records that the group cannot obtain. In such cases, a focus solely on legal policies would not capture the group's actual set of rights.

CITIZENSHIP REGIMES IN JORDAN AND LEBANON

Citizenship regimes are the culmination of social pacts or agreements between citizens and between citizens and the state, which comprise the totality of civil, political, social, and economic rights and duties.[21] These regimes reflect how a state constitutes its political community, including singularistic (favouring one particular group, typically one ethnic or religious group), pluralistic (including multiple, equal sub-groups that mediate one's citizenship), and universalistic (offering equal access to all individuals regardless of group affiliation) approaches.[22] This section engages these frameworks in discussing Jordan's and Lebanon's citizenship regimes over time.

Colonial–Local Alliances

The first modern citizenship regimes in the Arab World were based on colonial–local alliances in the early twentieth century.[23] These alliances stemmed from colonial officials propping up particular groups in the territory. These groups were more Westernised and adopted language about sovereignty, rights, and citizenship. Further, these groups enjoyed the benefits of colonial support and used them to cement their claims to power in the new states, even if they were not indigenous to those states' territories. In general, this colonial-based regime was elitist, exclusionary, and preserved pre-modern forms of state formation (e.g., tribal and religious structures).[24]

---

21 Ibid., 67.
22 Butenschøn, 'State, Power, and Citizenship', 16–27.
23 Meijer, 'Citizenship, Social Pacts'.
24 Ibid., 25.

Jordan's Colonial–Local Alliance

Jordan's first citizenship regime largely maps onto the colonial-influenced regime described above. However, Transjordan did not emerge as a separate country until the early 1920s, when Britain partitioned its Palestine Mandate.[25] In addition, King Abdullah I came from the Hijaz and secured his position through the British and his role in the Great Arab Revolt, led by his father Sharif Hussein. Further, King Abdullah I envisioned expanding Transjordan (later known as Jordan) to include Syria and Palestine. This vision played a key role in his decision to unify the East and West Banks (including Jerusalem) in 1950 and to give all Palestinians living in those areas Jordanian citizenship. This approach created a universalistic citizenship regime, where at least in law, all citizens were considered equal based on their individual status as a citizen, including many elites of Syrian origin.

Lebanon's Colonial–Local Alliance

In Lebanon, this colonial influence was much more prominent. The French protected and propped up the Maronite Christian minority based on their strong historical ties.[26] Specifically, the French supervised the creation of new political and administrative institutions in Greater Lebanon that favoured the Maronite community. In addition, the Constitution built on Ottoman rules to distribute public positions among sects, according to their demographic weight.[27] This paved the way for the National Pact in 1943, which divided power among the Maronites, Sunnis, and Shiʿis (i.e., Maronite President, Sunni Prime Minister, and Shiʿi Head of Parliament). This arrangement, organised by demographic weight, would forever remain based on the 1932 Census because of the political sensitivity surrounding the decline in Lebanon's Christian population in the following years. Thus, in law, a pluralistic citizenship regime emerged in Lebanon, where the main confessional groups shared power and where individual

---

[25] Morten Valbjørn, 'Like But Not Same As. . .: Arab Citizenship and the Jordanian Experience', in *The Crisis of Citizenship in the Arab World*, eds. Roel Meijer and Nils Butenschøn (Leiden: Brill, 2017), 175–202.

[26] Rania Maktabi, 'State Formation and Citizenship in Lebanon: The Politics of Membership and Exclusion in a Sectarian State', in *Citizenship and the State in the Middle East: Approaches and Applications*, eds. Nils Butenschøn, Uri Davis, and Manuel Hassassian (Syracuse, NY: Syracuse University Press, 2000), 146–78.

[27] Melkar el-Khoury and Thibaut Jaulin, 'Country Report: Lebanon', EUDO Citizenship Observatory, September 2012, 2.

legal status stemmed from belonging to one of these groups. However, this system would not incorporate the Palestinian refugees who arrived in 1948, and instead, left them firmly outside of the political community to this day.[28]

Institutionalising Pre-state Relations

The next citizenship regime in Jordan and Lebanon reflected the institutionalising of pre-state community structures, including those based on tribal and sectarian relations, by individuals empowered through the colonial–local alliance. With this regime, the state acquired sovereign political power and demanded political allegiance based on pre-existing local power relations, which helped shore up the state's legitimacy. In general, these relationships involved the state fostering economic development, maintaining the national identity, and protecting national interests, while the population received state jobs, education, housing, pensions and subsidies.[29] Basically, the state provided social goods, economic support, and security in exchange for limited civil and political rights.

However, this regime began to unravel in the 1980s as states were forced to address economic problems and reduce public spending.[30] This shift required states to rein in economic and social benefits, fostering public anger and unrest. To mitigate these pressures, states compensated their citizens with more civil and political rights. However, despite meaningful increases in civil and political rights in the beginning of this shift, the state quickly removed these new rights. This led to a new regime arrangement with fewer social and economic rights alongside limited political and civil rights.

Tribal-based Citizenship in Jordan

Jordan's citizenship regime reflected pre-existing tribal power structures by portraying the government as the provider of justice, security, and goods in exchange for loyalty and taxes. This regime particularly emerged in the late 1950s after King Hussein dodged a coup and popular anger led to the dismissal of British General John Glubb. During this time, the King dismissed the cabinet, dissolved Parliament, banned all political parties,

---

28 Except for some Palestinians of Lebanese or Armenian origin, Christian Palestinians, and Palestinian elites. See Maktabi, 'State Formation and Citizenship in Lebanon'.

29 Meijer, 'Citizenship, Social Pacts', 11.

30 Ibid., 1.

and declared martial law while empowering traditionally loyal East Bank tribes. This led to restrictions on civil and political rights that lasted until 1989.[31] At the same time, the government increasingly provided greater social and economic rights in the form of government jobs, public education, and public health care, especially during the 1970s economic boom.

The government continued to promote a universalistic approach to citizenship, though informally the state promoted a more singularistic citizenship regime favouring Transjordanians. This informal approach accelerated after Black September in 1970, which witnessed intense fighting between the Palestine Liberation Organization (PLO) and the Jordanian army. The legacy of this conflict, as well as the growing popularity of the PLO as the representative of the Palestinians, led to the government increasingly staffing the intelligence and security services with Jordanians of Transjordanian descent, while gradually removing Jordanians of Palestinian descent from these positions. The 1967 War also saw the arrival of refugees from Gaza (as well as displaced persons from the occupied West Bank), and in this political context, the Gazans were not provided citizenship or a path to obtaining it. This mainly occurred because Gaza was previously under an Egyptian mandate. However, the high population of Jordanians of Palestinian descent also influenced this decision because including the Gazans as citizens would have tipped the population balance in favour of those of Palestinian descent, making those of Transjordanian descent a minority.

Jordan saw a brief decline in this tribal-based citizenship in 1989, when the state was forced to accept a structural adjustment plan from the International Monetary Fund. This plan stipulated the removal of subsidies, increases in privatisations, and cuts in public sector employment.[32] These policies led to protests against the government in traditional tribal regime strongholds, like Ma'an, Karak, and Tafileh. In response, King Hussein allowed the first full parliamentary elections in decades, permitted political parties to form, and expanded freedom of the press.

This shift occurred just after Jordan's 1988 disengagement with the West Bank, which removed Jordanian citizenship from all Palestinians living in the West Bank at that time. The decision came after the first intifada and the failure of a confederal or federal deal between Jordan and the PLO. Although legally policies toward Jordanians of Palestinian descent on the East Bank did not change, Jordan witnessed a clearer shift toward privileging Jordanians of Transjordanian descent as a more loyal class.

---

31 Valbjørn, 'Like But Not Same', 8.
32 Ibid., 9–10.

This marked the strengthening of a gradual informal process of adopting a more singularistic citizenship regime favouring Transjordanians.

Jordan then saw the reinstatement of this tribal-based citizenship regime after the political openings in the early 1990s. For instance, despite holding relatively free and fair elections in 1991 and 1993, new election laws and restrictions on political parties later in the decade reversed this liberalising trend. During this period, the government also introduced more restrictions on Jordanians of Palestinian descent. For instance, placing fewer and fewer in cabinet and security positions as well as on rare occasions revoking their citizenship during administrative procedures (e.g., renewing a driver's licence). These citizenship revocations have come in waves since the 1990s,[33] with thousands of Jordanians of Palestinian descent losing their citizenship based on opaque changes to the terms of the disengagement, such as working in any form for the Palestinian Authority or failing to register a child's birth with Israeli authorities in the West Bank. These actions have turned thousands of Jordanian-Palestinians into stateless non-citizens overnight.

In addition, Iraqi refugees started entering Jordan in the mid-1990s, with another wave after 2003. The government opened its borders to them, though like other non-citizen refugees, they were viewed as temporary guests with limited social and economic rights. Altogether, these policies suggest that in law Jordan maintained a universalistic citizenship regime, though in practice it was increasingly bearing the markings of a singularistic regime favouring those originating from the East Bank and distancing itself from refugee populations.

Sectarian-based Citizenship in Lebanon

As French colonial influence declined, Lebanon's citizenship regime continued to reflect sectarian power structures by establishing a government that shared power between the state's three major religious sects: Sunni Muslims, Shia Muslims, and Christians. This created a weak, divided central government that offered few civil and political rights as well as encouraging citizens to access social and economic benefits through their sectarian affiliations. The civil war, lasting from 1975–1990, accentuated Lebanon's decentralised, sectarian approach to citizenship, where citizens literally divided against each other along sectarian lines. The role of the PLO in the civil war (after the group had been expelled from Jordan in

---

33 Luisa Gandolfo, *Palestinians in Jordan: The Politics of Identity* (London, New York: I.B.Tauris, 2012).

1971) made the Palestinians a convenient scapegoat for the conflict and helped enshrine their status as political outsiders. Similar to the colonial–local alliance, the law continued to support a pluralistic citizenship regime, though before the civil war, in practice, it looked more like a singularistic regime supporting the Maronite Christians above other groups.[34]

As in Jordan, there was a brief weakening of Lebanon's sectarian citizenship regime after the Ta'if Accords in 1989, which ended the civil war. Specifically, Ta'if called for the gradual abolition of confessionalism and the establishment of universal social and economic justice. In addition, the Ta'if Accords introduced reforms granting Muslims a greater role in the political process. These measures brought the population hope that the government would shift toward a more secular, universalistic citizenship regime.

However, also like Jordan, this brief opening was followed by a reinstatement of the previous regime, with the reversal of hopes for secular reform and the return of sectarian politics by the late 1990s. The fragility and weakness of the government, as well as a distrust of other sects, made it difficult for citizens and non-citizens to demand more rights.[35] Fears of descending into another civil war enabled the sectarian regime to remain in place and inhibited the adoption of new policies, especially those touching on sectarian divides or threatening to alter the country's demographic composition. This comes across in the cold welcome of Iraqi refugees after 2003, providing them with few rights and limited access to legal residency.[36] Thus, the pluralistic political system remained intact, though this time with weakened Christian executive powers.

Post-Arab Spring Security Regimes

Jordan's and Lebanon's citizenship regimes since the Arab Spring are similar to the reinstatement of the tribal- and sectarian-based regimes discussed above, but with the addition of a deeper concern with securitising citizenship. After the states made liberalising promises in response to protests inspired by the Arab Uprisings, the regimes gradually returned to their former citizenship regimes. External security threats, including neighbouring conflicts and terrorist groups, helped enable this retreat

---

[34] Butenschøn, 'State, Power, and Citizenship', 17–21.

[35] Faten Ghosn and Amal Khoury, 'Lebanon after the Civil War: Peace or the Illusion of Peace?' *Middle East Journal* 65 (2011) 3: 383–4.

[36] 'Rot Here or Die There: Bleak Choices for Iraqi Refugees in Lebanon', Human Rights Watch, Report, December 2007, accessed 1 December 2017, https://www.hrw.org/reports/2007/lebanon1207/.

by inserting a securitisation element into their citizenship regimes. This securitisation has fostered anxieties about real and imagined threats with the intent of affirming the state's role as an important provider of protection and security.[37] This process also involves associating threats, such as terrorism, crime, and unemployment, with categories of people, like refugees.[38] Thus, states claim to deal with these threats by introducing means of distinguishing between citizens and non-citizens, including through detention and deportation processes as well as biometric identification technologies.[39]

Jordan's Post-Arab Uprising Citizenship Regimes

Jordan follows this pattern of a brief weakening of the tribal-based citizenship regime after the protests in 2011 and 2012, when the state offered greater political and civil rights. Specifically, the state introduced constitutional amendments, removed some restrictions on freedom of assembly, created a constitutional court, and adopted new political party and election laws.[40] However, the state also retreated from these legal reforms by introducing regulations that limit their application and enforcement based on opaque security concerns. Further, the state has allowed media discourses connecting Syrian refugees to unemployment, crime, and terrorism to proliferate as well as deported refugees based on security concerns.[41] The Ministry of Interior (MOI) also emphasised its own registration process for refugees by distributing new biometric identification cards linked to individual iris scans and required for accessing humanitarian aid.[42]

---

[37] Peter Nyers (ed.), *Securitizations of Citizenship* (New York, NY: Routledge, 2009), 4.

[38] Didier Bigo, 'Security and Immigration: Toward a Critique of the Governmentality of Unease', *Alternatives* 27 (2002) 1 (Supplement): 63–92.

[39] Benjamin J. Muller, '(Dis)qualified Bodies: Securitization, Citizenship and "Identity Management"', *Citizenship Studies* 8 (2004) 3: 279–94.

[40] Valbjørn, 'Like But Not Same', 12.

[41] Alice Su and Karin Laub, 'Aid Officials Report Spike in Jordan Deportations of Syrians', *Associated Press* 12 May 2017, accessed 1 December 2017, http://abcnews.go.com/amp/International/wireStory/aid-officials-report-spike-jordan-deportations-syrians-47364075.

[42] 'Securing Status: Syrian Refugees and the Documentation of Legal Status, Identity, and Family Relationships in Jordan', Norwegian Refugee Council (NRC) and the International Human Rights Clinic at Harvard Law School, November 2016, accessed 1 December 2017, https://www.nrc.no/globalassets/pdf/reports/securing-status.pdf.

In addition, since roughly 2015, the government has enacted more restrictive policies toward Gazan refugees. These policies have shifted their treatment closer to that of foreigners, rather than as a special case of protracted refugee. For instance, Gazans have been blocked from economic sectors that they previously worked in (e.g., as private school teachers) and asked to pay four times more to renew their temporary passports (a shift from about $35 to $140 and twice the fee increase for citizens).[43]

Lebanon's Post-Arab Spring Citizenship Regimes

Unlike Jordan and other Arab countries, Lebanon largely avoided the Arab Uprising. One leading factor behind this is Lebanon's lack of a strong central government as well as its divisive sectarian politics. However, Lebanon has seen recent spikes in protest and hope for reform, including with the Cedar Revolution in 2005, which led to Syria's withdrawal of forces from Lebanon, as well as the 'You Stink' trash protests in 2015. Yet, the introduction of a pro-Syrian cabinet in June 2011 and limited government responses to the 2015 protests—including the government's inability to appoint a president from May 2014–October 2016—dampened hopes for secularising and democratising reforms. Further, the Syrian conflict has taken a toll on Lebanon, dividing Lebanese public opinion and sparking internal feuds. This situation reflects Lebanon's troubled history with Syrian political interventions.

Thus, Lebanon has seen a reinstatement of a sectarian-based citizenship regime, where the central state provides few civil, political, and social rights, leaving individuals to seek these rights through their sects. Within this context of a weak, sectarian Lebanese government, Syrian refugees have represented another burden and threat to the state.[44] However, Lebanon's approach to distinguishing them as non-citizens has been in refusing to recognise their status as asylum seekers and preventing the formation of formal refugee camps. These policies make life precarious for Syrian refugees because they are subject to detention and deportation. In addition, Syrian refugees are blamed frequently for increasing unemployment and spurring internal feuds, especially since most of these refugees are Sunni and opposed to the Syrian regime (threatening the power of

---

[43] 'Government to Lower Renewal Fees of Gazans' Two-Year Passports', *Jordan Times*, 23 February 2017, accessed 1 December 2017, http://bit.ly/2reQbDX.

[44] Rami Khouri, 'Has The Arab Spring Arrived In Lebanon?' WBUR Here & Now, 25 August 2015, accessed 1 December 2017, http://wbur.fm/2rqaBqL.

pro-Syrian Christian and Shiʿi sects). Thus, the government deals with Syrian refugees as a security threat that should be granted few rights and encouraged to leave.

NON-CITIZENSHIP REGIME FOR SYRIAN REFUGEES IN JORDAN AND LEBANON

The citizenship regimes described above come across in Jordan's and Lebanon's non-citizenship regimes toward Syrian refugees. On the one hand, these regimes provide similar sets of rights to Syrian refugees as to their citizens, including many social but few political rights. On the other hand, these regimes provide fewer civil and economic rights to these refugees than to their citizens. This combination of rights reflects both domestic and international laws and pressures.

For instance, although Jordan and Lebanon did not sign the 1951 Geneva Convention and its 1967 Protocol,[45] they are still bound to respect customary international law.[46] The most prominent example of this kind of law is the principle of non-refoulement, which stipulates that states should not return refugees 'to the frontiers of territories' where their lives or freedom would be threatened.[47] In addition, other human rights conventions that Jordan and Lebanon have signed afford refugees rights, including the International Covenant on Civil and Political Rights (1966) and the International Covenant on Economic, Social, and Cultural Rights (1966).[48] These international agreements have helped push Jordan and Lebanon to grant refugees social rights, including access to education and health care.

Further, both Jordan and Lebanon have signed a Memorandum of Understanding (MOU) with UNHCR. Jordan signed its MOU in 1998, which borrows most of its language from the 1951 Convention, excluding an unconditional commitment to non-refoulement and the possibility of

---

45 Like many countries around the world, Jordan and Lebanon largely refused to sign the Convention because of Article 34 on naturalising refugees, which is a sensitive demographic issue in both states.

46 In addition, neither country is party to the 1954 Convention relating to the Status of Stateless Persons or the 1961 Convention on the Reduction of Statelessness.

47 NRC, 'The Obligations of States towards Refugees under International Law: Some Reflections on the Situation in Lebanon', June 2016, accessed 1 December 2017, https://www.nrc.no/globalassets/pdf/reports/obligations-of-state.pdf.

48 Kate Jastram and Marilyn Achiron, 'Refugee Protection: A Guide to International Refugee Law', UNHCR, 2001.

refugee naturalisation. Jordan amended its MOU in 2014 to extend the time for UNHCR to process refugee applications from 30 to 90 days, and it extended the validity of refugee identification cards from six to 12 months, conditional on the refugees being repatriated or resettled.[49] The London Conference in 2016 strengthened this MOU by requiring the Jordanian government to offer 200,000 work permits to Syrian refugees over the coming years in exchange for international aid as well as easier access to European markets.[50]

The Lebanese government signed its MOU with UNHCR in 2003, which offered unprecedented legal assurances to refugees in Lebanon, including access to legal residency status.[51] The MOU, however, did not include a full commitment to non-refoulement and it clearly states that Lebanon does not consider itself an asylum country. Lebanon also considers the Syrian refugee crisis beyond the MOU's scope because of the number of Syrians and their definition as 'displaced persons', not refugees. These different MOUs help explain why Jordan has offered more accommodating policies toward the Syrians than Lebanon.

In addition, Jordan and Lebanon are party to two regional conventions concerning refugees: The Declaration on the Protection of Refugees and Displaced Persons in the Arab World (1992) and The Arab Convention on Regulating Status of Refugees in the Arab Countries (1994). These agreements, however, tend to focus on the conditions under which a country does not have to grant an individual refugee rights, including when governments deem such actions as threats to national security. On the other hand, these documents highlight the importance of protecting refugee women and children as well as treating refugees no worse than foreign residents. These conventions provide support for Jordan's and Lebanon's frequent security caveats when violating refugee rights, particularly their right to non-refoulement.

Neither Jordan nor Lebanon has a domestic law on refugees. Instead, both apply laws regulating foreign residents to refugees (in Jordan, Law No. 24 of 1973 on Residence and Foreigners' Affairs, and in Lebanon, the 1962 Law Regulating the Entry, Stay, and Exit from Lebanon). However,

---

49 Issam Saliba, 'Refugee Law and Policy: Lebanon', The Law Library of Congress, June 2016, accessed 1 December 2017, https://www.loc.gov/law/help/refugee-law/lebanon.php.

50 'Jordan Secures $1.7 Billion Grants, Grant Equivalents at London Conference', *Jordan Times*, 4 February 2016, accessed 1 December 2017, http://bit.ly/2qvTrYY.

51 UNHCR, 'Country Operations Plan: Lebanon', UNHCR Regional Office in Lebanon, 2004, accessed 1 December 2017, http://www.unhcr.org/3fd9c6a14.pdf.

the Jordanian Constitution does prohibit the extradition of 'political refugees'.[52] Similarly, Article 31 of Lebanon's 1962 Law prohibits deporting a political refugee to a state where his life or freedom is not secured, though Article 32 states that foreigners who enter Lebanon illegally can be fined and or imprisoned for 1–36 months.[53] Further, both the Jordanian and Lebanese governments avoid official recognition of refugees under their domestic laws and refer to Syrian refugees as 'asylum seeker certificate holders' who are pursuing asylum elsewhere.[54] In the media, Syrian refugees are also described as 'visitors', 'Arab brothers', or 'guests'.[55]

Although Syrian nationals automatically receive residence permits to stay in Jordan, this policy does not apply to Syrian asylum seekers and refugees. Syrians must register with UNHCR and the MOI if they want to obtain the documents necessary to access assistance for asylum seekers living outside of refugee camps, including education, health care, social assistance, and work permits.[56] These policies have become stricter over time, in part to enhance national security and in part to encourage Syrians to remain in or relocate to one of the Syrian refugee camps. Similarly, Syrians traditionally have been able to enter and reside in Lebanon with open borders and few documents. This changed when Lebanon closed its borders with Syria in 2014. Since then, Syrians have faced barriers to obtaining needed documentation in Lebanon, including birth, marriage, and asylum seeker certificates.[57] In addition, obtaining these certificates is more complicated and stricter than in Jordan.[58]

---

52 Suzan Akram, 'Protecting Syrian Refugees: Laws, Policies and Global Responsibility-Sharing', Talk at St. Joseph University in Beirut, 9 March 2015, accessed 1 December 2017, http://www.isp.usj.edu.lb/pdf/Talk%20of%20Suzan%20Akram2.pdf, 3.

53 Saliba, 'Refugee Law and Policy: Lebanon', 2.

54 Author interview with international development expert, 21 May 2017. Ghida Frangieh, 'Relations between UNHCR and Arab Governments: Memoranda of Understanding in Lebanon and Jordan' in *The Long-Term Challenges of Forced Migration: Perspectives from Lebanon, Jordan and Iraq*, ed. Ribale Sleiman Haidar. LSE Middle East Centre Collected Papers 6 (September 2016): 37–43.

55 Issam Saliba, 'Refugee Law and Policy: Jordan', The Law Library of Congress, June 2016, accessed 1 December 2017, https://www.loc.gov/law/help/refugee-law/jordan.php, 2.

56 'Securing Status: Syrian Refugees and the Documentation of Legal Status, Identity, and Family Relationships in Jordan'.

57 Zahra Albarazi and Laura van Waas, 'Understanding Statelessness in the Syria Refugee Context', Research Report, Institute on Statelessness and Inclusion and the NRC, 2016, accessed 1 December 2017, http://www.syrianationality.org/pdf/report.pdf.

58 Author interview with international development expert, 8 May 2017.

The diverse pressures from international laws and agreements as well as domestic laws and citizenship regimes explain the myriad of rights that Jordan and Lebanon have offered to Syrians. International pressures have pushed for greater refugee rights, especially social and economic rights. However, domestic laws do not guarantee these rights for refugees, and local citizenship regimes tend to frame refugees as guests and economic and security threats. This contradiction leads to sets of rights that exclude political rights and limit civil rights–both in defence of the country's physical and identity security–while offering many social and some economic rights. In addition, these conflicting pressures lead to divergences between the formal social and economic rights promised and those provided in practice. The next sections dive into the specific content of these non-citizenship regimes by looking at some of the formal and informal civil, political, social, and economic rights offered to Syrian refugees in both countries. This overview, though not exhaustive, provides a richer sense of Syrian refugee non-citizenship in Jordan and Lebanon.

CONTENT OF NON-CITIZENSHIP FOR SYRIAN REFUGEES IN JORDAN

Civil Rights

In its MOU with UNHCR, Jordan committed to respecting refugees' religious freedom, including to practise their religion, provide religious education, and live free from discrimination based on race, religion, or nationality–provided that these religious practices do not contradict Jordanian laws and regulations.[59] The MOU also grants refugees access to courts and legal assistance.[60] Further, Jordanian Islamic (*shari'a*) courts are open for Syrians to register births and marriages.[61] These rights have been upheld in practice, though Syrians without proper documentation may have trouble accessing these systems. For instance, if a couple does not have a marriage certificate (e.g., if the conflict in Syria prevented them from obtaining one), then the couple cannot obtain birth certificates for their children in Jordan.[62]

---

59 Saliba, 'Refugee Law and Policy: Jordan', 2.

60 Frangieh, 'Relations between UNHCR and Arab Governments', 37.

61 Ali Abdul Kadir Ali, 'Interview: Dr. Ali Abdul Kadir Ali', CBRL British Institute in Amman Podcast, 25 March 2017.

62 'Securing Status: Syrian Refugees and the Documentation of Legal Status, Identity, and Family Relationships in Jordan'.

Jordan also committed in the MOU to strengthening its asylum institution and respecting refugees' right to non-refoulement. However, the MOU falls short of guaranteeing non-refoulement, allowing forced repatriation of refugees when they pose a national security threat.[63] This has been the primary reason provided when development workers witness Syrian refoulement cases. There have been instances of refoulement since the beginning of the Syrian crisis, though initially they mainly consisted of Palestinian refugees coming from Syria.[64] Since 2015, these cases have increasingly concerned Syrians, including children, injured individuals, and entire families of suspected terrorists.[65]

In addition, Jordan adopted a no-entry policy that prevented PRS from crossing into Jordan in April 2012.[66] In 2016, Jordan expanded this policy to apply to all refugees coming from Syria after a terrorist attack in June on the border near al-Rukban camp in Syria. Further, the government increasingly has restricted the movement of Syrians within Jordan. In 2012, Syrians could enter Jordan and move freely. In 2014, refugees were directed immediately to refugee camps and could only leave legally through a sponsor's 'bailout'. In 2015, the bailout policy ended and refugees could not settle outside of the camps. Currently, the refugees already living outside of the camps must possess both an asylum seeker certificate and a new MOI card; those without these documents are at risk of being deported to a camp or back to Syria.[67]

Political Rights

Jordan has not agreed to offer Syrian refugees any political rights, and informally this absence of rights seems to be enforced in practice. This approach follows Jordan's policies to other non-citizen refugees, including the Gazans and Iraqis.

---

[63] Author interview with international development expert, 8 May 2017.

[64] Author interview with international development expert, 21 May 2017.

[65] Frangieh, 'Relations between UNHCR and Arab Governments'.

[66] Luigi Achilli, 'Syrian Refugees in Jordan: A Reality Check', Policy Brief, Migration Policy Centre, EUI, February 2015, accessed 1 December 2017, http://cadmus.eui.eu/bitstream/handle/1814/34904/MPC_2015-02_PB.pdf?sequence=1&isAllowed=y.

[67] 'Securing Status: Syrian Refugees and the Documentation of Legal Status, Identity, and Family Relationships in Jordan'.

Social Rights

Jordan offers many social rights to Syrian refugees, including access to education, health care, housing, and social assistance. First, in Jordan, Syrian refugee children whose families have a UNHCR registration certificate and an MOI identity card receive free access to primary and secondary public schools. However, UNHCR reports that only about half of Syrian children in Jordan are in school.[68] Although this figure remains low, it marks an increase since 2014 when only around 25 per cent of school-aged refugees were in school.[69] This continued discrepancy may stem from delays in getting UNHCR and MOI documents, lack of awareness about these policies among parents, school distance from homes, and limited seats in the education system.

Jordan's system for refugee health care is comprehensive and builds on previous experiences serving Iraqi refugees. In the beginning of the crisis, Syrian refugees were eligible for free primary health services in public facilities. However, since 2014, due largely to budget constraints, Syrian refugees now must pay the same fees as Jordanians without health insurance.[70] This situation has been mitigated by the government's introduction of a relatively cheap insurance system for refugees.[71] Those with secondary and tertiary health needs may receive treatment in public facilities with assistance from UNHCR and the Jordanian government. In addition, Syrian refugees have free access to primary, secondary, and tertiary health services from non-governmental providers.

Syrians can access housing in Jordan by living in a designated refugee camp. The camp population represents about 21 per cent of Syrian refugees, though the government would like to see this population increase because the camps keep refugees near the borders and facilitate refugee registration along with the distribution of aid.[72] Of the 80 per cent of

---

[68] Paolo Verme, Chiara Gigliarano, Christina Wieser, Kerren Hedlund, Marc Petzoldt, and Marco Santacroce, 'The Welfare of Syrian Refugees: Evidence from Jordan and Lebanon', World Bank Group and UNHCR, 2016, accessed 1 December 2017, https://openknowledge.worldbank.org/bitstream/handle/10986/23228/9781464807701.pdf?sequence=21&isAllowed=y, 127.

[69] Rochelle Davis and Abbie Taylor, 'Syrian Refugees in Jordan and Lebanon: A Snapshot from Summer 2013', Georgetown University.

[70] Author interview with international development expert, 8 May 2017.

[71] Verme et al., 'The Welfare of Syrian Refugees', 128.

[72] Dawn Chatty, 'The Syrian Humanitarian Disaster: Understanding Perceptions and Aspirations in Jordan, Lebanon, and Turkey', in *The Long-Term Challenges of Forced Migration: Perspectives from Lebanon, Jordan and Iraq*, ed. Ribale Sleiman Haidar. LSE Middle East Centre Collected Papers 6 (September 2016): 55–60.

refugees living outside of camps, 20 per cent live in substandard accommodation, such as garages, chicken coops, and tents. A smaller number of refugees reside in informal tented settlements spread throughout the country and often lacking basic services.[73]

Syrian refugees have access to social assistance programmes through UNHCR. Jordan's MOU with UNHCR stipulates that both parties will coordinate in responding to emergencies quickly by providing food, water, sanitation, shelter, medical treatment, and physical safety. The Jordanian government approves UNHCR's, along with other organisations', programmes based on certain conditions, but does not offer refugees access to its national social assistance programmes. Jordan typically approves basic relief projects, though it has been reluctant to approve youth centres and vocational training activities.[74] This may signal Jordan's desire to emphasise the temporariness of Syrian refugees.

Jordan provides many social rights to Syrian refugees that appear available in practice, notwithstanding everyday barriers to accessing them (such as transport costs and limited supplies). However, Jordan has been limiting UNHCR's refugee registrations since 2014 and has been operating its own registration process. Specifically, the government instructed UNHCR to stop issuing asylum seeker certificates, which are needed to obtain the MOI identity cards that grant refugees access to services, like public health care and education. Further, the government has instructed humanitarian organisations to serve only refugees with complete documentation, which has prevented many refugees in host communities from accessing needed services as well as exposing them to arrest and exploitation.[75] Altogether, these registration barriers prevent Syrian refugees from realising their promised social rights.

Economic Rights

In its MOU, Jordan committed to respecting refugees' right to work whenever its national laws and regulations permit.[76] The Jordanian Ministry of Labour also maintains a list of professions and industries in which only Jordanian citizens can work. These include medical, engineering, administrative, and legal professions.[77] However, in practice the private sector

---

[73] Achilli, 'Syrian Refugees in Jordan'.
[74] Davis and Taylor, 'Syrian Refugees in Jordan and Lebanon'.
[75] Achilli, 'Syrian Refugees in Jordan', 7.
[76] Frangieh, 'Relations between UNHCR and Arab Governments'.
[77] George Sadek, 'Legal Status of Refugees: Egypt, Jordan, Lebanon, and Iraq', The Law Library of Congress, December 2013.

does not always enforce these closed sectors, especially when Syrians will accept a lower wage without social security benefits. Syrians can also work in cooperatives, e.g., agriculture or handicraft cooperatives, without work permits. This enables them to work in the same field without being tied to one employer.[78]

Aside from these professions, Syrians must obtain legal work permits or investor cards to start their own businesses, though the latter card is difficult to obtain.[79] Syrian refugees, like all foreigners, with valid employment contracts and work permits should be registered with social security.[80] Further, as part of the 2016 London Conference, Jordan committed to granting 200,000 work permits to Syrians. However, there is some ambiguity about what this means, with Western donors viewing this as permits for 200,000 Syrians and the Jordanian government viewing this as 200,000 permits themselves (where one individual could obtain multiple work permits).[81] However, as of May 2017, only about 50,000 work permits have been issued, despite government efforts to facilitate this process.[82] This situation may stem from Syrians' difficulty accessing work sites (especially remote factories), disinterest in the permitted employment sectors, reluctance to interact with government institutions, and fears that they will lose UNHCR benefits if they register their employment.[83]

These policies followed a period during which the government would not issue new work permits for Syrians and pursued stringent penalties, business closures, worksite raids, and deportations to refugee camps for any Syrian violators.[84] However, some analysts have reported that Jordanian officials have been generally relaxed in their enforcement of these policies since 2012.[85] Altogether, Jordan has offered many economic rights to Syrian refugees who obtain the proper paperwork, though this registration process can be challenging and costly. Further, the state seems to enforce these policies, with some variation among officers depending on how sympathetic they are to the Syrians.

---

[78] Author interview with international development expert, 8 May 2017.

[79] Verme et al., 'The Welfare of Syrian Refugees'.

[80] Unless they are working in agriculture, which does not require social security registration.

[81] Ali, 'Interview: Dr. Ali Abdul Kadir Ali'.

[82] Author interview with international development expert, 29 May 2017.

[83] Author interview with international development expert, 28 November 2016.

[84] Davis and Taylor, 'Syrian Refugees in Jordan and Lebanon'; Chatty, 'The Syrian Humanitarian Disaster'.

[85] Ali, 'Interview: Dr. Ali Abdul Kadir Ali'.

CONTENT OF NON-CITIZENSHIP FOR SYRIAN REFUGEES IN LEBANON

Civil Rights

Unlike Jordan, Lebanon promises few civil rights to Syrian refugees. Since 2012, Lebanon gradually instructed UNHCR to limit the number of registered Syrians. In October 2014, the General Directorate of General Security (GSO) announced that Syrians would only be permitted to enter Lebanon with valid identity documents for an approved, evidence-based humanitarian reason (determined by the government and excluding international protection). Although it is unclear if the government formally adopted these instructions by issuing a Council of Ministers decree, as required by law, they came into effect in January 2015. These instructions stipulate different permitted lengths of stay and supporting documentation (e.g., if the humanitarian reason is to attend college, they must show university transcripts). They also note that these Syrians must sign a notarised commitment not to seek employment when renewing residency permits. Then, in May 2015, Lebanon prohibited UNHCR from registering new refugees.[86]

For UNHCR-registered Syrian refugees in Lebanon, the GSO announced in February 2015 that to renew their residency they must: present a UNHCR registration certificate, pledge not to work, housing commitment signed by the landlord and stamped by a local leader (*mukhtar*), lease agreement or real estate deed, yearly fee of 200 U.S. dollars, and declaration that the refugee will return to Syria when the permit expires or as requested by the Lebanese government. These policies resulted in more than two-thirds of Syrian refugees losing their legal status. This is critical because Syrian refugees lacking valid residence permits cannot register civil status events, like births. This is a violation of the Convention on the Rights of the Child, which Lebanon signed.[87]

Lebanon allows Syrian refugees with legal residency to move freely within the country. However, Syrians lacking valid residency cannot

---

[86] UNHCR, 'Universal Periodic Review: Lebanon', 2nd Cycle, 23rd Session, Human Rights Liaison Unit, Division of International Protection, UNHCR, March 2015, accessed 1 December 2017, https://www.google.co.il/url?sa=t&rct=j&q=&esrc=s&source=web&cd=1&cad=rja&uact=8&ved=0ahUKEwjglpCbpOnXAhVC6aQKHR3tAvIQFgglMAA&url=https%3A%2F%2Fuprdoc.ohchr.org%2Fuprweb%2Fdownloadfile.aspx%3Ffilename%3D2172%26file%3DEnglishTranslation&usg=AOvVaw2YOqmIafoz0eQQ3Qt-RW4O.

[87] Ibid.

move freely and are at risk of arrest and detention if caught.[88] This risk is heightened by Lebanon's refusal to guarantee non-refoulement–though this principle is customary international law and is included in human rights treaties Lebanon has signed. UNHCR has received reports of Syrian deportations and denied entries at the border since August 2014.[89] Lebanon also bans foreign nationals from owning real estate without official permission.[90] In addition, Lebanon does not explicitly grant Syrian refugees religious freedom or rights to a fair trial. Altogether, Lebanon provides few civil rights formally, which are limited to registered refugees. In addition, it offers some rights informally for all, including a general respect for non-refoulement (i.e., there were no cases before 2014).

Political Rights

Lebanon does not offer Syrian refugees any political rights, and they do not appear to have any political rights in practice. This is the case for all non-citizen refugees, including Palestinians who have been in Lebanon since 1948.

Social Rights

In line with its commitments to UNHCR, Lebanon offers some social rights to Syrian refugees. The government provides free or heavily subsidised access to public education and offers access to Lebanese universities after registering with UNHCR.[91] However, like Jordan, many Syrian children are not in school. This stems from beliefs that they will return soon, the need for child labour, overcrowding, school distance, and a lack of school supplies.

Lebanon provides free or subsidised public health care to Syrian refugees with funding from UNHCR. However, Lebanon has a weak public health system, which forces some cases to seek expensive private health care. The high cost and shortage of medicines is also a serious problem in Lebanon. The Ministry of Health and Iraqi Red Crescent helped address these problems by announcing in July 2013 that they would provide free medical services for Syrian refugees, despite shortfalls in international aid.[92]

---

88 Ibid.
89 Ibid.
90 Sadek, 'Legal Status of Refugees'.
91 Ibid.
92 Davis and Taylor, 'Syrian Refugees in Jordan and Lebanon'.

Lebanon has resisted building official camps for Syrian refugees, despite UNHCR's preference for camps. However, by 2015, there were over 1,000 informal Syrian settlements on the margins of towns and in unused agricultural fields, which housed about 10 per cent of Syrians.[93] Refugees in these informal arrangements typically access assistance through local patron–client relationships rather than through UNHCR.[94]

The Lebanese government allows UNHCR to distribute aid, but does not provide Lebanese social assistance to Syrian refugees. However, informally, some municipalities and local charities serve both Lebanese citizens and Syrian refugees, including informal, clientelistic social programmes.[95] Overall, Lebanon offers more informal social rights than formal, especially since there are municipal-level variations, where some villages adopt more accommodating policies than others.

Economic Rights

It is difficult for Syrians to obtain work permits in Lebanon. The government suspended an agreement with Syria in 2015 that guaranteed Syrians the freedom to live, work, and conduct economic activities in Lebanon. Since then, Syrian refugees, UNHCR-registered or not, find it nearly impossible to get work permits, except in construction, agriculture, and cleaning sectors. Further, under Lebanese law, they can be deported to Syria immediately if they are caught working without a permit.[96] However, Lebanese enforcement of these regulations is very weak, making informal access to work feasible.[97] This weak enforcement may stem from the economy's historic reliance on Syrian labour and the small number of officers policing this issue.[98] Thus, many Syrian refugees are working informally in Lebanon, despite the risk of detention, large fines, and deportation.

CONCLUSION

A detailed review of Jordan's and Lebanon's obligations and policies toward Syrian refugees highlights that the rights offered to Syrian

93 Akram, 'Protecting Syrian Refugees'.

94 Chatty, 'The Syrian Humanitarian Disaster'.

95 Ali, 'Interview: Dr. Ali Abdul Kadir Ali'.

96 Rasha Faek, 'Little Hope of Jobs for Syrians in Lebanon and Jordan', Al-Fanar Media, 25 February 2017.

97 Verme et al., 'The Welfare of Syrian Refugees'.

98 Ali, 'Interview: Dr. Ali Abdul Kadir Ali'.

refugees are similar to those offered to citizens. In Jordan, citizenship and non-citizenship for Syrian refugees has typically consisted of social and economic rights with few civil and political rights. Jordan also maintains a universalistic legal approach to Syrians refugees, treating them as individuals independent of their religion or sect.[99] Further, Jordan's tendency to offer more accommodating formal policies, even if these policies are not enforced in practice, mirrors its policies toward citizens. This tendency reflects a combination of demonstrating a liberal, democratic face to Western countries providing aid and addressing popular opinion against refugees.

In Lebanon, citizenship and non-citizenship for Syrian refugees involve Syrians depending largely on sub-state actors to access social and economic rights, while offering few civil and political rights. For citizens, this pluralistic regime deals with individuals as members of sub-state sects, through which they access rights. For Syrian refugees, where one lives in the country influences the kind of rights one has. Further, since most of these refugees are Sunni Muslim, the state treats them as a demographic threat based on this group identity. Lastly, the Lebanese government is too weak to enforce its policies toward Syrians, enabling them to operate informally with fewer legal problems than in Jordan. Citizens witness the opposite side of this formal–informal policy divide, where they cannot access promised rights, like public health care or trash collection, because of the government's incapacity.

Assessing Syrian refugee non-citizenship alongside host state citizenship regimes is useful because it highlights how states use similar strategies in dealing with non-citizen refugees and citizens. This comparison contextualises non-citizen rights. It also identifies barriers to refugees gaining more rights because these barriers are rooted in the state's citizenship regime. In addition, it demonstrates the utility of engaging the concept of non-citizenship as distinct from citizenship.

Acknowledgements

The authors thank the George Washington University Institute for Middle East Studies, Fulbright U.S. Student Program, and University of Jordan's Center for Strategic Studies for supporting this research as well as Kelly Connors, Sara Smith, Nathan Brown, and the book's editors for helpful feedback on earlier chapter drafts.

[99] Except for the PRS, though this Palestinian discrimination also mirrors broader citizenship policies in Jordan.

14. After the Arab Spring: toward women's economic citizenship

Valentine M. Moghadam

INTRODUCTION

The era of globalisation is characterised by a neoliberal model of capitalism based on the premise that 'human well-being can best be advanced by liberating individual entrepreneurial freedoms and skills within an institutional framework characterised by strong private property rights, free markets, and free trade'.[1] Key ingredients of this model are private sector development, entrepreneurship, labour market 'flexibility', and a reduction of the public sector wage bill. The role of the state is to facilitate the required conditions for capital accumulation, though it also may provide a 'safety net' for vulnerable social groups. This model, which gained traction during the 1990s and into the new century, has generated strong critiques of the growing income inequality, deteriorating public services, rising private service costs, and limits to national sovereignty that accompanied neoliberalism. With the Great Recession that followed the US mortgage crisis of 2007, mass social protests erupted across the globe for civil, political and economic rights. The Arab Spring of 2011 was one dramatic manifestation. It also occurred in the context of a region-wide women's rights movement that has prioritised family law reform, equal nationality rights, criminalisation of all forms of violence against women, and enhanced political and economic participation – or what women in francophone North Africa call *citoyenneté*.

In the countries of the Middle East and North Africa (MENA), women's economic participation and rights – as well as their civil and political rights – have been constrained by structural, institutional and normative features, including the oil economy, patriarchal family laws and conservative social norms. Paid maternity leaves and childcare facilities are not generous, creating a disincentive for many women, and especially

[1] David Harvey, *A Brief History of Neoliberalism* (New York: Oxford University Press, 2005), 2.

those from lower-income families, to join or remain in the labour force. As in other countries, MENA women are responsible for the care of the home and children, though wealthy women may resort to a nanny, usually from another country. Unlike women in other world regions, MENA women have yet to achieve labour market attachment; average labour force participation is just 30 per cent and women comprise a small share of the total salaried work force. Educated women are disproportionately represented in the formal labour markets, the poor make do with informal or precarious work, and Muslim Family Law (MFL) places women in a position subordinate to men in the family. In such a context, what are the possibilities for MENA women's economic citizenship?[2]

Informed by Thomas H. Marshall's conceptualisation of citizenship,[3] feminist analyses of care work,[4] and the decent work agenda,[5] this chapter addresses some key questions with respect to MENA women's economic status and social rights, and offers some recommendations for the achievement of women's economic citizenship. Sources of information and data are the literature on women, work, and family, personal interviews conducted in Morocco and Tunisia between 2013 and 2015, and national- and global-level data. Following this introduction, the second section elaborates on the concept of the social-economic rights of citizenship, and the third section explains how political economy and family law have limited women's economic citizenship. The fourth section describes some features of women, work and family arrangements on the eve of the Arab Spring; the fifth section discusses advocacy, activism and policy changes after the Arab Spring, with a focus on North Africa; and the final section offers some proposals.

WOMEN AND THE SOCIAL-ECONOMIC RIGHTS OF CITIZENSHIP

Social-economic rights constitute the third pillar of the rights of citizenship – the other two being civil rights and political rights – and include an

[2] This chapter refers broadly to MENA, which includes non-Arab Iran and Turkey, but the focus is on the Arab countries.

[3] Thomas H. Marshall, *Citizenship and Social Class* (Cambridge: Cambridge University Press, 1950).

[4] Ruth Lister, *Citizenship: Feminist Perspectives* (2nd edition, London: Macmillan, 2003); Nancy Folbre, *Valuing Children: Rethinking the Economics of the Family* (Cambridge, MA: Harvard University Press, 2008).

[5] ILO, *The Decent Work Agenda:* http://www.ilo.org/global/topics/decent-work/lang--en/index.htm, accessed 28 November 2017.

array of social and labour rights, from the right to organise and form trade unions to the rights to education, training, health and welfare. In Marshall's framework, social rights are those connected to education, training, a decent standard of living, and good work conditions; in his historical analysis, social rights followed the civil and political rights established in the course of democratic revolutions and struggles in the eighteenth and nineteenth centuries. They constituted the gains made by labour movements in the early twentieth century and their codification in the labour laws and social policies of welfare states, particularly around health, education, vocational training, and social insurance, including 'the right to a modicum of economic welfare and security to the right to share to the full in the social heritage and to live the life of a civilized being according to the standards prevailing in the society'.[6] Sometimes known as the 'stepchild' of the rights family, social-economic rights are under-emphasised in liberal capitalism and tend to be associated with robust social democratic welfare states. They are, however, inscribed in international standards and norms.

The International Labour Organization's (ILO) four core labour standards, represented by eight conventions, call for freedom of association and the prohibition of child labour, forced labour and discrimination in employment. The International Covenant on Social, Economic, and Cultural Rights (ICESCR, 1966) prescribes the right of people to a freely chosen job; equitable and equal wages for work of equal value; dignified working conditions for workers and their families; professional training; equal opportunities for promotion; protection for families, especially children; maternity protection; and protection of boys, girls and teenagers against economic exploitation.[7] References to women's economic citizenship and social rights are found in the UN Convention on the Elimination of All Forms of Discrimination Against Women (CEDAW), the Beijing Platform for Action, and most explicitly in the Charter of Women Workers' Rights of the International Confederation of Free Trade Unions (ICFTU, now the ITUC, or International Trade Union Confederation). Also relevant are ILO Conventions 100 (equal remuneration for men and women for equal work), 111 (non-discrimination), and 183 (maternity leave). Economic citizenship

---

[6] Marshall, *Citizenship and Social Class*, 72.

[7] See www.ilo.org; Valentine M. Moghadam, Suzanne Franzway, and Mary Margaret Fonow (eds.), *Making Globalization Work for Women: The Role of Social Rights and Trade Union Leadership* (Albany: State University of New York Press, 2011), especially the introductory chapter by the editors and Chapter 2 by Moghadam.

is conventionally tied to work and employment. In many countries, labour laws or social policies entitle women workers to paid maternity leave, crèches at the workplace with nursing breaks to feed their babies, subsidised childcare facilities in the community, and retirement several years earlier than men. Women also may be the beneficiaries of laws against discrimination in employment and pay, and against workplace sexual harassment.

The right to an occupation of one's choice spans civil and social-economic rights as it entails control over one's own body for freedom of movement and the ability to offer one's labour power for various occupations and professions. In a capitalist world, workers are free to move from one job to another, although there are restrictions on labour migration across international borders. For women, patriarchal structures have historically constrained their mobility; historian Alice Kessler-Harris underscored American women's right to move about as central to their search for equity and economic citizenship.[8] In certain cultural contexts, family laws place women under the protection – or control – of male kin and require that they obtain the permission of their fathers or husbands to seek employment, sign a contract, or travel.

Women's economic activities uniquely span the domains of formal labour and domestic labour, or the spheres of production and reproduction, and hence women's economic citizenship requires conceptualisation that pertains to both spheres. Nonetheless, the entry point for both research and advocacy is typically the position of women within the labour market, which is frequently studied as an empirical measure of women's overall status and their capacity for empowerment.[9] Access to remunerative work in the formal sector of the economy is regarded by many researchers in the field of women, gender and development as an important indicator of women's social position and legal status. Employed women tend to have greater control over decision-making within the family; households also benefit when women control income and spending, and the well-being of

---

[8] Alice Kessler-Harris, *In Search of Equity: Women, Men and the Quest for Economic Citizenship in Twentieth Century America* (New York: Oxford University Press, 2001).

[9] On conceptualising and measuring women's empowerment, see Naila Kabeer, 'The Conditions and Consequences of Choice: Reflections on the Measurement of Women's Empowerment' (Geneva: UNRISD Discussion Paper 108, August 1999), emphasising resources, agency, and achievements. For analysis of the tension between collective resistance and advancement as political idea on the one hand, and empowerment as an individual and psychological condition on the other, see Amalia Sa'ar, *The Quest for Inclusion: Economic Citizenship of Low-Income Women in Israel* (New York: Bergahn Books, 2015).

children is increasingly linked to female education and income.[10] Many women's rights advocates regard women's involvement in paid employment as a pathway to social and gender consciousness, autonomy and empowerment. This perspective is partly the legacy of arguments made by Karl Marx and Friedrich Engels to the effect that work in a capitalist economy is both a source of exploitation and a possibility for mobilisation, and that for women, employment is a prerequisite for involvement in political society.[11]

Enhancing and improving women's gainful employment has become a mantra within mainstream international policy circles and agencies. International agencies such as the World Bank, the International Monetary Fund, and various UN regional agencies draw attention to productivity and growth losses due to women's exclusion from paid labour, while investment in women's education and especially employment is increasingly understood as integral to building the national human resource base and increasing income and growth.[12] In a 2012 report, the United Nations Economic and Social Commission for Asia and the Pacific (of which Iran is a member), estimated that the Asia-Pacific region lost $42–47 billion annually from women's limited employment, compared to just $16–30 billion lost per year from educational inequality. According to World Bank president Jim Yong Kim, women's low economic participation created income losses of 27 per cent in the MENA.[13] Furthermore, international organisations

---

[10] Rae Lesser Blumberg, 'Introduction: Engendering Wealth and Well-Being in an Era of Economic Transformation', in *Engendering Wealth and Well-Being: Empowerment for Global Change*, eds. Rae Lesser Blumberg et al. (Boulder, CO: Westview Press, 1995), 1–14; Rae Lesser Blumberg, *Making the Case for the Gender Variable* (Washington DC: USAID, 1989); Rae Lesser Blumberg, 'A General Theory of Gender Stratification', *Sociological Theory* 2 (1984): 23–101; and Janet Saltzman Chafetz, *Gender Equality: An Integrated Theory of Stability and Change* (Thousand Oaks, CA: Sage, 1990).

[11] Karl Marx and Friedrich Engels, *The Communist Manifesto* (1848) and Friedrich Engels, *The Origins of the Family, Private Property, and the State* (New York: Pathfinder Press, 1972[1884]).

[12] Nadereh Chamlou and Massoud Karshenas (eds.), *Women, Work, and Welfare in the Middle East and North Africa* (London: Imperial College Press, 2015).

[13] UN, *Economic and Social Survey of Asia and the Pacific: Surging Ahead in Uncertain Times* (NY: UN ESCAP, 2007), 103. The World Bank president is quoted in David Cuberes and Marc Teignier, 'Gender Gaps in the Labor Market and Aggregate Productivity' (University of Sheffield Economic Research Papers, 2012), available at http://www.shef.ac.uk/economics/research/serps/arti cles/2012_017.html, accessed 28 November 2017. See also World Bank, *World Development Report 2012: Gender Equality and Development* (Washington DC:

have identified institutions that obstruct women's advancement, compiling data on access to land ownership, employment, inheritance, and the like as part of their assessment of women's empowerment or of gender equality. Such 'efficiency arguments' have been criticised as instrumental by feminist scholars who prefer rights-based arguments. Governments, however, are more likely to pay heed to analyses of efficiency and growth, especially when they are otherwise inclined to deny women equal citizenship on the grounds of cultural or religious norms.

CONSTRAINTS: POLITICAL ECONOMY AND FAMILY LAW

Why are MENA women from working-class or low-income households less likely to be part of the formal labour force? Could the provision of quality childcare, family allowances and paid maternity leave increase the labour force participation of married women with children? What role is played by political economy, legal/policy frameworks, human capital and social norms in the variations seen across the region? What is the role of the state in enhancing women's labour force participation, helping to secure work–family balance, and ensuring women's economic citizenship? How does women's collective action make a difference?

MENA countries are at different levels of economic development (industrialisation, urbanisation, social structure), and in terms of wealth they range from the rich Gulf Cooperation Council (GCC) countries to impoverished Yemen. Their political structures also vary, as do the size and strength of women's rights movements. Their authoritarianism and gender inequality have been attributed to the regional oil economy, the neopatriarchal state, or rentierism. There is indeed a long-standing literature on the economic and political effects of the 'rentier state'[14]

The World Bank, 2012). *The Economist* analysed the strongest factors promoting global GDP growth from 1985–2005 in an article entitled 'Forget China, India and the Internet: Economic Growth is Driven by Women' (5 April 2006), 16. Its conclusion reads, 'The increase in female employment in the rich world has been the main driving force of growth for the last couple of decades. Those women have contributed more to global GDP growth than has either new technology or the new giants, China and India'. See also Ana Revenga and Sudhir Shetty, 'Empowering Women is Smart Economics', *Finance & Development* (March 2012), 40–3, http://www.imf.org/external/pubs/ft/fandd/2012/03/pdf/revenga.pdf, accessed 28 November 2017.

[14] The early writings include the following: Hossein Mahdavi, 'The Pattern and Problem of Economic Development in Rentier States: The Case of Iran', in *Studies*

though less has been written about its impact on gender dynamics.[15] When a state depends on 'rents' (that is, revenues from state-owned oil, minerals, tourism, or waterways) it accrues vast wealth without needing to rely on income taxes. The implications are both economic, in that diversification is forestalled, and political, in that the state is less accountable to its citizenry.

During the heyday of economic development in the large MENA countries (1960s to1980s), oil wealth financed infrastructural development and state-owned industries, but in a lopsided fashion that also distorted the labour force. Male workers in the public sector were privileged, educated women found jobs in teaching and health, and governments instituted social security programmes and protective legislation for working mothers. Such policies were part of the *social contract* between the government and the governed, or what some scholars have called the *authoritarian bargain*. That is, at a time when civil and political rights were limited, the state provided social rights, at least to those employed in the state sector and their families.[16] Citizens in domestic work, the informal sector, agriculture, or migrant labour were outside the purview of labour law. The oil economy served to limit female labour supply and demand by privileging male workers through high wages, preventing diversification, and enabling labour migration and remittances.

The MENA model of state-led industrialisation and growth was swept aside in the 1990s with the global transition to the neoliberal economic policy model. Studies showed how ill-prepared MENA countries were for such a transition, whether in terms of the size and strength of the private sector and key economic institutions, or in terms of the quality, and gender composition, of its labour force.[17] The large-scale entry of women into certain economic sectors that had been observed in Southeast Asia and

---

in the Economic History of the Middle East, ed. Michael A. Cook (Oxford: Oxford University Press, 1972); Homa Katouzian, *The Political Economy of Modern Iran: Despotism and Pseudo-Modernism* (New York: New York University Press, 1981); Hazem Beblawi and Giacomo Luciano (eds.), *The Rentier State in the Arab World* (London: Croom Helm, 1987).

[15] Mary Ann Tetreault, *Stories of Democracy: Politics and Society in Contemporary Kuwait* (New York: Columbia University Press, 2000).

[16] Massoud Karshenas and Valentine M. Moghadam (eds.), *Social Policy in the Middle East: Economic, Political, and Gender Dynamics* (Basingstoke: Palgrave Macmillan, 2006), especially, 1–30.

[17] Massoud Karshenas, 'Economic Liberalization, Competitiveness, and Women's Employment in the Middle East and North Africa', in *Labour and Human Capital in the Middle East*, ed. Djavad Salehi-Esfahahi (Reading, UK: Ithaca Press, 2001), 147–69.

parts of Latin America, and theorised by Guy Standing[18] and others, was not present in MENA. Instead, a *patriarchal gender contract* prevailed,[19] the implicit and often explicit agreement that men are the breadwinners and are responsible for financially maintaining wives, children and elderly parents, and that women are wives, homemakers, mothers and caregivers. This understanding was codified in the region's *shari'a*-based family laws.

By codifying male responsibility for the maintenance of wives, female kin and children, MFL reinforces female financial dependence on male kin. Associated practices are the *mahr* (dower, or bride price), and in the Islamic Republic of Iran the *ujrat-ol-mesl*, or the concept of wages for housework and childcare in the event of divorce.[20] Under MFL women are required to obtain the permission of their fathers, husbands, or other male guardians to undertake travel, including business travel. Although wives – at least those who are educated and politically aware – may stipulate the condition that they are allowed to work in their marriage contracts, many wives make no such stipulations, and courts have been known to side with the husband when the issue is contested, as Amira Sonbol found in Jordan.[21] Traditional gender norms codified in MFL may discourage the adoption of policies and arrangements favourable to broad-based maternal employment, such as paid maternity leave and childcare centres. Research has uncovered the gap between *de jure* and *de facto* realities, but there does seem to be a connection between the prevalence of MFL and the historically low rates of female labour force participation and involvement in paid employment in MENA.

Family law has seen reform in MENA countries, but regressions have occurred as well, in Iran after the 1979 revolution, Egypt in 1985 and again after its 2011 political revolution, and southern Yemen following unification with the north in 1990. Only Tunisia's personal status code was relatively liberal from the start (1956) and was improved upon in the early

---

18 Guy Standing, 'Global Feminization through Flexible Labor: A Theme Revisited', *World Development* 27 (1999) 3: 583–602.

19 Valentine M. Moghadam, *Women, Work and Economic Reform in the Middle East and North Africa* (Boulder and London: Lynne Rienner Publishers, 1998), Chapter 1.

20 At first glance, the idea of wages for housework may appear progressive and indeed reminiscent of 1970s Marxist-feminist arguments. However, although the initiative was urged by Islamist women as a way to make divorce more costly for men, I am not aware of any study of its implementation and efficacy. Moreover, it is premised on the idea of women as homemakers and may also help to reproduce and reinforce the patriarchal gender contract.

21 Amira El Azhary Sonbol, *Women of Jordan: Islam, Labour, and the Law* (Syracuse, NY: Syracuse University Press, 2003), especially 89–99.

1990s. Even so, Tunisian feminists note the persistence of unequal inheritance laws. Indeed, under MFL across MENA countries, sons inherit twice as much as daughters, as they are expected to look after elderly parents (although the actual care work is done by female kin). Polygamy is not practised widely, but it does occur (especially in the Gulf countries), along with divorce. A deceased man's inheritance and his pension are divided between his widows, his children, and any other relatives that he may have been supporting. As a result, many widows receive insignificant pensions. Even though Islamic norms and some laws require that fathers and husbands financially support their daughters and wives, it is also the case that divorced, widowed or abandoned women without access to jobs or a steady source of income, especially among low-income social groups, are often left in a state of impoverishment. For low-income women, being divorced can mean loss of children and home, and a life of destitution.[22] Unequal inheritance puts women at a disadvantage, compared with males, when they attempt to start a business, but it remains a sensitive issue, given its mention in the Qur'an. Around the world, many countries have instituted laws that recognise marital property and a wife's right to half of the marital assets in case of divorce, but this principle has yet to be adopted in most MENA countries.

As in other regions, MENA women's formal rights of citizenship are based on two pillars: national legislation and international treaties and norms. As Table 14.1 shows, governments have signed a number of key international agreements pertaining to women's participation and rights. However, these are often weakly enforced, or they are rendered moot by virtue of their conflict with some national legislation or interpretation of *shari'a*. In the national context, one set of laws might contradict another set. Labour laws that signify women as workers with certain rights are contradicted by family laws that place women under the authority of male kin and deny them equal access to family wealth. Although the right to an occupation of one's choice is enshrined in the ICESCR, which has been signed by most MENA countries, that right is not enjoyed by women in all MENA countries. In Saudi Arabia and Iran, national legal frameworks do not give women the unqualified right to work, women require the written permission of a spouse or male relative to travel, and Saudi women were

---

[22] See, for example, Rahsa Abou Jalal, 'Palestinian Widows Lose Rights', accessed October 2014, www.al-monitor.com/pulse/originals/2014/10/widows-gaza-increase-confiscation-rights.html, which points out that many Palestinian women are unaware of certain inheritance rights, but also that a widow is entitled to just one-quarter of her dead husband's wealth. She is entitled to half the deceased husband's pension but forfeits it if she remarries.

Table 14.1 International conventions signed by selected Arab Countries, year of ratification

Convention	Algeria	Morocco	Tunisia	Egypt	Jordan	Bahrain	Kuwait	Qatar	Saudi Arabia	UAE
Convention on the Elimination of All Forms of Discrimination Against Women (CEDAW), 1979 (with or without reservations)	1996	1993	1985	1981	1992	2002	1994	2009	2000	2004
Beijing Declaration and Platform for Action, 1995	Adopted[a]	Adopted[a]	Adopted[a]	Adopted[a]	Adopted[a]	Adopted[a]	Adopted[a]	Adopted[a]	Adopted[a]	Adopted[a]
International Covenant on Economic, Social, and Cultural Rights, 1966	1989[a]	1979	1969	1982	1975	2007	1996			
International Covenant on Civil and Political Rights, 1966	1989	1979	1969	1982	1975	2007	1996			
International Convention on the Protection of the Rights of Migrant Workers and Their Families, 1990	2005	2003		1993						
UNESCO Convention: Discrimination in education, 1960	1968	1968	1969	1962	1976		1963		1973	
ILO Convention 111: Discrimination in employment/occupation, 1958	1969	1963	1959	1960	1963	2000	1966	1976	1978	2001

Table 14.1 (continued)

Convention	Algeria	Morocco	Tunisia	Egypt	Jordan	Bahrain	Kuwait	Qatar	Saudi Arabia	UAE
ILO Convention 100: Equal remuneration for men and women for equal work, 1951	1962	1979	1968	1960	1966				1978	1997
ILO Conventions 87 & 98: Freedom of association and right to organize, 1948	1962		1957	1957, 1954	1968	1961				
ILO Convention 182: Worst forms of child labor	2001	2001	2000	2002	2000	2001	2000	2000	2001	2001
ILO Convention 183: Maternity protection, 2000		2011								
ILO Convention 156: Workers with Family Responsibilities, 1981	–	–	–	–	–	–	–	–	–	–
ILO Convention 189: Domestic Workers, 2011	–	–	–	–	–	–	–	–	–	–

Note: Empty cells indicate no ratification.
[a] Made general and interpretative statements or expressed reservations.

Source: Compiled from 'A Summary of United Nations Agreements on Human Rights', http://www.hrweb.org/legal/undocs.html and the ILO NORMLEX Information System on International Labour Standards: http://www.ilo.org/dyn/normlex/en/f?p=1000:11001:0::NO::: (accessed July 2015; December 2017).

long prohibited from driving. ILO Convention 189 on domestic workers has not been signed.

In her historical study of states, women's rights, and kin-based solidarities in post-independence Algeria, Morocco and Tunisia, Charrad explained that patriarchal family law reflected very real social and political conditions, as it was founded on the strength of kin-based relations.[23] In most MENA countries today, social structures have changed so that the extended family unit is less prevalent than the nuclear family. Urbanisation and nuclearisation mean that most women cannot easily turn to female kin for help with childcare should they wish to seek employment outside the home. Nevertheless, although the female labour force in MENA remains small in comparison with other world regions, an expanding population of urban and educated women seeks employment or is increasingly responsible for family welfare. It is precisely this population that has produced women's rights groups calling for family law reform.[24] As a result, several countries, most notably Morocco in 2003–2004, have reformed their family laws, establishing more equitable rights and responsibilities within the family and releasing women for activities outside the home.

To summarise, during most of the twentieth century and into the present century, MENA women's civil, political and social rights of citizenship were limited by law and by tradition.[25] Challenges to the social contract, authoritarian bargain, and the patriarchal gender contract emerged in the late twentieth century, in the form of the structural adjustment policies of the 1980s and 1990s, which led to the privatisation of many social rights; women's rights movements critical of women's secondary citizenship; and broad globalisation processes that undermined state authority and encouraged civil society growth. As studies have documented, rights and privileges such as guaranteed public sector employment for graduates were withdrawn in the 1990s. School and university enrolment rates went up, but the quality of education deteriorated. The cost of living rose, income gaps widened, unemployment skyrocketed – especially among young, new college graduates and the women among them – and real wages stagnated. Between 2000 and 2010, many MENA countries increased their military

---

23 Mounira Charrad, *States and Women's Rights: The Making of Postcolonial Tunisia, Algeria, and Morocco* (Berkeley, CA: University of California Press, 2001).

24 See Collectif 95 Maghreb-Egalité, *Dalil pour l'égalité dans la famille au Maghreb* (Rabat: ADFM, 2003), available in English as *Guide to Equality in the Family in the Maghreb*, published in 2005 by the Women's Learning Partnership's Translation Series.

25 Suad Joseph (ed.), *Gender and Citizenship in the Middle East* (Syracuse NY: Syracuse University Press, 2000).

spending while spending on health declined. These are the socio-economic factors causally related to the Arab Spring protests.

WOMEN, WORK AND FAMILY ON THE EVE OF THE ARAB SPRING

According to a 2010 global index and ranking by the Economic Intelligence Unit (EIU), MENA countries provided few 'economic opportunities' for women. The EIU index and ranking were based on labour policy and practice, access to finance, education and training, women's legal and social status, and the general business environment. Of the 113 countries on the list, most MENA countries ranked 62 or lower (Israel was 28th; Saudi Arabia was 98th, Iran 103rd, and Yemen 112th). In the ranking of the highest-income countries, the rich GCC countries came last. Among the low-income countries, Yemen came last. Tunisia, however, ranked first among the lower-middle income countries on the EIU list.[26] In what follows, I summarise some of the characteristics of the MENA female labour force.

Impressive socio-demographic changes in the areas of female tertiary enrolments, age at first marriage, contraception prevalence, and fertility rates have not been accompanied by a significant growth in the female share of the labour force or their activity rates. The average rate of female participation grew only from 22 per cent in 1980–1985 to about 28 per cent in 2005–2010; this compares to activity rates that ranged from 45 to 62 per cent globally.[27] Data from the ILO's *Global Employment Trends*

---

[26] Economist Intelligence Unit, *Women's Economic Opportunity: A New Pilot Index and Global Ranking from the Economist Intelligence Unit* (2010), http://graphics.eiu.com/upload/WEO_report_June_2010.pdf, accessed 28 November 2017. It is telling that Vietnam – a country that endured a long and brutal American war and had to reconstruct itself from much devastation utilising all its human resources, including women – ranked first on the listing of economic opportunities for women among the low-income countries. As for the US, it ranked just 15; European countries with strong welfare systems usually rank higher than the US on gender and social indicators.

[27] Data from ILO 1990, table 1, 60, as well as from the ILO's *Yearbook of Labour Statistics 1981, 1985, 1991,* table 1. Figures for the 1990s are from the ILO's *Key Indicators of the Labour Market* (Geneva: ILO, 1999). On Lebanon, see *Al-Raida* 15 (1998) 82: 16, a special issue on women in the labour force, which reported that women's share of employment was 20 per cent. See also CAWTAR, *Globalization and Gender: Economic Participation of Arab Women* (Tunis: CAWTAR and UNDP, 2001).

for Women 2012 show that the female employment-to-population ratio was much smaller in the Middle East (15 per cent) and North Africa (19.7 per cent) than for the world (47.8 per cent). Even South Asia had a higher figure for women (30.4 per cent).[28] The female share of the total labour force rose between 1990 and 2010 in most MENA countries but declined in Egypt, Kuwait and Qatar. The dual-income family structure characteristic of Western countries and China remains atypical in MENA.

Employed women in MENA tend to be concentrated in professional occupations, mainly in community, social and public services; those with access to paid employment are largely educated women from the middle classes. Large proportions of employed women with higher education attainment are found in the West Bank and Gaza (a whopping 44.2 per cent), Oman, the United Arab Emirates, and Iran (roughly 30 per cent). Many of these women are employed as teachers, and in some countries they have come to constitute high proportions of the teaching staff at universities. According to data from the World Economic Forum's *Global Gender Gap Report 2011*, high percentages of female instructors at the tertiary level are found in Tunisia (42 per cent) and Algeria (38 per cent).[29]

Few women, however, occupy senior administrative and managerial positions. In 2010 Bahrain reported the highest proportion (22 per cent), followed distantly by Kuwait, Morocco, Egypt, Syria and the UAE (10–14 per cent); elsewhere in the region, the proportions were 5–9 per cent, with Yemen trailing behind with a mere 2 per cent female share of total legislators, senior officials and managers, according to the 2011 *Global Gender Gap Report*. These small percentages may be the reason why women's high rates of unemployment do not appear to preoccupy policymakers. Since the mid-1990s, the MENA region has been characterised by a feminisation of unemployment, especially among women with a university education. Female unemployment rates have been consistently high and higher than male unemployment rates.

In GCC countries, a common pattern is that the native female labour force is almost entirely concentrated in the public sector. This is made

---

28 ILO, *Global Employment Trends for Women* 2012 (Geneva: ILO, 2012), table 2, p. 12. See also ILO, *Women in Labour Markets: Measuring Progress and Identifying Challenges* (Geneva: ILO, 2010); and LABORSTA, available at http://laborsta.ilo.org/, accessed 28 November 2017 (Note: this database was replaced by ILOSTAT for data after 2008).

29 Ricardo Hausmann, Laura D. Tyson, and Saadia Zahidi, *Global Gender Gap Report 2011* (Geneva: World Economic Forum, 2011). The 1990s figures are from UNDP, *Human Development Report 1998* (New York: Oxford University Press, 1998), table 3, p. 134.

possible by the massive numbers of migrant labour for domestic chores and private services, including help for childcare and eldercare, cooks, cleaners, drivers and workers in retail and hospitality. (There is also a huge contingent of unskilled labour for construction, as well as a smaller proportion of skilled and high-level manpower for managerial positions in the many private firms in the Gulf.) Colton has stated that in Kuwait, on average, there are two domestic workers per home.[30] Al-Mughni notes that Kuwait's Labour Law, which specifies that a working day should be restricted to eight hours, does not apply to domestic workers, the majority of whom are women working long hours for low wages. Kuwaitis remain highly dependent on foreign labour – mostly from South and Southeast Asia – for domestic work.[31] The Gulf region as a whole has a very high presence of women migrant domestic workers, but so do Jordan and Lebanon.[32] The presence of household help is not a luxury enjoyed by all professional women across MENA, though the global care chain and rural–urban migration do enable cheap domestic help. For working-class Arab women, care work is entirely their own responsibility.

Countries in the region differ in patterns of women's involvement in clerical work, hotel, retail, restaurant, nursing, and factory work. Nursing was long considered an inappropriate occupation for women in the Gulf countries, which used to import nurses from abroad. With the exception of Morocco and Tunisia, few women work in factories. A study of the garment industry in Fez in the 1990s found that although the industry was overwhelmingly female, it attracted mainly young, unmarried women whose work conditions did not lead to labour force attachment or

---

[30] Nora Ann Colton, 'Social Stratification in the Gulf Cooperation Council Countries' (London: The Kuwait Programme on Development, Governance, and Globalisation in the Gulf States, London School of Economics' Global Governance Centre, Research Paper 14, January 2011).

[31] Haya al-Mughni, 'Kuwait', in *Women's Rights in the Middle East and North Africa: Progress Amid Resistance*, eds. Sanja Kelly and Julia Breslin (Washington, DC/Lanham, MD: Freedom House and Rowman and Littlefield, 2010), 232. See also Martin Baldwin-Edwards, *Labour Immigration and Labour Markets in the GCC Countries: National Patterns and Trends* (London: The Kuwait Programme on Development, Governance, and Globalisation in the Gulf States, London School of Economics' Global Governance Centre, Research Paper 15, March 2011).

[32] Simel Esim and Monica Smith, *Gender and Migration in Arab States: The Case of Domestic Workers* (Beirut: ILO Regional Office for Arab States, 2004); see also ILO, *Report of the Awareness-Raising Workshop on the Situation of Women Migrant Domestic Workers in Lebanon* (Beirut: Regional Office for Arab States, November 2005).

self-identification as workers.[33] In most MENA countries, women from working-class households or with high school education or less are missing from the salaried labour force. Could this be the result of inadequate institutional supports, especially for working mothers? Untoward workplace environments could constitute another reason.

This chapter emphasises the importance of salaried work for women, but economic citizenship entails what the ILO calls 'decent work'. In particular, care work – whether for children or for the elderly – should be regarded as socially useful labour that requires forms of support. Folbre has argued that 'the costs of producing future workers, developing their skills, maintaining their health, and providing for them in old age should be construed as part of the costs of producing human capital'.[34] What might support for that combination of productive and reproductive work look like?

Scholars have identified five categories of households with different earner–carer arrangements that have been – or should be – supported by the state, the market, or family relations: male breadwinner/female carer; male breadwinner/female part-time earner; dual earner/state carer; dual earner/marketised carer; dual earner/dual carer.[35] In the MENA region, where the social category of *dual earner* is not yet widespread and where gender relations do not yet reflect the *dual carer* model, the male breadwinner/female homemaker model is the most prevalent. Still, many lower-income households in which the wife/mother is involved in informal labour may be identified as falling into the male breadwinner/female part-time earner category. In addition, there is the female-headed household, and many such households fall near or under the poverty line. For GCC countries and, to a lesser extent, Jordan and Lebanon, with their

---

33 M. Laetitia Cairoli, *Girls of the Factory: A Year with the Garment Workers of Morocco* (Gainesville, FL: University Press of Florida, 2010); and M. Laetitia Cairoli, 'Garment Factory Workers in the City of Fez', *Middle East Journal* 35 (1999) 1: 28–43.

34 Nancy Folbre, 'The Political Economy of Human Capital', David Gordon Memorial Lecture, reprinted in *Review of Radical Political Economics* 44 (2012) 3: 281–92, 282.

35 Birgit Pfau-Effinger, 'The Modernization of Family and Motherhood in Western Europe', in *Restructuring Gender Relations and Employment: The Decline of the Male Breadwinner*, ed. Rosemary Crompton (Oxford: Oxford University Press, 1999), 60–79. If the categories were arrayed on a continuum, they would represent the range of gender relations from traditional to egalitarian. See Rosemary Crompton, *Employment and the Family: The Reconfiguration of Work and Family Life in Contemporary Societies* (Cambridge: Cambridge University Press, 2006), Fig. 101, p. 205.

prevalence of domestic help drawn from migrant labour, another category might be introduced: *male breadwinner/marketised carer*. Each of these categories would require a different set of support mechanisms, whether from the state or the market, including the following:

1. Employer-provided social security extended to wife/mother
2. Family or child allowance
3. Subsidised childcare and pre-school centres
4. Social support/labour rights for domestic workers
5. Paid maternity leave of at least four months with the possibility of longer parental leave
6. Elder care provision
7. Tax credit.

As seen in Table 14.2, statutory maternity leave policies across the MENA region have not been generous. In 2011, the length of paid maternity leave ranged from a low of 7–8 weeks or two months in Lebanon and Tunisia to 120 days or four months in Syria (and Turkey). Only Algeria, Bahrain, Jordan, Morocco and Tunisia (also Iran) provided maternity leave entirely covered by social security; elsewhere, maternity leave was an additional tax on the employer and a disincentive to hire women. An ethnographic study by Mona Hamade of women and work in the United Arab Emirates found that the issue of maternity leave and employment prospects upon returning to work post-pregnancy was raised time and again.[36] Paternity leave is almost unknown.[37] In contrast, Norway provided nearly a year of fully paid maternity leave with an additional 12 weeks provided for the father if he chose to take it, at full pay. MENA's maternity leave policies in 2011 were not substantially different from other countries in Table 14.2, such as Argentina, China, Japan and South Korea, but in those countries, female labour force participation was considerably higher than in MENA, and both Argentina and South Korea provided subsidised childcare facilities.[38]

Failing to provide mothers with paid maternity leaves of appropriate length, quality and affordable childcare, family allowances, and so on

---

36 See Denise Marray, 'What Emirati women need at the workplace', *GulfNews.com*, 6 March 2014, accessed January 2016, http://gulfnews.com/news/uae/general/what-emirati-women-need-at-the-workplace-1.1300023.

37 By 2016, Algeria and Morocco had instituted three days of paternity leave.

38 See, for example, Ito Peng, 'The Political and Social Economy of Care in the Republic of Korea' (Geneva: UNRISD Gender and Development Paper 6, October 2009).

Table 14.2 Policies on maternal employment, Arab countries and others 2011

Country	Length of maternity leave	Percentage of wages paid	Provider of maternity coverage (% covered)		Length of paternity leave	Percentage of wages paid for paternity leave
			Social security	Employer		
Algeria	14 weeks	100%	100%	0%	none	0%
Bahrain	45 days	100%	100%	0%	none	0%
Egypt	90 days	100%	75%	25%	none	0%
Iraq	–	–	–	–	–	–
Jordan	10 weeks	100%	100%	0%	none	0%
Kuwait	70 days	100%	0%	100%	none	0%
Lebanon	7 weeks	100%	0%	100%	none	0%
Libya	–	–	–	–	–	–
Morocco	14 weeks	100%	100%	0%	none	0%
Oman	none	0%	0%	0%	none	0%
Qatar	50 days	100	0%	100%	none	0%
Saudi Arabia	10 weeks	50 if working less than 3 years, 100 if working 3 or more	0%	100%	none	0%
Syria	120 days for first child, 90 days for second, 75 days for third	100%	0%	100%	none	0%

Table 14.2 (continued)

Country	Length of maternity leave	Percentage of wages paid	Provider of maternity coverage (% covered)		Length of paternity leave	Percentage of wages paid for paternity leave
			Social security	Employer		
Tunisia*	1-2 months	social insurance benefits paid to private sector employees for 30 days at a rate of 67% of average daily wage; 100% for civil servants	100% – national social security fund	0%	None	0%
UAE	45 days	100%	0%	100%	public sector only, 3 consecutive working days after birth	public sector only, 100%
West Bank and Gaza	–	–	–	–	–	–
Yemen	60 days	100%	0%	100%	none	0%

Other countries	Length of maternity leave	Percentage of wages paid	Provider of maternity coverage (% covered)		Length of paternity leave	Percentage of wages paid for paternity leave
			Social security	Employer		
Argentina	90 days	100%	Family allowance funds (financed through state/ employer contributions)	Family allowance funds (financed through state/ employer contributions)	none	0%
China	90 days	100%	Social insurance, % not given		none	0%
Iran	90 days	67%	100%	0%	none	0%
Israel	14 weeks	100%, up to ceiling	100%	0%	Father can take part of leave instead of mother from 6 up to 14 weeks	100%
Japan	14 weeks	30%) – upon return to work mother receives a further 10% of pre-leave wage for duration of leave taken as a re-engagement benefit	1/8 national treasury	7/8 employment insurance fund	none – except at corporate level	50%

Table 14.2 (continued)

Other countries	Length of maternity leave	Percentage of wages paid	Provider of maternity coverage (% covered)		Length of paternity leave	Percentage of wages paid for paternity leave
			Social Security	Employer		
Norway	46 or 56 weeks	100% or 80%	Social insurance, 100%	0%	12 weeks	100%
South Korea	90 days	100%	Employment Insurance Fund		3 days	0%
Turkey	16 weeks	67% for 12 weeks	100%	0%	Public sector only, 10 days	0%
Venezuela	18 weeks	100%	100%	none	none	0%

Note: By 2016, some (non-Arab) countries had introduced changes.

Sources: World Economic Forum, Global Gender Gap Forum 2012, http://reports.weforum.org/global-gender-gap-resport-2012/#=; * http://www3.weforum.org/docs/WEF_GenderGap_Report_2011.pdf.

constitutes an under-investment in the family that stalls societal progress.[39] Conversely, investing in the care economy is needed for women's full citizenship, and generates jobs, taxes and growth.[40] Arguments for 'human capabilities', 'an ethic of care', and 'gender justice' constitute an appeal for a world 'where the daily caring of people for each other is a valued premise of human existence' and for the establishment of institutions to reflect that value.[41] In MENA countries, institutional supports for care and work–family balance would attract and retain more women in the work force, especially those from working-class and lower-income households.

ADVOCACY AND ACTIVISM FOR WOMEN'S ECONOMIC CITIZENSHIP

Most MENA countries have women's organisations but nowhere are they as active or as effective in policy terms as in the Maghreb, where women's groups since the early 1990s have called for family law, labour law and penal code reforms to provide for women's full civil, political, and social rights of citizenship.[42] Calls for laws to prohibit sexual harassment in the workplace and gender-based employment discrimination led to policy changes in Morocco and Tunisia, and in all three Maghreb countries hotlines for women victims of sexual harassment and domestic violence (*centres d'écoute*) were set up. Algerian women's collective action forced the government to introduce some amendments to the conservative family law in 2005, although activism seeks an end to unequal inheritance and a ban on polygamy. The introduction of a gender quota resulted in a 31.6 per

---

39 Kenneth Dau-Schmidt and Carmen Brun, 'Protecting Families in a Global Economy', *Indiana Journal of Global Legal Studies* 13 (2006) 1: 165–205; and Folbre, *Valuing Children.*

40 See Lister, *Citizenship: Feminist Perspectives*; and Ipek Ilkkaracan, 'A Feminist Alternative to Austerity: The Purple Economy as a Gender-Egalitarian Strategy for Employment Generation', chapter 2 in *Economics and Austerity in Europe: Gendered Impacts and Sustained Alternatives*, eds. Hanna Bargawi, Giovanni Cozzi, and Susan Himmelweit (London: Routledge, 2017).

41 Joan Tronto, *Moral Boundaries: A Political Argument for an Ethic of Care* (London: Routledge, 1994), 178; Martha Nussbaum, *Women and Human Development: The Capabilities Approach* (Cambridge: Cambridge University Press, 2000).

42 See, for example, Association Démocratique des Femmes du Maroc, *Protection des droits des femmes: Agissons pour l'application effective de la législation du travail* (Rabat: ADFM, et al., 2004).

cent female presence in Algeria's National Assembly following the 2012 parliamentary election. Moroccan women's rights advocates in both civil and political society helped usher in the family law reform of 2003–2004, a new labour law provision to prohibit gender-based discrimination, and an electoral law to establish a quota to increase women's parliamentary presence. In April 2011 Morocco became the first Arab country to sign and ratify ILO Convention 183 on maternity leave. Since then, women's rights advocates have continued to work toward the harmonisation of national laws with the international conventions that Morocco has signed. Constitutional amendments approved in a July 2011 referendum included Article 19, which stipulates equal enjoyment by men and women of 'rights and freedoms of civil, political, economic, social, cultural, and environmental character . . . '.

In Tunisia, l'Association des Femmes Tunisiennes pour la Recherche et le Développement (AFTURD) and l'Association Tunisienne des Femmes Démocrates (ATFD) organised marches in 2011 and 2012 for 'liberty, dignity, equality', and insisted on women's full and equal citizenship. On May Day 2012, ATFD joined with the trade union Union Générale des Travailleurs Tunisiens (UGTT) to march for rights; a coalition *pour la citoyenneté* was formed by ATFD, AFTURD, UGTT and La Ligue Tunisienne des Droits de l'Homme. Activists from these organisations and the secular political parties defended constitutional language on *equality* between women and men rather than the proposed notion of *complementarity*. As one feminist trade unionist, a member of both the UGTT and AFTURD, and an official in the UGTT health sector, told me in 2014: 'On August 13, the national women's day, we had a big demonstration against the idea of *complémentaire*; for us, the woman is complete' (*pour nous, la femme est complète*).[43] The new constitution, adopted in January 2014, includes the following provisions for the social rights of citizens and equality of women:

> Article 38: 'Health is a right for every person' and the state shall 'guarantee preventative health care and treatment for every citizen and provide the means necessary to ensure the safety and good quality of health services'. The constitution promises 'free health care for those without support and those with limited income'.
>
> Article 40: 'Work is a right for every citizen, male and female. The state shall take the necessary measures to guarantee work on the basis of

---

43 Personal interview, Tunis, 5 March 2014.

competence and fairness. All citizens, male and female, shall have the right to decent working conditions and to a fair wage.'

Article 46: 'The State shall commit to protecting women's achieved rights and seek to support and develop them . . . The State shall guarantee equal opportunities between men and women in the bearing of all the various responsibilities in all fields . . . The State shall take necessary measures to eliminate violence against women.'

Tunisian feminists note that the constitutional guarantees provide an important legal and ethical framework, but the attainment of women's economic citizenship requires more specific laws and policies because, as one feminist trade unionist pointed out, *il y a des specificités femmes*. For her, these include women's enterprises and a more generous maternity leave policy. She told me that at the UGTT, the women trade unionists and their allies work for equality of public and private labour law; social insurance for all workers; crèches; a healthy workplace; an end to sexual harassment; and the ratification of ILO Convention 183 on maternity leave. The feminist movement and the labour movement, she explained, had much common ground, but 'we [feminists] emphasise women's citizenship'. She continued:

> Women's economic independence and control over income is very important. We want to have women's economic security, we are always mindful that *la citoyenneté complète* has to include the economic. Now when we say 'development' we mean full human rights . . . We live in a society where women are part of a family – that's where the idea of 'complementarity' comes from. But we want women's citizenship before family.[44]

One achievement was the removal of the CEDAW reservations in order to make national laws and international conventions more compatible. Another feminist trade unionist, active in the teachers' sector, told me that the new priorities included 'elaboration of Tunisian women's rights'. As she explained:

> The Constitution has to be translated into laws, especially for the private sector. Now that CEDAW reservations have been removed the next step is to insist on the adoption of ILO Convention 183 on maternity protection. The public sector provides two months of paid maternity leave plus more at half salary, while the private sector provides only one month. We want to campaign for a year, but our campaign has to be based on the values and spirit and articles of

44 Personal interview, Tunis, 5 March 2014.

> the constitution, especially articles 21 and 29. The values of *citoyennité* and of *liberté* – the laws must protect them. We must be faithful to the constitution [*nous devons être fidèle à la constitution*]. Even the Islamists voted for it, so they cannot oppose it! We need to have a strategic campaign drawn from the constitution to make a convincing case for the people and also to compel the government to adopt progressive legislation that would make it possible for more women to enter the work force and to stay there . . . We have to combat women's poverty, marginalisation, exclusion, and exploitation with a gender budget, which will make it possible for more women to access jobs.[45]

In 2015, women's rights advocates hoped that the new government and at least a large segment of the female members of Parliament – who after the October 2014 elections constituted 31 per cent of all members – would craft and adopt the necessary policies. Tunisia may well represent a model for citizenship campaigns elsewhere in the MENA region, but more research as well as more advocacy is needed, especially around women's double burden, as families continue to exercise the traditional sexual division of labour whereby the women in the family are responsible for domestic tasks, childcare and elder care. If current trends in female educational attainment and advocacy continue, it is likely that in the years ahead we will witness women's rights groups focusing their campaigns on working women's double burden, family ethics and social policies for work–family balance, calling on women parliamentarians to introduce the relevant bills. In the meantime, governments should take a closer look at the developmental and ethical imperatives of women's economic citizenship.

CONCLUSIONS AND PROPOSALS

Female labour force participation in MENA is still low in relation to that of other regions of the world and in relation to male labour force participation. Reasons lie in economic and non-economic factors and forces: the oil economy and absence of economic diversification; conservative social norms codified in the region's family laws; states that are not favourable to the advancement of women and their economic empowerment – especially when the state is constituted by men holding patriarchal attitudes concerning women, work and family. The neoliberal policy environment has not proved to be the great equaliser that its proponents argued it would be.[46]

---

45 Personal interview, Tunis, 12 March 2015.

46 Thomas Friedman, *The World is Flat* (New York: Farrar, Strauss and Giroux, 2005).

In the wake of the Arab Spring and in the context of democratic transitions, the challenges of the new governments include the integration of an increasingly educated female population and women's claims for economic participation in the new policy frameworks. At the time of writing, the Arab Spring had resulted in democratic transitions only in Tunisia and Morocco; elsewhere, countries affected by the Arab Spring had either descended into internationalised civil conflict (Libya, Syria, Yemen), repressed the civil society actors who protested (Bahrain), or reverted to military-led authoritarian rule (Egypt). Other MENA countries, notably Saudi Arabia, continue to allocate huge resources toward the purchase of arms from the US and Europe. The immediate future for social and economic rights, as well as for the civil and political rights of citizenship, does not appear bright. Nonetheless, I end with some proposals that could be of use to civil society activists and to those political parties that have modernising and progressive agendas. These proposals for women's participation and rights serve the goals of democratic development, a well-functioning labour market, poverty alleviation, and growth with equity.

New social and gender contracts premised on developmental, ethical, and equality goals should be on the agenda. Decent work and decent wages, along with policies and institutions that alleviate women's responsibilities for the care of children and the elderly – such conditions would encourage women from low-income households to seek and remain in employment. Legal and policy frameworks should be in alignment: constitutions, labour laws, family laws, social policies and international conventions should complement and not contradict each other.

Women's economic citizenship requires social provisioning sufficiently expansive to support households and families, the capacity of women to seek employment and enjoy family life, and the rights of citizen-workers. Shorter working days for parents of small children, and paid maternity leave of at least six months in duration with additional leave for fathers, and good quality and subsidised pre-school facilities would recognise care work as a social good, ensure parent–child bonding, enable women's labour force attachment, and be a pathway to gender equality. Parental leave could be financed through government, employer and worker contributions. Care for the elderly, who will become a growing proportion of the MENA population, should be compensated through family allowances or the provision of subsidised home care. Domestic workers should be protected under labour law.

To address the needs and rights of lower-income women, respond to the appeals of women's rights advocates for equality in the family, and offer an alternative to the patriarchal gender contract, governments should allocate family allowances to mothers and not exclusively to fathers, and remove inequalities in inheritance. Paid maternity leave should be part of social insurance and financed through general revenues. Ministries should create a gender budget from which women-specific programmes could be funded. Such policies would institutionalise social rights while also addressing the region's specific constraints on women's mobility.

The recommended measures and policies are, admittedly, costly for some of the poorer countries in the region and controversial in some circles in all the countries. As these policies are discussed in the legislatures and through social dialogues, advocates can reiterate the recommendations and calculations of international organisations regarding 'smart economics' and the economic growth benefits of female employment. Advocacy also can incorporate a push for the kind of 'Tobin tax' that progressives have long called for: a tax on global and transnational financial speculative transactions that could then be used for development and social provisioning purposes, including measures for women's economic citizenship.[47]

[47] For an interesting twist on the Tobin Tax, which would 'creat[e] a tax on global movements and transactions, thereby involving large numbers of people in cosmopolitan citizenship, and providing a material foundation for cosmopolitanism', see Engin F. Isin and Bryan S. Turner, 'Investigating Citizenship: An Agenda for Citizenship Studies', *Citizenship Studies* 11 (2007) 1: 5–17.

Index